Hacking MySQL

Breaking, Optimizing, and Securing MySQL for Your Use Case

Lukas Vileikis

Foreword by Louis Davidson

Apress®

Hacking MySQL: Breaking, Optimizing, and Securing MySQL for Your Use Case

Lukas Vileikis
Siauliai, Lithuania

ISBN-13 (pbk): 979-8-8688-0979-8 ISBN-13 (electronic): 979-8-8688-0980-4
https://doi.org/10.1007/979-8-8688-0980-4

Copyright © 2024 by Lukas Vileikis

This work is subject to copyright. All rights are reserved by the Publisher, whether the whole or part of the material is concerned, specifically the rights of translation, reprinting, reuse of illustrations, recitation, broadcasting, reproduction on microfilms or in any other physical way, and transmission or information storage and retrieval, electronic adaptation, computer software, or by similar or dissimilar methodology now known or hereafter developed.

Trademarked names, logos, and images may appear in this book. Rather than use a trademark symbol with every occurrence of a trademarked name, logo, or image we use the names, logos, and images only in an editorial fashion and to the benefit of the trademark owner, with no intention of infringement of the trademark.

The use in this publication of trade names, trademarks, service marks, and similar terms, even if they are not identified as such, is not to be taken as an expression of opinion as to whether or not they are subject to proprietary rights.

While the advice and information in this book are believed to be true and accurate at the date of publication, neither the authors nor the editors nor the publisher can accept any legal responsibility for any errors or omissions that may be made. The publisher makes no warranty, express or implied, with respect to the material contained herein.

>Managing Director, Apress Media LLC: Welmoed Spahr
>Acquisitions Editor: Shaul Elson
>Development Editor: Laura Berendson
>Editorial Assistant: Gryffin Winkler

Cover designed by eStudioCalamar

Cover image designed by Simon Mettler from Pixabay

Distributed to the book trade worldwide by Springer Science+Business Media New York, 1 New York Plaza, Suite 4600, New York, NY 10004-1562, USA. Phone 1-800-SPRINGER, fax (201) 348-4505, e-mail orders-ny@springer-sbm.com, or visit www.springeronline.com. Apress Media, LLC is a California LLC and the sole member (owner) is Springer Science + Business Media Finance Inc (SSBM Finance Inc). SSBM Finance Inc is a Delaware corporation.

For information on translations, please e-mail booktranslations@springernature.com; for reprint, paperback, or audio rights, please e-mail bookpermissions@springernature.com.

Apress titles may be purchased in bulk for academic, corporate, or promotional use. eBook versions and licenses are also available for most titles. For more information, reference our Print and eBook Bulk Sales web page at http://www.apress.com/bulk-sales.

Any source code or other supplementary material referenced by the author in this book is available to readers on GitHub. For more detailed information, please visit https://www.apress.com/gp/services/source-code.

If disposing of this product, please recycle the paper

I dedicate this book to developers sharing their knowledge who often do so free of charge – doing so necessitates a lot of effort, and without your effort, books like these wouldn't exist.

Table of Contents

About the Author xiii

Acknowledgments xv

Preface xvii

Foreword xxi

Part I: The Basics of MySQL 1

Chapter 1: The World of MySQL 3
The History of MySQL 3
The Architecture of MySQL 4
Basic Use Cases and Initial Considerations 6
Storage Engines 7
    Other Storage Engines 8
Summary 9

Chapter 2: Individual Storage Engines 11
The Modern King of Storage Engines 11
    InnoDB in MySQL and MariaDB 11
    Storage Engines in Percona Server 20
    Percona MyRocks and TokuDB 21
The Primary Contestant of InnoDB 24
    The Early Days of MyISAM 24
    MyISAM in the Present Day 25
Storage Engine Use Cases 26
    The MEMORY and TempTable Storage Engines 26
    The CSV Storage Engine 27
    The ARCHIVE and BLACKHOLE Storage Engines 28

TABLE OF CONTENTS

 The MERGE Storage Engine 29

 The Storage Engine for High Availability 30

 The FEDERATED and EXAMPLE Storage Engines 34

 Storage Engines Exclusive to MariaDB 35

Summary 37

Part II: Breaking MySQL 39

Chapter 3: What Breaks MySQL? 41

MySQL Use Cases 41

Problematic Use Cases 42

 Performance Hiccups 43

 Availability Issues 45

 Security Problems 46

Understanding Your Data 47

 Choosing the Proper Schema and Data Types 48

 Character Sets and Collations 51

Your Architecture Is a Mess 53

Communicating with MySQL Through Software 55

 Top Causes of Slow Query Performance 56

Summary 59

Chapter 4: How You Broke Your Queries 61

The Good, Bad, and the Ugly: Understanding Queries in MySQL 61

How You Broke Queries in MySQL 62

Types of Queries in MySQL 62

 Factors Breaking DML Queries in MySQL 63

 Factors Breaking DDL Queries in MySQL 65

 Factors Breaking DCL and TCL Queries in MySQL 68

Why Are Queries Slow? 68

Devising the Perfect Schema Design 74

Understanding Data Types 77

Understanding Character Sets and Collations 80
Understanding Indexes 84
Understanding Partitions 86
    Partitions and Big Data 89
    NULL Values and Pruning in Partitions 90
Things to Avoid When Optimizing Queries in MySQL 92
    Don't Blindly Trust Documentation 93
Summary 95

Chapter 5: Understanding Query Components 97

SQL Queries and Stored Procedures 97
Parsers and Optimizers 99
Queries and Error Messages 103
    Common MySQL Error Codes 104
Factors Disliked by Your Queries 106
    Isolate Your Columns! 107
    Get Rid of Duplicate Indexes 107
    Use EXISTS Instead of IN 108
    Make Use of Stored Procedures and Triggers 108
SHOW STATUS and EXPLAIN 110
Summary 114

Chapter 6: Understanding Your Server 115

Efficiently Using Server Resources 115
Understanding and Simulating Errors 117
Server Components and Their Interaction with MySQL 120
Coding for MySQL Performance and Security 124
What Not to Do 128
Summary 129

TABLE OF CONTENTS

Part III: Optimizing MySQL 131

Chapter 7: Optimizing Your Server for MySQL 133

Why Optimize Your Server for MySQL? 133

Common Webserver Issues Affecting MySQL 136

What Limits the Performance of MySQL? 138

Choosing Servers and Hard Drives 139

Configuring MySQL Parameters 140

Configuring MySQL I/O for Your Operating System 145

Testing Your Hardware 147

Taking Advantage of ACID Properties 150

Summary 153

Chapter 8: Optimizing Storage Engines, Schemas, and Data Types 155

Why Optimize Storage Engines and Data Types? 155

Optimizing Storage Engines 156

Data Types in MySQL 159

    String-Based Data Types 160

    Numeric Data Types 160

    Date, Time, Spatial, and JSON Data Types 161

    Storage Requirements for Data Types 162

    Choosing the Right Data Type 164

    Optimizing Schemas and Data Types for Big Data 165

Summary 167

Chapter 9: Optimizing Queries 169

Why Optimize SQL Queries? 169

Optimizing Specific Types of Queries 171

    The Query Cache 171

    Optimizing INSERT Queries 173

    Optimizing SELECT Queries 177

    Optimizing UPDATE Queries 187

TABLE OF CONTENTS

Optimizing DELETE Queries 191
Optimizing Queries for Big Data, Avoiding Deadlocks, and Other Query Optimization Tips 192
Summary 194

Chapter 10: Optimizing MySQL for Big Data 195

Can MySQL Deal with Big Data? 196
MariaDB and Big Data: Operations with Big Data Sets 197
    Inserting Big Data Into MariaDB 198
    Reading Big Data with MariaDB 200
    Updating Big Data in MariaDB 202
    Deleting Big Data From MariaDB 203
Storage Engines and Big Data 204
ACID and Big Data 205
Big Data Pitfalls and Known Issues 206
Summary 208

Chapter 11: Indexing MySQL 209

Why Index? Indexes Available in MariaDB 209
What and When to Index? 213
Indexing Myths, Misconceptions, and Fragmentation Issues 216
Your Hardware, Database, and Indexes 218
Types of Indexes 220
    B-Tree Indexes 221
    Covering Indexes 228
    Multicolumn (Composite) Indexes 232
    Prefix Indexes 235
    Spatial (R-Tree), Hash, and Clustered Indexes 236
Devising the Perfect Index Design 238
Indexing for Performance and Big Data 242
Summary 247

ix

TABLE OF CONTENTS

Chapter 12: Optimizing Partitions 249
Why Partition Data? 249
When to Partition Data? 250
Internals of Database Partitioning.. 252
Types of Partitioning in MySQL 254
Partitioning Tips: Subpartitioning, Limitations, NULL Values, and More 261
Summary... 268

Chapter 13: Optimizing Backups and Recovery 269
Why, When, and How to Backup MariaDB? 269
Backup Types and Tools 272
Backup Compression and Security 278
Backing Up Big Data Sets 280
Recovering MariaDB 283
    Recovering Big Data 284
Backup and Recovery Pitfalls 285
    Pitfalls for Big Data.. 286
Summary... 289

Chapter 14: Optimizing Replication 291
Understanding Replication... 291
Configuring and Implementing Replication... 292
Types of Replication 295
Replication Notes and Tips... 298
Securing Replication 299
Summary... 301

Chapter 15: Optimizing for Security 303
Understanding Security in MariaDB.. 303
Securing MariaDB upon Installation.. 307
General Security Measures 309
Summary... 310

TABLE OF CONTENTS

Part IV: Securing MySQL 311

Chapter 16: The World of Security in MySQL 313
General Security Guidelines and Measures Revisited 313
Access Control 316
User Security 320
MariaDB Components and Plugins That Keep Data Safe 322
Firewalling MariaDB 324
Summary 325

Chapter 17: Securing Your Database Instance 327
Security Guidelines for Specific Use Cases and Defense in Depth 327
Account Categories and Reserved Accounts 330
Password Management and Account Locking 331
SQL Injection, Input Sanitization, and MariaDB 334
    Corner Cases of SQL Injection 337
Other Attacks Targeting Your Database 337
Summary 339

Chapter 18: Security and Big Data 341
Security, Big Data, and Code in the Initial Phases of Your SDLC 344
Data, Script Kiddies & Co. 346
What Happens If…? 348
Summary 352

Appendix: Things You Wish You Knew, but Don't 355

Index 365

About the Author

Lukas Vileikis is an ethical hacker, a MySQL database administrator, and a frequent conference speaker. He has worked on MySQL since late 2013 and, since 2014, has found and responsibly disclosed security flaws in some of the most visited websites in Lithuania and abroad. Lukas honed his database administration skills while building and administering one of the biggest data breach search engines in the world: BreachDirectory.com, which is used by cybersecurity companies, individuals, as well as prominent universities worldwide. The website allows people to check whether they're at risk of identity theft and protect themselves on the Web, and protects more and more people from all walks of life every single day. BreachDirectory has been running on MySQL ever since its inception and has won numerous awards, including at World Summit Awards 2020, where BreachDirectory was a national nominee nominated by the Lithuanian government to represent Lithuania against an international jury evaluating the best digital innovations in the world, and at Technorama 2021, a tech product-based event organized by Kaunas University of Technology (KTU), where BreachDirectory was nominated as the best product in the security space by Bentley Systems.

Outside of BreachDirectory, Lukas produces content situated around database management systems. He has written articles for Severalnines, Redgate, DbVisualizer, Arctype (now part of ClickHouse), dbWatch, and other companies, as well as managed writers in some of those companies (Redgate, DbVisualizer, Arctype). Some of his written content has been also replicated by MySQL, MariaDB, and Percona. He also runs a YouTube channel under the moniker "Database Dive," where he distills complex database topics into relatable explanations in video format. Lukas also talks and runs workshops at conferences like Percona LIVE, MariaDB Server Fest and MariaDB Unconferences, DevTalks Romania in Bucharest, Big Data Conference Europe, and Build Stuff in Vilnius and can be found at TEDx events in Lithuania, talking at "Dirty AI" and other software events in Spain.

Lukas also runs his own blog at lukasvileikis.com and can be reached by email at lukas@lukasvileikis.com.

Acknowledgments

I'd like to thank a couple of people who, directly or indirectly, contributed to the content in this book, my knowledge that's shared within, or acted as catalysts. The first people that come to mind are Zach Naimon, Mikael Oldebäck, and Louis "Dr. SQL" Davidson.

Those people have played an especially important role in this book – whether by inspecting my work, criticizing me where necessary, or providing advice – and are never forgotten. Without them, parts of this book wouldn't exist.

Zach, thank you for being a great friend and an awesome person to work with; Mikael, thank you for pushing me forward where necessary and being a great manager; and Louis, thank you for writing the foreword too!

Jonathan Gennick and Dr. Charles Bell have been instrumental in helping me find out that an issue regarding an "@" sign on bigger data sets (I share details of it in the Appendix) is a bug within MySQL as well – a big thank you goes out to you two as well.

Those who taught development secrets all these years ago are never to be forgotten too: a special thank-you goes out to Gediminas Kiltinavičius, Artūras Lazejevas, and other people involved in shaping me as a person (and as a developer!) in the programming school in Lithuania.

Of course, a special thank-you goes to the Apress editors Jonathan Gennick, Shaul Elson, Krishnan Sathyamurthy, and the rest, without whom this book wouldn't have been able to see daylight in the first place.

Finally, a separate thank-you goes out to countless people who are contributing their advice, often free of charge, on forums and mediums like Stack Overflow, the DBA Stack Exchange, blogs, YouTube, conferences, and beyond – bits and pieces of advice on how to solve specific issues are always golden. Some of that advice helps developers in their darkest moments, some of it helps solve smaller issues, and some of it doesn't work at all, but regardless, the developer community rocks! A big thank you goes out to you as well. Whoever you are, whatever you do, sharing your knowledge is caring. Thank you for caring for the developer community and providing advice where necessary.

Preface

If I'm honest, the reason you've picked this book up is most likely because of the title, right? What kind of a book has "Hacking" as part of its title? That's crazy! As you can probably already tell by the title, this book isn't your average book about development or database management systems.

Traditional books about databases often focus on a specific thing – performance, indexes, or the like. That's not necessarily a bad thing, but what many of them lack is the explanation of how you broke your database to the point that you need optimizations described in the book in the first place. Here's where this book comes in. The aim of this book is to open your eyes to what's really possible in the realm of MySQL and that's why it is split into three distinct parts – "Breaking," "Optimizing," and "Securing." The first part of the book – breaking – will walk you through how you broke your database to such a point that you may need optimizations for it; optimization will tell you how to optimize your database to be highly performant, reliable, and secure; and the last part – securing your database – will help you understand how to secure your data you just optimized.

These days, hacking is everywhere – and I'm not only saying that because we live in an AI age. Hacking has a very wide meaning – and its meaning is not only confined to computer systems with information on it. Far from it – hacking down a tree or hacking your body at the gym also falls within that realm. And who could deny that hacking your career onto different heights isn't hacking, too?

I hope you will enjoy reading this book as much as I enjoyed writing it – ultimately, I do hope that the information within this book helps you in situations beyond the scope of this book.

Now make yourself some coffee, sit back, and enjoy. Not before walking yourself through the contents of this book though!

How Is This Book Organized?

Apart from a nice title, this book is purposefully split into three parts – breaking, optimizing, and securing – with an additional part acting as an introduction.

PREFACE

As I've already noted before, each of those parts serves three distinct purposes necessary to achieve three different objectives:

1) **Breaking** allows you to understand how to break your database, meaning that it will walk you through things you're doing wrong that probably impact your database performance, availability, security, or all of those things. OK, I'll come clear – it will walk you through how to intentionally break your database too. Such knowledge may be extremely beneficial for those running workshops, speaking at conferences, or just wanting to flex their MySQL wizardry on their friends.

2) **Optimizing** walks you through how to optimize your database instance for your specific use case.

3) **Securing** walks you through the necessary security measures to employ to secure your database instance and secure your data.

As such, each part of this book has its own remits, so I'd recommend you read it starting from the first part and ending at the last one – you may also elect to start reading from the optimization part, but it will likely contain analogs to the first part, and the third part is likely to contain analogs to the second part.

Tip It's not necessary to read this book from top to bottom, but as each part of the book serves a distinct objective that leads to the next, some things may become blurry if you read the book as you see fit. For those wanting quick advice, I'd advise you to skip to the specific problem in question using the index.

Who Is This Book For?

The primary audience of this book are database professionals, but that's not to say that other software professionals won't be able to apply the advice in this book.

This book is for everyone using MySQL – the catch here is a specific approach to the database management system as a whole. Instead of teaching you how to optimize database internals, this book tells you what you're doing wrong first and then tells you how to optimize these things and secure them for the future.

PREFACE

This book will build a solid foundation around MySQL both for junior database administrators and for experienced DBAs alike – juniors will learn what not to do to a database to avoid problems, while seniors will be provided useful tips that will help them deal with issues in everyday work or corner cases that may occur in the future.

Conventions Used in This Book

The conventions used in this book are as follows:

- Code formatting indicates parts of code and looks like so:

    code

- *Italic* indicates the names of files, directories, file extensions or URLs, emphasized text – everything in that realm. It also introduces new terms.

- **Text in bold** or underlined text reminds you of something you should be wary about.

This book also provides you with tips, warnings (cautions), or notes. These things will be outlined like so:

Tip   This is a tip.

Warning or Caution   This is a warning or a caution!

Note   This is a note.

Examples in This Book

The code examples in this book are based on MySQL 8.0 on a Windows architecture but should work well on other architectures too. To be on the safe side, avoid running code examples in this book in a live environment – test, verify, and only then push the code into production.

PREFACE

Be careful when using code examples – some examples may need additional context, some may slow down or even break your queries, and some will be shown as examples of what not to do. Make sure to read the notes preceding the code examples carefully and only run code examples in a safe environment with a full and thorough understanding of the implications of your actions.

Comments, Questions, and Concerns

If you have any comments, questions, or concerns regarding this book, feel free to contact me via email at lukas@lukasvileikis.com – I'm happy to be contacted regarding all sorts of queries, be invited to speak at conferences or to run workshops, or do other stuff, and I usually respond pretty promptly.

For more information about databases, security on the Web, or myself, visit

- My website over at lukasvileikis.com.

- A data breach search engine I've built by navigating to BreachDirectory.com (in case you're wondering, it's also based on MySQL!).

- If you desire, watch a video or two about database performance by visiting @DatabaseDive on YouTube or other mediums.

And now, let's dive into MySQL, shall we?

Foreword

I am pleased to write this note in front of Lukas' book *Hacking MySQL*. Over the past few years that I have worked with Lukas through his writing about MySQL for the Simple Talk website, where I am the editor, I have witnessed his knowledge and skill when it comes to working with MySQL.

The title of the book does sound ominous, but it isn't really about how to hack into a MySQL database, but in reality, what breaks MySQL and what keeps it from breaking and being broken into.

When you finish reading this book, you should be far more knowledgeable about all things MySQL and be more equipped to deal with all the common, and not so common, issues that come up when setting up and using MySQL for your production work.

I have learned quite a bit over the last two years from Lukas from his writing of articles on these subjects and his willingness to dive deep into the subject. I think you will get the same experience from this book, and a whole lot more.

Louis Davidson

PART I

The Basics of MySQL

CHAPTER 1

The World of MySQL

MySQL is one of the most widely used database management systems in the world. That's not without a reason – MySQL is a friend to many tech companies including, but not limited to, Facebook, Twitter, Netflix, and Uber.

The reason why so many companies elect to use MySQL as their primary database management system of choice is because of its robustness: MySQL supports multiple storage engines which makes MySQL flexible enough for an ever-changing world of data – those storage engines come with their features related to performance, availability, or security, features that can be exploited to get the most out of this database management system.

The History of MySQL

MySQL was originally developed in the 1990s by Michael Widenius, David Axmark, and Allan Larsson. The development of the database management system began in 1994, and it was first released to the general public a couple years later.

In expert circles, Michael is often referred to as "Monty," and it is said that Monty came up with the idea to build MySQL after he, while working in a small data warehousing company he and Allan Larsson founded in 1985, wrote a reporting tool using C. Sometime after, it is said that customers of the company wanted something akin to an interface to deal with their data and Monty, fed up with solutions that don't work, started writing a tool – the tool now known as MySQL. MySQL is a name derived from a combination of the name of Monty's first daughter (My) and SQL, the programming language.

Over the years, MySQL has advanced further and further. Many readers will know that these days, we have three choices to choose from when working with MySQL – we can use MySQL Server, MariaDB Server, or Percona Server.

Both MariaDB Server and Percona Server are variations of MySQL Server – they don't differ much, but offer some things the others don't. MariaDB is known for its storage engines, and Percona Server comes with many improvements to performance and functionality enhancements. MariaDB is named after Monty's youngest daughter – Maria – and includes features developed based on community feedback, while Percona is known for its database consulting prowess.

The Architecture of MySQL

As is the case with all database management systems, MySQL has an architecture unique to itself. The MySQL architecture has three main parts, them being as follows:

1. **Client**: The client part of the MySQL architecture; the part that users interact with when running MySQL.

2. **Server**: The "brains" of MySQL. The client passes the query through the server, which performs its own functions. Thread handling handles the query and distributes it toward the query cache and the parser, which, in turn, forwards it to the query optimizer.

3. **Storage**: Finally, once the client has worked on the query and passed it on to the server, the server passes everything on to the storage. Storage refers to the storage engines powering MySQL – at present, the most popular storage engine is InnoDB followed by MyISAM. All of those storage engines have their own pluses and minuses which will be discussed a little later.

The point here is very simple – the three layers described above always work in conjunction and oil your server for MySQL to work properly. Figure 1-1 will help you visualize how these components within MySQL interact.

CHAPTER 1 THE WORLD OF MYSQL

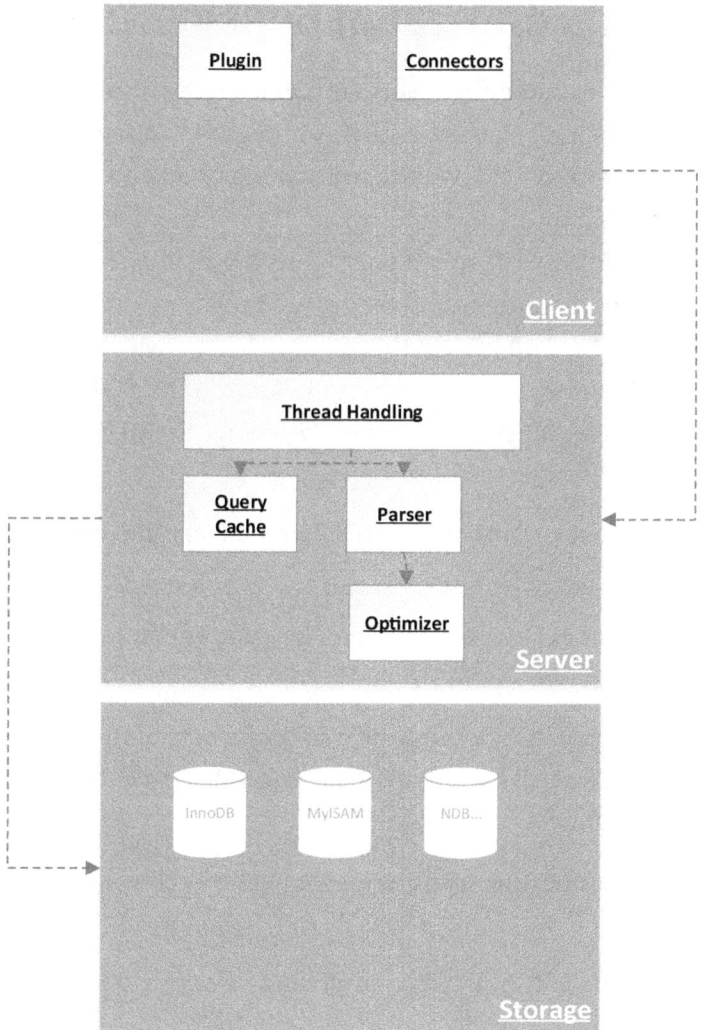

Figure 1-1. *Architecture of MySQL*

Walking yourself through the architecture of MySQL is the first step toward a better understanding of how your database is broken, optimized, and how it can be secured, too.

Once you understand how the architecture layers connect together, it's time to think about the use cases of MySQL. Don't worry if you don't understand much at this point, too – everything will become more clear as we go along.

5

CHAPTER 1 THE WORLD OF MYSQL

Basic Use Cases and Initial Considerations

MySQL consists of three architecture layers, and that's not without a reason – each of them is a necessity to properly execute requests in regard to our configuration.

MySQL can be configured with a configuration file titled "my" – the name of the file is "my.ini" on Windows architectures and "my.cnf" on Linux-based systems.

The configuration file consists of a set of different parameters. Some of them are listed below, but to properly understand them, you must also understand one crucial thing. Go back to Figure 1-1 and look at the very last layer – what does it say? Right, it says "Storage." Storage refers to the storage engines within MySQL. MySQL is built on the principle of storage engines, and at the present moment, the RDBMS offers eight storage engines to choose from:

- `port`: Defines the port of our MySQL Server. Defaults to 3306 can be changed.

- `key_buffer_size`: Defines the size of key (index) buffers in memory. Relevant to users of MyISAM.

- `max_allowed_packet`: Defines the maximum size of the packet that can flow through MySQL. The default value on a MySQL 8.0 instance is 1GB.

- `log_error`: Defines the location where log files relevant to MySQL are stored.

- `log_error_verbosity`: Defines what kind of errors to log:

    - A value of "1" only logs errors.

    - A value of "2" logs errors and warnings.

    - A value of "3" logs errors, warnings, and notes.

- `innodb_buffer_pool_size`: The most important parameter for the users of the InnoDB storage engine. This setting defines the buffer pool size for the InnoDB storage engine. The buffer pool caches table and index data as it's being accessed.

- `innodb_data_file_path`: The path toward the InnoDB data file – ibdata1.

As you can see, the configuration file consists of a set of different parameters. Here, we have a double-edged sword: my.ini on Windows provides developers with a lot of comments for them to understand how MySQL works at the expense of certain parameters being out of reach, while my.cnf on Linux doesn't provide as many parameters to start with and has no comments within itself, but it offers a wider realm in the sense of available functionality. The reason why Windows users have fewer choices than their Linux counterparts is very simple – Windows is not equipped for certain optimization operations to be completed (e.g., the InnoDB flush method of O_DIRECT is only available on Unix systems because it requires POSIX-based header files).

Interesting, yeah? Stick with me. Go back to Figure 1-1 and look at the very last layer – the Storage layer. Sounds familiar? Storage refers to the storage engines within MySQL. MySQL is built on the principle of storage engines, and at the present moment, MySQL 8.0 offers 10 storage engines you can choose from.

Storage Engines

At present, the main storage engines offered for use within MySQL are shown in Table 1-1.

Table 1-1. *Main storage engines*

Storage Engine	About
InnoDB	<ul><li>The main storage engine offered by MySQL since MySQL 5.5.</li><li>A general-purpose storage engine that is recommended for use in most projects using MySQL.</li><li>The only ACID-compliant storage engine in MySQL.</li><li>Offers support for foreign keys and, since MySQL 5.6, for full-text indexes.</li><li>When MariaDB is in use, InnoDB supports virtual columns.</li></ul>
MyISAM	<ul><li>MyISAM was the default storage engine until MySQL 5.5 rolled around – as such, it is the primary competitor to InnoDB.</li><li>MyISAM provides no ACID compliance and is based on the key buffer.</li><li>MyISAM offers support for full-text indexes by default.</li><li>MyISAM stores an internal table row count inside of itself and thus, while generally being a slower alternative to InnoDB, offers faster performance for COUNT(*) queries.</li></ul>

CHAPTER 1 THE WORLD OF MYSQL

Other Storage Engines

Aside from InnoDB and MyISAM, MySQL also has other storage engines you can choose from. Changing the storage engine of your MySQL infrastructure is not generally recommended unless you have a good reason to do so as InnoDB has been tried and tested extensively and determined to be the best storage engine for the vast majority of use cases, but if you're feeling a little adventurous, here's what your options are and why you may consider them.

Storage Engine	About
MEMORY (HEAP before MySQL 4.1)	• This storage engine stores all of the data in memory. • Provides tables with hash-based storage making exact data retrievals extremely fast, but with a downside of storing data in memory (once the server is shut down or the memory is cleared, data is gone). • Before MySQL 8.0, MySQL used the MEMORY storage engine to store data relevant to temporary tables. This engine was replaced by the TempTable storage engine for temporary table use cases starting from MySQL 8.0.
TempTable	• This storage engine is primarily used by the optimizer to create temporary tables and store data relevant to them.
CSV	• As the name suggests, this storage engine stores data in a CSV-like format. • No support for indexes or partitioned tables.
ARCHIVE	• Intended to be used as an archive for data that is no longer used or required for your application to function properly. • Has an extremely small footprint on the disk at the expense of not supporting DELETE, REPLACE, or UPDATE operations. • No support for indexes or partitions.
BLACKHOLE	• Any and all data inserted into this storage engine disappears into a blackhole, hence the name. • Intended to be used as a demo solution for sandbox projects.

(*continued*)

Storage Engine	About
MERGE (formerly MRG_MyISAM)	• This storage engine provides a collection of MyISAM tables that are merged and can be used as one table.
FEDERATED	• This storage engine enables for querying of remote data without replication or clustering.
EXAMPLE	• Intended to act as an example for developers building storage engines within MySQL.

MySQL is a serious beast, huh? So many storage engines without even counting the main one? Oh, and did you know that Percona has built an enhancement for the main storage engine – InnoDB – too? Their enhanced storage engine is called Percona XtraDB or simply XtraDB, and it's known for offering a wide variety of features suitable for those needing a high-performance environment.

That's the world of MySQL – you now have a good idea of how everything works together. Now, you will dive deeper into specific storage engines, and then, we will start breaking your MySQL instance to figure out how to optimize and secure it.

Summary

MySQL is a powerful, but very complicated beast – with so many features under its hood, it's no wonder why many developers get lost in its jungle.

The good news is that this beast can be tamed – once you learn more about the storage engines available MySQL, you will be able to determine how you broke your instance, then – how to optimize everything for it not to be broken again, and finally, how to secure your data from data breaches for your infrastructure to be more secure.

Now, go grab a coffee and make sure to refresh your memory about the storage engines in MySQL before you continue reading – this is where we dive deeper into the realm of storage engines.

CHAPTER 2

Individual Storage Engines

For many, the usage of MySQL is a means to an end – some of us create websites, while applications may take the cake for others. No matter what your specific use case is, you will need to make good use of storage engines within its infrastructure.

Go back to Chapter 1 and take a closer look at the MySQL architecture drawing in Figure 1-1 once again. The last layer provides an incomplete list of storage engines, and the layer is called "Storage." The storage layer consists of three objects – InnoDB, MyISAM, and NDB. These are the storage engines available in MySQL, and while one of them may be considered the "King," others are no less important too – all of them should be considered before you plan the next step in your journey.

The Modern King of Storage Engines
InnoDB in MySQL and MariaDB

As far as storage engines in MySQL are concerned, one of them – InnoDB – unequivocally takes the cake. Many of you have probably heard of InnoDB: the storage engine was introduced to MySQL in version 5.5.5 in July 2010 and is known to support many features that are used to tune MySQL servers for high performance and reliability.

Since its inception, InnoDB has replaced MyISAM as the primary and default storage engine – back in the day, MyISAM was still a viable choice for many developers, but as the time flew by and engineers introduced features previously only available in MyISAM into InnoDB, the engine has sunk into the past. MyISAM can still be found in MySQL, but the engine can be rightfully considered obsolete. With that being said, MyISAM has a feature that's worth your attention, but don't get distracted yet – InnoDB is a beast that needs to be dealt with properly, too.

CHAPTER 2 INDIVIDUAL STORAGE ENGINES

It all starts from the configuration – my.cnf on Unix systems or my.ini on a Windows architecture. The file can be found in various locations. Windows users will find the file in the binary folder: /bin/mysql/mysql*.*.** where the *.*.** is the version of your MySQL Server, and users of the Unix infrastructure will find the file in one of the following locations:

/etc/my.cnf
/etc/mysql/my.cnf
/var/lib/mysql/my.cnf
~/my.cnf

After finding the file in one of the specified locations, open it up and you will see a bunch of settings relevant to InnoDB. On a Windows architecture, the available settings will look like so (example based on MySQL 8.0.31. Older versions may have less available options – the most important options are emboldened):

innodb_adaptive_hash_index=on
innodb_buffer_pool_dump_now=off
innodb_buffer_pool_dump_at_shutdown=off
innodb_buffer_pool_instances=2
innodb_buffer_pool_load_at_startup=off
innodb_buffer_pool_size=1G
innodb_data_file_path=ibdata1:12M
innodb_default_row_format=dynamic
innodb_doublewrite=on
;skip_innodb_doublewrite
innodb_file_per_table=1
innodb_flush_log_at_trx_commit=1
innodb_flush_method=normal
;innodb_force_recovery=1
innodb_ft_enable_stopword=off
innodb_ft_max_token_size=10
innodb_ft_min_token_size=0
innodb_io_capacity=2000
innodb_max_dirty_pages_pct=90
innodb_lock_wait_timeout=600

innodb_log_buffer_size=16M
innodb_log_file_size=20M
innodb_log_files_in_group=2
innodb_optimize_fulltext_only=1
innodb_page_size=16K
innodb_purge_threads=10
innodb_read_io_threads=10
innodb_stats_on_metadata=0
innodb_strict_mode=on
innodb_thread_concurrency=16
innodb_undo_log_truncate=on
innodb_write_io_threads=4

Here's what the options mean, one by one:

Setting	Explanation
innodb_adaptive_hash_index	Enables InnoDB to act as an in-memory database. Once enabled and if an InnoDB-based table fits in the memory of your server, MySQL will enable a direct (and thus quicker) lookup of elements by automatically building hash indexes. May not be suitable for all projects – test before using in production.
innodb_buffer_pool_dump_now	Dumps the most recently cached pages in the buffer pool immediately.
innodb_buffer_pool_dump_at_shutdown	Dumps the most recently cached pages in the buffer pool when the InnoDB engine shuts down.
innodb_buffer_pool_instances	Defines the number of the instances of the buffer pool is divided into in InnoDB. If the InnoDB buffer pool is extremely large, tuning this value and increasing the number of instances may improve performance.
innodb_buffer_pool_load_at_startup	Whenever MySQL is started, the buffer pool is pre-loaded with the same amount of pages it had when it was shut down.

(*continued*)

Setting	Explanation
innodb_buffer_pool_size	Arguably the most important parameter in InnoDB. Specifies the size of the buffer pool in InnoDB – since the InnoDB buffer pool holds the data and indexes relevant to InnoDB tables, it's recommended to increase its value to be big enough to accommodate your data. Setting the value of this parameter to around 60% of the available RAM is a good starting point. Adjust as necessary.
innodb_data_file_path	The path toward ibdata1 – the file that holds data, metadata, and indexes derived from InnoDB-based tables.
innodb_default_row_format	Specifies the default format for rows in tables using InnoDB. Available values: 1. DYNAMIC. Default value starting from MySQL 5.0.3. InnoDB tables using this row format will store rows in a manner that enables your database to store more data on database pages that overflow. Otherwise, very similar to COMPACT. 2. REDUNDANT. The original row format that was available before MySQL 5 rolled around. 3. COMPACT. Very similar to REDUNDANT. This format requires less storage when storing data, hence the name. 4. COMPRESSED. Compresses as much data as possible, can store even more data on pages that overflow.

(continued)

CHAPTER 2 INDIVIDUAL STORAGE ENGINES

Setting	Explanation
`innodb_doublewrite`	Enables or disables doublewrite buffering. Available values – ON and OFF. Enabling this parameter will provide InnoDB with the ability to have a storage area to "play with" before writing database pages to ibdata1, thus potentially preventing half-written pages to be written to ibdata1.
`skip_innodb_doublewrite`	If left uncommented, makes InnoDB skip the doublewrite buffer.
`innodb_file_per_table`	`Enables InnoDB tables to be stored separately from the ibdata1 file by storing their data in separate files, thus preventing cluttering. Leave the value of this parameter ON unless you have a good reason to turn it off.`
`innodb_flush_log_at_trx_commit`	`Controls the balance between strict ACID compliance and higher performance at the expense of ACID.` `The value "0" will make InnoDB flush the redo logs to disk only once a second, a default value of "1" will make InnoDB ACID compliant, the value of "2" will write to logs upon commit and flush logs to disk once a second, and "3" will write logs to disk once they're prepared and once they're committed, thus making the process slower.`

(continued)

Setting	Explanation
innodb_flush_method	Describes the method InnoDB uses to flush logs at the transaction commit phase. Available values include 1. normal 2. unbuffered 3. async_unbuffered 4. fsync 5. O_DSYNC 6. nosync 7. littlesync 8. O_DIRECT 9. O_DIRECT_NO_FSYNC I'll explain what these values mean a little later, but for now, leave this setting at default for Windows architectures, and choose O_DIRECT for Linux.
innodb_force_recovery	Enables or disables the crash recovery mode for InnoDB. Available values include integers from 0 to 6.
innodb_ft_enable_stopword	If left ON (default value), will make InnoDB fulltext indexes have stopwords. Uses the built-in list of stopwords or takes them from the values set in innodb_ft_user_stopword_table or innodb_ft_server_stopword table.
innodb_ft_max_token_size	Specifies the maximum character length of words that can use a FULLTEXT index.
innodb_ft_min_token_size	Specifies the minimum character length of words that can use a FULLTEXT index.
innodb_io_capacity	Defines the number of I/O operations per second InnoDB can use for tasks completed in the background.

(continued)

Setting	Explanation
innodb_max_dirty_pages_pct	A percentage-based value that defines the acceptable percentage of dirty pages in InnoDB.
innodb_lock_wait_timeout	Amount of time in seconds that an InnoDB transaction will wait for a row lock before rolling an operation back.
innodb_log_buffer_size	The size of the buffer that's used when InnoDB is writing data to the log files. Default value – 16MB, making it larger may improve I/O performance.
innodb_log_file_size	The size of InnoDB log files. Recommended value – around a quarter (25%) of the buffer pool size. Deprecated starting from MySQL 8.0.30 – adjust the innodb_redo_log_capacity variable instead.
innodb_log_files_in_group	Specifies the number of InnoDB log files in a group. Deprecated starting from MySQL 8.0.30 – adjust the innodb_redo_log_capacity variable instead.
innodb_optimize_fulltext_only	Makes OPTIMIZE TABLE only optimize FULLTEXT indexes. Intended to be used for maintenance operations.
innodb_page_size	Specifies the data page size for tables running the InnoDB storage engine.
innodb_purge_threads	Defines the number of threads to be used once an InnoDB purge is underway.
innodb_read_io_threads	Specifies the number of I/O threads allocated for read operations (SELECT queries) in InnoDB.
innodb_stats_on_metadata	This parameter applies to the optimizer of MySQL when the optimizer statistics aren't persistent. Available values include OFF (default) and ON. Look into enabling this parameter if you work with bigger data sets and deal with SELECT queries.

(continued)

CHAPTER 2   INDIVIDUAL STORAGE ENGINES

Setting	Explanation
innodb_strict_mode	Makes InnoDB behavior more strict in the sense that warnings will be treated as errors if this variable is enabled.
innodb_thread_concurrency	The maximum number of threads in InnoDB.
innodb_undo_log_truncate	If an undo tablespace exceeds a certain threshold defined in the innodb_max_undo_log_size, the logs are truncated.
innodb_write_io_threads	Defines the number of I/O threads for write-based operations inside InnoDB.

Quite a lot of parameters you can optimize, right? However, while knowing what the parameters above do will act as a good starting point before we break our MySQL instances, most of you will probably not need to modify or even look at all of them – optimizing a couple of them will be more than enough, and the rest should be touched upon if you want to push InnoDB to its limits later on.

When initially optimizing InnoDB, pay attention at the seven emboldened values:

1) **innodb_buffer_pool_size**: Set the buffer pool size to 60–80% of the available RAM in your system. The bigger the buffer pool is, the more data and indexes InnoDB will be able to cache, and as a result, your SQL queries will complete faster.

2) **innodb_data_file_path**: This parameter may not seem very significant at first glance, but keep in mind that the data file (explained below) stores a whole host of data relevant to your tables. As such, if you're working on a big data-based project, it's crucial to set the data file path on a drive that lots of space.

3) **innodb_file_per_table**: Leave this parameter at its default value of 1. By doing so, you remove unnecessary clutter from the data file by enabling InnoDB to store tables in separate files, as well as provide yourself with more leniency for maintenance operations in the future.

4) **innodb_flush_log_at_trx_commit**: It is usually best to leave this parameter at the default value – 1 – to ensure your database stays ACID-compliant. It's possible to specify other values like 0, 2, and 3 as specified above, but those will sacrifice ACID for speed.

5) **innodb_flush_method**: As stated above, this parameter defines the method InnoDB will use to flush logs once a transaction is committed. Here's all of your available options:

   a. normal: Simulated asynchronous I/O, buffered I/O.

   b. unbuffered: Simulated asynchronous I/O, non-buffered I/O.

   c. async_unbuffered: Windows asynchronous I/O and non-buffered I/O. The default setting for Windows users.

   d. fsync: Makes InnoDB use the fsync() function to synchronize the state of the database and the server. The default setting for Linux users.

   e. O_DSYNC: Makes InnoDB use the O_DSYNC function to guarantee that both data and metadata have been written to the disk before flushing the log files. Usually a faster alternative to O_DIRECT at the expense of data consistency.

   f. nosync: Intended to be used for internal testing and unsupported for production use cases.

   g. littlesync: Intended to be used for internal testing and unsupported for production use cases.

   h. O_DIRECT: Imposes a hint toward InnoDB saying that you want the data to bypass the cache of the Linux kernel. Generally slower than O_DSYNC, but more stable and data consistent.

   i. O_DIRECT_NO_FSYNC: Imposes a hint toward InnoDB stating a desire to use O_DIRECT while skipping the fsync() function.

6) **innodb_log_buffer_size**: The log buffer size is crucial for quickly writing to the log files on the disk. Making the log buffer larger will enable larger transactions to be completed quicker and, thus, save disk I/O.

7) **`innodb_redo_log_capacity`**: An alternative to the now-deprecated innodb_log_file_size and innodb_log_files_in_group variables. If this variable is left undefined and the log file size and log files in the group are defined instead, the value of this parameter is calculated using a formula (innodb_log_files_in_group * innodb_log_file_size.) If not, InnoDB uses the value specified in this parameter.

The understanding of the parameters described above is crucial to achieve your performance objectives, but also bear in mind that these parameters would not be complete without the InnoDB system tablespace – ibdata1.

InnoDB also has a data file that is also referred to as "the system tablespace" as described above. The file is the aforementioned ibdata1 – it resides in the *bin* directory of your MySQL Server installation and acts as the backbone for everything related to the InnoDB storage engine. ibdata1 stores the data and indexes from all InnoDB-based tables, the undo space and rollback segments, the double-write buffer, changes to secondary indexes or insert buffers, and Multiversion Concurrency Control (MVCC) data. Enabling innodb_file_per_table will help alleviate the damage, but if ibdata1 is deleted or corrupted, your data is gone.

Aside from that, there's a lot that can be said about ibdata1 and related files – you will learn the specifics when we Break and Optimize our database. Before doing that, you must educate yourself about the rest of the storage engine choices available to you.

One thing you must keep in mind is that various flavors of MySQL come with different options for search engines, too – Percona Server is famous for its XtraDB offering, while MariaDB can enable you to store data in Amazon S3 servers or offer a crash-safe alternative to MyISAM. But about everything from the beginning…

Storage Engines in Percona Server

Percona Server can be thought of as an enhanced version of MySQL Server. The server is a free and an open source alternative to MySQL that's focused on offering blazing-fast performance.

Percona Server works similarly to its counterparts – it does support InnoDB in all its glory, but it has a trick up its sleeve, too: Percona is well known for its XtraDB fork too.

XtraDB is an enhanced version of InnoDB with custom built-in options to enhance performance. It's not anything magic, but if you're tinkering around with InnoDB, you will certainly hear about its brother XtraDB as well.

Contrary to popular belief, XtraDB can also be used in MariaDB and even was its default storage engine up until MariaDB 10.1 – that's no longer the case because starting from MariaDB 10.2, the team switched back to InnoDB as XtraDB had many improvements over InnoDB in older versions of the database management system, but over time, InnoDB has quickly caught up.

Some argue that with properly optimized options, XtraDB is only marginally better than InnoDB, but there are a couple of things you should know nonetheless.

XtraDB builds on the foundation of InnoDB and exploits its robust design while adding more features and metrics on top. Percona Server also supports two other storage engines not available in MySQL – MyRocks and TokuDB.

Percona MyRocks and TokuDB

MyRocks

MyRocks is a storage engine based on RocksDB – a key-value store for faster storage. It is known for its ability to take up less footprint on the disk and better I/O capacity. It should be known that to work with the storage engine, it's necessary to have Percona MyRocks installed and enabled on your server. A simple `sudo` command will do:

```
sudo apt install percona-server-rocksdb-OS
```

Here OS represents the option you need to specify depending on the operating system you find yourself using. If it's Debian or Ubuntu, specifying `5.7` is enough. For RHEL or CentOS, you'd have to specify `57.x86_64`:

```
sudo apt install percona-server-rocksdb-57.x86_64
```

Once RocksDB is installed, interact with Percona Server using the Percona Server admin – `ps-admin` – script like so, and you will be good to go:

```
sudo ps-admin --enable-rocksdb --u [username] --p[password]
```

Once that's done, you can start familiarizing yourself with RocksDB.

CHAPTER 2   INDIVIDUAL STORAGE ENGINES

The first thing you should be aware of is that while most of the storage engines within MySQL are based on B+ trees, RocksDB, unlike InnoDB, is an LSM-based storage engine. That means that it may not be a very good fit for read-intensive workloads, but at the same time, it also means that it's quite a decent choice if your use case is a write-intensive workload with bigger data sets that require efficient storage capabilities. Data in MyRocks requires less storage space too, but it doesn't come without downsides:

- MyRocks doesn't provide support for online DDL commands.
- No support for full-text or spatial indexes or foreign keys.
- No support for gap locks, transportable tablespaces, or group replication.
- MyRocks doesn't have any SAVEPOINT capabilities either.

If the downsides don't scare you and your use case is a write-intensive workload and a bigger data set, familiarize yourself with the available options. Some of the more interesting options offered by MyRocks include:

MyRocks Option	Explanation
rocksdb_bulk_load	One can tell MyRocks to ignore certain checks or skip the acquisition of locks by enabling the rocksdb_bulk_load variable. MyRocks also has a couple of options related to this that let you specify when to commit a transaction during a bulk load, etc.
rocksdb_create_checkpoint	The directory where checkpoint files will be created (default – none).
rocksdb_db_write_buffer_size	When the tables in the memory reach the value specified in this parameter, data is flushed to disk.
rocksdb_error_if_exists	Used when building new databases. A value of "1" enables an error to be displayed if a database already exists. Off (0) by default.
rocksdb_column_default_value_as_expression	Allows functions to be used as default values for columns.

A bulk loading functionality, functions as default values... Interesting, huh? Taking a glance at the settings available to be configured alone is enough to grasp the fact that this storage engine is for writing. Providing the storage engine with data isn't tricky as long as you remember a couple of key rules:

1. **Bulk loading**: Enable the `rocksdb_bulk_load` option, load data, disable the option. Enabling this option makes the loading of data faster because it enables MyRocks to skip certain operations, but it also means that your data may not be visible until the bulk load operation is completed.

2. **Secondary indexes**: If your table has any columns with secondary indexes on them, drop the indexes before providing the table with data. After that, restore them.

3. **Unsorted data**: If your data is not sorted by PRIMARY KEYs, enable the `rocksdb_bulk_load_allow_unsorted` option before loading your data, and disable it after.

4. **The memory**: Since MyRocks "memorizes" details about ongoing transactions (holds them in the memory), it is wise to keep the transaction size relatively small to avoid issues.

After that, keep up to date by familiarizing yourself with the information available in the documentation, and you should be good to go!

TokuDB

Up until Percona Server 8 and MariaDB 10.5, MySQL had another storage engine up its sleeve – TokuDB. The idea of TokuDB was to facilitate the work with bigger data sets where data is inserted and queried at the same time; however, as time went by, Percona understood that MyRocks provided similar benefits to TokuDB, eventually deprecating this storage engine in May 2021.

TokuDB is not the only storage engine that is considered to be deprecated – old-school fanatics of MySQL will remember MyISAM which was the default storage engine for MySQL until MySQL Server 5.5 rolled around.

CHAPTER 2 INDIVIDUAL STORAGE ENGINES

The Primary Contestant of InnoDB

Back in the day, MyISAM was the only storage engine provided by MySQL and had a lot of upsides to itself and was even considered a viable contestant to InnoDB for a long period – some developers can be still seen suggesting the usage of this storage engine, but DBAs will quickly tell you that InnoDB quickly caught up and threw MyISAM to the curb meaning that MyISAM is widely considered to be an obsolete storage engine by today's standards as it has no ACID support and is prone to crashes.

With that said, MyISAM does have two significant upsides to its counterpart InnoDB – it does not store its data in any file that cannot shrink (the same cannot be said about the InnoDB's tablespace – ibdata1), and it does provide an exact row count in all tables running the storage engine.

The Early Days of MyISAM

Back in the day, MyISAM was an awesome storage engine; it was the only storage engine provided by MySQL up until MySQL 5.5, and by the standards of these days, it performed its functions exceptionally well.

MyISAM is based on ISAM – an **I**ndexed **S**equential **A**ccess **M**ethod – that was developed by IBM to facilitate access to data sequentially. Such an access method allows for easy reading of database files starting from the first record and ending at the last with indexes pointing at the correct record in the file thus making the method easy and straightforward to understand for everyone involved.

MyISAM was cheap – the data didn't take up much space on the disk, tables in the database provided an exact row count due to the internal design of the storage engine, and there was no file "linked" to other files that could clutter the database if not dealt with properly as is the case with InnoDB's ibdata1. To add to that, MyISAM supported features that were not supported by InnoDB making it an extremely attractive choice for many developers. Even with MyISAM being a non-transactional storage engine, considering these factors it's no wonder why developers thought of MyISAM as a viable alternative for InnoDB for so long:

Feature in MyISAM	Feature in InnoDB
Support for full-text indexes.	Full-text indexes are supported starting from MySQL 5.6.
Support for portable tablespaces.	Portable tablespaces have been supported since MySQL 5.6.
Support for spatial indexes.	Spatial indexes became available in InnoDB since MySQL 5.7.
Support for the last update time in regard to tables running the storage engine.	The functionality was implemented in InnoDB since MySQL 5.7.

In general, the functionality was pretty okay, and everyone got on with it. But as with everything, MyISAM didn't come without downsides – and as time went on, they became more and more apparent.

MyISAM in the Present Day

These days, the main downsides of MyISAM are related to data inconsistency and no ACID compliance. Due to its design, MyISAM is a non-transactional storage engine meaning that the storage engine is incapable of supporting rollbacks or atomic operations, thus making it an Achilles' heel for many developers.

On the flip side, MyISAM has a very simple design, thus making functionality unavailable in InnoDB easily accessible in MyISAM – MyISAM stores the exact row count of tables running the storage engine inside of its metadata and displays the number of rows in any table running the storage engine, and deleting files associated with the storage engine deletes the data in full without any issues too. The same can't be said about InnoDB because of its tablespace file and the log files that are scanned through when we start the recovery process.

Ironically, the upsides of MyISAM make its downsides more painful as well. MyISAM takes much less footprint on the disk, but since MyISAM maintains no log files, it simply cannot look at them when recovering data from a crash and with MyISAM having no support for transactions, it cannot ensure their integrity thus coming with a very high probability of losing your data when writing to a database. Sounds like a nightmare? That's because it is.

These things stand to this day making MyISAM an awesome companion to InnoDB – but no longer making it a viable replacement option, which is why MyISAM is now deprecated.

If you find yourself running MyISAM, consider converting all MyISAM-based tables to InnoDB for ACID compliance:

1. First, obtain a list of tables running MyISAM by running the SQL query below – replace *database* with the name of your database:
   `SELECT TABLE_NAME FROM information_schema.TABLES WHERE TABLE_SCHEMA = 'database' AND ENGINE = 'MyISAM';`

2. Make all of those tables run InnoDB:
   `ALTER TABLE 'table_name' ENGINE = InnoDB;`

3. If necessary, repeat these steps for each of the databases in your database management system.

Woohoo! Now all of your tables run InnoDB – as easy as that. Time to learn the use cases of other storage engines available in our beloved DBMS!

Storage Engine Use Cases

There's no secret why there are so many storage engines for us to choose from – some storage engines hold our data in memory, some support an Excel-like format, some act as archives, some aim to act as blackholes for us to test the functionality of our code, and some are built as examples of how to build new storage engines within MySQL.

While InnoDB deserves to be the #1 storage engine for many general use cases and even for big data if it's optimized properly, some use cases may require you to get acquainted with different storage engines available in MySQL. We'll do that now.

The MEMORY and TempTable Storage Engines

Before MySQL 4.1, MySQL had a storage engine referred to as "HEAP" – the purpose of the HEAP storage engine was to store data in memory, and that's why starting from MySQL 4.1, the storage engine is called MEMORY.

The secret of the MEMORY storage engine is hidden in the name itself – the storage engine stores data in the memory, meaning that once we restart the server or if our database crashes for any reason whatsoever, our data is gone. Such a storage engine isn't a very practical choice for many applications in the modern world, but it can sometimes be useful for data to serve as a read-only cache in the memory.

In this realm, newer versions of MySQL do have another trick up their sleeve – starting from MySQL 8.3, the database management system builds all of its internal temporary tables based on the *TempTable* storage engine. The storage engine that's used for temporary tables can be swapped to the MEMORY storage engine by fiddling with the `internal_tmp_mem_storage_engine` variable.

The primary difference between the TempTable and MEMORY storage engines is that the TempTable storage engine stores all data and information related to the table inside of a file that's saved on the disk, while tables based on the MEMORY storage engine store data inside of the memory and the disk saves only the .frm – table definition – file. The TempTable storage engine is a good choice for storing larger object types.

The TempTable storage engine does have three main parameters that may be of interest to those fiddling with temporary tables: these are the `tmp_table_size` variable, the `temptable_max_ram` variable, and the `temptable_max_mmap` variable. The first variable defines the maximum size of temporary tables, the second variable defines the maximum size of a temporary table before it starts storing data on the disk (default value – 1GB), and the last variable defines the maximum amount of memory a TempTable-based table can accrue before it starts storing data on the disk. If TempTable starts storing data on the disk, data is stored using the InnoDB storage engine.

The CSV Storage Engine

The CSV storage engine is just what it sounds like – it stores all of its data in text files having an Excel-like format. Values are separated by commas, and tables always have a ".CSV" extension attached to them. Writing data into the table means writing data into the Excel file.

CSV-based tables can be created like usual tables; you just need to specify the appropriate storage engine at the end:

```
CREATE TABLE `demo_table` (
`id` INT NOT NULL,
`message` VARCHAR(225) NOT NULL,
`message_from` VARCHAR(225) NOT NULL,
`message_to` VARCHAR(225) NOT NULL,
`time_sent` VARCHAR(225) DEFAULT CURRENT_TIMESTAMP,
`time_received` VARCHAR(225) DEFAULT CURRENT_TIMESTAMP,
...
) ENGINE = CSV;
```

The CSV storage engine does have upsides and downsides – since data is not stored in any file other than Excel-based files, the data inside of the files can be modified by modifying data inside of the table or the Excel file itself or by modifying the Excel file – but the storage engine also has no support for indexing or partitioning.

The ARCHIVE and BLACKHOLE Storage Engines

The rest of the storage engines aren't rocket science either. The ARCHIVE storage engine is intended to act as an archive for your data – its row compression capability makes data based on the storage engine have an extremely small footprint on the disk, and your data can easily be backed up while it's stored using row-level locking capabilities. At the same time, the tables stored with this storage engine won't have any MVCC, B-Tree, foreign key, full-text, hash, or geospatial indexing capabilities.

The BLACKHOLE storage engine is intended to act as a blackhole and could be useful for those performing internal testing – data in the storage engine can only be written, but not retrieved as it's never stored anywhere in the first place, hence the name: all data written to tables based on this storage engine disappears at the blink of an eye. There are no files that are stored on the disk at any time either. This storage engine, just like ARCHIVE, provides no support for partitioning though it does support all kinds of indexes with the maximum available key length being 3072 bytes in size.

The internal functionality of the BLACKHOLE storage engine makes for a bunch of interesting use cases: while the storage engine doesn't store any files on the disk, it can copy SQL queries over to replica servers if statement-based binary logging is enabled which makes it a good companion in replication setups. Suppose you have a table based on the BLACKHOLE storage engine:

```
CREATE TABLE `demo_table` (
`id` INT NOT NULL,
`message` VARCHAR(225) NOT NULL,
`message_from` VARCHAR(225) NOT NULL,
`message_to` VARCHAR(225) NOT NULL,
`time_sent` VARCHAR(225) DEFAULT CURRENT_TIMESTAMP,
`time_received` VARCHAR(225) DEFAULT CURRENT_TIMESTAMP,
...
) ENGINE = BLACKHOLE;
```

Once you perform any (CRUD) actions on the table above, MySQL will write those to the binary log that will then be copied over to the slave servers. This means that if you make a table with the same structure on the slave server and set it to run the InnoDB storage engine, *MySQL will copy the changes from the binary log to the slave server, copying the inserted data as well.*

In other words, if you want to be able to avoid storing data on your master server but see it on your slave servers at the same time, BLACKHOLE is the storage engine for you – just make sure that tables on your slave server have the same structure and are based on a reliable storage engine that holds data instead of spewing it out.

Another popular use case of the BLACKHOLE storage engine is the verification of syntax in backup files – if your logical backups are swallowed into the abyss, their syntax is correct.

The MERGE Storage Engine

MySQL also has a storage engine dedicated to merging data derived from MyISAM – back in the day, this storage was known as MRG_MyISAM, but nowadays, it has a much simpler title depicting its use case – the storage engine is titled MERGE.

The MERGE storage engine is simple to explain: it's a collection of MyISAM tables that have the same structure. Once a table based on the MERGE storage engine emerges inside of your database, you will see no usual files having the ".MYD" or ".MYI" extensions on the disk – a file with the extension of ".MRG" (merge) will be created instead. The table format of these tables will be stored in the data dictionary, and the contents of any ".MRG" file will only contain the names of the tables that are running the MyISAM storage engine and will be treated as one MyISAM-based table instead.

You are unlikely to often use the advantages posed by the MERGE storage engine in MySQL, but some may cross your radar more often than you'd think:

- As the repair of MyISAM tables is inevitable due to MyISAM being a non-transactional storage engine, if you have a use case that necessitates the usage of large MyISAM tables, splitting them up into multiple MERGE tables and repairing many individual tables based on MERGE instead are likely to be much faster than repairing a single table based on MyISAM.

- MERGE can exceed the maximum file size limit set by your OS. For MyISAM, adhering to this limit is a necessity – for MERGE, it is not.

With that being said, MERGE does have some problems. `ALTER` queries will mess up the merge structure with associated tables, the reliable functionality of `REPLACE` queries is likely to be lost, and queries like `[ALTER|DROP|OPTIMIZE|REPAIR|ANALYZE] TABLE` or `DELETE` without a `WHERE` clause may provide incorrect results due to MySQL referring to the primary table and not the merged tables themselves.

All this makes the MERGE storage engine a flawed, though valuable addition even when MyISAM is obsolete.

The Storage Engine for High Availability

Aside from data being merged, your data needs to be highly available too. MySQL does offer a storage engine dedicated to just that – it's called NDB. The preceding "N" at the beginning is not there without a reason: the NDB storage engine stands for Network Database and comes with a shared-nothing architecture. NDB is a high-availability storage engine that is always connected to a data cluster, and that's why it's also referred to as NDBCluster.

Each instance of NDB has to have at least three nodes, them being the data node, the SQL node, and the management node:

1. The data node, as suggested by the name, stores the data relevant to the cluster. In a typical NDB setup, it is recommended you have two or more data nodes to provide redundancy for your database.

2. The SQL node is used to run SQL queries on the data node. In other words, we use the SQL node to access data on the data node using SQL.

3. The management node is used to manage all of the nodes within NDB.

Installing and Using NDB

It's worth mentioning that one can't create NDB-based tables using the usual engine definition so many people are used to. It isn't uncommon for people to run a SQL query similar to the one depicted below and come across the error #1286 with MySQL screaming "Unknown storage engine 'NDBCLUSTER'":

```
CREATE TABLE `demo_table` (
`id` INT NOT NULL,
`message` VARCHAR(225) NOT NULL,
`message_from` VARCHAR(225) NOT NULL,
`message_to` VARCHAR(225) NOT NULL,
`time_sent` VARCHAR(225) DEFAULT CURRENT_TIMESTAMP,
`time_received` VARCHAR(225) DEFAULT CURRENT_TIMESTAMP,
...
) ENGINE = NDBCluster;
```

The reason you come across such an error is that the NDB storage engine is not supported in the standard releases of MySQL – make sure to use MySQL NDB Cluster instead.

After you've successfully downloaded NDB and installed the downloaded files, you will usually need to create the data directories for the data nodes running MySQL and make sure that the directory is owned by mysql like so:

```
mkdir -p /var/lib/mysql/
chown [-R] mysql:mysql /var/lib/mysql/
```

Here, the `-p` option means "parents" (`mkdir` will create the directory and any other directories if they don't already exist), while the `-R` option in regard to `chown` will make it not follow symlinks.

CHAPTER 2   INDIVIDUAL STORAGE ENGINES

After, you will need to create a service for the NDB data node by running something akin to this:

`vi /etc/systemd/system/ndbd.service`

Once you have a service, you will want to edit your my.cnf file on all applicable nodes to configure NDBCluster. Add this below [mysqld]:

```
ndbcluster
ndb-connectstring=#
```

Here # is the IP of the management node.

You will also need to have a [mysql_cluster] section with the same ndb-connectstring specified there as well, so everything will look like this:

```
[mysqld]
ndbcluster
ndb-connectstring=#
[mysql_cluster]
ndb-connectstring=#
```

Don't forget to specify the IP of your management node in place of the hashtag.

Once you're done, run `systemctl enable ndbd` to enable the NDB service.

Afterward, you will need to create the management node. On that node, you will need to download and install the management server for NDB, then create a directory for the NDB Cluster, and finally, create the configuration file. Your configuration file should look something like this:

```
[ndbd default]
# Options affecting the ndbd processes on all data nodes
NoOfReplicas=2 # Number of replicas

[ndb_mgmd]
# NDB Management Node
hostname=127.0.0.1 # The IP of the management node
datadir=/usr/ndb-cluster/data   # The data directory
```

```
[ndbd]
# First Data Node
hostname=127.0.0.2 # The IP of the first data node
NodeId=2 # The ID of this data node
datadir=/var/lib/mysql/ # Data directory

[ndbd]
# Second Data Node
hostname=127.0.0.3 # Hostname/IP of the second data node
NodeId=3 # The ID of this data node
datadir=/var/lib/mysql/ # Remote directory for the data files

[mysqld]
NodeId=4
hostname=127.0.0.2 # NDBCluster Node 1

[mysqld]
NodeId=5
hostname=127.0.0.3 # NDBCluster Node 2
```

Now, create the NDB management service on the management node. Create a file called /etc/system/system/ndb_mgmd.service and make sure it consists of three parts – [Unit], [Service], and [Install]. You can easily find the structure of this file on a GitHub repository. Finally, enable the management service by running systemctl enable ndb_mgmd.

Perfect! Proceed to the last step and provide the location of the configuration file to your management node by running ndb-mgmd --initial --config-file=[location/of/config/file] on the management node, and then running ndbd on each of your data nodes or move into the config directory and start your data node using ndbd.

Finally, run service mysql start to start MySQL on every data and SQL node, and you're good to go.

Once you've set up NDB, you've unlocked a whole new world of opportunities. Now, you can set your tables to use the NDBCLUSTER or NDB storage engine and run SQL queries in parallel, enjoy multi-master replication capabilities, and more!

Use the management client by invoking ndb_mgm through the CLI, then check up on your cluster configuration by invoking SHOW once you're logged in.

CHAPTER 2 INDIVIDUAL STORAGE ENGINES

The FEDERATED and EXAMPLE Storage Engines

Aside from the NDBCluster, there are two more storage engines I need you to be aware of. Most of you have probably heard of them both, but never used them – and that's not a problem. These storage engines are not a necessity in your everyday work, but they are there lurking in the shadows and waiting for their next chance. A chance that rarely comes, indeed – those storage engines are FEDERATED and EXAMPLE.

The first one allows us to access data from a remote database, and the second one acts as an example of how to build new storage engines.

To make good use of the FEDERATED storage engine, make use of the CONNECTION option defining the table you create on another server like so – here `federated_user` is the user in the `remote_server`, 9306 defines the TCP protocol, the `database` defines the name of your database, and `demo_table` refers to the table on that database:

```
CREATE TABLE `federated_table` (
`message_id` INT(15) NOT NULL AUTO_INCREMENT PRIMARY KEY,
`message_title` VARCHAR(120) NOT NULL,
`message_user` VARCHAR(120) NOT NULL,
`message_contents` VARCHAR(255) DEFAULT NULL,
...
) ENGINE = FEDERATED
DEFAULT CHARSET = ...
CONNECTION = 'mysql://federated_user@remote_server:9306/database/demo_table';
```

Great! Now make use of this connection you just made by making an InnoDB-based table with the same structure:

```
CREATE TABLE `demo_table` (
`message_id` INT(15) NOT NULL AUTO_INCREMENT PRIMARY KEY,
`message_title` VARCHAR(120) NOT NULL,
`message_user` VARCHAR(120) NOT NULL,
`message_contents` VARCHAR(255) DEFAULT NULL,
...
) ENGINE = InnoDB;
```

CHAPTER 2   INDIVIDUAL STORAGE ENGINES

Good! Now, once you add data to the `demo_table`, the same data will also appear in the `federated_table`. Great, right?

There also is a way to create the same federated table using the `CREATE SERVER` query. An example would look like so:

```
CREATE SERVER demo_server FOREIGN DATA WRAPPER mysql OPTIONS (USER
'federated_user', HOST 'federated_host', PORT 9306, DATABASE 'demo_
database');
```

Here, `demo_server` is the name of your database server, `mysql` defines our DBMS, `OPTIONS` defines the username and the host, while `database` defines the title of your database.

Everything's much more simple with the EXAMPLE storage engine – it serves as an example of how to build new storage engines. The storage engine doesn't support any necessary CRUD operations, partitioning, or indexing, but is still there waiting for a chance to give birth to new storage engines in the future: find its directory in the `storage` directory of MySQL and check the `example` subdirectory.

Storage Engines Exclusive to MariaDB

That's it – now you know everything about the storage engines in MySQL! Well, almost everything.

You know *almost* everything because MySQL is not the only one with flesh in the game – I've already told you about its brother Percona Server, and My also has a sister called Maria, too. One of the things MySQL's sister MariaDB is known for is its storage engines. MariaDB provides support for all of the storage engines available in MySQL and more – including storage engines exclusive to MariaDB.

Those storage engines include Aria, the popular MariaDB ColumnStore storage engine, CONNECT, FederatedX, Mroonga, OQGraph, the S3 and Sequence storage engines, as well as SphinxSE and Spider. Oh, there's also MyRocks and TokuDB, too – you're already familiar with them.

Don't fret – many of the storage engines available in MariaDB are self-explanatory: Aria is a crash-safe version of MyISAM that's used by system tables starting from MariaDB 10.4, ColumnStore extends MariaDB with columnar storage, CONNECT enables MariaDB to "connect" with data in a different format, FederatedX is a spin of the FEDERATED storage engine to keep the features available in FEDERATED up to date and

CHAPTER 2   INDIVIDUAL STORAGE ENGINES

not bury the storage engine altogether, Mroonga is suitable to search through Korean, Japanese, and Chinese data with full-text search capabilities, OQGraph is suitable for those who store graphs and related data, S3 is perfect for those who store their data in Amazon S3 servers, and the Sequence storage engine allows for the storage of sequences of numbers. Sequences can be either ascending or descending.

There's also SphinxSE or Sphinx and Spider – Sphinx acts as an alternative to full-text search in MariaDB, while Spider "joins" different instances of MariaDB into one as if they would function on the same database instance.

Interesting, yes? Storage engines within MariaDB also have secrets unique to themselves – have you heard about the fact that there is no known way to create a table running the Sequence storage engine? Such tables are read-only too; you use this storage engine like so:

```
MariaDB [database_name]> SELECT * FROM seq_1_to_10;
+-----+
| seq |
+-----+
|   1 |
|   2 |
|   3 |
|   4 |
|   5 |
|   6 |
|   7 |
|   8 |
|   9 |
|  10 |
+-----+
10 rows in set (0.002 sec)
```

You can also specify steps and how many steps you'd like MariaDB to perform like so – if you do so, MariaDB will "skip" certain numbers – for example, here we display every third number from 10 to 1, thus skipping every 3 numbers:

```
MariaDB [tests]> SELECT * FROM seq_10_to_1_step_3;
+-----+
| seq |
+-----+
|  10 |
|   7 |
|   4 |
|   1 |
+-----+
4 rows in set (0.002 sec)
```

That's not it either – the S3 storage engine is home to amazing capabilities as well. To use S3, you must know your S3 access and secret keys, as well as the bucket and region your data should be stored in, but once that's known, configure the access to your bucket for the S3 storage engine via my.cnf, and you're good to go. Don't forget to specify the `s3-host-name`, `s3-bucket`, the `s3-access-key`, and the `s3-secret-key` as well as turn the `s3` variable to `ON` via my.cnf, the rest should work just fine. Now, you're free to move data from a table existing in MariaDB to S3 by simply switching engines like so – you can specify a compression algorithm too if you so desire:

```
ALTER TABLE data_table ENGINE=S3 [COMPRESSION_ALGORITHM=zlib]
```

I'll leave the rest up to you – explore the storage engine options in MySQL, MariaDB, and Percona Server, and get ready to break your own MySQL instances.

Summary

Storage engines are a key part of MySQL, and while some may not be used as often as others are, they all have their unique upsides and downsides. The primary storage engine employed by many developers and engineers is InnoDB, but there are many other options for you to choose from. For better or for worse, all of them have something to offer, and once you find yourself using MySQL with any storage engine whatsoever, it is vitally important that you employ their upsides to your advantage and avoid falling into performance traps.

Avoiding falling into performance traps is impossible without being aware of the ways databases are broken and torn apart, and now that you have refreshed your memory about storage engines, it's time to break them, too. Safely, of course.

PART II

Breaking MySQL

CHAPTER 3

What Breaks MySQL?

The reason why I've walked you through the history of MySQL and storage engines is for you to gain a deeper understanding of MySQL as a whole. The understanding of how MySQL functions under the hood will be vital as you continue reading this book; the history of MySQL is the foundation of the database management system, while its storage engines allow you to dive deeper into what MySQL can offer as a whole.

Now that you know what storage engines are and what can they offer to you as a developer, it's time to familiarize yourself with what factors break MySQL so you can better optimize your database management system. After all, what good does optimizing and securing do if you're not acquainted with the factors that shatter your MySQL instances in the first place?

MySQL Use Cases

Many of the readers of this book will know what MySQL is used for. After all, the use cases of MySQL aren't rocket science. The database management system has made its mark in many industries – cybersecurity, education, healthcare, recruiting, marketing, real estate, energy, finance, supply chains, retail, and even agriculture. Various companies in these industries make use of MySQL in one way or another, and while different industries may employ the DBMS in different ways, the core principles of the DBMS remain in place and are unlikely to change.

One of the main reasons why that happens is because MySQL is a very reliable database management system. It's reliable because its main storage engine is renowned as a home to ACID properties and because of the necessity to have a database model to make the database management system shine.

ACID is a set of properties that guarantee that MySQL remains functional despite errors and problems that would make NoSQL-based databases tremble. Those problems include electricity quickly going out, servers going down, and everything else in that realm. ACID ensures that our databases continue to function well despite these errors.

ACID translates to Atomicity, Consistency, Isolation, and Durability, and in the MySQL realm, everything translates to

- **A**tomicity: Ensuring that statements in any transaction operate as an indivisible unit and that their effects are seen either as a whole or not at all.

- **C**onsistency: Data consistency is ensured by the logging functionality exclusive to one of MySQL's flagship storage engines. Remember InnoDB and its architecture? One of the components of its architecture is the log files `ib_logfile*`, and that's not without a reason.

- **I**solation: Rows can be isolated – or locked away – from queries that may impact them. In other words, row-level locking.

- **D**urability: InnoDB maintains a log file that tracks all of the changes to the data.

In other words, MySQL – and, in this case, specifically InnoDB – is a very powerful beast that can help you in a wide variety of different scenarios and use cases from listing the pupils in a school to scanning through a billion rows in milliseconds. The problem here is that the storage engine has to be optimized to adhere to your specific use case and only then can you unleash its abilities for high performance and reliability at the same time. The only storage engine capable of adhering to ACID characteristics is InnoDB, too.

Problematic Use Cases

Ironically, even with MySQL being such a resourceful and powerful beast, many problems start to arise one after the other even if we think we have everything thought out. The problems come up because we avoid optimizing our database or say "The database is doing well enough – what is there to optimize?" and then get upset when our application takes ages to load.

Database problems can be conveniently split into multiple categories –availability, performance, and security are a good place to start. When walking yourself through the issues, keep in mind that the simplest things often cause the most headaches and the same is true for MySQL, and while the reasons behind these problems are, in most cases, more simple than you think, they must be addressed properly too.

Performance Hiccups

To start with, something that has plagued every DBA and developer working with MySQL (or any database management system for that matter) for ages are database performance problems. Database performance issues are at the heart of almost every slow-performing application, no matter what kind of skeleton (technologies) your database may be supporting.

No matter the application, database performance is rarely looked into initially. That's not to say that developers dismiss the importance of performance in open source databases – they almost certainly don't – but what frequently ends up happening is the developer only looks into performance from the side of an application. That means one or more of the following:

- Your server is doing more work than it should.

- Your database is resource-constrained.

- Queries running in your database are not optimized for performance and consume excessive or inadequate amounts of resources as a result.

- Your database structure is not optimized for the work you're asking your database to perform making your database ill-equipped to finish the work you're asking it to do. That may include columns in your database having no indexes or you not making use of them, no partitioning when it's necessary, etc.

See the pattern? It's not your database that's the problem – it's you not understanding what the tools you employ do to your database that's at the heart of the issue.

No worries – at the high level, everything's more simple than you could imagine. Seriously – all you need to do is optimize four types of queries. They're the CRUD neighborhood – Create, Read, Update, Delete. At the most basic level, everything works like so:

CHAPTER 3　WHAT BREAKS MYSQL?

Type of Query	How to Optimize?
Create – INSERT	Before executing an INSERT, make sure that table locks, consistency checking, and index updates are done after the INSERT query is complete and use bulk inserting capabilities. If that doesn't work, ditch INSERTs for LOAD DATA INFILE.
Read – SELECT	Read through as little data as possible.
Update – UPDATE	Keep in mind that MySQL updates the data and anything on top of it (indexes or partitions) too. Drop indexes and (or) partitions, if necessary, employ locking, and beware of NULL values too – if you insert such values into any partition in your table, they will reside in the lowest partition.
Delete – DELETE	Make use of the LIMIT clause and switch DELETE to TRUNCATE where feasible (TRUNCATE deletes all rows in a table.)

What if you would insert data into your database like so:

LOCK TABLE mysql_table;
INSERT INTO mysql_table VALUES ('demo', 'demo', 'demo'), **('data'**, 'data', 'data'), **('more data',** 'more data', 'more data');
INSERT INTO mysql_table VALUES ('more data', 'demo data', 'some data'), **('demo data'**, 'more demo data', 'something here too'), **('data'**, 'more data', 'more data');
...
UNLOCK TABLE mysql_table;

Read from your database like so:

SELECT **demo_column** FROM mysql_table **WHERE** some_column >= 500 **LIMIT 0,10;**

Update data in your database like so:

LOCK TABLE mysql_table;
UPDATE mysql_table SET column = 'value' **LIMIT 0,5000;**
UPDATE mysql_table SET column = 'value' **LIMIT 5000,10000;**
UPDATE mysql_table SET column = 'value' **LIMIT 10000,15000;**
...
UNLOCK TABLE mysql_table;

Or delete all data in a table like so:

```
TRUNCATE TABLE mysql_table;
```

What do you think would happen? Many of your database performance problems would start to disappear. See how easy everything becomes once you follow a couple of basic steps? We'll get into performance optimization in the third part of this book, but the aforementioned things will be a good starting point in terms of database performance.

Availability Issues

The next one on the list is availability issues. They're nothing new – if your database is down or application performance is grinding to a halt, you've got issues. Such issues are discussed very widely, and fixing them isn't rocket science – for your database to be available most of the time (let's be fair, some downtime will inevitably occur), choose a reliable server provider, make sure your application is routing its requests through CloudFlare or any other CDN, make sure to backup your data and test your backups frequently, optimize the queries running in your database, and if necessary, take a look into the way load balancers work in your database infrastructure.

To top it all off, replicate data across multiple servers if necessary, and you should be good to go! Don't stress over making your database accessible 100% of the time either – given the fact that even CDN providers can be taken down with DDoS attacks, 100% uptime of the service behind your database is never a guarantee; however, that doesn't mean you shouldn't do everything in your power to thwart such attacks to begin with.

In the database realm, availability issues occur because your database isn't optimized properly, so do remain vigilant and watchful over how the data in your database is being used, but once you make sure that your application is behind a CDN thwarting DDoS attacks, queries are optimized, data backups are reliable and tested, the application employs rate limiters, and you're behind a load balancer or two, relax – nothing's likely to happen. However, do remain vigilant – security breaches are just around the corner too.

CHAPTER 3   WHAT BREAKS MYSQL?

Security Problems

Once you're sure that your application is performing well and availability levels are acceptable to your organization or for yourself, it's time to ask your database another question – has the data in it ever been stolen?

Unfortunately, in many cases, the answer is "Yes" even if you've never heard of any data breaches hitting the infrastructure of your company or any companies related to it. The truth is that data breaches are rarely announced on the front page of your company – and if they are, they're almost certainly not the first data breach that your company has experienced.

To mitigate security issues, take care of the following aspects:

1. General security guidelines
2. User security and access control
3. MySQL security components and plugins
4. Enterprise-level security controls

Seemingly very few things to take care of, right? Don't get too excited because as with everything, the devil is in the details. That's why this book has an entire part of it dedicated to security – I'll tell you everything you need to know once we reach the security part of MySQL (that's the last part of this book), but for now, follow this advice:

Security Guideline	Advice
General security guidelines	Ensure that only the root user has access to the user table in the mysql database, never trust data provided by the user (that's the primary cause of SQL injection), and consider using a Web Application Firewall (WAF) to prevent attacks directed at your application and your database alike.
User security and access control	Use strong passwords and don't store them in plain text or using weak algorithms (look into BCrypt or Blowfish for that matter), don't grant more privileges than necessary for users to complete their actions, and take a look into account locking and unlocking.

(*continued*)

Security Guideline	Advice
MySQL security components and plugins	MySQL provides you with the ability to implement a password security policy where only passwords above a certain length can be employed, comes with an enterprise-level firewall specific to itself (see enterprise-level security controls), offers a keyring plugin to safely store sensitive information for retrieval later on, etc.
Enterprise-level security controls	Enterprise-level security controls include, but are not limited to, the MySQL Enterprise Firewall and MySQL Enterprise Audit functionalities for auditing and user security, data masking procedures, and the like.

That's the basics of security which we'll dive in deeper in the last part of this book, but we're not ready to get into the security part of your database just yet – you secure something that isn't safe and optimize something that's broken. For now, understand that under the MySQL hood, everything is simple if you tread the database road carefully and understand everything it involves. Databases involve data, data involves schemas (in the MySQL world, a schema is also a synonym for a database), and schemas involve data types, indexes, and the like. Understanding your data, schema, and the data types related to them may seem like a simple task, but it is far from a piece of cake: it does need careful consideration and attention to function properly both now and in the future – with improper schema and data types, you could be breaking your database without being aware of it! You're in luck because now I'll walk you through how to understand your data by choosing the proper schema, data types, and collations to avoid just that. How? Well, keep reading and find out.

Understanding Your Data

To understand your data, start by walking yourself through the necessities: chances are that you already have a lot of data in your database, right? Well, how did the data end up in your database? What did you think about before any data found its way into any of the databases within your MySQL Server? That's right – table schemas, data types, and collations. These three things are the three "musketeers" powering your data: table schemas define the overview of your tables, data types define what data can go into what column, and proper collations make sure that data isn't represented by signs you can't comprehend.

Essentially, table schemas, data types, and collations provide you with a highway for your data – you choose the speed limit. However, no matter the speed limit, if the highway is so badly made that your car can barely make its way through it, you won't reach your destination. That's why it's crucial to choose the proper schema, data types, character sets, and collations before embarking on any project – these things lay the foundation for any project.

Choosing the Proper Schema and Data Types

"Properly choose the right schema, character sets, and data types" might sound cool, but what does that mean? For you, it means the following:

1. **Evaluate your use case**: What are you using MySQL for? In many cases, your use case has a huge weight on your decision to choose one data type or collation instead of the other.

2. **Think about what databases and tables inside of them will be a necessity for your use case**: How many databases or tables do you need? Why?

3. **Brainstorm**: Think about the structure of your table, look into the available data types and collations for your version of MySQL, MariaDB, or Percona Server, and choose the one that feels closer to your use case. Schemas, data types, and character sets aren't set in stone and can change as time goes by, so choose wisely, but don't worry too much.

4. **Think about your server**: When brainstorming to choose the best data type or collation, think about your server – how much disk space do you have? Do you have plans to expand your software appliance in such a way that would necessitate changes for your data types or collations in the future? Keep in mind that different data types occupy different amounts of database space – while that may not be important now, 100 excessive bytes mean a lot when you have a million records or more.

5. **Choose**: Now that you have got these things out of the way, choose the proper data types and collations!

Properly choosing data types and collations can be tricky, and it helps to simplify the process. Use simple reasoning and think about the future.

When thinking about what data type to choose, think about what kind of data you intend to store and choose the simplest solution. Here are your options:

- **Data types for numeric data**

    - Data types to store general integer values: INTEGER or INT, SMALLINT, TINYINT, MEDIUMINT, and BIGINT. Here, everything's related to ranges of values. For example, SMALLINT can store signed integer values from -32768 to 32767 or unsigned values from 0 to 65535, TINYINT can store signed values from -128 to 127, or UNSIGNED values from 0 to 255. Refer to the tip below and the documentation for more information.

    - Data types to store exact numeric values: DECIMAL and NUMERIC. Use these data types when storing exact numeric values (e.g., data for accounting purposes).

    - Data types to store approximate and floating-point values: FLOAT and DOUBLE. MySQL needs four (4) bytes if you're storing single-precision values and eight (8) bytes if double-precision values are stored.

    - The BIT data type. Use BIT when storing bit values from 1 to 64, and define your range in brackets by defining BIT(number) where *number* is a number from 1 to 64.

- **Data types to store date and time values**

    - DATE, DATETIME, and TIMESTAMP data types. Use the DATE data type if you're storing YYYY-MM-DD dates without time, DATETIME will help you if you're storing such dates with a time value (YYYY-MM-DD hh:mm:ss), and TIMESTAMP works the same way, just with a smaller range: it only accepts values from 1970-01-01 00:00:01 to 2038-01-19 03:14:07. All values are in UTC.

    - The TIME data type for storing time values from -838:59:59 to 838:59:59.

    - The YEAR data type for storing year values. This data type has a data width of four characters.

- **Data types to store string values**

  - The CHAR and VARCHAR data types refer to *char*acter or *var*iable *char*acter values. These data types are similar, and that's the reason they're not being mentioned separately, but they differ in regard to maximum length and requirements for storage space. CHAR values are preceded with spaces to the length of your choice, and trailing spaces are removed once they're retrieved, while for VARCHAR that's not the case. When VARCHAR is in use, MySQL will issue a warning if spaces precede a value too.

  - The BINARY and VARBINARY data types refer to binary strings; otherwise, they're very similar to the aforementioned CHAR and VARCHAR data types.

  - The BLOB and TEXT data types refer to Binary Large Objects and larger text values. Such data types are similar, and their names as well as the maximum length of their values correspond. They also have the same storage requirements. There are four BLOB types, TINYBLOB, BLOB, MEDIUMBLOB, and LONGBLOB; the same goes for TEXT.

  - The ENUM data type refers to a list of permitted values that are enumerated.

  - The SET data type can have any value specified in a defined (set) list. This list can have up to 64 members.

- **Spatial (geospatial) data types to store geographic data**

  - GEOMETRY, POINT, LINESTRING, and POLYGON data types are intended to hold single geometric values.

  - MULTIPOINT, MULTILINESTRING, MULTIPOLYGON, and GEOMETRYCOLLECTION data types can be used to hold multiple geometric values. Refer to the documentation for more information.

- **The JSON data type is suitable to store JSON data.**

As you can see, your choices are broad – evaluate your use case, think into the future, and choose the simplest solution. In other words, if you intend to choose email addresses, a VARCHAR solution would probably work better than TEXT, SMALLINT will likely be enough if you store integer values that don't exceed 30,000, and DATETIME will probably be the option you're looking for if you store dates together with a time value, but DATE will suffice for storing dates instead. *In many cases, the simplest (smallest) data type is the best.*

Tip When choosing integer data types for numeric data, keep in mind that here, everything is related to the ranges of integers MySQL accepts and whether you store SIGNED or UNSIGNED values. Signed values mean 0, positive, and negative numbers, while unsigned values refer to 0 and positive numbers.

Character Sets and Collations

Once we've chosen our data types, we have to remember that every table has a character set and collation. Many developers conveniently forget about those – after all, character sets and collations are defined by default, so why bother?

And that's correct – MySQL does provide a character set and collation by default, but MySQL's choices often aren't the best. After all, no one knows your database better than yourself, right?

Starting from character sets, MySQL and MariaDB offer a wide set of character sets you can choose from – there's no need to even switch to a database to obtain the list of character sets you can use to power your data. Simply issue a SHOW CHARACTER SET query once you log in to MariaDB, and you will be provided with a list of all available character sets together with their descriptions, default collations, and maximum number of bytes required to store a single character. Take a look.

CHAPTER 3 WHAT BREAKS MYSQL?

```
MariaDB [(none)]> SHOW CHARACTER SET;
+----------+-----------------------------+---------------------+--------+
| Charset  | Description                 | Default collation   | Maxlen |
+----------+-----------------------------+---------------------+--------+
| big5     | Big5 Traditional Chinese    | big5_chinese_ci     |      2 |
| dec8     | DEC West European           | dec8_swedish_ci     |      1 |
| cp850    | DOS West European           | cp850_general_ci    |      1 |
| hp8      | HP West European            | hp8_english_ci      |      1 |
| koi8r    | KOI8-R Relcom Russian       | koi8r_general_ci    |      1 |
| latin1   | cp1252 West European        | latin1_swedish_ci   |      1 |
| latin2   | ISO 8859-2 Central European | latin2_general_ci   |      1 |
| swe7     | 7bit Swedish                | swe7_swedish_ci     |      1 |
| ascii    | US ASCII                    | ascii_general_ci    |      1 |
| ujis     | EUC-JP Japanese             | ujis_japanese_ci    |      3 |
| sjis     | Shift-JIS Japanese          | sjis_japanese_ci    |      2 |
| hebrew   | ISO 8859-8 Hebrew           | hebrew_general_ci   |      1 |
| tis620   | TIS620 Thai                 | tis620_thai_ci      |      1 |
| euckr    | EUC-KR Korean               | euckr_korean_ci     |      2 |
| koi8u    | KOI8-U Ukrainian            | koi8u_general_ci    |      1 |
| gb2312   | GB2312 Simplified Chinese   | gb2312_chinese_ci   |      2 |
| greek    | ISO 8859-7 Greek            | greek_general_ci    |      1 |
| cp1250   | Windows Central European    | cp1250_general_ci   |      1 |
| gbk      | GBK Simplified Chinese      | gbk_chinese_ci      |      2 |
| latin5   | ISO 8859-9 Turkish          | latin5_turkish_ci   |      1 |
| armscii8 | ARMSCII-8 Armenian          | armscii8_general_ci |      1 |
| utf8mb3  | UTF-8 Unicode               | utf8mb3_general_ci  |      3 |
| ucs2     | UCS-2 Unicode               | ucs2_general_ci     |      2 |
| cp866    | DOS Russian                 | cp866_general_ci    |      1 |
| keybcs2  | DOS Kamenicky Czech-Slovak  | keybcs2_general_ci  |      1 |
| macce    | Mac Central European        | macce_general_ci    |      1 |
| macroman | Mac West European           | macroman_general_ci |      1 |
| cp852    | DOS Central European        | cp852_general_ci    |      1 |
| latin7   | ISO 8859-13 Baltic          | latin7_general_ci   |      1 |
| utf8mb4  | UTF-8 Unicode               | utf8mb4_general_ci  |      4 |
| cp1251   | Windows Cyrillic            | cp1251_general_ci   |      1 |
| utf16    | UTF-16 Unicode              | utf16_general_ci    |      4 |
| utf16le  | UTF-16LE Unicode            | utf16le_general_ci  |      4 |
| cp1256   | Windows Arabic              | cp1256_general_ci   |      1 |
| cp1257   | Windows Baltic              | cp1257_general_ci   |      1 |
| utf32    | UTF-32 Unicode              | utf32_general_ci    |      4 |
| binary   | Binary pseudo charset       | binary              |      1 |
```

Figure 3-1. *A list of character sets and collations available in MariaDB*

While the most likely choice for you and your database will be a character set that supports UTF-8 unicode (that's utf8mb4 with a collation of utf8mb4_general_ci), some use cases may require other character sets to be used. Dealing with data in Greek? Use the Greek character set with greek_general_ci as your collation. Dealing with customers from Israel who interact with data inside of your database? Use the Hebrew character set with hebrew_general_ci as your collation.

For most general use cases, utf8mb4 is your reliable partner. Back in the day, some engineers initially preferred utf8, but as utf8mb4 became the standard collation method in MySQL, utf8 slowly drifted away. There's nothing "wrong" if you prefer to use utf8 over utf8mb4; it's just that the original implementation of utf8 doesn't support all Unicode characters – in most cases, you will be okay, but if come across scenarios where you need to store emojis or other characters, utf8 won't be enough since it only supports characters from the Basic Multilingual Plane (BMP) which doesn't account for all Unicode characters, hence the implementation of utf8mb4.

Take the maximum length of bytes required to store a character into account too – a difference of a couple of bytes may not seem like much, but if you're storing bigger data sets, the bytes will mount up quicker than you imagine.

Don't want to use utf8mb4 or have other plans for your database? Good news – the list given by MySQL is extensive, simple, and self-explanatory. Choose the character set and collation based on data you store in your database, think into the future, and you will be good to go.

Your Architecture Is a Mess

What do your schema, data types, character sets, and collations have in common? Right – they all form a bigger or smaller part of your database architecture as a whole. Your data, its schema, data types, character sets, and collations are all a part of your database architecture. Some of them make up a bigger part, some smaller, but they all play a role. To remember what the architecture of MySQL looks like, flick back to Chapter 1 and skim through the header "The Architecture of MySQL." I'll remind you that the architecture of your DBMS has three main parts them being the Client, the Server, and the Storage:

1. **Client**: We interact with MySQL using a CLI or by using a SQL client.
2. **Server**: Every query you run in your database management system is run through the server. Initially, your query passes through a thread handler, afterward – the query cache and the parser, the parser forwards everything through the query

optimizer. This is the part where the optimizations of your MySQL Server come into the game too: remember my.cnf? my.ini? There's a reason these files exist – these files contain the options used to make your MySQL Server able to consume a specified amount of resources on your server in the way you specify. Seems like a highway to paradise, right?

3. **Storage**: Finally, the storage engine running your database also has a point to make. For most of you, the storage part of MySQL will probably refer to InnoDB or Percona XtraDB and will be directly dependent on the options set in my.cnf.

When investigating the architecture of your database, it's crucial to look at the things *inside* your server. Imagine your server could speak – what would the databases and the data within them ask you?

- When was the last time you inspected the structure of your tables?
- Take a look at the structure of your tables again. Are all columns you have necessary for your use case?
- What indexes are visible once you inspect your table structure? Do you know why they are in place?
- What character sets and collations are used in your database? Why?
- If you have more than a couple million rows in your database, are your tables normalized? If yes, what normalization form do you use and why? If no, why?

Inspecting your database architecture isn't rocket science, and the questions you need answers to aren't complex. That's the entire beauty – you don't need to invent a bike when optimizing MySQL, but make sure that you use proper character sets and collations, employ indexes wisely, partition your tables if you run bigger data sets, and normalize your data where necessary. That's it – you're off to a good start!

Now you need to learn how to properly communicate with your database to access the data it employs. If your server and architecture are set up properly, you still need to know how to interact with your database through software appliances – you would be surprised how many mistakes developers make here too.

Communicating with MySQL Through Software

Knowing how to properly communicate with your database is half the battle. Many developers think that they know how best to talk to their database, but a glance at code interacting with MySQL will often tell you that it's rarely the case. Open up a piece of code belonging to a search engine and inspect some SQL queries – you will likely see something similar to the following:

1. SELECT * FROM `table_name` WHERE `column` = 'Search Query';
2. SELECT * FROM `table_name` WHERE `column` LIKE '%Search Query%';
3. SELECT * FROM `table_name` WHERE(`column`) MATCH('Search Query' [IN ANY FULLTEXT SEARCH MODE]);
4. SELECT `product_id`, `product_title`, `category_title` FROM `table_1` INNER JOIN `table_2` ON `products`.`cat_id` = `categories`.`cat_id`;

You could add some ANDs or ORs to the mix and voilà – that's almost the same query you run in your application to return results from a database!

"And what's wrong with those queries?" – I hear you asking. Nothing – these queries aren't "wrong" as-is, but each of them provides us with unique insight into what resources they're likely to consume in our database, and they act as an extremely good starting point once we have the need to understand what breaks our database, especially if some of those queries are slow.

Now stop and take a closer look into each query – I've underlined things worth an extra second of your attention:

1. SELECT * FROM `table_name` WHERE `column` = 'Search Query';
2. SELECT * FROM `table_name` WHERE `column` LIKE '%Search Query%';
3. SELECT * FROM `table_name` WHERE MATCH(`column`) MATCH('Search Query' [IN ANY FULLTEXT SEARCH MODE]);

4. SELECT `product_id`, `product_title`, `category_title` FROM `table_1` INNER JOIN `table_2` ON `products`.`cat_id` = `categories`.`cat_id`;

There are four queries in which I've underlined 11 things worth paying attention to. I've done that with a very good reason: each of those things comes with different performance implications both for your application and the database behind it. Each query is a task composed of smaller tasks: each of those tasks has an impact on performance. Performance is response time, and the faster it is, the better for everyone involved.

In other words, higher performance means a shorter response time and to achieve a good result – a performant database – we need our response time to be as low as possible. To achieve our goal, we need to understand what causes slow query performance, understand the internals of our problems, and eliminate them.

Top Causes of Slow Query Performance

Since we're after performance when communicating with MySQL through any software appliance, it's crucial to take some time and think about the structure of our SQL queries and that's why you see four different examples above. Developers make various performance hiccups, and the queries you see are a very good example.

Take a closer look into the same queries again: what potential performance hiccups can you spot? How many of them exist? I've spotted four:

1. **Query structure**: SELECT * FROM means that we're selecting every column from a table. Is selecting everything necessary? Probably not. If not, why are you using SELECT * instead of SELECT column? Can you imagine what your database goes through when selecting every column in a table with 10,000 records? 100,000 records? 1,000,000 records? The more records you have, the less recommended this approach becomes. In many cases, it's enough to issue a query like SELECT 'column' FROM to instantly see performance improve because our database scans through fewer rows to return results.

2. **Wildcards**: There's nothing inherently wrong in using wildcards for search operations, but using a wildcard *in front of a query* is just asking for trouble because you're telling your database "Search for anything in front of text I'll give you. Oh, the text may have anything after it, too." *If you do that, your database won't be able to use indexes* because it won't know the exact query you are concerned with. **Never use wildcards in front of a query – if necessary, employ them at the end.**

3. **Fulltext searching may be problematic**: Full-text search operations are an old friend of MySQL; there are many valid reasons to employ full-text search operations using the database management system. Full-text search operations provide MySQL with superpowers rivaled by very few things; however, such an approach may become problematic because MySQL doesn't prevent you from putting multiple kinds of indexes on the same column. Be wary of the kinds of indexes you use in your database management system, and also, keep in mind that queries using full-text indexes on bigger data sets may break MySQL 5.7 due to a bug inside of MySQL (see Appendix – Query that Breaks MySQL 5.7 for more information.) Newer versions of MySQL aren't affected by this issue.

4. **Is an INNER JOIN necessary?** There's nothing wrong with using INNER JOIN to help your query succeed, but keep in mind that in many cases, INNER JOINs mark the start of complex queries – it isn't unusual to see multiple INNER JOINs spanning one query and slowing down its performance as a result. After all, is an INNER JOIN the join type you need? There are four other JOIN types you may use – there's LEFT OUTER JOIN, RIGHT OUTER JOIN, SELF JOIN, and CROSS JOIN, too.

Many causes of slow SELECT query performance have something to do with the aforementioned performance hiccups. Others will have something to do with indexes being defined, but not used, your table not being normalized, or other things. Once your application completes the necessary queries, it's also vitally important to close the connections to not run out of the number of connections that MySQL can employ – that's what the `max_connections` variable does. In MySQL, the default number is 151, the minimum – 1, and the maximum is 100,000.

I will walk you through the ins and outs of optimization of SQL queries in the second part of this book – for now, understand that for your SELECT queries to be as quick as possible, you need to read as little data as you can while making use of indexes and partitions after fine-tuning your server resources for MySQL.

In other words, to speed the performance of SELECT queries up, select as little data as possible after allocating much of your server resources to MySQL.

Once you find yourself in the INSERT territory, the advice changes – for your INSERT queries to be effective, keep in mind that while indexes and partitions help SELECTs, they harm INSERTs, UPDATEs, and DELETEs because when data is inserted, updated, or deleted, the data in the index or partition has to be updated as well.

To optimize INSERT queries, aim to insert as much data as possible in one go using the bulk INSERT capability like so:

```
INSERT INTO `demo_table` (`col1`,`col2`,`col3`)
VALUES(1,2,3),(4,5,6),(7,8,9),...;
```

Aim to insert data when indexes aren't in place (if possible, add them after you insert data into your table), and if you find yourself working with bigger data sets, ditch INSERTs altogether and use LOAD DATA INFILE instead.

As far as UPDATEs are concerned, they work just as SELECT queries do with the overhead of INSERT queries. To optimize UPDATEs, beware of indexes, partitions, and NULL values:

- Beware that indexes will slow down UPDATEs if we modify columns that are indexed because of additional overhead (your database needs to update data itself and the data in the index as well.)

- Beware that UPDATE queries will be slower than usual if partitions are in use due to MySQL needing to update data in the partition and the data itself (and, if necessary, switch the partition where the data resides in, too.)

- Beware that NULL values have a caveat as far as updates are concerned, too – if you insert a NULL value into a partition, it will reside in the lowest possible partition.

Finally, to optimize `DELETE` queries, consider deleting data using the `LIMIT` clause, dropping indexes and partitions before deleting your data if deleting takes a lot of time, and finally, using `TRUNCATE` instead of `DELETE` if you're deleting all rows in a table: `TRUNCATE` queries will always be faster than `DELETE`s because instead of deleting records one by one, `TRUNCATE` queries will delete all rows in a table in one go.

Summary

As you discovered, MySQL has a layered architecture – those layers can be broken, and breaking any one layer impacts the performance of other layers. This chapter has walked you through ways to understand your data by properly choosing the schema and data types for your use case, as well as provided you with an understanding in regard to available character sets and collations in MySQL.

It's vitally important to build MySQL on a reliable architecture and choose a proper way to communicate with your database – but that's not enough. One should also write queries in a way that doesn't obstruct your database from helping you (e.g., if wildcard signs are found to be necessary, avoid using them at the beginning of your query, etc.) and close database connections once they're no longer necessary.

However, some of these tips are only applicable when the database is being built and may not necessarily be applicable once you've been working with it for some time. As time flies by, more and more database issues occur, and it's vital to know how to tackle them and prevent them from occurring too. Some of you may have been working with your database – and breaking your queries – for years too.

CHAPTER 4

How You Broke Your Queries

Understanding the reasons behind why your queries are slow and don't produce the necessary results is an essential skill for both novices and power users alike. After all, we optimize something that's broken – how can we optimize our queries if we don't even know what actions of ours broke them? This is what I'll help you explore in this chapter. This chapter will focus on the essentials of broken queries as well as some things you may not know, so make sure to read it carefully. Not all advice in this chapter may apply to your specific use case either – weigh the ups and downs of my advice, and take from it what you will. If you're not sure about something, you can always consult the latest version of documentation concerning your specific DBMS or ask your friendly neighborhood DBA.

The Good, Bad, and the Ugly: Understanding Queries in MySQL

You may think you understand your queries. After all, queries in MySQL aren't rocket science: there are only so many queries you count on in your daily work. These may be INSERT, SELECT, UPDATE, DELETE, and a couple of queries you turn to when these don't help. Seriously – that's kind of it. Yet, people still struggle to achieve performance: their SQL queries time out, MySQL greets them with errors, or customers contact them in regard to downtime headaches.

Much of that has to do with improperly written queries – we've gone through some examples in the last chapter where I walked you through some causes of slow query performance, but you'd be surprised at the things you do that break your queries from the inside. Some of you don't even think of them and they're there – hiding in plain sight.

CHAPTER 4   HOW YOU BROKE YOUR QUERIES

How You Broke Queries in MySQL

Contrary to popular belief, breaking your queries is easy. So easy in fact, that some of your colleagues are probably already breaking them without even knowing it.

You see, both developers and DBAs – no matter how senior they are – know how to write queries: who doesn't? The problems start when we start miscommunicating with our databases and biting off more than we can chew. Standard approaches are nice and good – until your application notoriety grows. With it grows the load onto your database and ways that helped you squash database issues before might be not applicable anymore.

I've walked you through a couple of such scenarios in Chapter 3: remember how I told you that you should take some time to think about your query structure? Properly choose data types and collations? Avoid using wildcards at the beginning of the queries having a LIKE clause? Each of these points of advice has merit – and the more points of relevant advice you adhere to, the faster you will bring your SQL queries back to their former glory. I will now walk you through the types of queries in MySQL, factors that are disliked by your queries, and explain why, how, and when that happens so you can head off performance issues.

Types of Queries in MySQL

MySQL has many types of queries available for you to use. These include the common set of four CRUD (Create, Read, Update, and Delete) queries, but also other SQL statements exclusive to DDL (Data Definition Language), DML (Data Manipulation Language), DCL (Data Control Language), and TCL (Transaction Control Language). In the MySQL world, such statements include, but are not limited to, the following data languages and statements:

Language and Explanation	Clauses and Statements
Data Definition Language (DDL)	ALTER, CREATE, DROP, RENAME, TRUNCATE
Data Manipulation Language (DML)	CALL, DELETE, DO, EXCEPT, INSERT, LOAD [DATA|XML], REPLACE, SELECT, UPDATE, UNION, VALUES, WITH (CTEs)
Data Control Language (DCL)	GRANT, REVOKE
Transaction Control Language (TCL)	COMMIT, ROLLBACK

In other words, queries in MySQL help you define, manipulate, or control your data or facilitate work with groups of statements that are handled as a single unit – these groups of statements are called *transactions*. As such, transactions cannot be inserted or deleted – they are either committed (saved in your database) or rolled back (restored to a previously defined state within your database.)

Factors Breaking DML Queries in MySQL

When it comes to understanding what breaks your queries, it's crucial to come back to the basics: remember what I told you in the last chapter? *Queries are tasks that are composed of other tasks. To make their performance faster, make the execution of those tasks faster or eliminate those tasks.* That's a piece of advice you can give to any developer who complains about inadequate query performance.

This piece of advice is a very good starting point – when you start to delve deeper into what it means, you start to understand what hinders and breaks your queries, and once you understand what hinders your queries from reaching their goal, you can start squashing problems.

Tasks are pieces of work that need to be accomplished to reach a goal. That goal differs depending on what query is in use: INSERT queries add data into tables in a database, UPDATE queries update the necessary columns in a table, and so on. Each query has a goal – a goal that you will have trouble achieving if your queries are broken.

Take the following table depicting messages sent between users.

```
MariaDB [(none)]> USE hacking_mysql;
Database changed
MariaDB [hacking_mysql]> DESCRIBE messages;
+-----------+-------------+------+-----+---------+----------------+
| Field     | Type        | Null | Key | Default | Extra          |
+-----------+-------------+------+-----+---------+----------------+
| id        | int(50)     | NO   | PRI | NULL    | auto_increment |
| message   | tinytext    | NO   |     | NULL    |                |
| sender    | varchar(50) | NO   |     |         |                |
| receiver  | varchar(50) | NO   |     |         |                |
| timestamp | timestamp   | NO   |     | NULL    |                |
+-----------+-------------+------+-----+---------+----------------+
5 rows in set (0.036 sec)
```

Figure 4-1. *Table used for demonstration purposes*

The table itself is nothing unusual – it's a simple table depicting sent and received messages with a timestamp. Tables with structures given above are a very common occurrence in various content management systems.

Many of you break your DML queries by using an improper structure of your tables and data types. Choose both of them carefully – improper structure means more work for all of your queries, and improper data types mean possible errors working with data.

The example you see above has four different data types: that's INT, TINYTEXT, VARCHAR, and TIMESTAMP. There's nothing wrong with that – at least not until you look into the future. Imagine your data set is getting bigger: naturally, you would want to add some partitions or indexes on top of it, right? By doing so, you would speed up read (SELECT) operations, and logically, you could add a couple of different partitions to account for messages sent within certain timeframes. Your SQL query would then look like so:

```
/* Adding a B-Tree Index on the Message Column */
CREATE INDEX message_idx ON messages(message);

/* Partitioning the Messages Table */

ALTER TABLE messages
    PARTITION BY RANGE ('timestamp') (
    PARTITION p0 VALUES LESS THAN (2018),
    PARTITION p1 VALUES LESS THAN (2019),
    PARTITION p2 VALUES LESS THAN (2020),
    PARTITION p3 VALUES LESS THAN (2021),
    PARTITION p4 VALUES LESS THAN (2022),
    PARTITION p5 VALUES LESS THAN (2023),
    PARTITION p6 VALUES LESS THAN (2024),
    PARTITION p7 VALUES LESS THAN (2025),
...
);
```

Except that you can't partition timestamp values – what a bummer!

```
#1659 - Field 'timestamp' is of a not allowed type for this type of partitioning
```

All inserted values must match the data type of your column, too – MySQL will scream if that's not the case.

Lesson Choose the structure of your tables and their data types carefully – improper structure or data types can be a highway to hell, at least figuratively speaking.

Another factor many of us overlook in this realm is syntax errors. Take a look at this example:

```
INSERT INTO `messages` (id, message, sender, `receiver`, timestamp)
SELECT id, 10, sender, receiver, timestamp
FROM `messages_old`
WHERE message_id = 1;
```

The problem here is that "10" is not the name of any column – it's a value that we wish to be inserted into our table.

Aside from INSERT queries, the next suspect would be SELECT queries – as I've already briefly mentioned before, you need to ensure that you select as little data as possible. To effectively do that, you would likely need to sacrifice the performance of SQL queries that insert, update, or delete data in your database, but that's the price you'll have to pay. GROUP BY and ORDER BY clauses also have a price. Remember – any additional operation has a performance cost. It may be small, but small things also add up quickly.

Some of you may also be fans of the UNION clause – the primary mistake here is having too many of them, and this has an undeniable impact on performance. Minimize the times you invoke the UNION clause and consider switching this clause to WHERE [condition] IN() instead.

Factors Breaking DDL Queries in MySQL

When it comes to DDL queries, the first thing we need to understand is that such types of queries help us define data hence their title, and in MySQL, come in five different forms helping us CREATE, ALTER, RENAME, DROP, or TRUNCATE our data.

Each of those clauses has different merits – `CREATE` helps us create databases that contain tables, `ALTER` helps us change the structure of our tables (move columns around, change their data types, rename them, or add, modify, or delete index structures), `RENAME` helps us rename tables containing our data, `DROP` removes our databases or tables within them, and `TRUNCATE` removes all of the data within our tables. As such, some queries are used more frequently than others, and consequentially, they are found to be broken more often. For example, you are likely to be modifying your tables with `ALTER` more often than you would be dropping them. Also keep in mind that `ALTER` has multiple equivalents, too: `RENAME` maps into `ALTER` as specified below, and when you find yourself creating things inside of your database, keep in mind that `CREATE INDEX` also maps into `ALTER TABLE ... CREATE INDEX`. Depending on your use case, dropping may occur more frequently than truncating or vice versa, and after you consider the upsides of DDL queries present to your database, you need to keep a couple of things in mind to understand why they might break.

`CREATE` queries are unlikely to be slow once you're creating a database or two; if you've noticed that they slow down, you're probably facing slower performance when building indexes. In that regard, `CREATE` queries are very similar to `ALTER`s. Keep in mind that when indexes are being built, both of these clauses modify – *alter* – your table in such a way that necessitates MySQL to re-create the same table, add data to it, and perform modifications on the table that was just created. MySQL then swaps the old table with the newly created table. None of these processes involve you seeing the table or data being added to it – you don't see a new table appear straight after you run these queries, and if you've noticed a drop in performance after running an `ALTER` or `CREATE`, that's the most likely reason.

When it comes to renaming tables, everything usually looks like this:

```
RENAME TABLE `old_table` TO `new_table`;
```

The same statement is equal to an `ALTER` statement:

```
ALTER TABLE `old_table` RENAME `new_table`;
```

I'll walk you through how to optimize your DDL queries in the Optimization part of this book, but for now, look into online DDL. If you find yourself using MariaDB Server, keep in mind that MariaDB provides support for online DDL operations where your database server performs some magic in the background to keep your tables accessible throughout those operations. For that, `ALTER TABLE` has two clauses – `ALGORITHM` and

CHAPTER 4   HOW YOU BROKE YOUR QUERIES

LOCK – that control how the DDL operation is performed (ALGORITHM) and how much concurrency is allocated for it to complete (LOCK). MariaDB supports various algorithms to facilitate online DDL, them being COPY, INPLACE, NOCOPY, and INSTANT. INSTANT is the most efficient algorithm, while COPY is the least efficient.

If you want to use the power of alter algorithms within MariaDB, specify the algorithm you want MariaDB to employ for an ALTER operation in a SET SESSION clause before you run an ALTER TABLE operation like so:

SET SESSION alter_algorithm='INSTANT';
ALTER TABLE `demo_table` ADD COLUMN `last_column` VARCHAR(120) DEFAULT NULL;

However, keep in mind that if you specify an algorithm other than COPY, MariaDB won't interpret it as "I must use the algorithm the user has specified." *Instead, it will interpret your decision for the algorithm as the least efficient algorithm you will accept* and that's why I've also mentioned the algorithms above: that means that if you've elected INPLACE as your solution of choice, MariaDB is free to choose the most efficient algorithm for the operation counting from INPLACE to INSTANT – in other words, *it can elect to use either of the three.* MariaDB does that because not all algorithms support certain operations. For example, if you find yourself adding columns to a table, MariaDB can only choose INSTANT if the column you're adding is the last column for that specific table.

When choosing locks for online DDL operations, everything's less complex – you only have four options, with the DEFAULT being the default one if none are specified:

1. DEFAULT: MariaDB chooses the least restrictive lock for your table.

2. NONE: MariaDB won't lock your table at all. All concurrent DML operations will run as expected.

3. SHARED: MariaDB will lock the table for reading while permitting concurrent DML, but only for read-only operations.

4. EXCLUSIVE: MariaDB will lock the table for writing and won't permit any concurrent DML operations.

When dealing with DDL and DML operations, increasing the innodb_buffer_pool_size might be of assistance too. Since the InnoDB buffer pool is a key component of the primary storage engine – InnoDB – and it's accountable for storing table and index data as it's accessed, the bigger it is, the faster your INSERT or ALTER operations are likely to complete, especially if the table you're modifying has indexes on it.

Factors Breaking DCL and TCL Queries in MySQL

When it comes to controlling data and transactions, factors breaking those things will be mostly related to you not granting users the necessary privileges (be honest – when was the last time you reviewed the privileges of all users within your database server?) or not revoking them once they're no longer necessary, not understanding that operations involving larger data sets can benefit from you delaying `COMMIT` operations by including `autocommit=0` before anything is inserted into your database and `COMMIT`ing your changes afterward, and the like.

Understand that rollbacks are not as scary as they sound either – they're just operations that return your database to the previous state, but they can also sometimes fail. If you've ever heard of a "runaway rollback," you know what I'm talking about. What if you try to terminate a process, but it just doesn't listen to you? If you ask your neighborhood DBA about their horror stories and they tell you that they had a process in a "Sending data" state, killed it, but it'd remained in that state, what do you call it? That's a *runaway rollback* because the reason your `KILL` operation takes ages is most likely due to rollbacks issued by InnoDB – to fix this issue, try employing `innodb_force_recovery` by setting it to 3 to skip rollbacks and then drop the table that's causing the problem. Make sure you've backed up your data beforehand, though.

Why Are Queries Slow?

Now we move toward perhaps the most frequently asked question in the database world – "Why are queries slow?" This question has plagued developers and DBAs for ages. To be honest, it most likely concerns the visitors or customers of your website too: have a look at your support tickets. Now search for "slow" or "doesn't load," and count the number of tickets you've received.

I'll guess that the number you've come up with is higher than 0 – and if it is, you've got problems on your hands. Slow queries mean slow response times, and slow response times are the pillar of slow performance. Remember what I told you earlier? *Performance is response time* – and the higher your response time is, the worse for your database, application, and everyone related to them.

Right, you got it – you need high-performing queries. Fast. I recommend solving such problems from the bottom – that means that the first question you must ask yourself is not "How to increase my query performance to < 1 second?" but "Why are my queries slow?"

CHAPTER 4   HOW YOU BROKE YOUR QUERIES

Think about it – to come up with strategies to increase your query performance, you have to understand what makes them slow in the first place, right?

So, back to where we started – why are queries slow?

The answer is simple, but complex at the same time – it depends. It depends because different developers shatter their queries in different ways – some break them when inserting data, some – when selecting data that has already been inserted, and some need assistance in updating data (that's especially the case when the data sets are bigger).

However, regardless of what kind of query you find yourself optimizing, there is a general answer – *queries are tasks that are composed of other tasks. Your query is slow because the subtasks your primary task is concerned with complete slowly.* To make your query performance faster, you need to make those subtasks complete faster or make your database ignore them altogether. That's all it is.

Right, now you've got an answer to why your queries are slow: that's because the subtasks within them are slow. So why are those subtasks slow and what are they? To understand what breaks your queries in that regard, you must employ some profiling, so that's what we'll do now.

First, we need to tell our database to enable monitoring for anyone who runs the query by enabling monitoring for your account, and optionally, disabling monitoring for everyone else. First, we disable monitoring:

```
UPDATE performance_schema.setup_actors SET ENABLED = 'NO', HISTORY = 'NO' WHERE HOST = '%' AND USER = '%';
```

After, we need to modify the `setup_actors` table in our performance schema to enable monitoring for our specific account (replace username with your username):INSERT INTO performance_schema.setup_actors (HOST,USER,ROLE,ENABLED,HISTORY) VALUES('localhost','**username**','%','YES','YES');

Once done, you need to enable logs for statements and their stages by running the following SQL queries:

```
UPDATE performance_schema.setup_consumers SET ENABLED = 'YES' WHERE NAME LIKE '%events_statements_%';
```

```
UPDATE performance_schema.setup_consumers SET ENABLED = 'YES' WHERE NAME LIKE '%events_stages_%';
```

69

CHAPTER 4 HOW YOU BROKE YOUR QUERIES

Then, enable the instruments allowing for the monitoring of your query:

UPDATE performance_schema.setup_instruments SET ENABLED = 'YES', TIMED = 'YES' WHERE NAME LIKE '%statement/%';

UPDATE performance_schema.setup_instruments SET ENABLED = 'YES', TIMED = 'YES' WHERE NAME LIKE '%stage/%';

Execute your queries as usual (make sure they're executed under the account you've just enabled monitoring on), then identify your query by running this one:

SELECT EVENT_ID, TRUNCATE(TIMER_WAIT/1000000000000,6) as Duration, SQL_TEXT FROM performance_schema.events_statements_history_long WHERE SQL_TEXT LIKE '%Your Query%';

Finally, to see the information in regard to your query, replace ID with your query ID and execute this query:

SELECT event_name AS Stage, TRUNCATE(TIMER_WAIT/1000000000000,6) AS Duration FROM performance_schema.events_stages_history_long WHERE NESTING_EVENT_ID = **ID**;

The results will provide you with a bunch of information you can use to profile your query. The results will contain multiple stages of your query and provide you with detailed information on how long a certain duration of the query took to execute properly.

Such an approach works on MySQL and MariaDB since profiling using SHOW PROFILE has been deprecated since MySQL 5.6.7. There also is a different approach that yields the same results and is easier.

To approach profiling from the other side, employ query profiling by setting SET profiling = 1, then running a query, issuing SHOW PROFILES to select the query you need to profile, and finally – SHOW PROFILE FOR QUERY x where x is your query ID. Here's how everything looks like.

CHAPTER 4   HOW YOU BROKE YOUR QUERIES

```
MariaDB [(none)]> USE hacking_mysql;
Database changed
MariaDB [hacking_mysql]> SET profiling = 1;
Query OK, 0 rows affected (0.000 sec)

MariaDB [hacking_mysql]> SELECT * FROM messages WHERE id = 4;
+----+----------------------+--------+----------+---------------------+
| id | message              | sender | receiver | timestamp           |
+----+----------------------+--------+----------+---------------------+
|  4 | The dinner is at 6PM.| Alissa | Christina| 2024-04-14 15:20:31 |
+----+----------------------+--------+----------+---------------------+
1 row in set (0.001 sec)

MariaDB [hacking_mysql]> SHOW PROFILES;
+----------+------------+------------------------------------+
| Query_ID | Duration   | Query                              |
+----------+------------+------------------------------------+
|        1 | 0.00090170 | SELECT * FROM messages WHERE id = 4|
+----------+------------+------------------------------------+
1 row in set (0.013 sec)
```

Figure 4-2. *Profiling an SQL Query: initializing*

```
MariaDB [hacking_mysql]> SHOW PROFILE FOR QUERY 1;
+--------------------------+----------+
| Status                   | Duration |
+--------------------------+----------+
| Starting                 | 0.000104 |
| checking permissions     | 0.000012 |
| Opening tables           | 0.000133 |
| After opening tables     | 0.000129 |
| System lock              | 0.000031 |
| table lock               | 0.000013 |
| init                     | 0.000054 |
| Optimizing               | 0.000068 |
| Statistics               | 0.000153 |
| Preparing                | 0.000008 |
| Unlocking tables         | 0.000009 |
| Preparing                | 0.000021 |
| Executing                | 0.000014 |
| Sending data             | 0.000043 |
| End of update loop       | 0.000006 |
| Query end                | 0.000003 |
| Commit                   | 0.000006 |
| closing tables           | 0.000004 |
| Unlocking tables         | 0.000003 |
| closing tables           | 0.000013 |
| Starting cleanup         | 0.000004 |
| Freeing items            | 0.000010 |
| Updating status          | 0.000056 |
| Reset for next command   | 0.000006 |
+--------------------------+----------+
24 rows in set (0.002 sec)
```

Figure 4-3. Profiling an SQL Query: results

We have 24 status codes to investigate – isn't that a lot? Keep in mind that for newer versions of MySQL, the results can also look a little different and include more rows in the set such as "Executing hook on transaction" and "waiting for handler commit," but here's what they mean:

ID	Status Code	Explanation
1	Starting	The database server is initializing the query.
2	checking permissions	The database server is checking whether our user has sufficient permissions to run the query. If that's not the case, we're presented with an error.
3	Opening tables	The database server ensures that all tables are open to conduct operations on them.
4	After opening tables	The database server is conducting miscellaneous operations after opening tables.
5	System lock	The database server is waiting for a system lock to be released if it's in place.
6	table lock	The database server is waiting for a table lock to be released if it's in place.
7	init	The database server performs initialization processes by flushing logs, etc.
8	Optimizing	The database server is performing internal work to determine how to optimize the query in the best way possible.
9	Statistics	The database server is calculating data related to statistics to develop the query execution plan.
10	Preparing	The database server is preparing to run the query.
11	Unlocking tables	Necessary tables are being unlocked.
12	Preparing	The database server is preparing to run the query.
13	Executing	The database server is executing the query.
14	Sending data	Our data is being sent to the server for it to return the necessary results.
15	End of update loop	The database server reaches the finish line after updating the data.
16	Query end	The database server finishes executing the query.

(continued)

ID	Status Code	Explanation
17	Commit	Commit operations are being run – data is saved inside of the database.
18 (2 of such values)	closing tables	Tables necessary for our query are being closed.
19	Unlocking tables	Tables are being unlocked.
20	Starting cleanup	The database server is starting the cleanup process.
21	Freeing items	The database server is freeing resources to deal with upcoming queries.
22	Updating status	The database server is updating its status.
23	Reset for next command	The database server is getting ready to accept upcoming queries.

See how many subtasks your query has to accomplish to execute? None of these subtasks are there without a reason – and none of them are unnecessary. The more queries you run, the more subtasks are on the list. I'll walk you through how to optimize these subtasks in the optimization part of this book – I'll do that once you understand the prerequisites for optimization. You cannot optimize anything that doesn't have a backbone – and for your database, that backbone is your database schema.

Devising the Perfect Schema Design

Ask 10 DBAs what goes into a perfect schema design, and you will hear 10 different things, but most of them will mention normalization, applying efficient constraints and indexes, proper relationships between database entities, minimizing disk space usage, using proper data types, and so on. The bottom line is that perfect database schema design means different things to different people – but is equally important no matter what your application is or what data you're dealing with. To devise the perfect schema design, understand the following:

- It's OK if your schema design isn't perfect now.

- You will likely make mistakes in implementing performance-related advice, and that's OK. That's not the end of the world.

- Experience is one of the best teachers you will ever have.

- Don't obsess over coming up with the best schema design ever – simple solutions are good, and every schema can be improved further.

Have a goal of what you're trying to achieve by modifying your database schema and go from there. For most of you, the goal will be related to performance improvement or restructurization.

Once you have a goal in mind, understand that a schema refers to the structure of your database. The structure of your database includes everything inside of your database – that includes database tables, column types and sizes, attributes, all kinds of indexes, partitions, and everything in between. In the MySQL world, databases can be also called schemas by themselves – and a schema is the backbone for your data. Likely, this backbone won't be completely straight once you start working on it and that's okay – your schema design isn't set in stone, and it will inevitably evolve once your data set grows and time goes by. Every schema can be improved further, but basic advice still stands.

To begin with, you can create a schema by writing all of its definitions yourself or let an SQL client or a framework generate them for you. If you find yourself using an SQL client, you will likely have an option to automatically create schemas, explore your tables as if they were spreadsheets, and so much more. Make use of these features because SQL clients are frequently designed by people who've been in the industry for at least a decade and who've seen databases survive through hot and cold. Their database design suggestions provided in the form of outputs in an SQL client are likely to supersede anything your neighborhood developers say. Such database design suggestions are likely to prevent mistakes you'd otherwise make – and if you find yourself using a paid version of the tool, chances are that you will also be able to contact a professional team of DBAs to help you during a consulting call or two. Did I mention that many such tools can generate ERD-like schemas designed precisely for this purpose? Here's how an ERD schema of a popular content management system for forums – MyBB – would look like.

CHAPTER 4   HOW YOU BROKE YOUR QUERIES

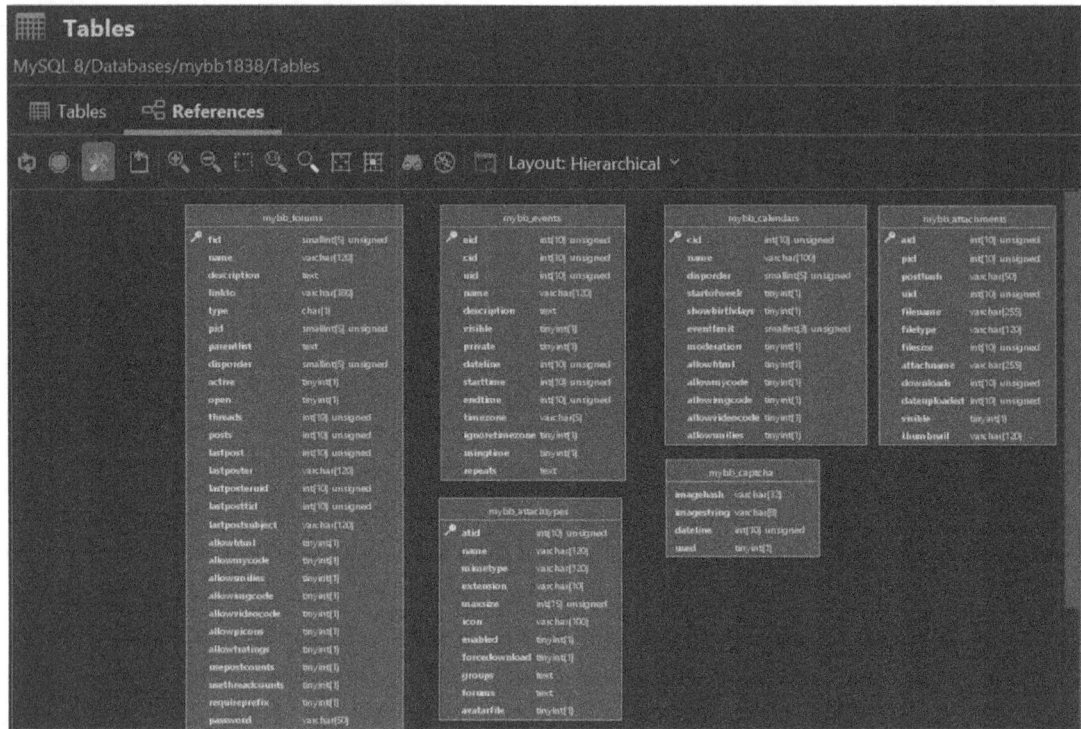

Figure 4-4. ERD schema of a couple of tables in MyBB

Did I tell you that most of the tables have been exempt from showing? You can drag and drop tables for better observability too!

ERD schemas can be an exceptionally useful tool when observing the posture of your databases or creating tables that will contain your most precious data.

The bottom line is clear – SQL clients can help you create database schemas and advise you what to do, make schema recommendations, tell you what things to avoid, and even consult you when necessary – but what if you don't have such a luxury? If that's the case, you need to create your database schema yourself.

To design a proper database schema, meticulously analyze the requirements of the software solution behind your database – consider your project scope, entity specifications, and the use case for your project itself. Come up with a sketch of your database schema. It doesn't have to be perfect for now.

The next step would be to somehow visualize your database schema for better clarity – here many will advise you to find an ERD tool that helps you bring clarity and coherence to your database design. ERD tools usually come by default in many SQL clients (see example above), but if you don't have one at hand, you can always search for a free equivalent: there are numerous ER diagram tools suitable for visualizing data in your database, and once you find one, try providing it a sketch of your structure and see how everything looks like. To refine your schema, follow this advice:

1. **Pick small data types**: Each data type has some weight inside of your database, so consider picking the smallest data type possible. Here, ask yourself questions – does your use case necessitate you choosing TEXT instead of VARCHAR? If you're using VARCHAR, is it necessary to have a maximum value of 255, or would 45 characters be enough? How much disk space can you allocate for your database? Do you have reason to believe that you find yourself working with bigger data sets in the future?

2. **Choose a simple column type**: Use numeric data types for numbers (SMALLINT would sometimes do more good than INT), VARCHAR for smaller text-based values, consider ENUM if you have a limited set of possible values, etc.

3. **Design your schema by looking into the future and designing it so that it accurately depicts the reality of your data**: Do you need that nullable column to be nullable? Do you need DEFAULT values on that column?

Follow these principles and you will be on the way toward performance heaven – I'll tell you more about database schema optimization in the optimization part of this book, but following these principles will ensure that neither you nor your database will get lost in the data jungle.

Designing efficient schemas is crucial because an efficient database schema design can be a matter of life and death when it comes to blazing-fast queries and index efficiency.

Understanding Data Types

Aside from database schemas (schemas, in the MySQL world, are synonyms to databases too), multiple other things are just as crucial to your database performance. One of those things is related to data types, which means that properly choosing data types for your database instance can be a matter of life and death for your databases too.

CHAPTER 4   HOW YOU BROKE YOUR QUERIES

MySQL supports several different data types:

1. **String data types**: These MySQL data types include CHAR and VARCHAR, BINARY and VARBINARY, BLOB and TEXT, and finally, ENUM and SET.

2. **Numeric data types**: Such data types include integer data types (INT, SMALLINT, TINYINT, MEDIUMINT, BIGINT), fixed-point data types – DECIMAL and NUMERIC, floating-point data types holding approximate values: FLOAT and DOUBLE, and bit-value data types, such as BIT.

3. **Date and time data types**: Such data types include DATE, DATETIME, and TIMESTAMP, and also the types depicting the TIME and the YEAR.

4. **Spatial data types**: Such data types include data types for holding singular geometric values, such as GEOMETRY, POINT, LINESTRING, and POLYGON, as well as data types reserved to hold multiple values – MULTIPOINT, MULTILINESTRING, MULTIPOLYGON, and GEOMETRYCOLLECTION.

5. **The JSON data type:** Such a data type, as its name suggests, is suitable to hold JSON values.

Aside from support for multiple different data types, all flavors of MySQL also provide its users with the ability to define how many characters they need stored in a specific column. Different data types have different amounts of characters that can be stored in a column powering that data type:

Data Type	Default Number of Characters or Numbers for Numeric Data Types	Maximum Value, Precision or Number of Characters
CHAR, BINARY	1	255
VARCHAR, VARBINARY	None. Must be defined	255
TINYINT	4	127 (signed) or 255 (unsigned)
SMALLINT	6	32767 (signed) or 65535 (unsigned)

(continued)

Data Type	Default Number of Characters or Numbers for Numeric Data Types	Maximum Value, Precision or Number of Characters
MEDIUMINT	9	8388607 (signed) or 16777215 (unsigned)
INT	11	2147483647 (signed) or 4294967295 (unsigned)
BIGINT	20	$2^{63}-1$ (signed) or $2^{64}-1$ (unsigned)
YEAR	4	2155
DECIMAL, NUMERIC	DECIMAL(10,0)	Maximum precision – 65
FLOAT, DOUBLE	Can't be defined	Can't be defined
BIT	1	64
JSON	None	No fixed limit

What an interesting database, huh? Some data types have a default number of characters, and some don't.

All that has a good reason – MySQL and its flavors provide you with a wide range of choices in regard to data types so you could choose the data type most suitable for your specific use case. Choose a data type after carefully considering

- **The kind of values you're going to store**: Think of the data you're working with – what kind of data goes into what column? How will the data be accessed?

- **The amount of space on the disk the data type requires**: Some data types occupy more space on the disk than others do, and that's one of the primary reasons why you see data types like TINYINT, SMALLINT, TINYTEXT, SMALLTEXT, and the like.

- **Whether you can index the column or not**: If you index TEXT values, bear in mind that you must specify an index length or use a full-text index, but at the same time, you will be able to store more data than in VARCHAR-based columns.

Some other things that would need your consideration include the row format you use to store your data (the default row format for InnoDB-based tables is DYNAMIC), but that's kind of it.

Aside from "ordinary" data types, MySQL also provides you with the ability to "dictate" values to a column using either the ENUM or SET data type. The ENUM data type takes a set of possible values into account like so:

`months_choose` ENUM(`March`, `April`, `May`,...);

The SET data type also allows you to specify valid values like so:

`availability_days` SET(`Mon`, `Wed`, `Fri`,...);

The difference between those two data types is that in ENUM, the user may only use one value of interest, while in a SET, the same logic applies, but the user may choose multiple values of interest instead. An ENUM column may contain up to 65,535 elements, and a SET column may contain up to 64 distinct values.

MySQL is also able to store JSON values with the JSON data type, and those are interpreted and stored as binary values for faster execution.

Choose your data types carefully – none of them are set in stone, but a good data type will do wonders for your database both now and in the future. However, data sets are only a piece of the equation.

Understanding Character Sets and Collations

Data types, as good as they may be, are only a singular piece of your schema equation. No matter what kind of data type you will elect to use, you will need to store data in it. Data – no matter what it may be – may be interpreted differently. Think of various countries – they speak English in the United States, but Spanish in Spain. They speak Finnish in Finland, Swedish in Sweden, and Turkish in Turkey. Now visit China, and I bet you won't have much luck communicating in either of those languages because they speak Chinese!

And with the world being so diverse, your databases need to evolve too. Well, not exactly – you won't need to come up with a plan to execute a revolution to deal with data from those countries – but you will need to know your way around character sets and collations.

Remember the time when you inserted data in a foreign language in a column and MySQL interpreted every character as a "?" sign? That's because it didn't understand the charset it was written in. Charsets are short for character sets – and collations are their friends.

Character sets define what sets of characters are accepted in a column, and collations refer to a set of rules that define how to sort everything that you provide to your columns. Together, they perform some magic, and characters are displayed as they should be displayed instead of you seeing ??? signs. To explore the character sets and collations available in MySQL, MariaDB, or Percona Server, log in to your database via the CLI and then execute the query SHOW CHARACTER SET – no matter what database you find yourself in (you don't even need to select a database to begin with – this query works the same way regardless), you should now see all of the available character sets and collations like so.

CHAPTER 4 HOW YOU BROKE YOUR QUERIES

```
MariaDB [(none)]> SHOW CHARACTER SET;
+----------+-----------------------------+---------------------+--------+
| Charset  | Description                 | Default collation   | Maxlen |
+----------+-----------------------------+---------------------+--------+
| big5     | Big5 Traditional Chinese    | big5_chinese_ci     |      2 |
| dec8     | DEC West European           | dec8_swedish_ci     |      1 |
| cp850    | DOS West European           | cp850_general_ci    |      1 |
| hp8      | HP West European            | hp8_english_ci      |      1 |
| koi8r    | KOI8-R Relcom Russian       | koi8r_general_ci    |      1 |
| latin1   | cp1252 West European        | latin1_swedish_ci   |      1 |
| latin2   | ISO 8859-2 Central European | latin2_general_ci   |      1 |
| swe7     | 7bit Swedish                | swe7_swedish_ci     |      1 |
| ascii    | US ASCII                    | ascii_general_ci    |      1 |
| ujis     | EUC-JP Japanese             | ujis_japanese_ci    |      3 |
| sjis     | Shift-JIS Japanese          | sjis_japanese_ci    |      2 |
| hebrew   | ISO 8859-8 Hebrew           | hebrew_general_ci   |      1 |
| tis620   | TIS620 Thai                 | tis620_thai_ci      |      1 |
| euckr    | EUC-KR Korean               | euckr_korean_ci     |      2 |
| koi8u    | KOI8-U Ukrainian            | koi8u_general_ci    |      1 |
| gb2312   | GB2312 Simplified Chinese   | gb2312_chinese_ci   |      2 |
| greek    | ISO 8859-7 Greek            | greek_general_ci    |      1 |
| cp1250   | Windows Central European    | cp1250_general_ci   |      1 |
| gbk      | GBK Simplified Chinese      | gbk_chinese_ci      |      2 |
| latin5   | ISO 8859-9 Turkish          | latin5_turkish_ci   |      1 |
| armscii8 | ARMSCII-8 Armenian          | armscii8_general_ci |      1 |
| utf8mb3  | UTF-8 Unicode               | utf8mb3_general_ci  |      3 |
| ucs2     | UCS-2 Unicode               | ucs2_general_ci     |      2 |
| cp866    | DOS Russian                 | cp866_general_ci    |      1 |
| keybcs2  | DOS Kamenicky Czech-Slovak  | keybcs2_general_ci  |      1 |
| macce    | Mac Central European        | macce_general_ci    |      1 |
| macroman | Mac West European           | macroman_general_ci |      1 |
| cp852    | DOS Central European        | cp852_general_ci    |      1 |
| latin7   | ISO 8859-13 Baltic          | latin7_general_ci   |      1 |
| utf8mb4  | UTF-8 Unicode               | utf8mb4_general_ci  |      4 |
| cp1251   | Windows Cyrillic            | cp1251_general_ci   |      1 |
| utf16    | UTF-16 Unicode              | utf16_general_ci    |      4 |
| utf16le  | UTF-16LE Unicode            | utf16le_general_ci  |      4 |
| cp1256   | Windows Arabic              | cp1256_general_ci   |      1 |
| cp1257   | Windows Baltic              | cp1257_general_ci   |      1 |
| utf32    | UTF-32 Unicode              | utf32_general_ci    |      4 |
```

Figure 4-5. *Character sets and collations in MariaDB*

CHAPTER 4 HOW YOU BROKE YOUR QUERIES

So many options across four columns! Yet, when you boil them down, everything becomes clear as water:

1. Charset refers to the character set you may choose.

2. Description helps you understand the use case where that charset may be useful by providing a short description of the character set in question.

3. Default collation describes the default collation mechanism for that specific character set.

4. Maxlen refers to the maximum number of bytes that your database server requires to store one character using that specific collation.

Think of SHOW CHARACTER SET as a companion to the documentation – it's easy to be lost in the jungle of documentation, and some of you may not even have time to read everything about every specific character set and collation. That's where SHOW CHARACTER SET comes in! Run this query, glance at the output, and the path should become clear. If it doesn't, turn to the docs, but most of what you need to know is explained there.

Most of you will have to wing a utf8mb4 charset together with a utf8mb4_general_ci or utf8mb4_unicode_ci collation or something along that realm, but be aware that MySQL does have a couple of "gotchas." For example, MySQL's UTF-8 isn't real UTF-8: real UTF-8 requires to support up to 4 bytes per character, while UTF-8 in MySQL only supports 3. Hence the introduction of utf8mb4: the main reason you will see utf8mb4 instead of utf8 in MySQL installations these days is because utf8mb4 offers full Unicode support meaning that its users can feel free to use emojis and other things. Unicode support also means that certain characters won't make MySQL error out and scream "Incorrect string value: '\x77\xD0' for column 'demo_column' at row 1" when you try to store them.

utf8mb4 might not be the primary choice for everyone though because every use case is different – however, no matter what character set and collation you intend to use, keep in mind that they're not rocket science; keep in mind that their primary purpose is to make data in various languages readable, and you should be good to go!

CHAPTER 4   HOW YOU BROKE YOUR QUERIES

Understanding Indexes

When you understand character sets and collations, the next thing that will inevitably pop up on your radar will be related to query performance in general. By now, you probably understand a little about the types of queries, the factors breaking them, and what makes them slow. You also know how to devise the perfect schema design, and I've also walked you through various charsets and collations for your schema perfection, but if you're interested in these things, you will also be interested in indexes.

Most of you probably already use indexes in one form or another and know what they are. For those of you who don't, think of indexes in your database as indexes in a book – they help your database quickly find things that it would probably take some time to find if they were not in place. The more data you have, the more important indexes become.

They become important because their primary purpose is to help your database quickly find rows and return them, but as such, indexes are not without their flaws and issues – they slow down queries that insert, update, or delete data in your database infrastructure as a result.

No matter what flavor of MySQL you use – MySQL Server, MariaDB Server, or Percona Server, you will always have options to choose from on the index front. I would lie to you if I said "All indexes are the same," "all indexes help your database," or "Index this column and you will never have to worry about query performance again" – that's not the case because indexes are not a holy grail – however, they're extremely good at two things they're primarily designed to do: occupying storage space and making SELECT queries faster.

Remember what I told you before? *Queries are tasks composed of other tasks*? That's right – indexes help your database sweep through some of those tasks with ease, and while all indexes serve a purpose, not all indexes are the same:

- **A typical index in MySQL is a B-Tree index**: Such an index will be used in operations where we're searching for a value with an exact match operator.

- **A descending index will store all rows in a descending order**: Such an index may be a necessity for those performing calculation operations or some sort of data analysis.

- **A unique index makes sure all of the values in a column are unique**: In other words, such an index makes sure that there are no duplicates within a column. If duplicate values are found, MySQL will error out (the error can be prevented by specifying an `IGNORE` clause, but I won't get into all of the specifics here – we'll have a chapter about indexes for that instead).

I would also like to note that a `PRIMARY KEY` is also an index – such indexes uniquely identify rows in a table and are often used together with the `AUTO_INCREMENT` clause to automatically increment column ID values once new rows are inserted. If a primary key index is in place on a column, a `NULL` value inserted in that column will manifest in the form of a row ID after MySQL calculates how many rows are in a table (e.g., if there are 1,499 rows in a table and we insert a row with a `NULL` value in a column that has a primary key, the `NULL` value will become 1,500).

Understanding indexes is crucial for any sort of performance operations – keep in mind that neither flavor of MySQL prevents you from using multiple indexes on the same column and nor does it show a message akin to "your index won't be used if you index this column – you should index another one instead." Of course, there are limitations and tips you can use to get the most out of the indexes that are in place in your specific DBMS; however, to get the most out of them, you will need to ensure that your indexes are being used in the first place. That's what bothers many databases without their owners being aware – "I've already indexed this column, why are queries still slow?!" Well, that's likely because the index isn't even used or considered by your database in the first place.

How do I know that? Simple – choose one query that has an indexed column and run an `EXPLAIN` operation on it. You will see two columns – `possible_keys` and `key` – and if any of those columns have a value that isn't the name of the index you want this query to use, you've got problems. Why? *Because keys are synonyms to indexes: keys can unlock the door toward a performance heaven for your queries, but they have to be used in a proper way to do that.*

For many developers, the main problem concerning indexes isn't that they're not in place – it's that they exist, but they are not even used by your queries! How did that happen? Well, simple:

1. You didn't search for an exact match using an equality operator.

2. You've conducted a wildcard search having a wildcard at the beginning of your query (remember when I told you that a wildcard at the beginning of a `LIKE` query makes it unable to use any indexes?).

3. If your column had multiple indexes in question, it wasn't the most selective one (it didn't find the smallest number of rows).

4. If your column had an index spanning multiple columns (a composite index), your query was not using the leftmost prefix of the index.

One or more of these four things are perhaps the core reason why your queries are performing slowly even though you have an index present on a column – just as not all developers are great, not all queries will use your indexes if certain things are not in place.

I'll walk you through some more of these things in a chapter dedicated to indexes later on, but wrap your head around these four things and you will be well-equipped to eliminate your index problems right then and there.

Understanding Partitions

What else improves query performance aside from indexes? Right – partitions!

Partitions are similar to indexes in a way that they minimize the amount of data your database has to sift through to find any row. Just as there are many types of indexes, there are many types of partitions, too – one can elect to partition by `RANGE`, `LIST`, `COLUMNS`, `HASH`, or `KEY`, or subpartition their tables too.

Partitions have an interesting function to perform – they too gobble up your disk space in return for your `SELECT` queries being faster. That's not their only purpose though – data existing in partitions can be purged by dropping that partition without having a dropping effect on your table as a whole because MySQL treats partitions as "mini tables" in and of itself. In other words, partitioning is the practice of splitting something rather large into smaller parts.

Those parts are stored as files on the disk – we refer to those files as partitions. Once partitions power your tables, MySQL will choose a partitioning function when data is selected or updated in any way. There are multiple ways to partition your tables:

1. **Partitioning by RANGE**: Such a partitioning method partitions a table in such a way that each partition contains values that fall within a given range.

2. **Partitioning by LIST**: This type of partitioning in MySQL is similar to partitioning by RANGE, just that partitioning by LIST takes a list of distinct integer values to define how data is split into partitions. If a table has no partition for a value, an error will be returned.

3. **Partitioning by COLUMNS**: This type of partitioning allows you to make use of multiple columns as partitioning keys.

4. **Partitioning by HASH**: This type of partitioning takes a column as a partitioning key. Alongside the column, the necessary number of partitions must also be defined. HASH partitioning partitions data evenly across all partitions and uses a hash function.

5. **Partitioning by KEY**: This type of partitioning is similar to partitioning by HASH. This type of partitioning also takes a column as the partitioning key, but instead of employing a column as the key or using a hash function, it makes use of an internal function within MySQL.

Partitioning types within MySQL are quite easy to understand – there's also subpartitioning meaning that users can elect to have partitions with partitions too, but MySQL will only allow subpartitioning to be in place when we're already working with partitioning by RANGE or LIST, and subpartitions are only allowed to use two partitioning types: our subpartitions must be of the HASH or KEY type.

One can start using partitioning after creating the table structure like so – here we define partitioning by range:

```
CREATE TABLE `demo_table` (
`id` INT AUTO_INCREMENT PRIMARY KEY,
`username` VARCHAR(122) DEFAULT ''
) PARTITION BY RANGE(id) (
PARTITION `p0_title` VALUES LESS THAN (10),
```

```
PARTITION `p1_title` VALUES LESS THAN (15),
PARTITION `p2_title` VALUES LESS THAN (20),
...
);
```

Subpartitions can be defined like so:

```
CREATE TABLE `demo_table` (
`id` INT,
`regdate` DATETIME
) PARTITION BY RANGE(YEAR(regdate))
    SUBPARTITION BY HASH(TO_DAYS(regdate)) (
        PARTITION part_0 VALUES LESS THAN (2015) (
            SUBPARTITION sub_0,
            SUBPARTITION sub_1
        ),
        PARTITION part_1 VALUES LESS THAN (2020) (
            SUBPARTITION sub_2,
            SUBPARTITION sub_3
        ),
        PARTITION part_2 VALUES LESS THAN MAXVALUE (
            SUBPARTITION sub_4,
            SUBPARTITION sub_5
        )
    );
```

Bear in mind that when you define VALUES LESS THAN in RANGE partitioning, the values of partitions must be increasing. If your first partition specifies values less than 2015, none of the other partitions can specify lower values because for RANGE partitioning, values must be strictly increasing to avoid this error:

`#1493 - VALUES LESS THAN value must be strictly increasing for each partition`

Each partitioning type is different, and I've explained their core differences above – the exact type of partitioning you will use will directly depend on your use case and requirements.

No matter what kind of partitioning type you elect to use though, you must be aware of key mistakes applicable to everyone using MySQL partitions. Not being aware of these issues may make your experience with partitions in MySQL sour.

Partitions and Big Data

The first thing you should be aware of is that partitions are not used without a reason. For many, that reason is clear – partitions split data into smaller tables that are still treated as one table by the SQL layer of your database. Such functionality of partitions within your database means that partitions are a frequent friend of those who build big data-based applications, such as search engines. Data breach search engines are a perfect example of this – the purpose of such search engines is to provide a quick and hassle-free way to check whether anyone's identity is at risk by allowing them to sift through massive troves of data breaches that have been made public at some point in time to educate people about the fact that they should change their passwords frequently and raise awareness about data breaches that have occurred in the past to not fall victim to identity theft. With data breaches being so rampant and with data breach search engines such a heavy task to accomplish, partitions play a big role.

From personal experience, I can tell you that to acquire "good" query performance (we're talking anywhere below or equal to 0.1sec. to complete all SQL queries relevant to the searching capability) for my own data breach search engine, I had to partition every data breach into 27 parts as per the English alphabet (26 partitions for each of the letters and 27th – for everything that remains using the capability of `MAXVALUE`) and add indexes on the columns that were searched for – that accounted for the fact that tables now occupy significantly more space on the disk (I have to make use of 8TB disk drives even when all of the data is fully parsed and set up for searching), but also for the fact that queries are blazing fast even during stress on the server.

Such is the truth about the partitioning world – you aren't likely to need partitions for every project, but when you do, it won't do good for your hard drive. Accounting for the space your partitions will occupy on the disk is as crucial as accounting for the values that will be inserted in them.

CHAPTER 4   HOW YOU BROKE YOUR QUERIES

NULL Values and Pruning in Partitions

As far as values are concerned, be especially wary of NULL values inside partitions when using MySQL. MySQL partitions are built in such a way that if you insert NULL values into your table that is partitioned by RANGE, these values will reside in the lowest possible partition. MySQL also treats NULL values as "less powerful" than ordinary values.

I'll let you in on another secret too – if there's one thing partitions are extremely beneficial for besides splitting data into separate tables that are still treated as one by MySQL, that's the pruning of data. Remember how I said that *each partition is represented as a file on the disk that has a specific weight*? Everything works the other way around, too – if you drop that partition, the file will be deleted, and your data will occupy less space on the disk. Partitions can be truncated too. Poof – gone. Think about search engines again – let's say your table is partitioned by range like so (such a way of partitioning might be beneficial for those searching across bigger data sets with values from A to Z – *partitioned values can also be strings*):

```
CREATE TABLE `demo` (
`structure` VARCHAR(115) NOT NULL DEFAULT '',
`nicely` VARCHAR(60) DEFAULT NULL,
`please` VARCHAR(70) DEFAULT '',
`define_partitions_too` VARCHAR(90) NOT NULL
) ENGINE = InnoDB COLLATE utf8mb4_unicode_ci
PARTITION BY RANGE COLUMNS(define_partitions_too)
(
PARTITION partition_a VALUES LESS THAN ('a'),
PARTITION partition_b VALUES LESS THAN ('b'),
PARTITION partition_c VALUES LESS THAN ('c'),
...
PARTITION partition_max VALUES LESS THAN (MAXVALUE)
);
```

For the purposes of this example, I'll create two tables – one with partitions, and one without, but with both tables having an identical structure.

CHAPTER 4   HOW YOU BROKE YOUR QUERIES

```
Run SQL query/queries on database hacking_mysql:

 1  CREATE TABLE `demo` (
 2  `data_int` INT(117) DEFAULT NULL
 3  ) ENGINE = InnoDB COLLATE utf8mb4_unicode_ci;
 4
 5  CREATE TABLE `demo_partitioned` (
 6  `data_int` INT(117) DEFAULT NULL
 7  ) ENGINE = InnoDB COLLATE utf8mb4_unicode_ci
 8  PARTITION BY LIST (data_int)
 9  (
10  PARTITION partition_1 VALUES IN (1,2,3,4,5),
11  PARTITION partition_2 VALUES IN (6,7,8,9,10),
12  PARTITION partition_3 VALUES IN (11,12,13,14,15)
13  );
```

Figure 4-6. *Tables with and without partitions*

After these queries have been executed, we'll have two tables.

Table	Action						Rows	Type	Collation	Size	Overhead
demo	⭐	Browse	Structure	Search	Insert	Empty	Drop	0	InnoDB	utf8mb4_unicode_ci	16.0 KiB	-
demo_partitioned	⭐	Browse	Structure	Search	Insert	Empty	Drop	0	InnoDB	utf8mb4_unicode_ci	48.0 KiB	-

Figure 4-7. *Tables with and without partitions differ in size*

If you can't already tell, the partitioned table will be bigger than the non-partitioned one, and the more partitions you will have the bigger the difference will become. Anyway, back to where we started. Partitions can be pruned.

I've now populated both of the tables with records.

Table	Action						Rows	Type	Collation	Size	Overhead
demo	⭐	Browse	Structure	Search	Insert	Empty	Drop	12	InnoDB	utf8mb4_unicode_ci	16.0 KiB	-
demo_partitioned	⭐	Browse	Structure	Search	Insert	Empty	Drop	12	InnoDB	utf8mb4_unicode_ci	48.0 KiB	-

Figure 4-8. *Two InnoDB tables with records*

I'll now showcase how dropping partitions impact your database:

```
MariaDB [(none)]> USE hacking_mysql;
Database changed
MariaDB [hacking_mysql]> SELECT data_int FROM demo_partitioned WHERE data_int = 11;
+----------+
| data_int |
+----------+
|       11 |
+----------+
1 row in set (0.001 sec)

MariaDB [hacking_mysql]> ALTER TABLE demo_partitioned DROP PARTITION partition_3;
Query OK, 0 rows affected (0.029 sec)
Records: 0  Duplicates: 0  Warnings: 0

MariaDB [hacking_mysql]> SELECT data_int FROM demo_partitioned WHERE data_int = 11;
Empty set (0.005 sec)
```

Figure 4-9. Dropping a partition in MariaDB

The point here is simple – our row resided in the third partition (see table structure), and once we've dropped the third partition, the row is no longer there. We've pruned data – woohoo!

Things to Avoid When Optimizing Queries in MySQL

Cool – now you know a thing or two about partitions too. Now that you know what breaks your queries, you should be aware of things to avoid when optimizing them too – I'll walk you through the things you need to know for optimization in the Optimization part of this book, but dipping your toes in the water before swimming never hurts.

Avoid repeating bad practices – you will be aware of a set of bad database practices as you go along. They're on almost every SQL blog; they're mentioned in conferences, workshops, meetups, etc. They're everywhere – almost every vendor will have a blog or two about bad practices that you should not repeat now or in the future too. In the database world, these include the fact that you should avoid selecting all columns if they're not necessary (`SELECT column` instead of `SELECT *`), the fact that you should avoid using `LIKE` with leading wildcards, use `ORDER BY` on large sets cautiously (employ `LIMITer`s), avoid using `COUNT(*)` with large data sets or on InnoDB tables as a whole (MyISAM is an exception to the rule since it stores an internal row count inside of itself – InnoDB does not), avoid `DISTINCT` on big data sets (look into `sort -u file.txt` on Unix – more on that in the optimization part), and keep in mind that MySQL doesn't keep you from putting multiple types of indexes on the same column.

Avoid complicating things – SQL is based on standards. ACID has been here for decades and is unlikely to go away any time soon either. The same can be said about almost all SQL queries you will find yourself using, the same about backups, security, and so on. Things change – but basic things remain the same. Why reinvent the wheel to achieve a goal when you can employ advice that has been tried and tested hundreds of times?

Avoid over-optimizing your database. Seriously – there are so many people suggesting you optimize your database that way, optimize another way, don't use that, etc., and you can be pretty confident that as time goes by there will be a lot more of those people giving you advice. Not all of that advice is credible – keep in mind that even MySQL makes mistakes sometimes (if you want some proof of that, have a glance at thousands of MySQL bugs here), so before taking any advice, ensure that you receive it from a credible source. Once you receive the advice you think is necessary to solve your problem, make sure to apply it as shown (if you don't, you risk running into further issues), run the code in a local environment first to make sure it runs without any issues and doesn't corrupt production data in the process, and trust your previous experience too. If adding an index on a column solved a certain performance-related problem last time, try it now. See if it works.

Always compare the advice you receive to the recent version of the documentation – and while there are instances where the documentation may mislead you (example below), in most cases, it's written by competent people who have multiple decades of experience in the field that have close ties to the people who built the product in the first place. Trust, but verify.

Don't Blindly Trust Documentation

Documentations are awesome – they help us to better understand products; there's no question about that. That's what they're supposed to do! One thing you will hear when you are after advice of any sort concerning query performance is that you should read the documentation of the product in question. This piece of advice is not bad at all – after all, the documentation should be written by the people who work at the company that built the product, right?

CHAPTER 4   HOW YOU BROKE YOUR QUERIES

That's not always the case: I want you to dig into an older example about the concurrency of InnoDB together with me. The situation occurred more than a decade ago, but is still relevant to illustrate that not everything that's documented is 100% correct all the time – the situation was as follows:

1. A person, we'll call him person X for the sake of simplicity, asked a question on StackOverflow: when does a multi-threaded database become more useful than a single-threaded database?

2. Multiple people chimed in to help person X. Most of them offered credible and noteworthy advice saying that usually the bottleneck of performance is the disk, that most databases create a temporary table for dealing with data, etc.

3. Finally, there's one person who touched upon multithreading capabilities in InnoDB (remember – InnoDB is the primary storage engine offered by MySQL and its counterparts), and he said that thread concurrency in InnoDB can be set by fiddling with the `innodb_thread_concurrency` variable in MySQL.

4. At this point, some may turn to documentation about InnoDB thread concurrency which at that point, said something along the lines of "set the thread concurrency to 5 to set the upper bounds of concurrent threads that can be open within InnoDB to 5," etc. but in another answer about InnoDB, the same person noted that despite the documentation, a MySQL expert at a Percona LIVE conference in NYC in 2011 said that despite what's said by the documentation, it's best to leave the `innodb_thread_concurrency` variable at its default value – 0 – so that InnoDB could decide what's the optimal number of `innodb_concurrency_tickets` to open for a MySQL database setup. He then also said that if you set both `innodb_read_io_threads` and `innodb_write_io_threads` to their maximum values of 64, you should be able to engage more cores (assuming you run a reasonable number of them – you may want to avoid this advice if you run a 16-core machine.)

See what I mean? Documentation is written by people – people make mistakes. Those mistakes can be costly!

So, to recap, avoid

1. Repeating bad practices.

2. Overcomplicating things.

3. Over-optimizing your database (only optimize what you understand, and make sure you know how that thing works).

4. Always compare the advice you receive to the recent version of the documentation.

To top it off, take advice from reputable sources, run code in a local environment first, and trust your experience from the past – learn from the mistakes you've made for a better and prosperous future for both your application and your database.

Summary

In this chapter, I've walked you through the factors that break your queries. You now understand what makes queries slow and how to go about building the perfect schemas for your database. You also understand how data types, character sets, and collations work too. I have walked you through indexing and partitioning, unraveled a couple of secrets surrounding partitions, NULL values, and pruning, and walked you through some things to avoid when optimizing queries in MySQL.

I've done this with a goal in mind. This chapter helps you understand what makes your queries go awry and that understanding will become more and more vital as you read and learn along.

The understanding of how to break queries in your database infrastructure is vital because it bolsters your understanding of how to optimize and secure your database too. We're not done breaking though. Before optimizing your queries and the infrastructure related to them, we must understand query components and your server. We'll do that now.

CHAPTER 5

Understanding Query Components

Now that you understand what factors break your queries, it's time to understand their components – tasks inside of them. Here we come back to something I've mentioned dozens of times throughout this book already – *queries are tasks composed of other tasks.* To ensure these tasks will execute successfully, we have to understand their components. Sounds simple enough, but if it were that simple, we would have way fewer people complaining about query performance, right? That's why understanding query components is so crucial – a proper understanding of query internals can make or break your database instances.

SQL Queries and Stored Procedures

From the outset, SQL queries look simple and uncomplicated. Under the hood, they're not a child's play – they're composed of many small tasks that all need to work in unison so that your database can achieve perfection. Flick back to the last chapter and read through the "Why Are Queries Slow?" heading, and you will quickly understand what I mean – with so many tasks to complete, it's reasonable to assume that queries reading through bigger data sets would take more time than those who haven't got as much data to sift through. Each type of query completes a different task (queries insert, select, update, or delete data), but under the hood, they all work similarly.

As I've already mentioned in the last chapter, there are multiple types of queries in MySQL – those include DML (Data Manipulation Language) queries, DDL (Data Definition Language) queries, and also DCL (Data Control Language) and TCL (Transaction Control Language) queries. Most of these queries work similarly – they execute 20 or so subtasks before returning any results. Those queries are often bundled

CHAPTER 5   UNDERSTANDING QUERY COMPONENTS

together in the sense that once the user using your application acts on a form or anything similar to it, an SQL query executes in the background. More savvy developers might even be aware of stored procedures to help them succeed!

To understand why query components are so crucial to your SQL queries, I'd like you to take a look at stored procedures as an example. In MySQL, stored procedures are implemented with the `CALL` statement – the statement calls (invokes) a stored procedure that has to be created using `CREATE PROCEDURE`. Procedures in MySQL are sets of SQL queries stored inside the database (and are thus known to the server) and executed once procedures are invoked using `CALL procedure` or `CALL procedure()`.

Procedures can have two parameters – one that goes `IN`, and another that goes `OUT`. Users can pass values to the procedure in the column defined in the `IN` parameter and the column defined in the `OUT` parameter passes values from the procedure back to the user. One can define procedures like so.

```
1 DELIMITER //
2 CREATE PROCEDURE CityCounter
3 (IN defined_countrycode VARCHAR(2), OUT count_cities INT)
4 BEGIN
5 SELECT cities INTO count_cities FROM all_cities WHERE country_code = defined_countrycode;
6 END //
7 DELIMITER ;
```

Figure 5-1. *Defining procedures in MariaDB*

Here, we changed the delimiter to "//" for MariaDB not to interpret the ending of our query as the end of the procedure, then defined the procedure and told it to put its results into a variable called `count_cities`. One can make use of the stored procedure in the following way.

```
MariaDB [(none)]> USE hacking_mysql;
Database changed
MariaDB [hacking_mysql]> CALL CityCounter('GB', @cities_in_gb);
Query OK, 1 row affected (0.001 sec)

MariaDB [hacking_mysql]> SELECT @cities_in_gb;
+---------------+
| @cities_in_gb |
+---------------+
|            76 |
+---------------+
1 row in set (0.001 sec)
```

Figure 5-2. *Calling a procedure in MariaDB*

CHAPTER 5   UNDERSTANDING QUERY COMPONENTS

We have the number of cities in Great Britain! Great.

The components of stored procedures are the statements within them meaning that stored procedures will be as quick as they are.

As you can see, procedures in MariaDB are pretty simple to work with – and since procedures consist of queries "remembered" by your MySQL instance, the performance of those procedures will also be directly dependent on the performance of those queries.

Query performance is directly dependent on how quickly your database can execute query components – which, remember, there are slightly over 20 of. Those components depend on the query execution plan, which depends on parsers and optimizers.

Parsers and Optimizers

Internally, every SQL query is turned into an execution plan. Before coming up with the execution plan, MySQL checks whether the syntax and grammar of the SQL query are correct during the parser phase – it checks for errors by examining all characters in the query one by one, matches them against rules, and if everything's OK, turns the query to the optimizer.

For you to imagine how a parser works within your database, take any query and split it into pieces. Take a look at this one if you want an example:

```
SELECT sender,COUNT(*) FROM messages WHERE message LIKE '%What time%';
```

```
MariaDB [hacking_mysql]> SELECT sender,COUNT(*) FROM messages WHERE message LIKE '%What time%';
+-----------+----------+
| sender    | COUNT(*) |
+-----------+----------+
| Christina |        1 |
+-----------+----------+
1 row in set (0.001 sec)
```

Figure 5-3. *SQL query in MariaDB*

For such an SQL query, the parser would interpret everything. Yes, every word and character! These words and characters would be as follows:

1. SELECT

2. sender

3. ,

4. COUNT

99

CHAPTER 5   UNDERSTANDING QUERY COMPONENTS

5. (
6. *
7.)
8. FROM
9. messages
10. WHERE
11. message
12. LIKE
13. '
14. %
15. What time
16. %
17. '
18. ;

See a pattern? The query parser has to split any SQL query, no matter how simple or complex, into pieces and evaluate them one by one. After it has gotten the OK sign from MySQL, it turns to the query optimizer.

The query optimizer in MySQL tries to predict what query execution plans would execute the quickest and choose the best option available for MySQL to use. In this scenario, I'd like you to think of everything in terms of price – MySQL even has a variable called `Last_query_cost`.

CHAPTER 5   UNDERSTANDING QUERY COMPONENTS

```
MariaDB [(none)]> USE hacking_mysql;
Database changed
MariaDB [hacking_mysql]> SELECT sender FROM messages WHERE message LIKE '%What time%';
+-----------+
| sender    |
+-----------+
| Christina |
+-----------+
1 row in set (0.013 sec)

MariaDB [hacking_mysql]> SHOW STATUS LIKE 'Last_query_cost';
+-----------------+-----------+
| Variable_name   | Value     |
+-----------------+-----------+
| Last_query_cost | 25.799000 |
+-----------------+-----------+
1 row in set (0.002 sec)
```

Figure 5-4. *Last_query_cost in MariaDB*

The variable `Last_query_cost` shows the "cost" of the last compiled query for the query optimizer. The variable is scoped by session, and its default value, 0, means that no queries have been run during this session. A value in the variable is the "cost" of the query. Costs are assigned to different possibilities and are based on how MySQL "thinks" internally and that means that it's unlikely to give you any incredibly useful feedback for the last query you executed, but it will be useful as a measurement variable. Keep in mind that according to the documentation of MySQL, if you employ this variable anywhere pre-MySQL 8.0.16, you'd be hard-pressed to get any results if you run any queries aside from a simple `SELECT`, but that doesn't negate its usefulness. Some say that the value doesn't even match the actual cost of executing your query, but flies somewhere "within the orbit" of the actual value. Nonetheless, this variable is certainly something you should be cautious about as far as parsers and optimizers are concerned. MySQL also has a similar variable – `Last_query_partial_plans` – that shows the *iterations* made by the query optimizer when preparing a plan for the query you just ran.

The role of the *query optimizer* stands behind the name itself and is not that hard to quantify: its task is to find the best approach to execute a query. The optimizer distills the complex parts of your query, evaluates different query execution plans, and determines the best way to execute a given SQL statement. The query optimizer will decide, among other things:

- **What's the best way to access your data?** It's the task of the optimizer to determine the way your data is accessed – will your data be accessed using a table scan or an index scan? Ask the query optimizer!

- **How to employ the power of indexes or partitions?** It's up to the optimizer to decide whether to use indexes to locate relevant rows and if so, what index and when to employ. Optimizers are the reason why you see the "possible_keys," "key," and "key_len" columns once you add an EXPLAIN clause in front of your query. The optimizer can also decide to ignore indexes altogether and perform a full-table scan if it thinks that's the better option, too.

- **What's the best order to execute JOIN queries if they are present?** It's the optimizer's task to decide the most efficient order to execute JOIN queries. That may come down to "deleting" tables not used by the join from the operation, etc.

- **How to use GROUP BY and ORDER BY?** The query optimizer has to decide whether to use indexes for GROUP BY and ORDER BY operations.

- **How to work with subqueries?** If you happen to execute any subqueries within your SQL query, you're also asking the optimizer to simplify them in a way your database can understand and also determine whether their results can be cached.

In other words, the query optimizer will decide on the best approach to optimize a query so that it executes as quickly as possible. The task of the optimizer is to help your database find a way to execute your query in a performant manner. The optimizer is called that way because it has a much bigger task than the parser – while the parser checks the syntax, the optimizer needs not only to deliver the results but also do so as quickly as possible.

The optimizer in MySQL can be accessed by digging into EXPLAIN – the EXPLAIN clause shows you the query plan part of the optimizer so you can better understand the reasons why your database does what it does. If you're a developer, EXPLAIN should be a part of your vocabulary regardless so I'll dig into the functionality of EXPLAIN a little later: a proper understanding of what EXPLAIN does will be necessary to distinguish the factors that make or break your queries. You should also keep in mind that it's not the only tool to understand query components because during the time MySQL has been on the market, there have been numerous companies trying to produce query performance metrics including Percona, MariaDB, and others, but since query components are essentially the smaller tasks we've talked about previously and they can tell a lot of secrets too, you can dig into them even if you don't have access to the tools developed by the professionals. A good starting point for many of you facing issues would be an understanding of the internals of what MySQL is telling you via error messages shown after you run certain queries.

Queries and Error Messages

You know that feeling when you click a button and your app returns with the "MySQL Error #XXXX?" Yeah. That's your database saying your code has messed up.

No one likes to see an error message after they run an SQL query. That's a certainty – what's also a certainty is the fact that error messages exist to help us; they're not some devious plot MySQL has come up with to harm your database, but rather, they exist to tell us why a specific decision we made was wrong and help us improve it. Yes, they may seem scary – and they sometimes are – but they're not the end of the world.

Errors in MySQL follow a specific format. Each MySQL error comes with:

- **An error number**: Each error has a particular corresponding number.

- **An error message**: Each error comes with a specific error message that tells you in detail what you did and why the action you just took went wrong.

- **An error condition in the form of an SQLSTATE value**: An SQLSTATE value is a five-character string that defines what SQL state the error has reached once it's been displayed.

Here's what errors look like.

```
MariaDB [(none)]> USE no_db;
ERROR 1049 (42000): Unknown database 'no_db'
MariaDB [(none)]> USE hacking_mysql;
Database changed
MariaDB [hacking_mysql]> SELECT * FROM no_such_table WHERE message = 'Data';
ERROR 1146 (42S02): Table 'hacking_mysql.no_such_table' doesn't exist
MariaDB [hacking_mysql]> SELECT * FROM messages WHERE no_column = 'Data';
ERROR 1054 (42S22): Unknown column 'no_column' in 'where clause'
MariaDB [hacking_mysql]> SELECT * FROM messages WHERE sender = Jack;
ERROR 1054 (42S22): Unknown column 'Jack' in 'where clause'
MariaDB [hacking_mysql]> SELECT * FROM messages WHERE sender = 'Jack"'
    -> ;
Empty set (0.002 sec)
```

***Figure 5-5.** Errors in MariaDB*

See how many errors we have? "Unknown database," "Table doesn't exist," "Unknown column in where clause...." Below, you will also find the "holy grail" hackers search for when probing for SQL injection flaws.

```
MariaDB [hacking_mysql]> SELECT * FROM messages WHERE;
ERROR 1064 (42000): You have an error in your SQL syntax; check the manual that corresponds to your MariaDB server version for the right syntax to use near '' at line 1
MariaDB [hacking_mysql]>
```

Figure 5-6. *A MariaDB syntax error*

"You have an error in your SQL syntax..." Oh, shoot! This is the error attackers search for when probing for injection vulnerabilities because it means that once they add a couple of quotes, escaping characters, and a semicolon or two, you can say goodbye to your database. Or at least the data in it. Poof – gone! These things happen because developers like to hold the doors wide open to welcome user input in your SQL queries and that's a road to disaster, but I'll tell you more about that in the last – Securing – part of this book.

Coming back to errors in general, understanding the MySQL error format is a necessity when trying to troubleshoot errors. That's pretty much the entire reason errors exist in the first place – an error message tells us what went wrong in a manner that's understandable to both developers and database experts, an error number lets us search for solutions to the error via documentation or other manners, and an error condition in the form of an SQLSTATE value provides developers with the ability to ask other developers what went wrong and ask for assistance in solving the problem. Win-win!

Common MySQL Error Codes

For your errors to end in a win-win situation, you have to have a grasp on at least a small set of MySQL error codes that can arise during your work with the DBMS. Here are a couple:

- **Error 1040: Too many connections:** This error means that the MySQL Server has reached the maximum number of client connections, so it cannot accept new ones. An easy solution to this problem is to make sure all of the queries that you run inside of your database are finished – closed – properly.

- **Error 1045: Access denied:** Do you have the proper permissions to run the SQL query you just attempted to run? Double-check the permissions for the user that attempted to run the SQL query, and once you're 100% sure they're in place and correct (in that they permit this user to run specific queries), use a `FLUSH PRIVILEGES;` statement to save your changes.

- **Error 1064: Syntax error:** This MySQL error denotes a syntax error. Check the syntax of the query you ran that caused this error.

- **Error 1114: Table is full:** This error denotes a shortage of space on the disk. Such issues mostly occur when the tables in your database are super large, when running `ALTER TABLE` queries for large tables, or when creating backups for large databases.

- **Error 1659: Field "timestamp" is of a not allowed type for this type of partitioning:** A column (field) called "timestamp" doesn't have the allowed data type for a specific type of partitioning. We've come across this error in the last chapter when I told you that you can't partition timestamp values, remember?

- **Error 2006: MySQL Server connection closed:** This error denotes that the MySQL server has timed out and closed the initialized connection. Check on the value of the `wait_timeout` variable and make sure the value is acceptable to both you and your database.

- **Error 2008: Client ran out of memory:** This error means that the MySQL client has run out of memory when performing a specific task. A very frequent cause of this problem is queries that return millions or even billions of results; if you need to return so many results, it's reasonable enough that MySQL would start screaming, beeping, or making other noises. Beep boop.

- **Error 2013: Lost connection during query:** This error is also quite self-explanatory. If you see this error, that's MySQL telling you that it has lost connection to the database during query execution. Are you sure that your database isn't taking too long to respond to queries? If you are, make sure that your Internet connection is stable, and you're

CHAPTER 5   UNDERSTANDING QUERY COMPONENTS

- **Packet too large:** This is one of those errors without code that often eludes developers, but is rather simple to understand once you get to the bottom of it: this error has to do with the `max_allowed_packet` variable that denotes the maximum possible packet size for the server and the client alike. If you face this error, increase the size of the maximum allowed packet size by fiddling with the `max_allowed_packet` variable.

- **Can't create/write file:** This error usually appears when your database is unable to create or write to a file in a temporary directory. Make sure that the directory for temporary files is defined properly in the `tmpdir` variable and ensure that MySQL has the ability to write to the directory specified therein.

not facing any connectivity issues, or try increasing the number in the net-read-timeout variable (this variable denotes the number of seconds MySQL will wait for data from a connection before aborting read operations).

Errors aren't something terrible – most of them can be squashed within minutes, and while some do require configuration changes (changes to the values in variables, etc.), they aren't the end of the world either. As time goes by and you will become acquainted with error codes, you will understand that errors are nothing to be afraid of: dig into the documentation and find out what error codes like HY000, 42000, or others mean, then consult the same documentation or your friendly neighborhood DBAs for advice on how to solve the issue. I'm sure you will squash the problem sooner than you think.

Factors Disliked by Your Queries

Query components are directly impacted by factors within your server, application, and database, and all queries you run come with a distinct weight toward your database too – you already know that to make your queries performant, you need to minimize their effort by minimizing or eliminating the number of tasks they perform, but that be made even more effective if you avoid certain things that SQL queries dislike.

Isolate Your Columns!

The first thing to keep in mind has to do with search – SELECT – queries. If you find that the column you run search queries on has an index, is properly partitioned, and you run SELECT column instead of SELECT * to select data inside of your database but it is still running slow, you may want to check if the column after the WHERE clause is isolated, too. That means that queries like the one below certainly won't fly:

SELECT * FROM `demo_table` WHERE column + 786 = 4425;

They won't fly because if the column after the WHERE clause isn't isolated ("left alone" if you will), your database won't be able to use the index. As such, your query may slow down. To avoid such an issue, make sure that the columns after the WHERE clause aren't "conspiring together with someone" to achieve a result. Leave them alone – MySQL will decide how best to return results.

Get Rid of Duplicate Indexes

MySQL or any of its flavors won't protect you from using duplicate indexes on the same column either. Take a look at this example:

```
CREATE TABLE `demo_table` (
`incrementing_id` INT(25) NOT NULL AUTO_INCREMENT PRIMARY KEY,
`column_2` VARCHAR(120) NOT NULL DEFAULT '',
`column_3` VARCHAR(125) NOT NULL DEFAULT '',
...
INDEX(incrementing_id),
UNIQUE(incrementing_id)
);
```

This one may become a tough nut to crack for inexperienced users – some may think that this SQL query makes the `incrementing_id` column increment automatically (it should, hence the name), adds an index on the same column once the columns are defined, and also makes sure that all values in the column are unique (there are no duplicate values). All fun and roses, right?

Experienced DBAs will quickly notice that something's up. Indeed, we have *three* indexes on the same column! MySQL implements the PRIMARY KEY and UNIQUE constraints with indexes, so we have two indexes right then and there. And since our column is indexed, too, that adds another index on the same column. Three indexes on one column? And then devs wonder what's up with their database structure.

Keep in mind that MySQL doesn't "protect you" from appending multiple indexes on the same column, so choose the types of indexes carefully.

I'll walk you through the ins and outs of indexes in an upcoming chapter, but for now, please don't make your columns (and your database as a result) suffer – employ indexes wisely.

Use EXISTS Instead of IN

Some of you may elect to use IN together with a subquery like so:

```
SELECT * FROM `demo_table` WHERE id IN (SELECT id FROM `demo_2` WHERE date >= DATEADD(day, -7, GETDATE()));
```

Such a subquery would find records within the last week, but it would also likely require MySQL to perform a full-table scan to return the necessary result set. Not good!

Consider switching IN to EXISTS to avoid a full-table scan on the subquery. If we switch the IN clause to EXISTS, we would now have a query like so:

```
SELECT * FROM `demo_table` d WHERE EXISTS (SELECT 1 FROM demo_2 d2 WHERE d2.id = d.id AND d2.date >= DATEADD(day, -7, GETDATE()));
```

No more full-table scans. Woohoo!

Make Use of Stored Procedures and Triggers

Many developers also face the necessity to complete the same task multiple times and so they craft similar queries again, again and again, wasting their time and effort (and putting additional strain on databases too) – your databases don't like that either.

There is a way around that – look into stored procedures and triggers!

Stored procedures can help you complete certain tasks, and they are an extension of the SQL language. Making use of stored procedures allows you to employ procedural language within MySQL – they're SQL code chunks with IFs and loops.

No matter if you're an SQL expert or not, chances are that you will be able to understand 90% or even more of what they have to offer. They can be extremely useful if you have to break down complex SQL logic into manageable and reusable modules that can be used on demand.

Here's where triggers come into the picture too – triggers are essentially objects within your database that activate when a particular event takes place. They may be used for a variety of different purposes, but most of their use cases come down to maintaining the integrity of data within your database. Make use of them! They can also be used for calculation purposes or, admittedly, to do some weird stuff, too. At the basic level, their syntax looks like this:

```
CREATE TRIGGER trigger_name
[AFTER|BEFORE] [operation]
ON table_name FOR EACH ROW
BEGIN
--define trigger here
END;
```

In this case, operation means any INSERT, UPDATE, or DELETE operation, and triggers need to also be row-based, hence the row definition.

All this means that triggers can be used to do a range of different stuff that may (or may not) make sense. Look at the one below:

```
CREATE TRIGGER slowinsert_trigger
BEFORE INSERT ON users
FOR EACH ROW
BEGIN
DO SLEEP(RAND() * 10);
END;
```

This trigger will make any and all INSERT operations on the users table slow down by generating a random number, multiplying it by 10 times to make the number bigger, and then making your database sleep (wait) for this number of seconds after every INSERT operation. May be useful if you want to make yourself a cup of coffee before INSERTs of a big data set complete, you know.

Make use of stored procedures and triggers to minimize the amount of repetitive SQL queries you run within your database – they exist for a reason. Even if that reason may be something fun!

SHOW STATUS and EXPLAIN

Coming back to serious topics, you should look into both SHOW STATUS and EXPLAIN, too. These two are crucial to maintaining high performance – SHOW STATUS will walk you through the status of your database, while EXPLAIN will explain everything your queries go through when executing.

SHOW STATUS can be invoked standalone as well as with LIKE or WHERE expressions. The primary purpose of SHOW STATUS is to provide information related to the status of your server (hence the name): it can provide you with the amount of currently open tables, aborted connections, a bunch of information on InnoDB and performance schema, the number of queries that have run in your database, and so on. In MariaDB, invoking SHOW STATUS in a vanilla form is likely to return hundreds of entries ranging from internal InnoDB variables to SSL and uptime.

```
| Ssl_session_cache_hits              | 0    |
| Ssl_session_cache_misses            | 0    |
| Ssl_session_cache_mode              | NONE |
| Ssl_session_cache_overflows         | 0    |
| Ssl_session_cache_size              | 0    |
| Ssl_session_cache_timeouts          | 0    |
| Ssl_sessions_reused                 | 0    |
| Ssl_used_session_cache_entries      | 0    |
| Ssl_verify_depth                    | 0    |
| Ssl_verify_mode                     | 0    |
| Ssl_version                         |      |
| Subquery_cache_hit                  | 0    |
| Subquery_cache_miss                 | 0    |
| Syncs                               | 19   |
| Table_locks_immediate               | 56   |
| Table_locks_waited                  | 0    |
| Table_open_cache_active_instances   | 1    |
| Table_open_cache_hits               | 0    |
| Table_open_cache_misses             | 0    |
| Table_open_cache_overflows          | 0    |
| Tc_log_max_pages_used               | 0    |
| Tc_log_page_size                    | 0    |
| Tc_log_page_waits                   | 0    |
| Threadpool_idle_threads             | 0    |
| Threadpool_threads                  | 1    |
| Threads_cached                      | 0    |
| Threads_connected                   | 1    |
| Threads_created                     | 5    |
| Threads_running                     | 1    |
| Transactions_gtid_foreign_engine    | 0    |
| Transactions_multi_engine           | 0    |
| Update_scan                         | 0    |
| Uptime                              | 4042 |
| Uptime_since_flush_status           | 4042 |
+-------------------------------------+------+
540 rows in set (0.014 sec)

MariaDB [(none)]>
```

Figure 5-7. Output of a Vanilla SHOW STATUS Query in MariaDB

"540 rows in set"! Nuts, isn't it? So many things to take care of. Geez.

That's why SHOW STATUS supports the WHERE and LIKE clauses – they are supported so you can filter what's important to you! Such clauses are very useful when you want to observe specific information like the number of queries that have been executed since the database has been up or information about the query cache.

```
MariaDB [(none)]> SHOW STATUS LIKE 'Qcache%';
+-------------------------+---------+
| Variable_name           | Value   |
+-------------------------+---------+
| Qcache_free_blocks      | 1       |
| Qcache_free_memory      | 1031344 |
| Qcache_hits             | 0       |
| Qcache_inserts          | 0       |
| Qcache_lowmem_prunes    | 0       |
| Qcache_not_cached       | 0       |
| Qcache_queries_in_cache | 0       |
| Qcache_total_blocks     | 1       |
+-------------------------+---------+
8 rows in set (0.003 sec)
```

Figure 5-8. *Information about the query cache*

Unfortunately, only knowing your way around SHOW STATUS won't be enough to bring your database to perfection. Observing statistics is awesome, but you should act for things to change; observing metrics isn't enough. That's why SHOW STATUS has a brother (or a sister, if you will) called EXPLAIN: it can't be invoked standalone like SHOW STATUS can (if you will, you receive an error), but it can be used in front of SELECT, INSERT, DELETE, REPLACE, or DELETE SQL queries. Here's EXPLAIN in action.

```
MariaDB [hacking_mysql]> EXPLAIN SELECT timestamp FROM messages WHERE sender = 'Jack' and message = '%';
+----+-------------+----------+------+----------------------------------------------+---------+---------+-------+------+-------------+
| id | select_type | table    | type | possible_keys                                | key     | key_len | ref   | rows | Extra       |
+----+-------------+----------+------+----------------------------------------------+---------+---------+-------+------+-------------+
|  1 | SIMPLE      | messages | ref  | message,sender_idx,message_ft,sender_idx_ft  | message | 3074    | const |    1 | Using where |
+----+-------------+----------+------+----------------------------------------------+---------+---------+-------+------+-------------+
1 row in set (0.002 sec)
```

Figure 5-9. *EXPLAIN in action*

When SELECT queries are being profiled, EXPLAIN will return a couple of columns depicting all sorts of information:

Column	About	Possible Values
id	The ID of the query.	Numeric IDs
select_type	The SELECT query type. If our SELECT is not using subqueries or the UNION clause, the SELECT query type will be SIMPLE; if the UNION clause is used, we will see UNION; if our select is the first select in a subquery, we will see SUBQUERY, etc.	SIMPLEPRIMARYUNIONDEPENDENT UNIONUNION RESULTSUBQUERYDEPENDENT SUBQUERYDERIVEDDEPENDENT DERIVEDMATERIALIZEDUNCACHEABLE SUBQUERYUNCACHEABLE UNION
table	The table of concern.	The table that we're running our queries on.
partitions	Any applicable partitions.	NULL for non-partitioned tables, otherwise the name of the partition.
type	The type of the JOIN query if one is used.	systemconsteq_refreffulltext... See the documentation for all possible values.
possible_keys	What keys (indexes) can MySQL use to help the query?	Any applicable index names.
key	The key (index) that was used.	The name of the index that was used.
key_len	The length of the key (index) that was used.	The length of the key (index) that was used.
ref	What columns are compared to the index to select rows?	Any applicable column names or func if the value is a result of a function.
rows	The number of rows examined by MySQL to execute the query.	The number of rows that MySQL believes must be looked at for the query to execute.
filtered	The estimated percentage of rows in the table that were filtered by a condition.	0–100%
Extra	Any additional information that may be useful to know how MySQL executed the query.	Backward index scanconst row not foundDeleting all rowsDistinctFirstMatchFull scan on NULLkeyNo matching min/max row...See the documentation for all possible values.

Both SHOW STATUS and EXPLAIN can be very valuable additions to your database toolset – use them when you see fit, but don't forget that they're not the only tools that can help your database when times become hard.

Summary

Understanding SQL query components is an essential task for everyone who cares about their database. As each SQL query is a task composed of many different tasks that help your database, understanding how queries look under the hood and what they consist of, what their parsers and optimizers do, and walking yourself through the explanatory outputs and error codes provided by your database is an essential step toward a brighter and better future for your application, server, and database.

Contrary to popular belief though, components aren't the only thing that makes your database tick; your database is only a part of the bigger puzzle that includes your application and your server. Understanding how both of these things and your database work in conjunction is an essential step to achieving database harmony – and that's why I now invite you to understand your server before telling you how you should optimize your database and everything within.

CHAPTER 6

Understanding Your Server

Before jumping into optimization, you need to understand your server and the components within it. No matter what's happening inside of your database, your server can become the biggest bottleneck of your database – understanding what server you use and how its components work together will allow you to understand how best to work with the server to achieve your goals. Some servers will tie your hands by default (think shared hosting), but if you have access to the internals of your server by using a VPS or a dedicated server, you have a chance to modify their parameters as you wish.

To understand your server, you have to efficiently write queries, simulate errors, understand server components and their interaction with MySQL, configure MySQL for your server, code for MySQL performance and security, and avoid the things you shouldn't be doing.

Efficiently Using Server Resources

The first thing related to your database would probably be the queries running inside of it. These have to be written efficiently, and this saying may have a different meaning depending on what kind of server you find yourself using.

When talking about shared hosting, there's not that much that can be done – you're given a small part of a single physical server together with hundreds of users keeping your hosting expenses low, but also keeping the space your application (and your database) moves in relatively confined. As far as your database is concerned, chances are that you will be moving around in a single database too.

That's why the best thing you can do for your database in a shared hosting environment is modify the things "on top of it" without touching its internals (you wouldn't be able to touch them if you wished): keep a close eye on the structure of your tables and monitor resource usage. Don't forget about things outside of your database either – use a CDN, limit the use of plugins (you're using a couple, aren't you?), and compress files where necessary.

Some performance advice wouldn't apply here: partitioning is likely to be unnecessary (one wouldn't have enough space to store bigger data sets to necessitate partitioning to begin with), but indexes would do their part. Keep your database clean too – don't store too much unnecessary data and you should be good to go.

The game changes when everything comes to a VPS or a dedicated server – now we have access to the internals of our database and can query the server to know what we're dealing with in the first place:

- To display the number of processor units on your server, utilize `nproc`.

- To view the CPU information of your server, issue `lscpu` or, if you're feeling fancy, `cat /proc/cpuinfo`.

- To check on the memory capacity, issue the command `free -h`.

- Don't forget to check on the version of your back-end language of choice. Those using PHP will need to employ `php -v`.

In many cases, these statistics will also be readily available upon logging in to your account on your hosting provider of choice, and these details are crucial because they determine to what extent you can optimize your database and work with your application. Users of smaller VPS services will likely have around 2-4GB of RAM and 30-50GB of space in their solid-state drives, while power users will have more room to move in, but regardless, any VPS will allow you to open and edit your my.cnf file and look into the buffer pool, the size of your log files, the query cache, the number of tables that can be stored in the cache, and the join buffer (it will help JOIN queries complete quicker. Before running queries, do that: find your my.cnf file (it's most likely located in the `/var/lib/mysql` directory – if not, search for it in `/etc/`, `/etc/mysql/`, or the `~/` directory), open it up and fiddle with the following:

- `innodb_buffer_pool_size`: Set the InnoDB buffer pool to approximately 60-80% of available RAM within your operating system (leave some room for the processes running in the background, too).

- `innodb_log_file_size`: Set it to approximately a quarter (25%) of the InnoDB buffer pool size.

- `table_open_cache` and `max_connections`: These variables impact the number of open tables for all threads and the maximum amount of simultaneous client connections your server can handle respectively.
- `join_buffer_size`: This variable depicts the maximum size of the buffer that's used when `JOIN` queries that perform full table scans are running.

Also, remember what MySQL looks like from the inside – from top to bottom, we have the file system (data, indexes, logs, and other files), storage engines such as InnoDB and the like, the optimizer, the parser, the SQL interface, the connection pool, and the connectors. Oh, and the global and engine-specific caches and buffers somewhere in between storage engines and the connection pool to the side of the optimizer, parser, and the SQL interface. In other words, we have `mysqld` and his files, connectors, the optimizer, caches, table engines, and other tools (I'll share an illustration with you soon) – we have lots of things to optimize, don't we?

That's why this book has an entire part of it dedicated to optimization; but before jumping into optimization, we have a bunch of other things to take care of, too!

Understanding and Simulating Errors

Once you're sure that you're using database resources properly, you may want to look into errors. Errors are a huge part of any project, especially those projects concerning databases; depending on the error condition, we can learn a lot about what went wrong and how to fix the problem. When tuning your server, there will likely be situations where you will benefit from the ability to simulate errors, too.

To understand errors in our beloved database management system, we have to understand that errors in MySQL have a lot to do with the values of a return code called SQLSTATE: This code consists of 5 bytes and is divided into two parts:

1. The first and second bytes have to do with the class of the error.
2. The other three bytes contain a subclass.

Each error class can have one of four categories:

1. Category S (class 00): Such error classes denote success in doing something.
2. Class W (class 01): Such error classes denote a warning.

117

CHAPTER 6   UNDERSTANDING YOUR SERVER

3. Class N (class 02): Such errors inform us that no data was returned, hence the letter.

4. Class X (all other classes): All other errors have to do with some exceptions, hence the letter X.

SQLSTATE codes denote the successful completion of a task, various kinds of warnings, dynamic SQL errors, connection and action exceptions, unsupported features, invalid and/or malformed SQL statements, data exceptions, integrity constraint violations, invalid transaction states, and much more. Here's what some of the SQLSTATE codes mean:

SQLSTATE Code	Meaning
01006/01007	Privileges not revoked/granted
08006	Connection failed
42000	Syntax error or access rule violated
23001	Integrity constraint violation
25000/25001	Invalid transaction state or invalid transaction state with an active transaction
25006	Invalid transaction state: read-only SQL transaction
2C000	Invalid charset name
40000	Transaction rollback

Attentive readers may notice a pattern – there's a number depicting the general error and an additional number at the end depicting what went wrong specifically. And if you're one of them, you're right! If we dig deeper, we quickly notice that SQLSTATE codes fall within certain ranges:

SQLSTATE Range	Explanation
00000	Successful completion of operations
01000-0102F	Warnings (class 01.)
02000 & 02001	No data (class 02.)
07000-46130, HW000-HW007, HV000-HV091, HY000-HY108 and HYC00	Exceptions (classes 07,08,09,0A,0D-0Z, 10, 20-28, 2B-2H, 30, 33-36, 38 and 39, etc.)

CHAPTER 6 UNDERSTANDING YOUR SERVER

Each SQLSTATE has a category, class, and subclass. Cool, yeah? Many of you probably never even thought of it!

The good news is that you don't have to memorize what every SQLSTATE state means to help your database (is that even possible?) – having a good grasp of what's involved is enough, and the path you should take will come clear through experience.

Now that you know what certain SQLSTATEs mean, here are some of the MySQL error codes you should be aware of, too:

MySQL Error Code (mysql_errno)	Explanation
1004	Cannot create or copy a file.
1005	A table cannot be created.
1007	Cannot create a database. The database already exists.
1008	Can't drop a database because it doesn't exist.
1016	MySQL can't find the table inside of the InnoDB data files.
1022	The table has a duplicate key.
1036	The table is read-only.
1037	The server is out of memory.
1040	Too many connections – inspect and/or adjust the max_connections variable.
1044/1045	The user you're using to access a database hasn't got enough privileges.
1046	No database has been selected.
1047	Unknown command.
1048	Column cannot be null.
1049	Unknown database.
1050	A table with such a title already exists.
1051	Unknown table.
1052	Ambiguous column.
1053	The database is shutting down.

See how many error codes we have? And that's not even an exhaustive list! I bet that some of the aforementioned SQLSTATE and MySQL error codes will seem familiar.

Some of you may get funny ideas here, and yes, you can simulate errors on purpose too. Remember triggers? What about a trigger like so:

```
CREATE TRIGGER insert_trigger
BEFORE INSERT ON users
FOR EACH ROW
BEGIN
SIGNAL SQLSTATE '45000' SET
MYSQL_ERRNO = 32000,
MESSAGE_TEXT = 'Your INSERT query has failed. Haha, what a surprise!';
END;
```

Such a trigger would prevent any INSERTs on the user table – such an idea may not be genius, but it may be useful if you want to flex your SQL wizardry on your friends or if you're running a workshop or two (you may also need to specify a delimiter at the beginning and before the end of the query too).

Server Components and Their Interaction with MySQL

After you have a good grasp of the errors you may encounter, you should familiarize yourself with your server components and how they interact with your database. You already know your way around my.cnf; however, my.cnf is only as effective as your server is; your disk, RAM, CPU, and everything else involving your server can slow your queries down as well.

Here's what the entire MySQL infrastructure looks like:

CHAPTER 6 UNDERSTANDING YOUR SERVER

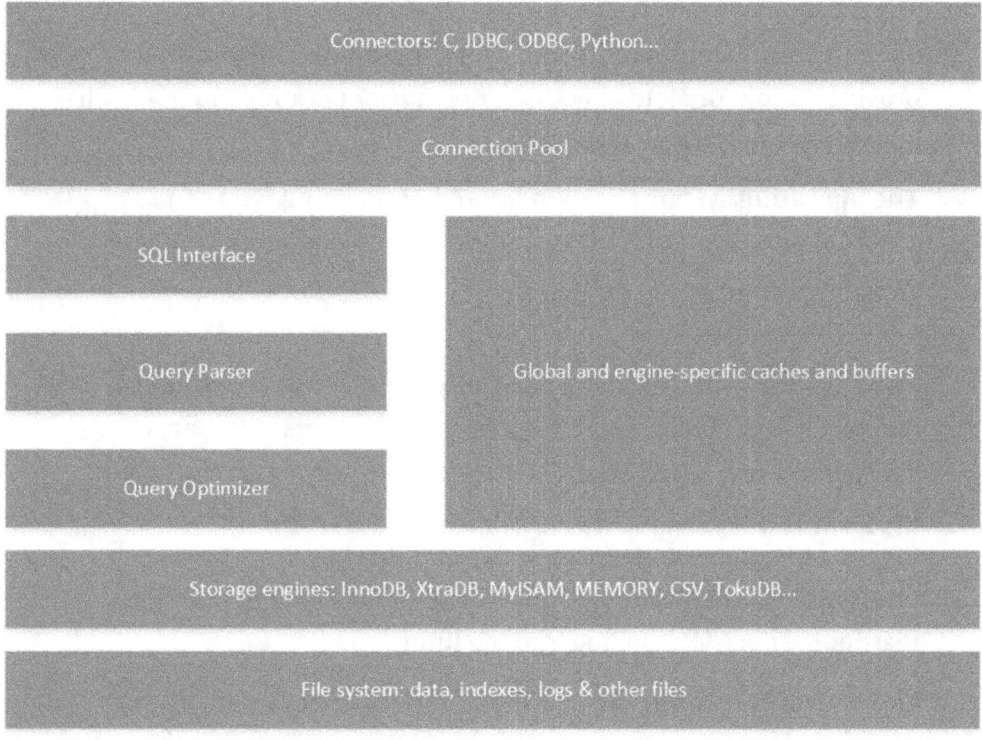

Figure 6-1. *MySQL infrastructure*

As you can see, almost everything is backed by your server – the data, indexes, and logs are stored in the /var/lib/mysql/[data] directory. Depending on what storage engine you use, you will likely see some .ibd files in the data directory depicting the data of the table and the metadata too.

The rest of the settings (the parser and the optimizer, global and engine-specific caches and buffers, etc.) are directly dependent on your server settings, too: if you're using InnoDB, your data and indexes will most likely be separated from the main tablespace (ibdata1), and ibdata1 will only consist of metadata – with it, you will also see files ib_logfile0 and ib_logfile1 that would be used to restore data in MySQL after a crash.

To choose a server for MySQL, consider:

- **The processor:** Keep an eye on modern CPUs from Intel or AMD and choose a CPU based on parameters of importance to you – look into clock speed, cache size, and other things.

- **The amount of operating memory:** How much memory does your use case necessitate? When choosing a server from any hosting provider, don't forget to check on how much operating memory will be available for you to "play with."

- **The operating system:** Keep in mind that the things you can optimize and change will slightly differ depending on the operating system that your server is running. With that being said, most of the differences are minor.

- **Hard drives:** Your hard drive has a direct impact on performance: it impacts how quickly your operating system starts, it impacts the speed of SQL queries, and it also dictates how much data your database can store. Many things are at play here – the good news is that storage space is cheap, and it's nothing you should over-obsess about: keep yourself educated on basic concepts and make a reasonable decision looking into the future.

- **How much bandwidth do you have?** For some of you, bandwidth would also be of concern – consult your hosting provider before making a choice, and keep in mind that CDNs can help your server save bandwidth where necessary.

It will also help if your server can be scaled automatically – if you are reaching the bounds of free hard drive space, just drop another hard drive into the mix!

I'd also like to stress the need to test your InnoDB flush method – just because your neighborhood DBA uses the `O_DIRECT` option for his project, doesn't mean that you should use the same option as well: `O_DIRECT` will open the data files with `O_DIRECT` and use `fsync()` to flush data and logs. To skip the option, you can use `O_DIRECT_NO_FSYNC`, and to use the `O_DSYNC` option to open and flush the log files and `fsync()` to flush the data files. Want to use the `fsync` system call for everything involving flushing? Set the flush method to `fsync`. Changing the flush method will change how MySQL performs flushing operations, and as such, you will able to observe how your database acts when different levels of flushing are involved.

Able to put your database through varying levels of load? Even better! For that purpose, use `mysqlslap`. We will run three iterations of the MySQL stress testing tool:

CHAPTER 6   UNDERSTANDING YOUR SERVER

1. `mysqlslap --user=root --host=localhost --auto-generate-sql --verbose`

2. `mysqlslap --user=root --host=localhost --concurrency=100 --iterations=10 --auto-generate-sql --verbose`

3. `mysqlslap --user=root --host=localhost --concurrency=50 --iterations=100 --number-int-cols=5 --number-char-cols=20 --auto-generate-sql --verbose`

The first stress-test iteration ran an auto-generated SQL code in a verbose output mode. The second one was a little more complex with 100 concurrent connections and 10 iterations for the SQL query. Finally, the third one utilized 50 concurrent connections with 100 iterations with 5 numeric columns and 20 character-based columns. The results?

```
mysqlslap --user=root --host=localhost --auto-generate-sql --verbose
Benchmark
        Average number of seconds to run all queries: 0.015 seconds
        Minimum number of seconds to run all queries: 0.015 seconds
        Maximum number of seconds to run all queries: 0.015 seconds
        Number of clients running queries: 1
        Average number of queries per client: 0

mysqlslap --user=root --host=localhost --concurrency=100 --iterations=10 --auto-generate-sql --verbose
Benchmark
        Average number of seconds to run all queries: 0.307 seconds
        Minimum number of seconds to run all queries: 0.078 seconds
        Maximum number of seconds to run all queries: 1.125 seconds
        Number of clients running queries: 100
        Average number of queries per client: 0

mysqlslap --user=root --host=localhost --concurrency=50 --iterations=100 --number-int-cols=5 --number-char-cols=20 --auto-generate-sql --verbose
Benchmark
        Average number of seconds to run all queries: 0.340 seconds
        Minimum number of seconds to run all queries: 0.141 seconds
        Maximum number of seconds to run all queries: 1.203 seconds
        Number of clients running queries: 50
        Average number of queries per client: 0
```

Figure 6-2. *Results of mysqlslap*

Not too bad, right? I'll walk you through the possible optimization techniques in the optimization part of this book (which is coming up right after this chapter) – slap your database around for now, and then don't forget to wrangle your code around the database properly too.

CHAPTER 6   UNDERSTANDING YOUR SERVER

Coding for MySQL Performance and Security

Once you understand how your server interacts with MySQL and adjusted a parameter or two to help your infrastructure (you've increased your InnoDB buffer pool size and adjusted the size of the log files, haven't you?), don't forget to write code in such a way that helps your database too. You'd be surprised how many developers still write code that traumatizes their databases – and some of you may make mistakes on this front too.

Remember a couple of key things:

1. **Never pass user input directly to a database** (do I need to say this?): Passing user input straight into a database is the highway toward SQL injection.

2. **Terminate connections when they finish, use rate limiters, and load balancers**: It seems basic, but operators of search engines, API appliances, and similar applications may be privy to situations where they've noticed their application running slow just to notice that the sluggishness was caused by the number of queries running in a database. Welp. If you run an application that's heavy on the reading spectrum, definitely rate limit the number of queries that can be executed in a given period and let load balancers balance out the rest if necessary. You don't need to invent genius-level rate limiters here: a couple of lines of PHP code should do the trick.

3. **Benchmark and profile**: Benchmarking is a unique way to determine what happens once you give your application work to complete. Many developers had situations where they plan for plan A, plan B, and plan C, and then life gives them lemons and they need to make use of plan D. Well, well, well... That's why you need to benchmark your application and databases – benchmarking will help you understand whether the expectations for your database are realistic, it will help you measure what your app and database can handle, and plan for growth. I'll walk you through benchmarking and profiling tactics once we get into optimizing MySQL.

CHAPTER 6   UNDERSTANDING YOUR SERVER

4. **Choose server components wisely**: Many think that to achieve great performance, one should use the greatest components ever. Sure, using the newest components for your server would be great if you have the means to afford them, but since great components also come at great cost, many don't have such a luxury. Choose components wisely and research your options – if you run a big-data-based search engine and need a lot of space on the disk, do you really need multiple terabyte-size NVMe drives? Perhaps grab a bigger HDD and purchase more RAM or get a better CPU? Remember the example of InnoDB using more cores: utilize components smarter, not harder. Choose components wisely and look into the future, and you will be able to push your server further than you think.

5. **Index for high performance**: If you're using an index, it's a safe bet that you're not using it for no reason, right? Indexes improve the performance of SELECT queries; however, dropping an index on the first column after a WHERE clause isn't always the smartest thing you can do. Various database management systems come with various types of indexes, and as such, you have a load of indexing strategies you can employ to achieve your performance goals. Profile your queries and index wisely.

6. **Nail down problematic pieces of code with code profilers**: What if I told you that databases aren't the only things you can profile? PHP users may want to look into xhprof – the tool profiles CPU cycles and memory usage and can help you figure out the causes of bottlenecks. Other programming languages will have similar appliances.

7. **Look into the advanced features of MySQL**: You don't need to be a power-user of MySQL to use advanced features. Those include triggers, stored procedures and functions, partitioning, prepared statements, full-text searching, and even the way you define character sets and collations. These exist for a reason – triggers can be used to "call" something automatically when we modify data in a table while stored procedures are to be called manually, partitioning helps your database split data into multiple

underlying tables while still treating a partitioned table as an indivisible unit, full-text searching enables you to search with explicit capabilities where certain different characters may have a different meaning for your query and utilize different search modes, while character sets and collations enable your database to understand data in different languages and display symbols.

8. **Backup your data**: No matter what project you run, backups should always be top of mind. Backups are something you rarely think about until disaster strikes – and then everyone's like "oh no, when did we last back up our database? Are our backups even restorable?" and that's why you need to think of them beforehand. Not only think of them – back up your data with `mysqldump`, `mydumper`, or other methods (we'll talk about backups later on) and make sure your backups are restorable too.

9. **Look into CSRF tokens**: Do you know how many CSRF attacks are blocked in BreachDirectory? Sometimes hundreds every week on the search engine page alone. Surprising? Shouldn't be. Some people are assholes – and once your app gets a little traction, you will certainly notice the full extent of that. Now while I fully understand why people would initiate searches through a search engine from a different place (that's the cause of some of the blocks), there's an API on the service for a reason. CSRF tokens are not only useful for search engines, and they can be of immense use if your application allows a user to change passwords, confirm a purchase by clicking on a link, etc. – anything that could make a nefarious party think "hmm, and if I send a request, maybe I'll benefit from this too?" CSRF tokens prevent CSRF attacks in that they're unique for each request/session and consist of a random value that's impossible to guess. I'll walk you through how to implement them in the security part of this book.

10. **Write clean code**: Clean code can contribute to the longevity of your databases as well. Anyone who's ever had to remake a legacy codebase knows exactly what I mean: you're going through the code base, and you're like "Why did *that* get included here?!"

> Avoid overcomplicating things and keep things simple: keep
> your code well-organized and well-structured, and you will see
> numerous benefits: it's likely to run faster, use less memory, and
> your database, application, and your future self will thank you too.

Adhere to those 10 things, and your application and database will surely thank you. With that being said, keep in mind that these things aren't a panacea, and they will only work if your application (and database at that) is built properly. You will make mistakes (who doesn't?) – learn from them.

Ever heard of the Brachistochrone curve experiment? It proves that a ball can roll along a curved line faster than on a straight line – take note of that: your mistakes are likely to move you further than other people who take a "straight" path. Learn and move quickly: mistakes will be inevitable, but they're not the end of the world.

When coding any application making use of MySQL, take a special interest in your server and data storage. Using the best architecture possible isn't always the wisest choice: great components also have a great cost, and experience in fiddling with MySQL components is sometimes likely to yield better results than throwing money at architecture.

Aside from that, keep an open mind toward security and memorize one thing: there's no such thing as a "completely secure application" or a "completely secure database." You won't ever achieve 100% security, but that doesn't mean you should discard the security of your database or application as a whole. Avoid providing user input to a database and use PDO where possible, educate yourself on the top 10 attacks in the OWASP list, use web application firewalls to prevent the most prevalent attacks, and don't forget the human factor either.

Think of your application as a castle: how would you defend it? Using multiple methods, of course! You'd have security guards guarding the perimeter, moats, and bridges that can be destroyed if an enemy is advancing, and inside the castle, you'd also have a bunch of security cameras to notify you about everything that's going awry. Now use that analogy for your application and database: security guards may mean firewall rules that block a request once they are triggered, moats may refer to CDNs and rate limiters to throttle the number of requests coming into your server, and bridges would mean server processes that work together to facilitate access to data in your database. The castle is your application, and inside of it, you have a database protected by cameras – triggers, a firewall appliance, and logs.

The database is the heart of your castle, and being the heart it necessitates special attention – protecting your application from injection, broken authentication, and sensitive data exposure is great, but learning how to protect your application from these attacks alone will not be sufficient. Secure the accounts you use to access MySQL – ensure they all have a password, that password is strong, never store passwords inside any of your databases in plain text, and ensure you use a one-way hashing function like Bcrypt or Blowfish, and don't forget the fact that you shouldn't grant any users access to the user table in the `mysql` database (except for the `root` user).

Always remember that there are ways to breach defenses and no application is 100% secure – don't neglect the human factor either.

What Not to Do

When working with your server and the database within, don't forget that there are things you should avoid doing to not harm your database. First, we have the documentation – don't take advice from the documentation on MySQL 8.0 if you run MariaDB 11.5: while the two database management systems are similar, one has distinct differences from the other, and even tools that have a similar name may work differently. While it's true that many tools available in MySQL will act as a symlink to the same tools in MariaDB (a prime example of this is the `mysqlslap` tool which is a symlink to `mariadb-slap`), in most cases, it's best to base your knowledge on the flavor of the database management system you find yourself using.

Next, we have optimization advice – some people will tell you that you should increase your buffer pool size if your INSERT queries are still slow after increasing it once, that you should make your query cache bigger than some percentage and it should be increased again if your queries aren't making use of it, etc. Before taking any tuning advice to heart, ensure it makes sense to begin with: solely increasing the buffer pool size isn't likely to make your INSERT queries 100 times faster; however, ditching INSERTs and using LOAD DATA INFILE would make more sense because LOAD DATA INFILE doesn't have that much overhead as INSERTs do. The cache hit ratio has nothing to do with the cache size either, and it depends on the effectiveness of the I/O operations within your server.

Avoid testing anything on a live server – even if you're 99% sure that nothing can go wrong and that you run a code block exactly the way it was intended to be run, something can go awry depending on your application, database, or server configuration. Don't assume that if you see a code block execute successfully in a tutorial, it will also execute the same way on your operating system. Test in a staging or demo environment, and then push the changes out to production. Trust, but verify.

The Internet is a great place, and Stack Overflow contains a lot of awesome advice too, but you shouldn't take everything you find there for granted either. Many people give advice, but it's not always easy to distinguish who is qualified to provide it. Sources affiliated with your database management system of choice are a good place to start – look around Planet MySQL and Planet MariaDB, identify vendors from there, and take advice from them. That's not to say you should blindly trust the documentation from official vendors either – test everything before rolling anything out to production!

Never say "This has a small chance of happening, so it probably won't happen to me" either: many of you probably heard of stories where developers told themselves something along the lines of "this infrastructure never failed in 5 years, so it won't fail anytime soon either," and they lost data to a power failure or other incident. Expect the best, but prepare for the worst.

The last thing to remember is that not everyone will have your best interest at heart – some people will provide you with advice because they're jealous or just to make themselves feel better by putting others down. Some people are jerks, and if you're a novice, that can make things particularly hard for you and that's why you should always base decisions on research and facts found in official sources (documentation, blogs of official vendors, etc.) or reputable people after you test and ensure that the advice works as specified.

Summary

Understanding how the components within your server interact with one another is an essential task for any developer and database administrator: we must efficiently use the resources within our server, understand how MySQL works from the inside, understand the causes of errors and what the database wants to say when errors are produced and choose the components of our servers carefully.

CHAPTER 6   UNDERSTANDING YOUR SERVER

Once we're already writing performant and secure code, we mustn't forget how our database can be optimized and use the necessary tools and knowledge to fine-tune our database and provide our database with the tools necessary to ride the high-performance highway.

Now that you know what your server looks like from the inside, how it works, and what resources it's using, it's time to understand what you can make your database do to perform at the best of its ability by optimizing it.

PART III

Optimizing MySQL

CHAPTER 7

Optimizing Your Server for MySQL

Oh, optimization. A favorite among many DBAs and the cause of headaches for many developers. Optimization is a necessity for every database – a well-optimized database is the reason why your application loads quickly, searches are blazing fast, and customers come flowing in. Everything can also work the other way around – run a slow, sluggish, and underperforming database, and the best products will dive into the ground. Your database is the primary force powering your application and everything related to data: data that is inserted, displayed, updated and transformed, and sometimes deleted.

Your database needs help: and by help, I don't mean therapy, but rather, your understanding of how your server works put to use to assist your database in performing required operations. Think about it – if you have 64GB of operating memory in a dedicated server together with disk drives of terabytes in size, is it really useful to build an app upon your database with default settings? The answer is obvious – no. But before grabbing an extremely powerful server, first, you have to understand what can be optimized and what should be left as-is. That's where your database configuration comes into play – for some, the benefits of optimization are obvious, and such people are likely to optimize their database before it even sees daylight, but many others are puzzled with a burning question to answer – why should I optimize my server for MySQL in the first place?

Why Optimize Your Server for MySQL?

"Why should I optimize my server for MySQL?" After all, your server is a powerful beast, and MySQL runs without any issues as-is, right? You're not facing any downtime or lag, perhaps you've already been running MySQL for a while, and you don't notice any slow-running queries either, so why optimize?

CHAPTER 7 OPTIMIZING YOUR SERVER FOR MYSQL

I bet that deep inside you already know the answer – you need to optimize your server for MySQL because if it is the primary database management system you find yourself using, chances are that it powers 110% of your application. It's the backbone of your application, and if things go sour with your database, they go sour for everyone: the users using your application, customers paying you money, visitors, developers working on the application, yourself, and even your accountant may start calling you up and saying "What's happening? The tax authorities cannot reach your website to inspect what you're up to." Yes, things will go sour for hackers too, but you shouldn't be happy – is there any point in hacking something that doesn't work properly in the first place?

Think of a castle again – you fortify the security measures around it to make access to it for a nefarious party harder. You do it ahead of time because if an enemy is marching toward the castle, fortifications need to help keep him as far away for as long as possible. Fortifying your castle as you're getting attacked is not a very smart idea because you will likely be eliminated if you do so – fortifications won't provide a 100% guarantee that you won't be eliminated, but they will certainly win you some time so you can prepare for what's going to happen next.

Now come back to your database: you need to optimize things ahead of time to help keep the experience for the users using your application as smooth as possible. If you're using a search engine, do you know how many searches it will go through every single day? 10? 100? Perhaps 10,000? You can presume, but it's impossible to know ahead of time. That's where optimization comes into play – you weigh all of the parameters to keep your database running smoothly no matter if 10, 100, or 10,000 queries are being run. A properly optimized database keeps your plan A from failing – and if your plan A is good enough, plan B isn't necessary.

Of course, you already know that there are loads of people willing to give you optimization advice – that's not a bad thing, but before taking it in, you need to be 100% sure that the advice is credible, and there's no better way to know that for sure than knowing some of the optimization secrets yourself. Knowing your way around optimization doesn't mean that you won't need advice – it means that you will have a good basis to weigh what's credible and what's not.

To properly optimize your server for MySQL, you have to choose a good server first. Here we come to the first dilemma – what makes a server "good"? From there, we have additional questions – how do you know how much operating memory will your use case necessitate? How do you know if you need an AMD or Intel processor? How to presume how much hard drive space will count as enough? That comes from experience. Do you know why your colleague took a look at the server list and came up with a solution that seemed to tick all of the boxes 3 minutes in? He's experienced in this field. Many choose servers without much thinking either and that's because of the same reason – experience.

Obtaining experience is relatively easy. Mistakes cost almost nothing to fix, and many servers can be upgraded as you go too. Below, you will find a list of rough guidelines that will help you choose a server:

1. **Did you make a choice previously?** Did you build any previous projects with any use case? What servers did you choose and was your choice wise? If the decision has satisfied you, look into buying a similar server, and chances are that you won't regret your choice here either.

2. **Evaluate your use case:** If you need a new server, think about how much data will your application produce/work with daily, think about the data types and character sets, what kind of people will use your application, and the types of applications your database will be supporting. How many apps do you plan on running? What kinds of databases will they use? Is concurrency an option?

3. **Consider server location and maintenance requirements:** Considering the location of your server is key – CDNs help, but if you primarily serve customers in the United States, a server in Japan isn't a good option. You may also want to choose a server with included maintenance and upkeep – you're likely to face problems with your server as time goes by (just ask any server administrator for his horror stories), and the outsourced maintenance team will help keep your headaches to a minimum.

4. **Flexibility:** Take into account whether the server offered by an organization is flexible, too. If you plan to host big data-based apps and you won't be able to expand your hard drive as necessary, you'll have problems on your hands.

5. **Budget:** Of course, everything comes down to finances too. You will likely have a budget, and the smaller it is, the more stress you will be required to put up with. Smaller budgets may mean your server and application being offline for some time with less traffic

to support. In this case, expanding your budget to thousands of dollars every month wouldn't be wise too – try to find a golden medium by researching the server (and the company) before choosing one, asking your colleagues for assistance in choosing the server, or talk to the hosting provider itself. Support channels exist for a reason – use them!

Didn't make a choice yet? Don't fret – once you walk yourself through common server issues affecting MySQL, know how to remove blockers limiting the performance of your DBMS, and configure your database management system to make use of I/O capabilities and other superpowers inside of your server, you will be able to choose server components with ease – once that's the case, you will be able to take full advantage of ACID properties within InnoDB or XtraDB if you use Percona Server, and you will be well on your way to a prosperous future for your database.

Common Webserver Issues Affecting MySQL

You know what your application, your database, and your server have in common? Issues! Issues that are the primary cause of customer complaints, slow-running queries, or even downtime. Some issues will affect your database directly, others won't, but be certain – all issues will alert you of their presence. Remember errors in MySQL? Once you see them, be certain – something's wrong.

All MySQL errors will alert you of something happening inside of your database, and some won't forget your server either. Making mistakes is inevitable, but ensure that your mistakes aren't the ones listed below – the price if they're exploited can be too much to bear:

- **You're running old, outdated versions of software**: This one will affect everything: run an old version of PHP, and you won't be able to upgrade plugins in WordPress; don't upgrade plugins in WordPress, and you will risk getting hacked. If you find yourself saying "WordPress is only a blog on my website so I don't need to pay much attention," you are asking for trouble. I won't even mention what kind of nasty security flaws your entire infrastructure would be exposed to! Your database would quickly become the least of your worries.

CHAPTER 7   OPTIMIZING YOUR SERVER FOR MYSQL

- **You avoid optimizing your application**: If your application is used badly, it can consume a lot of resources. I'll begin with the fact that if your Apache configuration is configured badly, you're likely to end up with many unnecessary processes. In case you find yourself using an appliance like `mod_security` for a firewall, keep in mind that it consumes resources too – why not look for proxy server-based alternatives like the same CloudFlare or Sucuri? Heck, you can even build a firewall yourself and it isn't that complex – I've built one and I didn't know that much about security at the time!

- **You avoid using a CDN, and your server gets overloaded**: CDN providers offload some of the traffic to themselves: serve CSS or JS through them and avoid load toward your database. Some providers like CloudFlare, Sucuri, and Imperva are known to be able to protect your entire infrastructure, no matter big or small, from DDoS attacks too. DDoS attacks happen more frequently than you'd think – even a small kid can start attacking your entire infrastructure with a script he'd found online or made using a tutorial. Neglected a CDN? Face the consequences.

- **You're low on disk space**: This is a big one and can arise even if you're confident that you have lots of disk space; it all can change very quickly – think of `ALTER` queries. These make a copy of the table on the disk; you won't "see" that unless you're paying attention to your drives as an `ALTER` query moves along, and if you find yourself adding an index to a large table, be 300% sure that you will have more than enough disk space – aim for the table size and additional 20-30% of free space as a minimum. Granted, there are ways to avoid running out of disk space when updating data if you're stranded – I'll walk you through them – but keep the amount of available disk space in mind at all times.

- **You don't have a backup strategy**: Backing up data is vital. No matter how you back up your precious data, you must ensure that you do so reliably and with a minimal impact on your database: backing up data at 1 AM is likely to have less impact than backing up at 1 PM, and make sure to test your backups properly too. Restore the backups

137

you took from time to time – is all data restored the way you expected it to be restored? How did the restoration process go? Once disaster strikes, data you backed up (or neglected to back up) will likely be your first line of defense.

Once you see one or more of these issues, glance back at your server – are you sure you're not running out of disk space? How is your CPU doing and how much operating memory did you allocate to the buffer pool? Did you remember to leave some memory for internal processes of your server? The reason we did not jump straight into performance optimization – or tuning as many like to call it – is because if you tune your database without understanding your server, your application is going to drown. It's going to be overwhelmed and drown because in that case, you wouldn't know what to ask your database for, and without knowing how to help you, your database wouldn't be up to the task no matter what it's asked for. Everything's a downward spiral from there, so it would be unwise to neglect any arising issues, big or small: even the smallest of issues can destroy the future of your database if neglected. Everything comes down to infrastructure, and once you're sure how to avoid limiting the performance of your database, you can feel free to choose where to turn to without performance, security, or availability implications. Pay attention to errors before errors pay attention to you.

What Limits the Performance of MySQL?

Contrary to popular belief, the first limiter for your database isn't the way you write your queries – sure, you may forget a couple of indexes here and there or invent a bike where an ordinary `LIMIT` would suffice, but that isn't what limits your database performance – at least that's not the primary culprit.

Your database performance is limited by the settings of your database – and the settings of your database are directly dependent on your server capabilities. That's why properly choosing a server is so vital for everyone involved: a server can become a bottleneck for high-load databases, but it can also be a significant overkill. Choose a golden medium, and then optimize. And no, you don't need to be a genius system administrator to choose the proper gear – search engines are storing upward of 10 billion rows on MariaDB and completing searches within milliseconds without resorting to the newest NVMe drives or other cream-of-the-crop gear, so everything's possible.

Even an old server can squeeze an impressive performance out of MySQL – it all depends on how your database is optimized. Of course, your app has a say here too: you will need to adhere to best coding and security practices if you want to survive in the wild (data breaches happen and you need to be ready), but if you're not using Laravel to build an app and are winging something yourself or find yourself using an old VPS and don't have the means to upgrade, not everything's lost either.

Choosing Servers and Hard Drives

When choosing a server, start from the things I've mentioned before: look at your previous choices, carefully evaluate your use case, consider server location and maintenance, flexibility, and your budget. These things will provide you with a rough outline of what servers you can look at – they will define whether you need a shared server, a VPS, or a dedicated server, and your use case will dictate the components that must be in place in your server for your app to run properly. Your server harbors the database that is then configured via my.ini or my.cnf depending on the OS you find yourself using. Settings can also be specified through the command line, but the bottom line remains the same – settings will help your database work in conjunction with your server to reach your goals.

A server will always be a limiting factor for your database, no matter if you find yourself using MySQL or other database management systems. Your database will only perform well if it's configured to make use of the components available in your server – and one of the main limiting points in regard to your database is hard drives and the I/O capability that goes through them, as well as your CPU.

Choose hard drives carefully – an NVMe SSD would be the fastest option, but it's also the most expensive one. In many cases, a simple SSD might make the cut, while in cases where bigger data sets are involved, one could use HDD storage to store terabytes of data. When in doubt, many would advise you to choose the golden medium – an SSD – as it'd be faster than HDD storage, but again, "good speed" may mean different things to different people: don't forget that a hard drive is only one part of the equation, and it won't solve all of your problems anyway, so there's no need to invent a bike here. At the same time, you should weigh the upsides and downsides of an HDD, SSD, and SSD NVMe against your use case, and choose wisely: choose an HDD if you intend to store bigger data sets (more than a couple of terabytes of data), an SSD NVMe if you're striving for high performance and can sustain a higher price point, and an SSD for general use cases.

When it comes to a CPU, choose a processor with multiple (preferably 4 or more) cores and a decent processor (a speed of 3.5 GHz is a good starting point). Keep in mind that both MySQL and its counterparts are multithreaded, so you shouldn't need additional configuration to make MySQL use multiple cores.

Before making a choice, make sure to consult the hosting company if possible too – people working there will have a good grasp of what servers are available, and once you tell them your use case and detail the requirements, they will be likely to direct you to a server and offer a money-back guarantee if you don't like the server you've chosen.

Configuring MySQL Parameters

After you've made a choice, inspect whether MySQL is already installed on your server. For some users, MySQL will likely already be installed, and others will have to install it themselves.

After you find time to scratch the surface of your server, shut MySQL down so you can configure it. Take a copy of the configuration file so you can restore default settings if/when necessary (Linux users will find the configuration file in the /etc/, /etc/mysql/, /var/lib/mysql, or ~/ directories, and for Windows users, the file will likely reside in the database management subdirectory of the bin directory), then decide what storage engine will you be using (most of you will choose InnoDB), and configure the options relevant to it.

Once the configuration file is opened up, Windows users will notice that it contains a bunch of different comments all mashed together.

```
 7   ⌐; The MariaDB server
 8   [wampmariadb64]
 9   ;skip_grant_tables
10   port =3307
11   socket = /tmp/mariadb.sock
12   skip_external_locking
13   key_buffer_size = 256M
14   max_allowed_packet = 1M
15   table_open_cache = 256
16   sort_buffer_size = 2M
17   net_buffer_length = 8K
18   read_buffer_size = 1M
19   read_rnd_buffer_size = 4M
20   myisam_sort_buffer_size = 64M
21   basedir="c:/wamp64/bin/mariadb/mariadb10.10.2"
22   log_error="c:/wamp64/logs/mariadb.log"
23   datadir="c:/wamp64/bin/mariadb/mariadb10.10.2/data"
24
25   ;Path to the language
26   ;See Documentation:
27   ; https://mariadb.com/kb/en/mariadb/server-system-variables/#lc_messages
28   lc_messages_dir="c:/wamp64/bin/mariadb/mariadb10.10.2/share"
29   lc_messages=en_US
30
31   ; Set the SQL mode
32   ;sql_mode=""
33   ;sql_mode="STRICT_ALL_TABLES,ERROR_FOR_DIVISION_BY_ZERO,NO_AUTO_CREATE_USER"
34
35   ; The default storage engine that will be used when create new tables
36   default_storage_engine=InnoDB
```

***Figure 7-1.** my.ini with comments*

InnoDB users will need to scroll further (while scrolling, adjust the default storage engine to InnoDB if it's not already adjusted), and below the storage engine, they will find a bunch of options.

```
113   ; The InnoDB tablespace encryption feature relies on the keyring_file
114   ; plugin for encryption key management, and the keyring_file plugin
115   ; must be loaded prior to storage engine initialization to facilitate
116   ; InnoDB recovery for encrypted tables. If you do not want to load the
117   ; keyring_file plugin at server startup, specify an empty string.
118   innodb_adaptive_hash_index=on
119   innodb_buffer_pool_dump_now=off
120   innodb_buffer_pool_dump_at_shutdown=off
121   innodb_buffer_pool_load_at_startup=off
122   innodb_buffer_pool_size=1G
123   innodb_data_file_path=ibdata1:12M:autoextend:max:500M
124   ;innodb_default_row_format=dynamic
125   innodb_doublewrite=on
126   ;skip_innodb_doublewrite
127   innodb_file_per_table=1
128   innodb_flush_log_at_trx_commit=1
129   innodb_flush_method=normal
130   ;innodb_force_recovery=1
131   innodb_ft_enable_stopword=off
132   innodb_ft_max_token_size=10
133   innodb_ft_min_token_size=0
134   innodb_io_capacity=2000
135   innodb_max_dirty_pages_pct=90
136   innodb_lock_wait_timeout=600
137   innodb_log_buffer_size=16M
138   innodb_log_file_size=20M
139   innodb_max_dirty_pages_pct=80
140   innodb_optimize_fulltext_only=1
141   innodb_page_size=16K
142   innodb_purge_threads=10
```

Figure 7-2.   InnoDB settings in my.ini

So many options! The good news is that you're unlikely to modify every one of them – the bad news is that some parameters need to be changed without question.

Linux users will have it easy because Linux's version of my.ini – my.cnf – will likely only provide the necessary parameters relevant to InnoDB, but all of those parameters apply to Linux users nonetheless. For a comprehensive explanation of what each parameter does, come back to Chapter 2 and refer to the heading "InnoDB in MySQL and MariaDB" – once you've refreshed your memory, optimize these parameters to make the InnoDB engine sing:

Parameter	Why Optimize?
innodb_buffer_pool_size	This is the size of the InnoDB buffer pool that stores data, indexes, and MVCC data related to InnoDB. Set this parameter to at least 60% of the available RAM in your system.
innodb_log_file_size	This parameter depicts the size of the log files within InnoDB. Log files are sifted through upon restoration – set this parameter to approximately a quarter of the buffer pool size. A larger log file size is better for performance, but larger log files will also force InnoDB to take a longer time to recover.
innodb_flush_log_at_trx_commit	This parameter controls the balance between ACID compliance and high performance: a value of 1 means ACID compliance, while values of 0 or 2 will allow for more speed, but increase the risk of losing up to one second of transaction data.
innodb_flush_method	Depicts the data flushing method that InnoDB uses to flush data to the disk. Some values are available only to Linux users.
innodb_data_file_path	Depicts the file name and the size of the main InnoDB tablespace – the ibdata1 file. The file can, indeed, have any name – and can be split into separate files if we so desire.

I've already covered most of the parameters relevant to InnoDB in Chapter 2 of this book, so I won't repeat myself here: what I do want you to pay attention to, however, is the main system tablespace within InnoDB – the ibdata1 file. It exists for a reason and contains multiple classes of data vital for InnoDB to function correctly including data, indexes, Multiversion Concurrency Control (MVCC) data, undo space, rollback segments, and two types of buffers – the insert buffer and the double-write buffer. The buffers have a dual purpose: the insert buffer will be used to "buffer" many updates to database pages and perform a single big update at once, and the double-write buffer is used to receive data flushed from the buffer pool: the InnoDB storage engine will only write data to the disk if the data in the double-write buffer is flushed to the disk beforehand.

The purpose of ibdata1 is to act as a "castle" that parts of your data are saved in. This castle keeps your data separated from itself by saving data related to InnoDB-based tables in two separate files: one under a ".frm" extension, the other under ".ibd." This feature is called the "file-per-table" feature: it's controlled by fiddling with the `file-per-table` variable in InnoDB (acceptable values include the default value – 1 – and 0), and a default value of 1 starting from MySQL 5.6 enables InnoDB to separate data relevant to InnoDB tables from ibdata1 due to issues that can arise if the data is held together. *A value of 0 would "glue" both data and metadata into ibdata1 and that can be the cause of a very frustrating problem: one wouldn't be able to delete data from InnoDB to make the size of its tablespace smaller.* The only way to delete data from InnoDB without a trace on the disk (and therefore shrink the ibdata1 file) would be to delete the data in the database or drop the database itself and then delete ibdata1 and the associated log files ib_logfile*. By doing so, however, we would inevitably destroy everything InnoDB-related altogether, so it wouldn't exactly be an ideal approach. A value of "1" splits data related to InnoDB tables into two files – one holding the table data (.ibd file) and one holding table metadata (.frm file.)

This is one of the primary ways that InnoDB keeps our data safe and declutters ibdata1 and also differs from other storage engines – while the data in InnoDB is also saved in files similar to MyISAM's ".MYD" for table data and ".MYI" for indexes within, MyISAM doesn't have a file to "rely on" to power the ACID capability while InnoDB does. This makes deleting the data in MyISAM easier (we can just delete the .MYD files to get rid of MyISAM tables or .MYI files to delete indexes within them), but ironically, at the same time, this makes MyISAM almost unusable for most modern workloads due to instability and frequent data corruption issues.

Aside from that, ibdata1 can be renamed or split into multiple different files by fiddling with the `innodb_data_file_path` variable – advanced users will know that the file can extend automatically too. A definition like so:

`innodb_data_file_path=ibdata1:10M:autoextend`

Would make the InnoDB data file 10MB in size and allow it to increment in size (8MB every time) each time more space is required. One can also define multiple data files that InnoDB would store data in together with their sizes like so (in this case, we would have three files – ibdata1, ibdata2, and ibdata3, all with varying sizes):

`innodb_data_file_path=ibdata1:10M;ibdata2:100M;ibdata3:500M:autoextend`

Remember that when `file_per_table` is enabled (and it will be enabled unless you disable it manually), those files would only store metadata related to the tables within your infrastructure, so they wouldn't need to be big either.

CHAPTER 7 OPTIMIZING YOUR SERVER FOR MYSQL

Configuring MySQL I/O for Your Operating System

Once InnoDB is taking the first steps on its own, you should turn your eye toward the disk I/O. Disk I/O can become an Achilles heel for your database because it's impossible to run away from I/O operations, and if they aren't optimized properly, they can be a source of much pain and confusion.

You already know some of the ways disk I/O can be optimized – you've increased the size of the buffer pool, perhaps adjusted the flush method, and perhaps used storage devices facilitating faster access to data (NVMe drives instead of SSDs of SSDs instead of HDDs, etc.)

Do you know why these ways optimize disk I/O? Everything's simple:

- *A bigger InnoDB buffer pool size allows your queries to access the buffer pool for a longer period* without performing any disk-bound operations, thus reducing disk I/O.

- *Setting the InnoDB flush method to O_DIRECT* – a default option starting from MariaDB 10.6 and only accessible on Unix infrastructure – allows your database to avoid the OS cache and allows for more data consistency. Granted, you have other options such as O_DSYNC which is a faster option than O_DIRECT, however, when such an option is in use and your database experiences latency or a crash, no data consistency would be guaranteed. For a refresher about the flush methods available in InnoDB, please go back to Chapter 2.

- *Using modern drives (think SSD and/or NVMe drives) reduces seek time.* This is a no-brainer: since SSDs and NVMe drives don't have any moving parts, their seek time can be significantly reduced. That's why some of us put our OS on NVMe drives – we do it for our systems to boot up quickly. According to numerous sources, modern hard drives have a seek time of around 5-7 milliseconds, while SSDs have a seek time of around 0.10 to 0.20 milliseconds.

These tips are the bare minimum – to further improve disk I/O, you would have to look into a couple of additional parameters:

- `innodb_io_capacity` and `innodb_io_capacity_max`: The first variable defines how many I/O operations are available to InnoDB, and the second one defines the maximum number of I/O operations InnoDB can use when flushing activity lags behind the specified capacity.

- `innodb_page_size`: Database pages are the backbone of every database providing a unit of data storage. Rows of data are stored in database pages, and each page has a size – and for InnoDB, that size can be controlled by fiddling with the `innodb_page_size` variable. To further optimize InnoDB's I/O capacity, adjust its page size to be close to the sector size of your hard drive.

- `innodb_flush_neighbors`: Enable this parameter to help InnoDB optimize disk I/O for hard disk drives. Disabled by default.

Aside from these parameters, one could consider making their log files larger, perhaps as large as the buffer pool itself. Such an action would necessitate MySQL to take its time when restoring your data as log files need to be read through when restoring it, but on the other hand, this could reduce disk I/O during InnoDB checkpointing operations.

Also, in regard to the buffer pool, you can configure InnoDB in such a way that allows it to perform operations that read data ahead of time to "warm the buffer pool up" to bring data in memory so that reading it wouldn't necessitate access to the disk. Such behavior is already the default starting from MySQL 5.7 – MySQL will save the contents of the InnoDB buffer pool and load it on startup.

Many of you will also know that InnoDB saves a quarter (25%) of the most frequently accessed database pages in its buffer pool based on the `innodb_buffer_pool_dump_pct` variable.

```
MariaDB [hacking_mysql]> SHOW VARIABLES LIKE 'innodb_buffer_pool_dump_pct';
+-----------------------------+-------+
| Variable_name               | Value |
+-----------------------------+-------+
| innodb_buffer_pool_dump_pct | 25    |
+-----------------------------+-------+
1 row in set (0.002 sec)
```

Figure 7-3. *The default value of the innodb_buffer_pool_dump_pct variable*

Since the definition of this parameter is to define the percentage of the recently used database pages for a buffer pool to read, this parameter can have a value between 1 and 100, and the value of this parameter is a percentage, setting to a value of a 100 is also possible and that would mean that InnoDB will try to access all of the data in memory without a disk read. Before you set this value to 100%, be aware that this variable would only save the percentage of data in the buffer pool, but not the entire buffer pool itself, for example, if you have a buffer pool of 100GB in size and the buffer pool contains 20GB of data, setting this variable to 100% would only save 20GB of data.

Aside from optimizing disk I/O, keep in mind that certain options in MySQL are only available for those using a Unix architecture. The aforementioned O_DIRECT mode would enable a direct mode for I/O throughput which would bypass the cache of the operating system using an option unavailable to be used in Windows.

Finally, keep in mind that everything running in your operating system is feeding on memory, too. Your database is certainly not the only one using your memory, and it is said that Windows usually uses more memory than Linux does due to all of the additions that come pre-installed with it, but if you install thousands of additional appliances on Linux, these will consume memory too. Avoid installing applications you don't need, and you will have more memory you can allocate to your database and your application.

Testing Your Hardware

No matter what kind of operating system you use, hardware is often the limiting factor for many databases. No matter if you have billions of rows or if you're just starting out – if your hardware will be a limiting factor, interacting with them can become difficult as time goes by. Difficulties can be overcome by properly configuring your database, but even that can become a hard task if your hardware doesn't allow for it. Many databases will have certain limiters – and many of those limiters have to do with the hardware on your system.

CHAPTER 7   OPTIMIZING YOUR SERVER FOR MYSQL

If you've read this far, chances are that you've already taken steps to optimize your database based on the hardware that is in place inside of your server: one of the most reliable ways to test what your hardware is capable of now is to interact with your data. Work with your application for a week or two – what do you notice? Do any problems occur? Do clients or users contact you about anything database-related?

When interacting with your database, remember that it's vitally important to strike and keep a balance between memory and disk resources. Who wouldn't want all of their data to be read from the memory for blazing-fast performance? Unfortunately, memory is much more finite than hard drive space is; but even with that being the case, there are many other things at play: we have query caches, reading and writing, flushing, I/O operations, and many other things, and each of them can help us make our database and our hardware work in conjunction.

There are tools that you can use to test your MySQL setup – one of those is the aforementioned `mysqlslap` (or `mariadb-slap` in MariaDB) which helps you emulate multiple concurrent connections toward MySQL or MariaDB and helps see how your database deals with issues, users of CentOS can make use of `sysbench`, and there's also `mysqlshow` and the `mariadb-show` equivalent in MariaDB that displays information relevant to the databases, tables, and columns within them so you can understand where to turn. Let's take `mariadb-show` for a spin.

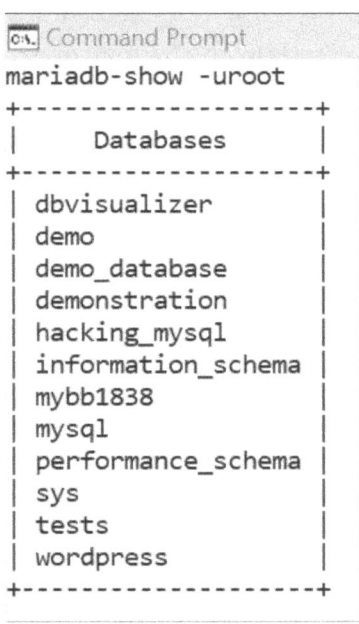

Figure 7-4. *Default behavior of mariadb-show*

148

CHAPTER 7 OPTIMIZING YOUR SERVER FOR MYSQL

By default, this tool will only show the databases in our database server. One can dig into a specific database by providing its name as part of the options list. I'll do that with the MyBB database.

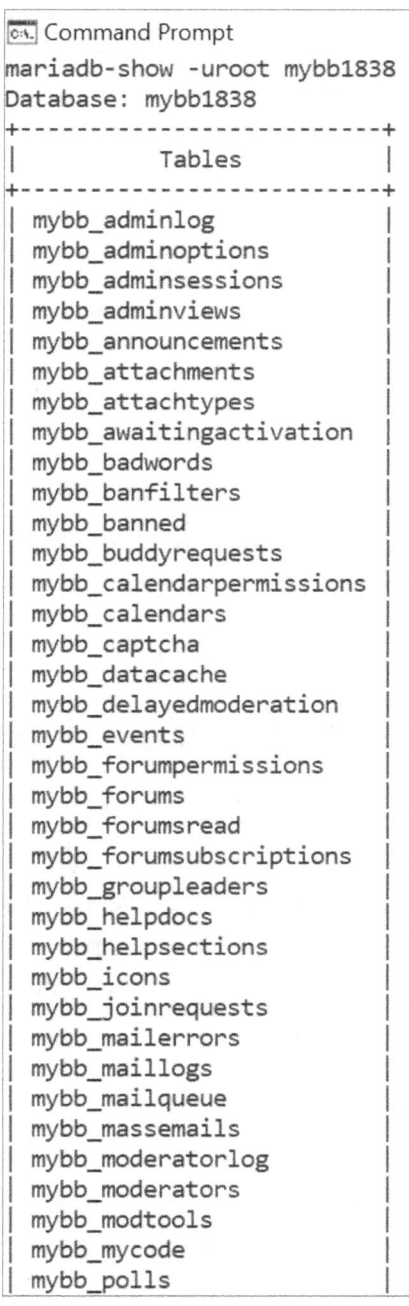

Figure 7-5. Digging into the MyBB 1.8.38 database in MariaDB

Both `mysql-show` and `mariadb-show` have a lot of options that let us dig into our table structure and the data within. Running a query like so:

`mariadb-show -uroot mybb1838 --count --status --keys`

Would provide us with a lot of information ranging from the row count (`--count`), extra information about the MyBB 1.8.38 table (`--status`), and some information about the indexes (`--keys`).

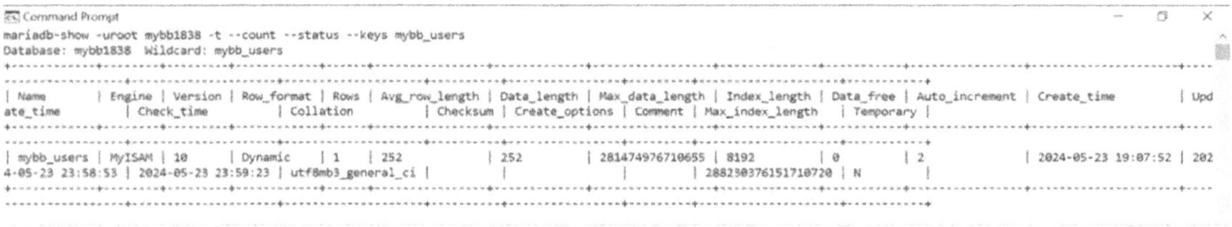

Figure 7-6. mariadb-show in action

Glean some information from tools like `mariadb-show` and `mysqlslap` to gain information on how best to optimize your server to use everything in its power to help your queries succeed, but don't forget the importance of basic database standards and properties either.

Taking Advantage of ACID Properties

Last but not least, what good databases would do if they wouldn't adhere to standards and properties? Who would trust databases to store their most precious data? Data must be stored reliably – that's a fact. And if we look at everything from a birds-eye-view, all databases store data safely, right? After all, what company would store data in a database knowing their most precious asset can come crashing down at any time?

All databases let you store data safely – but there are fundamental differences between the models that databases are based on. There are two models – one that strives for better data consistency, and one that strives for higher availability. Those two models are ACID and BASE, and only one of those models can be used at a given moment. ACID will be used in relational database management systems and NoSQL-based systems will make use of BASE, so you can't make use of the upsides of both – but that's their entire beauty at the same time.

ACID is an acronym that lives together with relational database management systems helping them achieve atomicity, consistency, isolation, and durability. That's precisely what this acronym stands for – and that's why you see relational databases like MySQL still standing after electricity goes out or a disaster strikes while many BASE-based databases will need to have their data restored; ACID helps us ensure that our data remains consistent and durable even in the event of a disaster.

Various relational database management systems implement ACID a little differently because no two databases are the same, but for MySQL, the process is as follows:

- **Atomicity** is handled by the `COMMIT` and `ROLLBACK` statements – it ensures that all queries in a transaction operate as a team.

- **Consistency** is handled by the MySQL logging mechanism and the log files (ib_logfile0 and ib_logfile1) that record all changes inside InnoDB. Once data needs to be restored, log files are scanned through.

- **Isolation** refers to the row-level locking available in InnoDB.

- **Durability** is ensured by the nature of error logs and other log files – for some, these files are the first point of defense against database errors.

ACID is the reason why sometimes you see developers saying that "changes to the data should be committed" and wonder what that means – to "commit changes to data" means to save them inside of the database files. Once changes are committed, they are permanently saved and become visible to other sessions.

ACID is the backbone of the InnoDB storage engine within all flavors of MySQL, and that's one of the reasons why the InnoDB storage engine is the default storage engine available in MySQL and MariaDB: its ability to adhere to ACID properties is rivaled by very few (RocksDB supports ACID too), and its support for features previously only accessible in MyISAM makes it well-suited for even the most demanding workloads.

In MySQL, ACID compliance can also be turned off in exchange for more speed and more risk of losing up to one second's worth of data and that can be done with the parameter `innodb_flush_log_at_trx_commit`. By default, InnoDB will flush data to the log files at the time transactions commit, thus ensuring ACID compliance (that's why this variable is set to the value of 1 to begin with), but some geeks will know that this variable can also have other values – 0, 2, and if MariaDB is in use, 3. Each of those values performs different tasks:

- **A value of 0 has to do with the redo log.** If `innodb_flush_log_at_trx_commit` is set to the value of 0, the redo log is written to and flushed to disk only once per second, thus guaranteeing no ACID compliance, but more speed.

- **A value of 1 has to do with ACID compliance.** If `innodb_flush_log_at_trx_commit` is set to the value of 1, InnoDB will be ACID-compliant.

- **A value of 2 has to do with committing and flushing operations.** If `innodb_flush_log_at_trx_commit` is set to the value of 2, InnoDB will write data to the log files once transactions are committed, but flush data to disk only once every second.

- **A value of 3 has to do with MariaDB.** If `innodb_flush_log_at_trx_commit` is set to the value of 3, MariaDB will flush the data to disk once it's prepared and once it's committed thus potentially making the operations slow.

Most of you will not need to change the `innodb_flush_log_at_trx_commit` parameter to anything else, but if the need to dig into data atomicity, consistency, integrity, or durability arises or if you need to exchange ACID for speed, you know who to call.

ACID also has a sister called BASE – BASE properties ensure high availability with eventual consistency. In other words, BASE means that a database puts in effort to ensure that our data is basically available, in a soft state, and can eventually become consistent. The BASE model has a focus on high availability, while ACID focuses on data consistency and integrity:

- **Basically available**: BASE-based databases ensure the high availability of data by copying it across multiple data nodes.

- **Soft state**: The BASE model is also known for its temporary nature and that's what Soft State refers to. Data in a non-relational database is likely to evolve and change very frequently. The state of data may change regardless if any action is taken or not.

- **Eventually consistent**: Databases based on the BASE model will put in their best effort to ensure the consistency of data; however, it's never a guarantee.

BASE sacrifices data consistency for high availability, while ACID will ensure that data remains consistent in almost any scenario. ACID databases will focus on committing your data to ensure it's consistent while providing you with a structure to work with, while BASE databases will have no need for a database model or structure and will give their best attempt to ensure eventual consistency of data with a focus on high availability.

Summary

Every database runs on a server – and no matter what kind of server you find yourself running, there is always something that can be improved upon. For most developers, optimizing a server for MySQL becomes a simple task once they understand what components are used by their database, what issues limit the performance of their database, once they properly choose hard drives and other components, and configure options related to InnoDB disk I/O. After that's done, it's safe to say that a database is in safe hands.

Optimizing a server for a database involves many more things than just disk I/O, the amount of available memory, or fiddling with your CPU – no one database management system is the same, and all databases have lots of internal options that can be optimized to achieve database performance goals: for MySQL, it all starts from storage engines.

Once a proper storage engine is chosen and understood, we can proceed to optimize our schemas, data types, and finally – SQL queries for a wide variety of use cases including big data.

CHAPTER 8

Optimizing Storage Engines, Schemas, and Data Types

Storage engines are the backbone of MySQL – they power our data and tell our database how to interact with it. I've told you about them in Chapter 2 of this book. Storage engines don't walk alone: they harbor database schemas, data types, collations, indexes, and other things, and each of those things has its remits on one side and downsides on the other. Regardless, storage engines were, are, and will be the spark that starts a fire; the fire that makes your data warm, and the users of your application happy.

For that fire to continue burning and for users to be happy, there are numerous things you should adhere to when working with your data – your storage engines should be optimized, the databases within them should hold data safely, and you should pay extra attention to the data types that are being used.

Why Optimize Storage Engines and Data Types?

First, we have storage engines. Put simply, storage engines are components within MySQL that allow MySQL to use certain operations for a variety of data types. MySQL supports a wide variety of storage engines, and the internal functionality of those storage engines can be modified by modifying my.ini on Windows, or my.cnf on Linux.

Open up the configuration file pertaining to your operating system, and you will quickly notice that not all MySQL storage engines have options available to them; the configuration file for Windows users will be much more generous in regard to options and comments, while most of the users using Linux will have few options to choose from and most of these options will likely pertain to the main storage engine – InnoDB – to begin with.

CHAPTER 8   OPTIMIZING STORAGE ENGINES, SCHEMAS, AND DATA TYPES

Regardless, InnoDB can be optimized as much as your hardware allows: you might want to flick back to Chapter 2 to find out what the function of each of the variables within the storage engine is, but regardless of what parameters or storage engine you find yourself using, the fact is that you will use the storage engine to store data inside of it; data comes in a variety of shapes and forms and while data types may seem like small fish in a pond, as more and more data will be introduced into your databases, their significance will only grow. No production database will come without tables inside of it; tables inside of the database signify data residing in them, and data residing in them signifies one or more data types that it's being powered with. Data types aren't set in stone: they can be made bigger, smaller, or changed altogether, but no table will come without them.

Optimizing Storage Engines

For many production environments running MySQL, the optimization of storage engines comes down to the optimization of InnoDB. Its companion MyISAM may appear here and there, but it should not be your priority. I've already told you about the parameters that can be optimized to make InnoDB tick in Chapter 2 of this book, but there are also other things you should know before you start building applications based on them. These things include ways to optimize InnoDB for appliances running a lot of tables, optimizing InnoDB for read-only applications, optimizing InnoDB redo logs, and properly dealing with transactions within the storage engine.

To begin with, if you're using InnoDB for applications with a lot of tables inside of them, you're doing so with a good reason – regardless of what that reason is, it's crucial to do so with a goal in mind and effectively. To work with lots of tables inside of InnoDB, consider:

- **The collation of your database**: Strings are matched and sorted according to a collation. A good collation isn't a golden ticket that solves all of your problems, but it's a key that unlocks a door to a better future for your data.

- **Data types and character sets**: Do all of the tables within a database use the same character set? Why/why not? What data types are in use?

- **Ways to load/extract data into/from MySQL-based tables**: This will depend on your use case, but do think about the way you load and extract data from a database, too. Many developers complain about their data loading slowly, and your database is only partly at fault. The rest of the responsibility for this is on you.

- **The type of data/data classes you work with**: Carefully choose the data classes you find yourself working with. Adhere to all regulations you and/or your company may be privy to (don't store private data if not necessary), and be careful when choosing data length too.

- **A backup strategy**: Carefully backup your data. Backing up tables in a database is simple, but if you have a lot of data, things may get a little more complex. You may make use of a loop of SELECT ... INTO OUTFILE queries to back up raw data – I'll walk you through these kinds of queries in the chapter Optimizing MySQL for Big Data, and I'll cover more on backups in a chapter dedicated to them.

To optimize InnoDB for read-only operations and properly deal with transactions, consider a couple of points:

- **Craft and select indexes carefully**: MySQL and its counterparts can offer a bunch of indexes you can choose from, and choosing the right type of index and employing them carefully can be the difference between life and death for your queries and database alike. For indexing advice, turn to the chapter concerning indexes.

- **Partition your data where necessary**: You already know the power of partitions and partitions combined with indexes can form an incredibly powerful team. I'm talking billions of rows being scanned through in milliseconds – if your storage engine is optimized, indexes are in place, but queries through bigger data sets still complete slowly, indexes may be the culprit.

- **Look at the buffer pool and the log files of InnoDB**: Ensure that the size of the InnoDB buffer pool and the log files is large enough. I've already mentioned this numerous times, but doing so would help relieve InnoDB from unnecessary disk flushing and other activities.

CHAPTER 8   OPTIMIZING STORAGE ENGINES, SCHEMAS, AND DATA TYPES

Older versions of MySQL had variables called innodb_buffer_pool_
read_requests and innodb_buffer_pool_reads that depicted the
number of requests to read the buffer pool and how many reads were
made to begin with that would've been useful too, but if you're using
newer versions of the DBMS, these options are likely to be long gone.

- **Make use of the START TRANSACTION READ ONLY statement**: It's not
well-known, but an important update was introduced in MySQL 5.6
for those running read-only transactions: MySQL did intentionally
reduce overhead in InnoDB for read-only transactions by avoiding
setting up the transaction ID. It's a small change, but since the
transaction ID is only needed for write operations or operations with
locked reads, read-only transactions can be made faster.

- **Help InnoDB detect read-only transactions**: That can be done by
making use of the aforementioned read-only statement or by turning
on the autocommit setting and running non-locking select queries.

- **Turn off autocommit when inserting large amounts of data, and
then enable it once all data is inserted**: After you do this, InnoDB
will no longer commit every time rows are inserted – instead,
commits will be made after all transactions complete, thus making
your INSERT queries faster.

Finally, to optimize redo logs within InnoDB, consider increasing their size (look
at the innodb_redo_log_capacity variable), keep your log buffer large enough, and
consider modifying the InnoDB log spin variables (these variables can help reduce
latency.)

InnoDB has a lot of variables, and some of those include variables you wouldn't even
think about – at the same time, not all of them are necessary even if you find yourself
working with incredibly big data sets.

In case you find yourself necessitating the use of MyISAM (I hope that's to
supplement InnoDB, not to replace it), look into its key_buffer_size (that's the innodb_
buffer_pool_size equivalent in MyISAM), thread_cache_size defines the number of
reusable threads available for the MyISAM cache, making the bulk_insert_buffer_size
larger may help make bulk INSERT operations faster on tables that aren't empty, and
read_buffer_size and sort_buffer_size will help with increasing read and sort buffer
sizes for MyISAM. Use MyISAM cautiously and weigh your decision before taking any

action. Finally, remember that following best practices is often enough – the catch is that those practices are incredibly nuanced and to follow them, you have to know your way around databases and your storage engine internally.

Data Types in MySQL

One of the database best practices has to do with data types: they're directly responsible for the size of your data, and the bigger your data sets become, the more important data types will be. As already mentioned in Chapter 3 of this book, MySQL has a variety of data types, but these can be dumbed down into a couple of categories the main ones being string, numeric, and date and time.

Each column in a table will have a data type, and depending on what that data type is, your database will be told what data it should store in that specific column. Also, keep in mind that values stored in any table will be affected by character sets regardless of what data type they use – depending on the character set you find yourself using, MySQL may allocate more or fewer bytes per character stored. Latin1 or ASCII character sets are unlikely to require more than 1 byte of storage per character, utf8-based character sets may take 3 bytes, while since utf8mb4 covers all Unicode characters, it takes up to 4 bytes of space to store one character.

To fully understand data types, you have to go a lot further than just scratch the surface – data types exist for a reason and all data you insert into your columns has an impact on the maximum column size, too. By default, MySQL's column size is limited to 767 bytes, and that's one of the main reasons behind errors like these:

```
Index column size too large. The maximum column size is 767 bytes.
```

Such an error occurs where the index column size is above 767 bytes – in other words, such an error may be encountered when we have `VARCHAR` or `TEXT`-based columns with around 200 characters and a collation that necessitates more than 3 bytes per character. Such errors can be overcome by setting the format for InnoDB tables to either `DYNAMIC` or `COMPRESSED`, but truthfully, if you are facing such errors, the issue is likely to be much deeper: why do you need to index a column bearing 200 characters in the first place? What read operations benefit from such a lengthy column? In other words, *what's your use case?* You would be surprised how many developers just put "255" when defining column length. As if that'd be the only value defining length. Can you deal with fewer characters in a column? Sure you can – why don't you set the column length to the actual maximum length that you expect? Setting the column length to 60 or even 40 characters may be the sweet spot saving you disk space, preventing errors, and saving you headaches as a result, too.

String-Based Data Types

As far as string-based data types go, if we look at MySQL, and then MariaDB, we will notice that most of the data types are the same, but if we look closely, we will notice that MariaDB supports a bunch of string data types that MySQL does not and those include LONG and LONG VARCHAR (these are synonyms for MEDIUMTEXT), the ROW data type for stored procedures, as well as the UUID data type and INET4 or INET6 data types, too.

MariaDB is unique in such a wide string data type offering, and while MySQL doesn't offer such data types directly, people can employ certain functions to achieve similar goals.

The string data types offered by MariaDB are indeed unique: the UUID data type offered by the DBMS lets us store **U**niversally **U**nique **Id**entifiers which are 128-bit 36-character strings that uniquely identify objects, and the INET4 or INET6 data types are suitable to store IPv4 or IPv6-related data.

Aside from data types unique to MariaDB, the DBMS also supports "ordinary" string data types like VARCHAR and TEXT, too. Some may wonder if MariaDB's support for string-based data types differs from the approach taken by MySQL, and the quick answer is yes, but only in some cases where it makes sense. For example, since MariaDB supports engines not supported by MySQL such as ColumnStore, if we're using the VARCHAR data type in ColumnStore, our defined number would no longer represent the maximum amount of characters that can be stored – it would represent the maximum length of the column in bytes. This makes sense because ColumnStore is suitable for incredibly big data sets (petabytes), and if you're storing such amounts of data in MariaDB, bytes are likely to be more important than the number of characters in a column.

Numeric Data Types

Aside from string data types, MariaDB also supports numeric data types. Here, things are a little less complex: while support for data types not available in MySQL exists, these data types aren't revolutionary, and they depict synonyms rather than new data types that can't be found anywhere except MariaDB.

Such synonyms include the data types INT1, INT2, INT3, INT4, and INT8. These data types are synonyms for TINYINT, SMALLINT, MEDIUMINT, INT, and BIGINT respectively. Numeric data types aren't anything impressive either, but keep in mind that their types (TINYINT and the like) don't exactly have a "direct map" to their string equivalents: for example, TINYTEXT will support a maximum of 255 characters, while the size of TINYINT won't be from 0 to 255, but rather, it's from -128 to 127.

You don't need to remember the size of every data type, but do remember that INT isn't the only solution to your problems: you would be surprised how many developers define INT as a data type when TINYINT would suffice. Pay attention to the structure of your tables and think ahead – data types aren't set in stone, but defining a well-thought-out data type ahead is likely to do you a lot of favors in the future, no matter if that data type is text or integer-related.

Date, Time, Spatial, and JSON Data Types

Aside from string and integer data types, some data types are also a very good fit for various other purposes. Such purposes may include the storage of time values, geographic constraints, or JSON arrays.

The number of use cases facilitating the use of numerous data types inside of a database management system is countless, and that's why MySQL's support for string or integer data types doesn't mark the end: many applications track the time when a user performs an action for internal purposes, and that's done with the help of data types depicting date and time values. Perhaps the most popular of such data types would include TIMESTAMP and DATETIME data types, and some data types provide support for specific formats too: the DATE data type would enable you to store dates in a YYYY-MM-DD format, the TIME data type would store exact times to the millisecond in the format of HH:MM:SS.ssssss, while the YEAR data type would be able to store years. Geometric – or spatial – data types such as GEOMETRY or POINT would assist in storing spatial data, while the JSON data type would enable developers to fiddle with their JSON-based data sets too.

Support for JSON data type also isn't something out of the ordinary: developers do work with JSON data and, naturally, need to store it inside of their databases. Advanced users of MySQL will know that in MariaDB, JSON is the same as LONGTEXT due to compatibility issues with MySQL and issues with SQL standards. Regardless, MariaDB provides full support for JSON data and even provides its users with functions that allow it to check for structure validity before inserting any data into a table. For that to work, we need to create a table with a CHECK constraint working in conjunction with the JSON_ VALID function that checks for the validity of data in a column. Everything would look something like this:

```
--First, we create a table with the CHECK constraint:
CREATE TABLE `json_demo` (
  `json_col` JSON
  CHECK (JSON_VALID(`json_col`))
);
--Our database will allow JSON values like this:
INSERT INTO `json_demo` VALUES ('{"id": 1, "information": "This book is cool!", "extra": "Read on and learn more things."}');
--But prohibit invalid, non-JSON values like the following:
INSERT INTO `json_demo` VALUES (`Invalid value`);
```

Figure 8-1. Example of JSON column validation

Storage Requirements for Data Types

Data types don't come alone – they have a significant overhead you must account for: that overhead has to do with storage requirements. Storage requirements aren't dependent only on data types either and they also depend on the storage engine you find yourself using, and they do differ depending on if you find yourself using InnoDB or NDB.

The primary difference you must account for is the way storage engines store data: InnoDB is famous for its row storage formats that have a variety of different characteristics and that's why people "overcome" problems like "Index column size too large" by switching the row storage format up; to understand why a switch to a

CHAPTER 8 OPTIMIZING STORAGE ENGINES, SCHEMAS, AND DATA TYPES

different InnoDB row format may solve issues, we have to understand the characteristics of various InnoDB row formats. Some InnoDB row format characteristics can be found below:

InnoDB Row Format	Characteristics
DYNAMIC	The default row format in InnoDB. Similar to COMPACT in that it has the same storage requirements. Includes support for large index prefixes.
COMPACT	Offers support for compact storage, but no large index prefix support. The same storage requirements as DYNAMIC.
REDUNDANT	This row format is redundant because it's mostly unusable; its purpose is to provide support for older versions of MySQL.
COMPRESSED	Famous for its support for data compression for tables and indexes, otherwise, acts the same way as the DYNAMIC row storage format.

Row formats can be changed either globally (for that, we would need to modify the ROW_FORMAT variable within my.ini or my.cnf and set it to one of the available values shown above) or per database/table with an ALTER TABLE query like so:

ALTER TABLE [table_name] ROW_FORMAT=[format here];

Row formats also have two sisters – Antelope and Barracuda. Those two sisters refer to the file formats available in InnoDB and work in conjunction with row formats: as far as InnoDB is concerned, Antelope supports the COMPACT and REDUNDANT row formats, and in the old days, it was the default file format available in MySQL. Barracuda supports all of the row formats available in InnoDB and is the default file format available in both MySQL and MariaDB of the present day.

Now that you understand that file and row formats are also at play, it's time to look into the actual storage requirements for specific data types. To simplify the presentation, I'll use two letters – B for "column length in bytes" and C for "column length in characters":

CHAPTER 8   OPTIMIZING STORAGE ENGINES, SCHEMAS, AND DATA TYPES

Data Type	Storage Requirements
VARCHAR(C) and VARBINARY(C)	B + 1 bytes if C is lower than 255 characters. B + 2 bytes otherwise.
TINYBLOB|TINYTEXT|BLOB|TEXT|MEDIUMBLOB|MEDIUMTEXT|LONGBLOB|LONGTEXT|JSON	B + 1 bytes|B + 2 bytes|B + 3 bytes|B + 4 bytes
TINYINT|SMALLINT|MEDIUMINT|INT|INTEGER|BIGINT	1, 2, 3, 4, and 8 bytes, respectively.
YEAR|DATE|TIME|TIMESTAMP|DATETIME	1 byte, 3 bytes, 3 bytes, 4 bytes, and 5 bytes, respectively. TIME, TIMESTAMP, and DATETIME also require some bytes to store fractions of seconds.

The table above doesn't cover absolutely all data types, but it will provide you with a good starting point. After you've started in a good place, understand that storage requirements are likely to change depending on how many characters you store in a column and what character set you use because some character sets may use more than one byte to store one character because of various reasons.

Choosing the Right Data Type

To choose the right data type for your use case, look at your database and the tables within from a birds-eye view: what data is stored? How often is it updated? Are indexes in use? Any partitions that data is spread across?

The answers to these questions will let you drift toward a data type path that's acceptable both for you and your database. For example, indexes are great if you use them properly – but not all of them may be used in the same way with all data types. Be aware of rules that apply once indexes are in place:

- **If you index columns with BLOB or TEXT data types, be aware that you won't be able to index them in full:** Such data types necessitate the usage of prefix indexes instead. Prefix size depends on what kind of row format is in use – if we use the COMPACT or REDUNDANT row storage format, they can be up to 767 bytes long, and if we use the default (DYNAMIC) or COMPRESSED row storage format, the length limit jumps to 3072 bytes. For those of you indexing on MyISAM, the limit will be set to 1000 bytes.

- **Data types impact index size:** The smaller the size of your index, the fewer paging operations are required. Also, if comparison operations are necessary, comparing integer values will likely be faster than comparing variable character (VARCHAR) values.

Rules also apply for partitioning and other operations running within your database – operations that are directly dependent on your use case. However, inventing a bike here won't be necessary: choosing the proper data type isn't rocket science, and all you need to do is *choose the most precise storage unit for your use case.* In other words, refer to the documentation before making decisions on what data type to choose for values you intend to store in the column in question. For example, if you intend to store integer values from 0 to 100, look into TINYINT. Intend to store larger text values and have a need to index the entire column? Look into VARCHAR, etc.

Optimizing Schemas and Data Types for Big Data

When bigger data sets are involved, the game changes. You don't need to look far to understand that a negative connotation exists: "MySQL with big data? You're crazy?!"

If we take a step back, it isn't hard to understand that everything is possible if you optimize your server and the data within properly. Sure, you may be hard-pressed to run bigger data sets if you find yourself using shared hosting, the rest of it comes down to experience, reading, and learning as you go along, and it isn't hard to run big data sets even on a normal-sized VPS to begin with. I'll give you a great example below:

Out of the following things, what would be the first thing to look at when optimizing your database for big data on a mid-sized server?

1) How many tables are in the database.
2) The amount/variety of queries running within the DBMS.
3) The configuration file (my.ini or my.cnf).
4) Data types.
5) Indexes.

Think for a second: what's the most logical answer? Right – *you will look at the configuration file.* Why? Because that's where everything begins. You may already have answers to all of the most pressing questions (Are your INSERT queries slow? Switch them to LOAD DATA INFILE, etc.), and it's only after you understand the internals of these answers – once you understand what makes them tick – that you're able to understand what makes your database perform the best.

All the things in the list are important, and there's no denying that – we'll get into working with big data in a chapter dedicated to it later on in the book, and you will find out just how crucial the synergy of all of those things working together is for your database – but for now, come back to the schema and data type realm. How do you optimize them for big data?

The question is complex: the answer is simple – you do that by keeping your approach simple and avoiding complex decisions. Keeping things simple will save you a lot of headaches in this realm – you have a lot of data to begin with, so why do you need additional problems? The rules are simple:

1. Structure your tables carefully and with a look into the future.

2. Choose a general use case collation if you don't need anything specific.

3. Keep data types simple.

4. Index what's necessary.

5. If you partition, look into the nuances of partitions and choose the partitioning type most suitable for your use case.

Keep things simple and be aware of the internals of data types to keep yourself out of trouble. Always remember examples – storing integers from 0 to 100? Look into TINYINT. The same applies to other data types – consult the documentation and your colleagues to make informed decisions, and choosing data types for bigger data sets won't seem like such a big problem to solve.

Making informed decisions involves many other things apart from data types, and these actions may become harder when bigger data sets are involved, and that's why this book has an entire chapter dedicated to big data: there's so much more that's needed to be said, so be curious and follow along – I'll tell you about big data sets after you learn to optimize your queries.

Summary

Optimizing storage engines, schemas, and data types isn't an easy task, but it's necessary to complete to advance query performance. Storage engines, schemas, and data types make up the part of the iceberg that's invisible, but crucial to understand for those striving to achieve high performance in their everyday work with MySQL or MariaDB.

High performance can seldom be achieved without optimizing queries themselves, and there's a lot that goes into their internals – now, I'll walk you through how to do just that as well.

CHAPTER 9

Optimizing Queries

Optimizing SQL query performance is a big task to perform. To properly understand why, we have to come back to the basics: data can be inserted, updated, selected, and if necessary, deleted. These four tasks necessitate the existence of four types of SQL queries: those queries are INSERT, UPDATE, SELECT, and DELETE. There are other queries, too, but those four queries form a "CRUD triangle": a triangle of queries that can *Create*, *Read*, *Update*, and/or *Delete* data.

To optimize these queries, we need to understand a simple truth that has been repeated many times throughout the book already to begin with: *queries are tasks – to optimize their performance, we optimize the performance of those tasks or get rid of them.* To begin optimizing task performance or getting rid of them, we must get to know those tasks and to get to know them, we must familiarize ourselves with their internals. Flick back to Chapter 4 – there, we've already familiarized ourselves with the profiling of SELECT queries. I will come back to them a little later, but first, I'll answer the burning question.

Why Optimize SQL Queries?

"I'm so happy my SQL queries are slow today!" said no one ever. Slow SQL queries are the cause of many headaches for you as a developer, the reason for bad reviews for your company, or the cause of lost customers for your boss. In many cases, slow SQL queries are the basis of any slow-performing application: and if we don't optimize them, we can forget about improved database efficiency and performance.

You already know what factors may break your queries: your schema design isn't perfect, data types live in your database without a care in the world, or perhaps you have too few (or too many) partitions or indexes. The answer depends on the type of query you find yourself running. Chapter 4 has shown a way to profile query performance by making use of SHOW PROFILES: profiles include the tasks performed by a query. Profile your queries – profiles will provide a good starting point. After you do that, remember the following:

- *To optimize INSERT queries, delay "informing the database" (commit operations) for as long as possible.* Ideally, commit only after you've inserted a batch of data into the database, then repeat. You want to avoid as much overhead as possible and make use of disk I/O while remembering the basics. Consider inserting data using SELECT queries if the necessary data is in a different table, running SELECT operations when creating a table (example below), and remember that raw data inserting will be significantly faster than inserting data using INSERT.

- *To optimize SELECT queries, make sure your database scans through as little data as possible.* That's it, really – use SELECT column instead of SELECT * (avoid fetching data from all columns inside of a database), don't fetch more rows than needed, and avoid fetching the same data repeatedly.

- *To optimize UPDATE queries, update data in bulk.* Make use of locking, beware of NULL values, keep the load of your database in mind, and make use of WHERE and LIMIT clauses. Sometimes, you can also make use of the DEFAULT clause. More on that in a second.

- *To optimize DELETE queries, run DELETE queries with WHERE or LIMIT clauses, or switch DELETE to TRUNCATE altogether.* Keep in mind that MySQL always provides you with the ability to wipe fractions of data, and the storage engine you use has an impact too.

Some of you may turn to query optimization if you see that a particular query looks rather complex. If you see subqueries, JOINs, functions, GROUP BY operations, and God knows what in one query, the first question that may cross your mind may be "Should this SQL query be chopped up into pieces?" and to answer that question, you will have to remove unknowns from the equation. What is your table structure? What's the path your query takes? Does it use indexes? What indexes does it use and how? etc., and once you remove unknowns from the equation, solve it with knowledge – knowledge on how to optimize specific types of SQL queries.

Optimizing Specific Types of Queries

Right – now how do you optimize specific types of SQL queries? Provided the settings in your my.cnf (or my.ini) file are optimized for a specific storage engine, you need to make use of basic advice and advice specific to your storage engine. That may not make sense for now, but follow along and you will quickly see what I mean.

First, the basics. Once we execute an SQL query, MySQL follows a four-step process:

1. MySQL client sends our SQL query to the server.
2. The database server checks for a hit inside of the query cache.
3. A query execution plan is prepared and executed.
4. Results are returned.

The query cache is the first stop – weird? Shouldn't be; the query cache is the primary reason why some applications making use of MariaDB or MySQL return results in an instant. Commercial search engines can even use this as a marketing trick – "Hey, our search engine returns results within milliseconds! Watch…" The query cache caches result sets corresponding to specific SQL queries: a result set is used anew if a match is found. If the database server cannot return results from the query cache, it will follow a query execution plan and return results.

The Query Cache

If the first thing MySQL stops for is the query cache, can't we just return as many results from the query cache as possible? Well, no, but we can make use of the modes available within the SQL query cache. If we specify SQL_CACHE within a SELECT statement, we enable the DEMAND mode:

```
SELECT SQL_CACHE customer_id, cat FROM products;
```

We can also tell MariaDB that we don't want to use the SQL query cache whatsoever with the SQL_NO_CACHE statement:

```
SELECT SQL_NO_CACHE customer_id, cat FROM products;
```

CHAPTER 9   OPTIMIZING QUERIES

In general, the SQL query cache has three modes – ON, DEMAND, and OFF. ON will allow queries to be cached, while DEMAND will allow you to cache queries on demand, turning the query cache OFF (or setting the have_query_cache variable to NO) will disable the query cache. In MariaDB, 7 variables work with the query cache, and these are as follows.

```
MariaDB [hacking_mysql]> SHOW VARIABLES LIKE '%query_cache%';
+------------------------------+---------+
| Variable_name                | Value   |
+------------------------------+---------+
| have_query_cache             | YES     |
| query_cache_limit            | 1048576 |
| query_cache_min_res_unit     | 4096    |
| query_cache_size             | 1048576 |
| query_cache_strip_comments   | OFF     |
| query_cache_type             | OFF     |
| query_cache_wlock_invalidate | OFF     |
+------------------------------+---------+
7 rows in set (0.006 sec)
```

Figure 9-1. *Variables having something to do with the query cache in MariaDB*

Here's what they mean:

Variable	Meaning
have_query_cache	Does the MariaDB query cache exist? Available values include YES and NO.
query_cache_limit	Results exceeding this size limit won't be cached.
query_cache_min_res_unit	The query cache will have this minimum size in bytes.
query_cache_size	The size of the SQL query cache.
query_cache_strip_comments	Specifies whether to remove all comments from a query before caching it.
query_cache_type	The aforementioned SQL query cache type.
query_cache_wlock_invalidate	If a lock for writing operations is acquired, the SQL queries in the query cache will be invalidated.

While I don't advise relying on the SQL query cache alone, saying that the query cache is not a helpful companion wouldn't be OK either. The query cache is the first stop – the second stop is the query execution plan. The query execution plan will put your queries to the test, and it will show what your database is capable of.

Optimizing INSERT Queries

Our first stop has to do with INSERT queries. Data inside your database appears for a reason: someone inserted it! What a surprise. One can insert data into a database by

1. Using ordinary INSERT queries
2. Using bulk INSERT capabilities
3. Combining SELECT with INSERT
4. Making use of the LOAD DATA INFILE query

Now, from the beginning – first, we have ordinary INSERT queries like this one:

```
INSERT INTO 'demo_table' [col_1,col_2,col_3,...] VALUES ('Value 1',
'Value 2', 'Value 3',...);
INSERT INTO 'demo_table' [col_1,col_2,col_3,...] VALUES ('Value 4',
'Value 5', 'Value 6',...);
```

Such INSERT queries can also be written like so:

```
INSERT INTO 'demo_table' [col_1,col_2,col_3,...] VALUES ('Value 1',
'Value 2', 'Value 3'), ('Value 4', 'Value 5', 'Value 6'), ...;
```

As you can see, specifying the columns is also optional provided values are inserted into all of them at once. The first query is the default INSERT query you will see given as an example in many software engineering and database tutorials – the second one is what you'll most likely see when inspecting a backup. Those two queries do the same thing – they insert data – but the second one is more powerful than the first one, and that's because rows are separated by commas (",") which means more of them can be inserted in one go.

If you want to speed up INSERT query performance even further, look into the `autocommit` parameter. This option can be used to delay COMMIT operations to the very last moment making INSERT query performance faster as a result. A perfect example can be seen below.

CHAPTER 9   OPTIMIZING QUERIES

```
 1  DROP TABLE IF EXISTS `demo_data`;
 2  CREATE TABLE IF NOT EXISTS `demo_data` (
 3    `id` int(20) NOT NULL AUTO_INCREMENT,
 4    `country` varchar(60) NOT NULL DEFAULT 'Not Specified',
 5    `country_code` varchar(100) DEFAULT NULL,
 6    `username` varchar(120) NOT NULL,
 7    `gender` varchar(20) NOT NULL,
 8    `ip_address` varchar(100) NOT NULL DEFAULT '',
 9    PRIMARY KEY (`id`)
10  ) ENGINE=InnoDB AUTO_INCREMENT=11 DEFAULT CHARSET=utf8mb4 COLLATE=utf8mb4_bin;
11
12  autocommit=0;
13  INSERT INTO `demo_data` (`id`, `country`, `country_code`, `username`, `gender`, `ip_address`) VALUES
14  (1, 'England', 'GB', 'randomuser', 'Male', '127.0.0.1'),
15  (2, 'Ukraine', 'UA', 'randomuser2', 'Female', '127.0.0.1'),
16  (3, 'Sweden', 'SE', 'randomuser3', 'Male', '127.0.0.1'),
17  (4, 'Finland', 'FI', 'randomuser4', 'Male', '127.0.0.1'),
18  (5, 'Norway', 'NO', 'randomuser5', 'Male', '127.0.0.1'),
19  (6, 'Denmark', 'DK', 'randomuser6', 'Male', '127.0.0.1'),
20  (7, 'Hungary', 'HU', 'randomuser7', 'Male', '127.0.0.1'),
21  (8, 'Argentina', 'AR', 'randomuser8', 'Male', '127.0.0.1'),
22  (9, 'Germany', 'DE', 'randomuser9', 'Male', '127.0.0.1'),
23  (10, 'Japan', 'JP', 'randomuser10', 'Male', '127.0.0.1');
24  COMMIT;
```

Figure 9-2. autocommit=0 inside of a backup

Only a single INSERT too! Isn't that cool?

You can also make use of locking and unlocking. To do that, first lock your table by making use of LOCK TABLE [table_name], then insert your data, and finally, unlock the table by making use of UNLOCK TABLE [table_name]. If you find your rows to have longer VARCHAR columns, insert a smaller number of rows at a time.

The next way to improve INSERT query performance would be to combine INSERTs with SELECT queries like so.

```
MariaDB [hacking_mysql]> CREATE TABLE demo_data LIKE mock_data;
Query OK, 0 rows affected (0.044 sec)

MariaDB [hacking_mysql]> INSERT INTO demo_data SELECT * FROM mock_data;
Query OK, 20000 rows affected (0.834 sec)
Records: 20000  Duplicates: 0  Warnings: 0
```

Figure 9-3. INSERT INTO ... SELECT

Inserting 20k rows takes less than a second – not bad, huh? Use a SSD or a NVMe, and you will likely see even faster results. Needless to say, INSERT INTO ... SELECT queries will likely be slower than ordinary SELECT queries because our example will write to a temporary file, where SELECT queries will read data from a file on the disk, but this example is a certainly viable option for those scattering their data across multiple tables/databases.

If you find yourself working with bigger data sets (>=100M rows), neither approach will work; that's because INSERT queries come with a lot of overhead that must be removed for the best performance on bigger data sets. LOAD DATA INFILE is an awesome fit for the task – it is a query specifically designed to load big data sets from a file into the disk by

- Requiring little overhead for data parsing
- Allowing users to skip lines or columns
- Allowing users to load data only into specific columns
- Handling errors related to duplicate keys

LOAD DATA INFILE with some of the most frequently used options looks like this:

```
LOAD DATA [LOCAL] INFILE [REPLACE|IGNORE] INTO TABLE `demo_table`
[PARTITION (p1)] [CHARACTER SET charset] [FIELDS|COLUMNS TERIMNATED BY '|']
[IGNORE number LINES|ROWS];
```

As you can probably tell, LOAD DATA INFILE is a powerful beast. Let's tame it by breaking it down:

- The optional LOCAL option specifies that the file is located on the host owned by the client rather than the server.
- REPLACE or IGNORE options will let you replace characters or ignore certain lines/rows.
- The PARTITION option will load the data into a specific partition if any is specified.
- The CHARACTER SET option will use a specified character set when loading the data into the database.
- The FIELDS|COLUMNS TERMINATED BY option will allow you to specify what character denotes another column. In other words, what character would tell MySQL/MariaDB that the data should be inserted into another column?
- The IGNORE number LINES|ROWS option will let you specify the number of lines or rows that should be ignored. Useful when the first line denotes the structure of the file, etc.

CHAPTER 9 OPTIMIZING QUERIES

There are many more options, and those options combined with the capability of MySQL/MariaDB instances being configured for InnoDB make `LOAD DATA INFILE` a really powerful force that should be reckoned with.

If you are working with bigger data sets, keep in mind that you can also make use of the `DEFAULT` keyword when creating tables. This keyword lets you specify a default value of the column, and as such, MySQL/MariaDB will pre-fill the column with a specified value without you needing to run any `UPDATE` queries afterward, saving you time. Look at the example above once again – *when creating the country column, I've also specified that by default, its value should be set to "Not specified."*

Last but not least, one can insert data into MyISAM tables by switching data files from one server to another. Remember – MyISAM doesn't come with an attached filespace (the same cannot be said about InnoDB), which means that if you find yourself working with data and/or index files like so.

Name	Date modified	Type	Size
db.opt	4/14/2024 15:14	OPT File	1 KB
demo.frm	5/29/2024 2:26	FRM File	1 KB
demo.ibd	5/29/2024 4:55	IBD File	64 KB
demo_data.frm	7/4/2024 1:49	FRM File	4 KB
demo_data.ibd	7/4/2024 1:50	IBD File	10,240 KB
demo_partitioned#p#partition_1.ibd	5/29/2024 4:55	IBD File	64 KB
demo_partitioned#p#partition_2.ibd	5/29/2024 4:55	IBD File	64 KB
demo_partitioned.frm	5/29/2024 2:33	FRM File	1 KB
demo_partitioned.par	5/29/2024 2:33	PAR File	1 KB
demo_table.frm	6/30/2024 18:42	FRM File	1 KB
demo_table.ibd	6/30/2024 19:55	IBD File	64 KB
json_demo.frm	6/30/2024 18:02	FRM File	1 KB
json_demo.ibd	6/30/2024 19:55	IBD File	64 KB
messages.frm	7/4/2024 3:34	FRM File	5 KB
messages.MYD	7/4/2024 3:34	MYD File	5 KB
messages.MYI	7/4/2024 3:34	MYI File	22 KB
messages_old.frm	5/20/2024 20:12	FRM File	2 KB
messages_old.ibd	5/20/2024 23:17	IBD File	80 KB
mock_data.frm	7/4/2024 1:46	FRM File	4 KB
mock_data.ibd	7/4/2024 1:46	IBD File	10,240 KB

Figure 9-4. *MYD and MYI files belonging to MyISAM*

You can copy/move them between servers without any hassle: that means that if you have two servers and need to store data based on the MyISAM storage engine, you can create a MyISAM-based table, insert data/work with it there, and copy underlying the data and index files to copy/move the data to another server. Cool – but only for `COUNT` queries.

Optimizing SELECT Queries

Once INSERT queries are out of the way, look at someone they've formed a very close relationship with over the years – SELECT queries. SELECT queries are pretty self-explanatory: they select data from tables within our database. The functionality of these SQL queries is rather simple, and many of us understand that they're only a small part of our database; nonetheless, slow SELECT query performance can have a drastic impact on the performance of both your database and your application.

One day, I was working on the BreachDirectory data breach search engine as usual, and then I noticed that pages started to load abnormally slowly. I've started searching for a cause and determined that there was a customer who had provided BreachDirectory with a file containing more than a million accounts and had asked the database to check whether all of them were at risk of identity theft at once. A million accounts at once – and I thought the rate limiter was working correctly. Not in this case. The issue was promptly fixed, but it just goes to demonstrate that SELECT query performance is no joke: a couple of mistakes here and there could spell doom for your database.

Have a look through the core functionality of your application and search (CTRL+F) for "SELECT ... FROM": what queries do you see? What data do they ask your database to provide and what functionality within your application do they account for? It'd be a safe bet that your application uses a bunch of SELECT queries: It'd be a safe bet because almost everything within a modern application is stored inside of a database and provided to an application from the database too. Remember SHOW PROCESSLIST? Start from there. I'm using a local MariaDB server, so I've employed mysqlslap for load emulation and used another CLI to check the load of the database at the same time, so my results look pretty awful formatting-wise, yours will look nicer.

```
mysqlslap --user=root --host=localhost --concurrency=100 --iterations=10 --number-char-cols=5 --auto-generate-sql
Benchmark
        Average number of seconds to run all queries: 1.017 seconds
        Minimum number of seconds to run all queries: 0.296 seconds
        Maximum number of seconds to run all queries: 1.688 seconds
        Number of clients running queries: 100
        Average number of queries per client: 0

-
```

Figure 9-5. Emulating load on MariaDB with mysqlslap

CHAPTER 9   OPTIMIZING QUERIES

```
MariaDB [hacking_mysql]> SHOW PROCESSLIST;
+------+---------------------+------------------+---------------+---------+------+----------------+---------------------------------------------------------------------------+
| Id   | User                | Host             | db            | Command | Time | State          | Info                                                                      |
|      |                     |                  |               |         |      |                | Progress                                                                  |
+------+---------------------+------------------+---------------+---------+------+----------------+---------------------------------------------------------------------------+
| 1011 | root                | localhost:54151  | hacking_mysql | Query   |    0 | starting       | SHOW PROCESSLIST                                                          |
|      |                     |                  |               |         |      |                | 0.000                                                                     |
| 1012 | root                | localhost:54152  | mysqlslap     | Sleep   |    0 |                | NULL                                                                      |
|      |                     |                  |               |         |      |                | 0.000                                                                     |
| 1214 | root                | localhost:54355  | mysqlslap     | Query   |    0 | Sending data   | SELECT intcol1,charcol1,charcol2,charcol3,charcol4,charcol5 FROM t1       |
|      |                     |                  |               |         |      |                | 0.000                                                                     |
| 1216 | root                | localhost:54354  | mysqlslap     | Sleep   |    0 |                | NULL                                                                      |
|      |                     |                  |               |         |      |                | 0.000                                                                     |
| 1217 | root                | localhost:54357  | mysqlslap     | Query   |    0 | Commit         | INSERT INTO t1 VALUES (15314,'zI3eHq5asS64S6RF7xrPqk1IzIM8xQZ5yqBgdi93Sm   |
| KHNQq5mmApfDMIKHbvC6qpFWxOFF |         |                  |               |         |      |                | 0.000                                                                     |
| 1218 | root                | localhost:54358  | mysqlslap     | Sleep   |    0 |                | NULL                                                                      |
|      |                     |                  |               |         |      |                | 0.000                                                                     |
| 1219 | root                | localhost:54359  | mysqlslap     | Query   |    0 | Writing to net | SELECT intcol1,charcol1,charcol2,charcol3,charcol4,charcol5 FROM t1       |
|      |                     |                  |               |         |      |                | 0.000                                                                     |
| 1220 | root                | localhost:54363  | mysqlslap     | Sleep   |    0 |                | NULL                                                                      |
|      |                     |                  |               |         |      |                | 0.000                                                                     |
| 1221 | root                | localhost:54360  | mysqlslap     | Sleep   |    0 |                | NULL                                                                      |
|      |                     |                  |               |         |      |                | 0.000                                                                     |
| 1222 | root                | localhost:54362  | mysqlslap     | Sleep   |    0 |                | NULL                                                                      |
|      |                     |                  |               |         |      |                | 0.000                                                                     |
| 1223 | root                | localhost:54361  | mysqlslap     | Query   |    0 | Commit         | INSERT INTO t1 VALUES (12300,'SFtC2wd9sJc1Mr00yKKPTohiEDqiggkLJcltpRESzk  |
| qoxxPQANBAp4f3FkHemrERt97gP4 |         |                  |               |         |      |                | 0.000                                                                     |
| 1224 | root                | localhost:54364  | mysqlslap     | Sleep   |    0 |                | NULL                                                                      |
|      |                     |                  |               |         |      |                | 0.000                                                                     |
| 1226 | root                | localhost:54366  | mysqlslap     | Query   |    0 | Sending data   | SELECT intcol1,charcol1,charcol2,charcol3,charcol4,charcol5 FROM t1       |
|      |                     |                  |               |         |      |                | 0.000                                                                     |
| 1225 | root                | localhost:54365  | mysqlslap     | Query   |    0 | starting       | INSERT INTO t1 VALUES (23290,'nyXm5LuWFnfqvjJaokZoe0RODDYqImkwTxddJYFP6x  |
| mEvWQ2Ftc6ywjafhPEOOj9wduRm3 |         |                  |               |         |      |                | 0.000                                                                     |
| 1227 | root                | localhost:54368  | mysqlslap     | Sleep   |    0 |                | NULL                                                                      |
|      |                     |                  |               |         |      |                | 0.000                                                                     |
| 1229 | unauthenticated user| connecting host  | NULL          | Connect |    0 | login          | NULL                                                                      |
|      |                     |                  |               |         |      |                | 0.000                                                                     |
```

Figure 9-6. *Output of SHOW PROCESSLIST after running mysqlslap*

It's worth noting that SHOW PROCESSLIST also has a couple of states allowing you to understand what state your database is in regard to a certain query. These states can tell you a lot of information, especially if you include the FULL statement. Here are a couple of states that SHOW PROCESSLIST can provide

- starting means that a query is just starting and hasn't performed any tasks yet.

- Sending data means that a query is sending data to a server and waiting for a response from it. If you see this state and your application performance is grinding to a halt, queries with this state should be suspect.

- Commit means that a query is committing data to a server.

- Writing to net means that a query is writing packets to a network interface.

- Waiting for source to send event means that the database is waiting for a source to send data.

- Has read all relay log; waiting for the replica I/O thread to update it means that a query has read the relay log (events describing changes in the database) and is waiting for the I/O processes of the replica.

- NULL means that the database is doing nothing in regard to the query (it's probably just in the list because your SHOW PROCESSLIST query "caught" it just before it finished).

Familiarizing yourself with SHOW PROCESSLIST is a necessity – only once you understand which state your queries are in when observing them as they run in your database can you start to optimize them.

Once you understand the state your queries are in, you can start to investigate. The investigation process shouldn't take long: identify the problematic query by looking at all of the columns, identify the source of the query, and start crunching through the code. As you crunch through the code, search for answers to the following questions:

1. **What's the state of your query?** What query state does SHOW PROCESSLIST depict? Why did the query stop there?

2. **What data does the SQL query work with?** Why is the query running in your database in the first place and what are you trying to achieve?

3. **What is the SQL query reading?** Take a close look at your query – what data are your SELECT queries reading?

4. **Does the SQL query run multiple times?** Does the query run as part of a loop? How many times does the loop repeat and what is it used for?

5. **Is the same column queried multiple times?** There have been cases where multiple queries would query the same column to obtain similar data – is that the case for you?

6. **Is the query using indexes or partitions?** If yes, what indexes and partitions are in use, and if not, is there anything that could hinder the performance of such a query type?

7. **Is the query using subqueries/stored procedures?** If yes, why and what kind of subqueries/stored procedures are being used?

8. **What parts of the query do *you* think would be problematic for the database?** After all, you have something to do with the application – ask your gut!

The answers to these questions will provide you with a great starting point and will likely lead you to a destination from where you can start optimizing your query performance. Start from the top: the state of your SQL query alone should be enough for you to realize what makes the query "stuck" and, as a result, slows down the performance of your application. Then, dig into the data your query works with: I'd be unsurprised if you told me that what you have is a query like so:

```
SELECT * FROM `demo_table` INNER JOIN `demo_table2` ON `demo_table`.`col` = `demo_table2`.`col`;
```

Once you have a query, dig into things surrounding it with EXPLAIN and understand whether the query runs multiple times, whether it uses indexes or partitions, subqueries or INNER JOINs, and anything in that realm. Once that's cleared, approach everything in small steps:

1. **Investigate the table(s):** How many rows does it have and what does its structure look like? For those using SQL clients like DbVisualizer, DBeaver, or appliances like phpMyAdmin, this step will be made easier, but those using the CLI will make use of the DESCRIBE statement (see example below).

2. **What's happening with your columns?** How many columns are you using? What data types and collations are being used? Why? What's your use case and are your data types and collations optimized for it?

3. **Does your query try to help you?** Is your query running in a "vanilla" way or does it use indexes or partitions? If yes, what types of indexes or partitions are used? What path does your query take?

```
MariaDB [hacking_mysql]> DESCRIBE demo_table;
+-------------+---------+------+-----+---------+-------+
| Field       | Type    | Null | Key | Default | Extra |
+-------------+---------+------+-----+---------+-------+
| varchar_col | char(1) | YES  |     | NULL    |       |
| int_col     | int(11) | YES  |     | NULL    |       |
| text_col    | text    | YES  |     | NULL    |       |
+-------------+---------+------+-----+---------+-------+
3 rows in set (0.089 sec)
```

Figure 9-7. DESCRIBE in action

CHAPTER 9   OPTIMIZING QUERIES

4. **How much data are you asking your database for?** This is the most likely mistake of yours. Is it that surprising that your database is grinding to a halt when you are asking it for millions of rows in one go?

Few questions – a lot of answers. The answer to the first question will determine the scope of your actions concerning the table structure, and the table structure determines the course of action for your SELECT queries. After you identify what columns are being used by your query, take into consideration the indexes or partitions in use – once that's out of the way, look into how many rows are returned.

To understand SELECT queries on a deeper level, remember the SQL query profiler. In other words, remember the tasks your SELECT query goes through – to optimize the query, you have to optimize the tasks in that query, right? Go back to the fourth chapter of the book for a bit – there, I have provided you with an image depicting a simple SELECT SQL query and provided explanations on the 24 tasks it goes through when marching toward completion.

To optimize those tasks, you need the following:

Task	How to Optimize the Task?
Starting	Have a database server with an Internet connection (hey, basics are important.)
Checking permissions	Make sure the user you use to run the SELECT query has the necessary permissions to run it – a SELECT permission will be necessary unless your SELECT doesn't access any tables.
OptimizingExecutingSending data	Make sure your SELECT scans through as little data as possible.
Query endCommit	To make COMMIT operations faster, enlarge the size of the InnoDB buffer pool.

Now that you remembered the internals, look into the output of a basic SELECT query using EXPLAIN once again.

CHAPTER 9   OPTIMIZING QUERIES

```
MariaDB [hacking_mysql]> EXPLAIN SELECT * FROM demo_data WHERE username = 'mebrallg';
+----+-------------+-----------+------+---------------+--------------+---------+-------+------+-----------------------+
| id | select_type | table     | type | possible_keys | key          | key_len | ref   | rows | Extra                 |
+----+-------------+-----------+------+---------------+--------------+---------+-------+------+-----------------------+
|  1 | SIMPLE      | demo_data | ref  | username_idx  | username_idx | 482     | const |    1 | Using index condition |
+----+-------------+-----------+------+---------------+--------------+---------+-------+------+-----------------------+
1 row in set (0.001 sec)
```

Figure 9-8. *Basic SELECT query*

Flick back to Chapter 5 to remember what each of those columns means in detail, and then remember how SELECT queries are optimized. Remember how your query looks like and what constraints mean the world for your SELECT clause, and then optimize those constraints.

Optimizing Indexes and Constraints

The first stop for optimizing SELECT query performance involves adding indexes onto a column. You've probably used indexes before, and if your SELECT queries are still slow, that's because it still doesn't know the quickest path to your data. Indexes help your database provide the SELECT query with the path toward your data – but they have a couple of types, and they must be chosen properly. I'll get into the details involving indexes in a chapter dedicated to them, but to properly understand them, you would need to brush up anyway. Basics first:

- An index is a synonym for a key and vice versa.

- All indexes have a name or a title.

- All indexes have a length – that's the size of the index in bytes (not unique rows within the index or anything like that.)

- Indexes have a couple of types. To make SELECTs faster, most of you will use B-Tree indexes, and I'll let you in on the secrets of all of the available index types in the chapter specific to indexes later on.

- Indexes act as pointers toward data allowing our database to eliminate unnecessary rows from consideration.

- Most of you using an index will benefit from a faster table scan.

- An index scan is always faster than a disk scan, but not all index appliances allow for an index scan.

- Indexes must be applied properly and account for the fact that MySQL doesn't error when multiple indexes of the same type are in place on the same column.

As far as indexes are concerned, keep in mind that the default type of indexes available in MySQL refers to B-Tree indexes and that B-Tree indexes are sorted beings. B-Tree indexes being sorted means that they can traverse trees from top to bottom recursively, and since that's the case, they make searches with exact search operators as fast as never before at the same time crumbling down on disk space. These specifics of indexes allow for multiple different properties to be built around them, and MySQL has many available index profiles (types) including spatial indexes, unique indexes, fulltext indexes, descending indexes, and primary keys, but to make SELECT SQL queries faster, we're going to focus exclusively on B-Tree indexes for now and dig into the others in the chapter dedicated to indexes.

B-tree indexes are a short abbreviation for Balanced Tree indexes. These types of SQL indexes are the default index type available in MySQL Server and all of its counterparts like MariaDB and Percona Server. On a high level, such indexes are lists of ordered values that are divided into a couple of ranges.

B-Tree indexes are useful for SELECT queries because they associate rows with components that help reach them in a quick fashion – keys. That's the precise reason why such indexes will facilitate the speed of our search engines or anything search-related.

Having a B-Tree index on a column doesn't mean that MySQL will use it though: MySQL will use indexes according to rules and only if our queries adhere to certain standards, but in general, MySQL will consider using B-Tree indexes for queries that are searching for exact matches of data. Such queries include comparison operators with the dominant equality sign ("=") as well as queries utilizing the less than/more than signs. In other words, B-tree indexes can satisfy most of those SELECT queries:

```
SELECT ... FROM 'hacking_mysql' WHERE 'column' = 'value' <...>;
SELECT ... FROM 'hacking_mysql' WHERE 'column' < value <...>;
SELECT ... FROM 'hacking_mysql' WHERE 'column' > value <...>;
SELECT ... FROM 'hacking_mysql' WHERE 'column' =< value <...>;
SELECT ... FROM 'hacking_mysql' WHERE 'column' >= value <...>;
SELECT ... FROM `hacking_mysql` WHERE `column` => value <...>;
```

Note how I didn't say that B-Tree indexes can satisfy all of those queries because the last one wouldn't be satisfied either way – MySQL would return a syntax error because of our use of the "=>" operator. As a workaround, you may consider using the "equal to or less" ("=<") operator or the "equal to or more" operator ("=>") to achieve the necessary objectives.

Also, take note that not all of the compared values are strings and that all of the aforementioned queries have signs notifying you that they're incomplete – that's because you're unlikely to see "simple" SQL queries in the wild, and every operation completed in addition to equality checks will provide some more strain for your indexes and database as a result.

Anyway, back to B-Tree indexes: the reason they speed SELECT queries up is because they provide a "key" for our database to faster access required data. They unlock doors and when combined with other things that improve the performance of read-based queries and proper database design, they can improve our query performance by tens, hundreds, or even thousands of times, and that's because they exchange disk space for speed and if our queries are using them, we can avoid a table scan and use index scan or index seek operations instead: an *index scan* occurs when our database accesses index pages to help us access our data while an *index seek* refers to our database accessing selective rows. If you find yourself in the shoes of making SELECT queries faster, understanding this will be crucial.

For advice on *how* to index for performance, turn to the chapter on indexing, but here's some high-level advice to increase the performance of your SELECT queries. I'll start from a list, then I'll elaborate further down the line:

- **Access as little data as possible**: Switch SELECT * to SELECT 'column' if possible.

- **Look into JOIN operations**: The usage of JOIN operations would necessitate MySQL to filter data from the first table and the second table. That's not to say that JOIN operations would automatically be slower than ordinary SELECT queries (timing queries is always a good idea), but I've heard of cases where tens of SELECT statements were optimized into a couple of JOIN queries and those JOIN queries had improved overall performance drastically.

- **Be wary of condition-based filtering**: When condition-based filtering is used (i.e., when your table has the AND, BETWEEN, and/or other clauses), additional strain on your SELECT query is applied. Look into the data you require your database to retrieve and examine the character sets and tables, then think: perhaps there is a way to split the query into multiple SELECT queries? If yes, would all SELECT queries be a necessity to complete your selected task? If no, is that AND/BETWEEN/IN() condition necessary?

- **Be aware of the BETWEEN ... AND and the IN clauses**: Many say that BETWEEN should outperform IN if your database is optimized for read operations, but again, take this advice with a grain of salt: performance would depend on whether an index can be used or is your database necessitating a full-table scan.

- **Be aware of nuances with** NULL: Many of the readers of this book will know that NULL necessitates certain functionality within partitions to work differently in that NULL values may be inserted into the lowest possible partition and that statement has truth in itself, but you should also keep in mind that MySQL may treat IS NULL no differently than other clauses in your database. Try running the EXPLAIN clause on a query that's searching for NULL values within your database: it wouldn't take long to notice that your database will likely optimize the query in the same way as it would optimize a SELECT query with an equality operator. Interesting, right?

- **Index to help the** ORDER BY **clause**: If your index contains all of the columns you're ordering by in the order you're ordering by (i.e., INDEX(a,b) will satisfy ORDER BY a,b), the database optimizer may avoid sorting thus making SQL queries faster.

- **Make use of the** LIMIT **clause**: The LIMIT clause is (unsurprisingly) used to limit the rows that are returned. For ordinary SELECTs where the LIMIT clause isn't specified and the table is rather huge, MySQL would only return 25 rows per page and allow you to flick to other pages. In this case, returning only one row (LIMIT [any number],1) will be significantly faster no matter how much data exists in a database, and you may also want to omit the HAVING clause from a query that has the LIMIT clause to see if it runs faster. If you find yourself using LIMIT together with ORDER BY, consider using an index on the ordered columns to speed up the query too.

- **Use tricks to avoid full table scans**: For SELECT queries, full table scans are rarely a great idea. Use EXPLAIN with the ALL clause and observe the type column to tell when MySQL decides to use a full table scan, and you can also take a look into FORCE INDEX to force MySQL to use an index instead of conducting full table scans.

- **Be wary of the DISTINCT clause**: If DISTINCT is used in conjunction with ORDER BY, your database may necessitate the usage of temporary tables. If you have a lot of data to search through and need to use the DISTINCT clause, perhaps it could be better to create a separate table containing distinct values, index a column or two, and use the table instead? Also, see the explanation below.

For those of you who work with really big data sets, the DISTINCT clause may be the cause of even more issues; if you have hundreds of millions of records or even more, look into the uniq statement in Unix (the statement would also be available on a Windows architecture if Cygwin or a similar appliance would be installed).

This command would be very useful to remove duplicates for those that take backups using SELECT ... INTO OUTFILE or work with raw data to begin with – then, you would improve the performance of your SQL queries "on three fronts":

1) The size of your backups would be significantly smaller (LOAD DATA INFILE/SELECT ... INTO OUTFILE doesn't contain any INSERT statements.)

2) Since there would be no INSERT statements and your database would deal with raw data, your database would deal with less overhead (raw data is always "lighter").

3) Since uniq would read raw data, it would be able to deduct duplicates from files with billions of records within milliseconds.

See how easy everything becomes? Of course, to properly optimize SELECT queries, you would also need to dive deeper into indexes and partitions, but that's no problem either – this book has separate chapters on those, too. The problem is related to your UPDATE and DELETE queries – don't forget to optimize those too.

Optimizing UPDATE Queries

To optimize UPDATE queries, one needs to follow the advice provided by MySQL as well. The problem on this front is that MySQL isn't exactly clear on how to do that: the documentation provides users with three paragraphs of information essentially saying "optimize UPDATEs like you would optimize SELECTs with an overhead for INSERTs." Confusing, right?

It gets a little less confusing when you understand what UPDATE queries do – they update the data in the tables within our database. So, how do we make the updating process faster? First, let's look into the internals of a basic UPDATE query:

UPDATE 'demo_table' SET [column] = ['value'] WHERE [details] [LIMIT x];

Here:

- **The column after SET defines a specific column we need to update.** If we need to update a singular column, specifying the column here is enough. If we're updating the values of multiple columns, these need to be specified after we specify the first value of the first column (before the WHERE clause.)

- **The details after the WHERE clause let us refine what data we need to update.** We can specify that we only want to update fields that have ID values higher than 500, etc.

- **The LIMIT clause lets us define how many rows we want to update.** A LIMIT 0,50 clause would update the first 50 rows, LIMIT 50,100 would update 50 rows starting from the 50th row, etc. Essentially, the LIMIT clause lets us define an offset we need to start the update and limit its reign, hence the title.

CHAPTER 9   OPTIMIZING QUERIES

Now, how exactly to optimize UPDATE queries in our database? First, there are a couple of tips we have to keep in mind:

- **Indexes will likely slow your queries down**: That doesn't mean "remove all indexes on all columns you're updating data in," but rather, be wary of the internal functions of indexes and UPDATE queries. In other words, be mindful of how UPDATE queries interact with indexes. For example, if you're working with a rather small number of rows, indexes aren't likely to be a very big deal, but if your data set is larger and as the UPDATE query needs to update the data and the index itself, it will likely take a while to complete. There are workarounds around this (I'll let you in on a secret in a second), but always be wary of such behavior before you optimize such types of queries.

- **Partitioning will have nuances**: Partitions are likely to slow down UPDATE queries too because if partition A holds integer values from 0 to 1000 and partition B holds integer values from 1000 to 2000, and we update a column to specify that its value would be 1700 like so:

  ```
  UPDATE 'demo_table' SET 'int_partitioned_column' = 1700;
  ```

  if the previous value was lower than 1000, our database will need to switch the values from partition A to partition B. This will take some time as the partition will need to be updated together with the data, and you would also need to keep in mind that the updated data will now reside in a different partition than usual.

- **Keep locking in mind**: If you see that your UPDATE queries are underperforming, one thing you could try is locking the table, performing many updates one after the other, and then unlocking it. Such an approach is likely to be faster than running a single UPDATE at once and would look like so:

  ```
  LOCK TABLE [READ|WRITE] `demo_table`;
  UPDATE `demo_table` SET `column` = 'value' LIMIT 0,10000;
  UPDATE `demo_table` SET `column` = 'value' LIMIT 10000,20000;
  UPDATE `demo_table` SET `column` = 'value' LIMIT 20000,30000;
  ...
  UNLOCK TABLE `demo_table`;
  ```

Think of this approach as turning autocommit to 0, inserting many rows, and then committing a transaction in INSERT queries.

For those updating bigger sets of data (think millions, billions of rows), things change; if you don't find much luck in locking and unlocking and need to update all rows in a column at once, keep in mind that there's also a neat workaround you can use to replace the UPDATE clause and avoid the overhead that comes with inserting data into tables, too.

Suppose you have a table with millions of rows inside of it – I'm using 20,000 as an example – and want to have one column with the same value, but have little space on the disk (using ALTER to update data is likely to make a copy of the table on the disk if the table is rather large.) Here's how to approach the problem:

1. Make a copy of the table using a method that doesn't come with much overhead when reimporting the data (back up raw data instead of INSERT statements using SELECT INTO OUTFILE – I've talked about this before):

```
MariaDB [hacking_mysql]> SELECT * FROM demo_data INTO OUTFILE 'C:/wamp64/tmp/demodata.txt' FIELDS TERMINATED BY ':';
Query OK, 20000 rows affected, 1 warning (0.080 sec)
```

2. Create a table identical to the table you're working with by making use of a SHOW CREATE TABLE statement or just running CREATE TABLE `another_table` LIKE `present_table`, and before you insert data into that table, make sure that the column that you need to update has a value that's necessary by default (for this example, I set this column to a value of "Good Value").

```
CREATE TABLE `demo_data` (
  `id` INT(20) NOT NULL AUTO_INCREMENT PRIMARY KEY,
  `country` VARCHAR(50) NOT NULL,
  `country_code` VARCHAR(50) NOT NULL,
  `username` VARCHAR(50) NOT NULL,
  `gender` VARCHAR(50) NOT NULL,
  `ip_address` VARCHAR(50) NOT NULL,
  `column_you_need_to_update` VARCHAR(50) NOT NULL DEFAULT 'Good Value'
) ENGINE = InnoDB;
```

Figure 9-9. Default value on a column

CHAPTER 9   OPTIMIZING QUERIES

3. Create the table, and then re-import the data without specifying the column that has the default value (it will be populated by default) – you may also want to add an IGNORE clause before the INTO TABLE statement to ignore any errors that might arise in connection with this query.

```sql
CREATE TABLE `demo_data` (
  `id` INT(20) NOT NULL AUTO_INCREMENT PRIMARY KEY,
  `country` VARCHAR(50) NOT NULL,
  `country_code` VARCHAR(50) NOT NULL,
  `username` VARCHAR(50) NOT NULL,
  `gender` VARCHAR(50) NOT NULL,
  `ip_address` VARCHAR(50) NOT NULL,
  `column_you_need_to_update` VARCHAR(50) NOT NULL DEFAULT 'Good Value'
) ENGINE = InnoDB;

LOAD DATA INFILE 'C:/wamp64/tmp/demodata.txt' INTO TABLE demo_data FIELDS TERMINATED BY ':'
(id,country,country_code,username,gender,ip_address);
```

Figure 9-10. *Importing data into a table with a column with a default value*

4. Import the data, and then observe the value of the column you need to update – it should be set to "Good Value" (or any other value you specify) by default – now, there's no need for an additional UPDATE.

ip_address	column_you_need_to_update
127.0.0.1	Good Value
127.0.0.2	Good Value
127.0.0.3	Good Value
127.0.0.4	Good Value
127.0.0.5	Good Value
127.0.0.6	Good Value
127.0.0.7	Good Value

Figure 9-11. *A column with an updated value*

Be aware of the internals of ALTER too – for some developers, it's an issue of concern when they, "for no reason," run out of disk space when ALTER queries are being run. If you update a Table X:

1. A copy of the Table X is made. Let's call it Table Y.

2. Data existing within Table X is copied into Table Y.

3. All of the updates are performed within Table Y.

4. Table Y is switched with Table X and destroyed.

That's the reason your ALTERs may run out of disk space – be wary of their internals.

For those of you still using MyISAM, remember that MyISAM isn't "connected" with any tablespace unlike InnoDB, and that means you can make use of multiple "tactics" impossible to use in InnoDB. One of those tactics has to do with moving MyISAM data to another server that has "better gear": more RAM, better processor, or other things and is optimized for MyISAM, updating data there, and moving the data (the .MYD data file itself) back into the original server – your data will be updated. Stupid? Perhaps. Working? Yes.

Optimizing DELETE Queries

When it comes to deleting data, it's really nothing revolutionary either – we use the DELETE query. Well, not in all cases – one can delete all of the rows in a table by making use of the TRUNCATE SQL query, and it will be significantly faster than DELETEs, but in many cases, we're deleting subsets of data and not wiping the entire table off the face of the earth.

To optimize the deletion of data:

1. **Make use of the WHERE and LIMIT clauses**: WHERE can be used to filter out specific data we do/don't want to delete, whereas LIMIT can help us limit the number of rows that are deleted.

2. **Be mindful of the impacts of indexes and partitions**: Again, be wary that indexes and partitions will slow down the data deletion process for the same reasons they slow down updates.

3. **Be mindful of storage engines**: Remember MyISAM not being related to a tablespace? That means that one can delete the .MYD in the directory of a database to delete a table, delete the .MYI file to delete an index on a table, etc.

4. **Wipe fractions of data if necessary**: If you have a lot of data, consider creating a new table with the AS clause to avoid the DELETE clause altogether, then drop the old table. For example, `CREATE TABLE x AS SELECT a,b FROM table_y;` would make the table X only consist of two columns – a and b – from the table Y. No other data.

Again, DELETEs are nothing revolutionary – make sure to explicitly tell your database what data you're deleting and on what terms (use the available WHERE and LIMIT clauses), and you should be good to go.

Optimizing Queries for Big Data, Avoiding Deadlocks, and Other Query Optimization Tips

When it comes to bigger data sets, remember how you've optimized your database to deal with big data: what did you do? You've most likely increased the size of the InnoDB buffer pool and the InnoDB log files to adhere to the amounts of data you're storing in a database, right? Did you make any other changes? What parameters/parts of your database were impacted by those changes?

You didn't optimize your database for no reason – make use of those changes! To work with queries involving bigger data sets, make use of the query optimization advice provided above, and always remember to approach everything in small steps: only select data that's necessary for you to use, insert bigger data sets while avoiding overhead posed by INSERT queries (use LOAD DATA INFILE instead), update data in chunks, and delete data making use of the WHERE and LIMIT clauses and other advice.

No matter what kind of advice you elect to follow, if you want to become a seasoned DBA, you will need to trek through hot and cold. Sometimes your database will hit you with something that looks completely out of the ordinary like a deadlock or two: what then? Deadlock situations occur when our database is completing different transactions, but none of them can proceed because each of them is holding resources that are necessary for the other transaction to complete. Transaction A is unable to proceed because it's waiting for transaction B, and transaction B is unable to proceed because it's waiting for transaction A. Deadlocks are essentially locks "with no way out."

How to solve such issues? Easy – follow the advice in the documentation of your specific DBMS in question and remember that the most complex problems often require the simplest solutions – deadlocks are not an exception to the rule. To solve issues posed by deadlocks, restart a transaction and make sure that the so-called *Coffman's conditions* aren't present in your database – those conditions often create opportunities for deadlocks to manifest:

1. **Mutual exclusion**: One or more resources should be held in a manner that prevents itself from being shared with other resources.

2. **Holding of resources**: One or more processes should hold a resource and request more resources, some or all of which should be held by another process.

3. **Inability to "release" resources**: The process holding resources shouldn't be able to "let go" of them.

4. **Circular wait**: Finally, the final predicate for deadlocks is a circular wait. A circular wait is an occurrence where one process is waiting for another process to finish, while another process is waiting for the first process to finish, etc.

To help your queries be the best version of themselves, avoid these conditions – by avoiding them, you will avoid deadlocks.

Deadlocks are not the only thing you should worry about though – to boost query performance, avoid using unnecessary subqueries in WHERE or HAVING clauses, execute SQL queries in batches, make use of the SQL query cache if you're in a read-heavy environment, consider caching content on a CDN level to reduce the load on the database, avoid utilizing functions in predicate statements (that way, your database won't be able to make use of indexes), and use aggregate functions like AVG, SUM, or COUNT sparingly to minimize the amount of data your database has to process.

These tips will be a great place to start not only when optimizing the performance of queries on an infrastructure with a low-to-mid-load, but for some instances of big data workloads as well.

CHAPTER 9   OPTIMIZING QUERIES

Summary

Many people think that optimizing query performance is a rather gruesome task, but in reality, it's a completely normal occurrence, but one that requires familiarity with the things happening "under the hood." Sure, optimizing query performance can be tough until you "crack the nut" and gain some experience, but I can assure you that gaining that experience will be worth it in the long run. No matter what type of queries you find yourself optimizing – be it `INSERT`, `SELECT`, `UPDATE`, or `DELETE` queries, all of them have something special to them. At the same time, optimizing their performance is not a flight to Mars – we have many tools available for us to use to gauge their performance under specific circumstances, and with local copies of our application and database always being able to help us, we can get rid of many pressing issues rather quickly.

Gaining experience is fun because once we're experienced, we can start helping our less-experienced colleagues and have a bigger "belt" of problems we can solve. Experience is gained by working on all sorts of projects, and for some of us, those projects may eventually become rather big – so big that ordinary measures to optimize SQL query performance would no longer suffice. Once that happens, we need to carefully evaluate our database architecture once again and then use measures to optimize our database for bigger data sets.

CHAPTER 10

Optimizing MySQL for Big Data

Once you've optimized your database instance and some time has passed, you may start to notice that the measures you've used to optimize your data for the SQL queries behind it are no longer sufficient. They may start to be insufficient because your data is growing – and as your data is growing, the measures to deal with that growth should grow together with it.

As your data is growing, you will have a lot of things to consider: from disk space and hosting to index and data fragmentation. None of those things are something that cannot be worked on, and all of them can be amended and changed as time goes on. The point here is that amending them is likely to require a lot of time and effort, and that's not even taking into account the monetary costs. Optimizing your database can be a tedious task – and as more and more data is introduced into that database, the task is likely to grow out of proportion if you're not ready for what's to come.

Not everyone has to optimize their database for big data, but it's always a good idea to keep optimization techniques at bay should you need them. When problems knock at your door, many engineers and DBAs turn to StackOverflow to ask questions, and I know of DBAs who use Secure Notes within password managers such as 1Password to remind themselves of database optimization secrets they find on the web too: doing so might be a great idea if you find yourself making use of password managers to keep your passwords safe; if not, keep this book somewhere within reach and come back to this chapter as your data grows.

CHAPTER 10　OPTIMIZING MYSQL FOR BIG DATA

Can MySQL Deal with Big Data?

There are a lot of misconceptions about the state of databases – and one of the primary ones is related to relational databases and bigger data sets. Many say that MySQL and its counterparts (MariaDB, Percona Server) aren't a fit for big data sets at all due to them being based on a relational database model, but that's not the problem – improperly optimizing databases for big data is.

Optimizing MySQL for big data is not that different from optimizing MySQL for data sets of an ordinary size; data is still data, there's just a lot of it. Granted, when data sets get bigger, one may have to employ different methods to deal with it, but that doesn't negate the effectiveness of database management systems as such.

The core of the saying "MySQL is not fit for bigger data sets" may stem from the premise that non-relational database management systems don't follow the relational database model, and as this model is swapped for a relational model followed by MySQL and its counterparts like MariaDB or Percona Server, a pattern emerges – you will hear people say

- MySQL is only a fit for applications where the ratio between read/write operations is no bigger than 80%/20%.

- NoSQL databases are meant to serve big data by default!

- Only NoSQL databases provide you with a performance benefit for bigger data sets; they're the only option!

While non-relational databases like MongoDB and its counterparts may be of great use for bigger data sets due to their flexible data model and ability to scale out when necessary, the bottom line is that MySQL is an extremely capable database management system and MySQL *can* deal with big data just as well as other database management systems can – it's just our configuration or use case that is the problem. Once your data gets bigger, irrespective of the database vendor, it's all about your server, database configuration, schema, and query design. Don't get me wrong – your database still has to be *optimized* to make use of the setup of your server – but that doesn't mean that MySQL is the worst option you can pick.

MySQL, MariaDB, or Percona Server will always be an option for bigger data sets if you just answer the question "What's my big data use case?" and *if your big data use case necessitates data being stored in databases and tables or rows and columns and doesn't necessitate a flexible data storage model*, you should certainly look into MySQL or MariaDB.

CHAPTER 10   OPTIMIZING MYSQL FOR BIG DATA

Big data and MariaDB would especially ring a bell for those who run cybercrime analytics or open source intelligence tools – think something akin to a data breach search engine. In that space, MariaDB is used more frequently than you could imagine because such solutions often work with data that's "ingested" through hacking forums, and such data rarely, if ever, consists of `CREATE` or `INSERT` statements.

It all starts to make a lot of sense when you start to understand how hackers operate; hackers usually take copies of databases with the data of hundreds of millions of users to sell them on the web (for the buyers, that presents an "upside" in that the data can be used for credential stuffing attacks), and if you'd ever glance at such data, you would quickly notice that 90% of such data is formatted by terminating the columns with the ":" sign. From an attacker's perspective, it all makes a lot of sense as "exfiltrating" data this way takes little time. Time can be used to "clean up" (remove traces of a hacker being in a system), and data sold in such a manner can be "put to use" to harm other users more quickly. What a surprise, everything's for "convenience…"

Of course, not every one of you will work with breached data, but the premise is the same – I find it unlikely that your systems would ingest millions of rows of data built on `INSERT` or `CREATE` queries for the same reason (that doesn't mean you won't have to ever deal with them, but they won't be your primary concern when importing larger troves of data), and MySQL, MariaDB, and Percona Server are capable to insert data in bulk. So, the answer to the question "Can MySQL deal with bigger data sets?" is yes if it's optimized properly and if your use case necessitates a "strong" data structure (data should be stored in rows and columns).

MariaDB users also have ColumnStore which is a columnar storage engine meaning that there's no need for a separate install either. If your use case necessitates big data processing and linear scalability or the insertion of larger volumes of data with close to no updates/deletes, ColumnStore is also a viable option.

MariaDB and Big Data: Operations with Big Data Sets

After you've made a choice to use MySQL or MariaDB to support bigger data sets, inevitably you will have to optimize the database management system for big data too. Contrary to popular belief, optimizing MariaDB for bigger data sets is not at all different from optimizing your database management system as a whole. That's why I've already walked you through the methods you can use to optimize your database for performance – once you're working with big data, you're going to have to make use of the settings you've just optimized. There's nothing new here – really, you don't have to invent a bike or a rocket. With that being said, ordinary INSERTs won't cut it, and there are a few things you must know for your work with bigger data sets to not become an absolute nightmare – that's why we're jumping into methods to help facilitate your work with big data.

Before working with big data, give your data a specific definition: when do you consider your application/database to cross the realm into big data? This question may seem weird, but people have so many definitions for big data that it's close to absurd. For these examples, we will consider big data "big" once it crosses the mark of 100 million records.

Inserting Big Data Into MariaDB

Before you go ahead and insert bigger data sets into MySQL, there are a couple of things you should keep in mind:

1. Most of the time, your data insertion will have nothing to do with INSERT queries. This is because INSERT queries come with unnecessary overhead.

2. The files you will insert data into your database from will most likely be text files, thus having a smaller size than logical/physical backups.

3. The columns within your data set(s) are most likely to be terminated by the ":", "|", "-" signs, or the comma sign (",") if Excel (CSV) files are in use.

4. You will be able to use your database as your data is inserted into it – your storage engine is unlikely to show the row count at first – the row count will show up after all of the data is inserted.

5. If you need partitions, partition your table before inserting data into it. If you need indexes, it is advisable you index after the data is inserted.

When inserting big data sets into your database, the query you will work with will likely concern the `secure-file-priv` variable too. Make sure the variable is set to a directory that's not readily accessible (i.e., outside `public_html`) and that the directory resides in a hard drive with plenty of space. Space concerns both the file you will be loading the data into your database from, the copies of the table/data your database will possibly make (I'm referring to the internal functionality of ALTER queries), and the amount of space required to store all of your precious data in the first place.

> **Note** The file you will be loading data into your database from will most likely be a text (.txt) or an Excel (.csv) file – not all of the columns in the file may be necessary for your use case either, but the size of text or excel files will be smaller than the size of the table containing your data regardless for various reasons starting from the collation and the character set of your choice and ending up with the partitions and indexes you may elect to use. Make sure you're equipped and ready to sacrifice disk space for speed on big data. *It is going to hurt.*

After `secure-file-priv` is out of the way, you will insert data into your tables using the LOAD DATA INFILE query. I'm not giving an ultimatum here, but the problem is that you have no other option – INSERT SQL queries will work fine until you have 10-20 million records, and then while waiting until your data inserts, you will make coffee, go grocery shopping and come back, watch an episode of your favorite TV show, run errands, and you will find that it's still not even half done. Sure, power users won't leave their server (or PC if that's a local workstation) on all the time as Linux users will be acquainted with the nohup – "no hangup" ("&" at the end of a query has the same effect) – command that ignores the HUP ("hangup/halt") command after a Linux user logs out so that your INSERTs run all the time, but that'd be just hiding the problem. A bunch of INSERT queries running in the background are sure to obstruct operations – what then? SHOW STATUS, KILL? Crap. Only half of your data got imported. Are you starting over next week? You know, when there are 2 additional days where you're sure that no one will use your application or your local MariaDB powerhouse won't need shutting down. Talk about a small problem growing into a nightmare scenario.

Seriously, switch INSERTs into LOAD DATA INFILE already – it inserts raw data without any fuss and allows you to define collations for a specific file you're importing, only import data into a specific column, skip lines/columns, and all that jazz. Flick back to the previous chapter to keep yourself up to date, and you will quickly agree – `LOAD DATA INFILE` has everything you need to deal with importing big data sets into MariaDB, and you will notice that backups of bigger data sets don't come in the form of logical backups either – big data comes in a form that's perfectly suitable for `LOAD DATA INFILE`! So what are you waiting for? *Use* `LOAD DATA INFILE` *with any raw data set that's separated by any character you can imagine (the separation is necessary for MariaDB/MySQL to determine where one column ends and another begins) which is in the form of a text or an Excel file.*

Regardless, some of you may have to use of the `INSERT` command – if you insert millions of rows, make use of the tips for `INSERT` queries outlined in previous chapters and always, *always* account for disk space. Done? Cool – time to read your big data sets!

Reading Big Data with MariaDB

Once you're about to run `SELECT` SQL queries through your big data set, you may be surprised to know that reading bigger data sets isn't much different than reading ordinary data. Take a look at this piece of code depicting a `foreach` loop within PHP.

```php
<?php
foreach(explode(',', $Results['tables']) as $Upcoming_Table) {
    $Search_Query = $Database->prepare("SELECT * FROM `$Upcoming_Table` WHERE $Column = :SearchQuery [LIMIT ...];");
    $Search_Query->execute(array(":SearchQuery" => $SearchQuery));
    $Results = $Search_Query->fetch([PDO::FETCH_ASSOC]);
}
?>
```

Figure 10-1. *SQL query in a loop*

This loop does a couple of things:

1. It takes a set of tables separated by the comma (",") sign and treats every table separately (that's a necessity to "feed" the `SELECT` query).

2. Provides the name of a table to a `SELECT` query, takes the column specified earlier on with the `Column` variable, and binds his search request to the SQL query.

3. Fetches ("retrieves") the result set and puts the results into a `Results` variable, which is then accessed and worked on as necessary.

The reason why this query is in a loop is because we have a lot of tables to query through, and new tables may be added into the database as time goes by: that way, when tables are added, no piece code needs to be updated. There's no SQL injection either – since there are only 4–5 search types and they're all whitelisted (no other values are possible to be provided), we're OK on that front too.

Such SQL queries can do the work when dealing with massive data sets – the thing that makes them stand out is the fact that they're as simple as they can get. Really – there are no massive JOIN operations, 500 UNION operations, or anything like that. There isn't even a LIKE clause present. Those clauses *can* be present, and there's nothing wrong if your SELECT does have them as long as you adhere to the rules that make them perform at their best (refer to the previous chapter for advice), but for this specific use case, there's no need for them – that's exactly what makes queries like the above so efficient: *a no-fuss approach to operations through a well-optimized database.* Are these queries slow? Make them read through less data by adding a LIMIT and/or an OFFSET clause, add an index or a partition or two on the column in question, and the SQL query will return results faster than you will blink. Everything's pretty basic, isn't it?

Granted, your SELECT queries may necessitate the reading of data from different databases/tables using the JOIN clause and you may want to make use of UNION queries, too. Look at this query as an example:

```
SELECT a.user_id, a.owner, a.pc_id AS computer_id,
o.m_id as monitor_id, o.m_inch
FROM computers AS a
LEFT OUTER JOIN monitors AS b
ON a.owner = b.owner and a.user_id = b.user_id and b.m_inch = 22
WHERE a.cpu_ghz >= 3.4
```

Look at the way the query is formatted to start with – what does the formatting of this SQL query tell you? Because of the formatting, it's visible what data is selected first, and what data we're after once the first operation completes: first, we select data from the computers table, then we select data from the monitors table.

Assuming both tables have hundreds of millions of rows, how would you optimize such an SQL query? That's right – you'd split the query into pieces, inspect the structure of both of the tables, then run an EXPLAIN query to dig into the specifics, and optimize the SQL query just like everything else keeping in mind the advice in the last chapter. Revolutionary, right?

The same goes for all other SELECT queries you have really. It's a common misconception that querying through bigger data sets necessitates millions of operations that your database finds difficult to complete and thus, MySQL should be thrown out the window – dig into the internals, read through as little data as possible, and don't forget the basics. You're good to go!

Updating Big Data in MariaDB

Updating bigger data sets isn't rocket science either – remember the UPDATE clause?

```
UPDATE `demo_table` SET [column] = ['value'] WHERE [specific details],
[update multiple columns here] [LIMIT x]
```

There's no specific UPDATE FOR BIG DATA clause – here, things are the same too. No matter how big your data sets are, UPDATE clauses don't change – their internal functionality remains the same, they look the same and accept the same parameters – they just update different amounts of data. Sure, there are life hacks you can employ to avoid them altogether such as creating a table and assigning a column a DEFAULT value so it gets pre-filled by default without you needing to mess with the clause altogether, but aside from that, best practices for UPDATE queries on big data sets include

- **Locking tables, updating data in chunks, and then unlocking them**: Such a practice is likely to make UPDATEs through bigger amounts of data faster.
- **Using the WHERE, OFFSET, and LIMIT clauses**: Those clauses will let you minimize the work your database has to do to complete the update query.
- **Staying alert about the load on your database**: Updating data at 2 AM will likely be a better option than updating the data within your tables at peak usage times.

That's it, really – in most use cases, standard practices are golden. Your UPDATEs are likely to be a little slow if you're running updates on bigger data sets, and you will have to wait depending on how big your InnoDB buffer pool is – I'm not promising that if you follow all of the advice I give you they will complete in milliseconds – but they will not put as big of a strain on your database and their speed will remain reasonable given the amount of rows in your database.

If you find yourself using MyISAM (that may be a necessity for those of you counting rows in a table – I'll get into how storage engines interact with big data sets in a second), you may also want to look into the `key_buffer_size` within the storage engine.

Deleting Big Data From MariaDB

As far as deleting goes, `DELETE` queries don't change either. Yes, deleting big chunks of data is likely to be painful, and that pain will only corroborate on partitions or indexes – that's why it's important to keep things simple and avoid performing many operations at once: things may get a little difficult if you're performing CRUD operations and counting or providing your database with another task at the same time – those operations will take some time, but again, even if they do, you can put all of the necessary SQL queries into a file and "feed" your database with the file for it to run the queries and return results in text files or something like that.

When deleting big data sets, keep in mind that such operations are not a piece of cake for MariaDB: deleting 1,000,000 rows may be a task your database would take on, but I'd lie if I said that deleting 50,000,000 rows from MariaDB is easy – truth be told, deleting that many rows may as well be game over for your database (I've heard you like partitions and indexes too...), *but not for Linux.*

In this realm, queries like `sed` or `sort` will be much, much faster than standard SQL counterparts, they will act on raw data files meaning that those files will be smaller in size, and best of all, they will not require much of a strain for your PC or server – you won't need a NASA-level infrastructure to complete tasks. What if instead of `DELETE FROM `demo_table` WHERE `column` = `string`;` you would export the raw data (even the data within that specific column) from your database with `SELECT ... INTO OUTFILE`, then used something like `sed -i `/string/d` data.txt`? Yes, perhaps you would wait for 10–15 minutes – operations would still need to be completed – but 10 minutes isn't a week: `-i` would modify the file without showing the results via the CLI, `d` would instruct `sed` to delete data, `string` would be the string you need to delete, and `data.txt` refers to the file name of your file.

`sort -u` (a sort operation with a unique flag) would replace the need for a unique index too: exporting raw data, then running a `sort -u` query on the file you've received from your database would drop duplicates within minutes, not days.

Finally, if you need to delete all rows within a table, keep in mind that queries like `TRUNCATE TABLE `table_name`` will be significantly faster than `DELETE` queries.

Removing indexes and partitions will take a while regardless unless you use MyISAM – if you use MyISAM, you're free to delete the .MYI file(s) associated with your table and the index related to that specific table will be gone for good unless the file is re-instated. That's only one upside of using different storage engines for bigger data sets.

Storage Engines and Big Data

Remember storage engines? I've covered them in the second chapter of this book. MySQL is almost unique in the aspect that it allows us to choose from multiple storage engines for our use case – PostgreSQL supports only one storage engine conveniently named "PostgreSQL," MongoDB and other database management systems do offer more choices, but rarely choices are as extensive as with MySQL. And with MySQL having a couple of flavors including MariaDB and Percona Server, our choices are even wider.

Most of those of you using MariaDB will make use of InnoDB – it's the primary storage engine offered by the relational DBMS – but there are other options, too. One of those options is MariaDB ColumnStore – a storage engine leveraging the benefits of columnar storage within MariaDB. By using the benefits provided by columnar storage, MariaDB is able to avoid storing data like so:

ID	Name	Position
52777	Josh Doe	Head of Marketing
52778	John Surnamey	Marketing Manager
52779	Alissa Surname	Influencer Marketing Manager
...	...	...

And store data like so instead:

52777	52778	52779
Josh Doe	John Surnamey	Alissa Surname
Head of Marketing	Marketing Manager	Influencer Marketing Manager
...	...	...

The method of storing data – and, consequentially – the storage engine you will need to access bigger data sets – is directly dependent on your specific data access pattern.

Row-based databases and storage engines such as InnoDB are ideal for transactional processing that involves running online transaction processing (OLTP) queries and accessing data by rows, while column-based databases are based on the OLAP – Online Analytical Processing – model. MariaDB's ColumnStore will also always be ACID-compliant and provide the ability for online schema changes, high availability, and come with a version buffer that will be used to roll back transactions, store data that is being modified, etc.

MariaDB will also provide all of you with the option to stay with the "vanilla" storage engines available within itself which means that choosing columnar storage is an option, not a necessity. That also means that you can force MariaDB to fold to your needs – not the other way around.

One of those needs may have to do with ACID compliance – a basic concept for many database management systems and the reliable guard of your database and the data within.

ACID and Big Data

One aspect that's going to be of crucial importance when you find yourself dealing with big data within any database management system is the consistency and durability of your data. The last thing you want is your customers/users complaining about data being corrupt, inaccessible, or impossible to work with, right?

MariaDB has a solution – ACID. Most of you know what it is and how it works and I've mentioned it throughout this book already, but as your data gets bigger, this concept could become more and more important. Some of you may come to the point where you'd ask yourself *does your database even need ACID?* Maybe. Maybe not. I'm aware of cases where engineers would turn off ACID compliance to experiment, forget that they've done so, and leave the speed trade-off running for weeks, even months. Did their database being speedy, but not being ACID compliant burn their data down? No – turning ACID off won't necessitate the end of your database as long as you understand what you're doing.

At the same time, if some of you expect me to say "Switch ACID to speed and the speed of your database writing data will increase by 852% at the expense of durability," that's not likely to be the case. Your INSERT queries will be significantly faster, but the thing is, if you've optimized your database for bigger data sets as I've already shown you, chances are that you will use `LOAD DATA INFILE`, not `INSERT`, to begin with. Even if you're unable to use `LOAD DATA INFILE` for any reason, the risks will rarely be worth the rewards – but at the end of the day, you're the master behind your decisions. Feel free to switch the `innodb_flush_log_at_trx_commit` variable to 0 or 2 to exchange ACID for speed and observe the results, and then decide if the risk is worth the reward.

Big Data Pitfalls and Known Issues

With all of the upsides big data brings to your infrastructure, be aware that it doesn't come without downfalls either. What comes up, must come down, right? When dealing with big data-enabled projects, many of you will quickly notice that big data means that you will sometimes have a hard time working with your data. You won't go through nightmares, but you must be aware of bottlenecks before they snap your database and data in half – I'll start from `LOAD DATA INFILE`.

`LOAD DATA INFILE` is your friend – it helps load data into a database in a rapid fashion. That's what it's supposed to do, but it doesn't come without nuances. Many of you who've made use of this query in the past could've noticed that this query slows down after a bunch of data is inserted; in the past, people would argue that the solution to this problem would be to switch InnoDB to MyISAM, run queries like `DISABLE KEYS`, and then try again, but such pieces of advice would be ill-suited and outdated for those running such queries in the present day. `DISABLE KEYS` doesn't work with InnoDB because the storage engine is simply not designed to make use of such a clause – MyISAM is. However, using MyISAM with bigger data sets is an absolute nightmare. Even if your use case does necessitate the need for an exact row count, exporting data with `SELECT … INTO OUTFILE` and then counting the rows in the file using EmEditor or any other editors that can open bigger data sets (Notepad++ is out of league for this – it will crash) is likely to be a better option.

Your best bet to make `LOAD DATA INFILE` as fast as possible is running InnoDB, relying on the InnoDB buffer pool, and if necessary, splitting the data you import into InnoDB into many small chunks (for decent performance, aim for a single file to have somewhere in the range of 50–100M rows), or fiddling with `autocommit` before `LOAD DATA INFILE` completes its mission.

Also, how many of you need primary indexes on that ID column that has hundreds of millions of rows? How much disk space does that column alone occupy? 30GB? 40GB? That's 30GB of free hard drive space should that column be removed.

With columns in mind, you'd be surprised how many of us follow "vanilla" advice for data when running big data sets. The advice isn't necessarily "bad," but when our data grows, there would be a need to think outside the box. Unique indexes are a perfect example of this – they may be an option if you have up to a million rows, but for data in the space of hundreds of millions, they'd likely be a nightmare: you would clog your database! Dig into Linux options – even if you're using Windows, install Cygwin and you will have access to almost all of them. Use them on raw data – chances are that they will be significantly faster than vanilla SQL queries through the CLI.

Years ago, I saw a thread on a forum where people talked about data or a certain kind of a search engine. I remember someone commenting something about data parsing – something along the lines of "How do you save the data in the database? How do you analyze the data and what are you using to make queries quick?" and the author replied with something along the lines of *"Data within the search engine is all in a parsed format and would be much larger otherwise <…> Thankfully, by using MySQL in the backend we can let the database take care of all of the necessary parsing for us – we remove unnecessary data before the data even hits our production server <…> By making sure data is parsed and available locally, we save disk space and use the local copy to perform data analysis <…>"* which makes me mention another crucial point – *data parsing*.

Parsing is nothing revolutionary, but it's an absolute necessity to extract information of interest to you. It helps you transform data into a structured format for easy reading, usage, and if necessary, analysis.

Data analysis is another point worth mentioning – if you have bigger data sets and need to, say, count the times a specific string in a column appears in a table, you can divert the task to MariaDB by putting all of the queries relevant to data analysis into a file, making them create separate files depicting results when they complete, and running that file through MariaDB on a local environment – you will have to wait, but MariaDB will analyze data for you and write results to a file – isn't that amazing? Here's an example:

```
SELECT SUBSTRING_INDEX(column, '[CHARACTER]', -1) AS x, COUNT(*) AS total
FROM `demo_table` GROUP BY `column2`
INTO OUTFILE '/tmp/demodata_analysis.txt';
```

The SQL query above will obtain everything to the right of a specific character (negative values obtain everything to the right side, positive values work the other way around), put everything into a variable titled x, and then count and group the occurrences of everything before or after a specified character into a file. That means that you're free to go make yourself a coffee as MySQL is analyzing your data and writing the results to a file.

Such methods of data analysis may not be suitable for everyone, but for some use cases (e.g., counting the times a specific email TLD was used, etc.), they may be golden and that's why you have to choose and use the methods to work with your data yourself by being aware of their upsides and downsides. Big data analytics will always take time, but at the same time, you can make MariaDB do all of the work and go do something else instead.

Many big data pitfalls are also related to the usage of indexes, too – that shouldn't come as a surprise as indexes are primarily used to speed up `SELECT` queries, which make up most of many big data applications. They must be used adequately, too – that's what we're going to get into now.

Summary

Optimizing MySQL or MariaDB for bigger data sets isn't that different of a task than optimizing MariaDB for ordinary use cases. Those who run bigger data sets within MariaDB have to be aware that it's sometimes not feasible to run certain operations through the database, and operations may complete faster if the equivalents of those commands are run on a Linux architecture (the same commands can be run on Windows if we use an appliance like Cygwin).

Regardless, there are certain things we should be aware of when working with bigger data sets within a relational database management system – but none of those include throwing MariaDB to the curb in favor of a non-relational database management system. MariaDB, MySQL, and Percona Server are all perfectly capable of crunching big data if we follow best practices. Indexes are one of those best practices – and the bigger your data sets get, the more prevalent they will become. That's what we're getting into now.

CHAPTER 11

Indexing MySQL

Indexes are a crucial part of any database. Many would even say that database performance without indexing is a myth – and that's not without a reason. Indexes are data structures that facilitate faster access to data by making use of hard drive space in the process; thus, they aren't exactly revolutionary, but at the same time, the reason why this book has an entire chapter dedicated to keys (keys are a synonym to indexes) is that when used properly, these keys can unlock doors toward the database performance heaven in ways you couldn't even imagine.

Indexes don't help with everything – they can make SELECT queries faster, but at the same time harm the performance of INSERTs, UPDATEs, and DELETEs.

I'll repeat – indexes *can* make queries faster, but there's no guarantee that they *will*. Optimizing SELECT query performance is a task too – for your indexes to make SELECT queries faster, they have to be used by your database in the first place. This chapter will help you understand how, why, and when to use indexes to make your query performance faster.

Why Index? Indexes Available in MariaDB

Before you do anything in life, it's necessary to have answers to the question of why you do it. The same thing applies to indexes – why do you index data? What makes you think "Indexes may help here?" The answer is simple – indexes act as pointers to data facilitating faster access to that data.

Think of an index as an index in a book – if you want to read a specific chapter, what do you do? You turn to the beginning of the book and observe all of the chapters inside of it, then see what page the chapter begins from to see what page you should turn to. There's a good reason why you do it – if there are more than 400 pages, an index being unavailable would make the task of searching for that chapter much harder, but after you know that the chapter about indexes starts from page 157, you turn to page 157 and start reading.

CHAPTER 11   INDEXING MYSQL

When it comes to databases, things are a little more complex – different types of database management systems may offer different types of indexes you can choose from. Thus, indexing advice may differ from database to database. At the same time, advice may differ from DBMS to DBMS, but its main aspects remain the same as time goes by – understanding the core principles of indexes will always put you ahead of the curve, and thus, you need to be well-acquainted with the types of indexes that are available for you to use at all times.

At the same time, indexes are not a cure for all of your problems, and they may also create problems in the long run, but they're extremely good and adept at solving speed problems when reading data.

The types of indexes in MySQL, MariaDB, and Percona Server are as follows:

1. **B-Tree indexes**: B-Tree indexes refer to Balanced Tree indexes, and such indexes are the most frequently used index type within MySQL. Such indexes will be in use once our query is searching for exact matches of data with the equality operator and also if we're using the LIKE or BETWEEN operators. For queries to make use of such an index, we have to ensure that our queries specify an exact match by using operators like =, <, <=, >, or >=.

2. **R-Tree indexes**: R-Tree indexes are referred to as spatial indexes. Such an index type within MariaDB and its partners is used exclusively to index geographical objects.

3. **Hash indexes**: Such indexes can be used only with the MEMORY storage engine, and they can only be used in conjunction with SQL queries that use the equality operators. Queries using such indexes will be blazing fast, but such indexes can only be held in the memory and not on the disk, so the hash indexes have limited use cases.

4. **Covering indexes**: Covering indexes within MariaDB "cover" all of the columns necessary for a query to execute. They're a special type of index within MariaDB in that if such indexes are implemented correctly, your database will read data from the indexes and not from the disk, thus drastically reducing the time needed to access your data.

5. **Clustered indexes**: Clustered indexes in MariaDB are PRIMARY KEYs, or if none are present within the table, UNIQUE indexes.

6. **Composite indexes**: Composite indexes cover multiple columns, and thus, they're sometimes referred to as multicolumn indexes. If an index resides on multiple columns at once, it is a composite, or a multicolumn, index.

7. **Prefix indexes**: Lastly, prefix indexes allow us to only index a small part of a column. Such practice may be very welcome for those who have a lot of data to work with and don't want to index the entire value in a specific column.

Keep in mind that PRIMARY KEY constraints are also indexes, as are UNIQUE indexes. As you can tell, each type of index solves a different problem; thus, most of you won't need to use all of them, but knowing your way around them is necessary. Also, keep in mind that every index (key) comes with a couple of aspects related to it:

1) **What's the title of the index?** All indexes will have a title assigned to them – you have the choice of assigning a custom title or making the database assign a title under the index name instead.

2) **What's the type of the index?** The index type determines the rules your queries should follow when accessing data.

3) **Is the index compressed?** Index compression helps indexes to take less space on the disk.

4) **What column does the index reside on?** The column the index resides on will dictate your actions when forming SELECT queries after a WHERE clause.

5) **What's the cardinality of the index?** In other words, how many unique values does the index have? The higher the cardinality, the better.

6) **Comments**: Each index can have comments related to it to ease the understanding why they were defined. Comments are optional and may or may not be displayed when certain SQL clients are in use.

These aspects of indexes within MariaDB let you understand how they work – they are data structures, and every data structure has nuances. Given that all indexes can be deleted just as easily as they can be created, their aspects are not a big deal, but each aspect uncovers a piece of the puzzle related to your database performance and after solving that puzzle, you will be able to make the performance of any database skyrocket, no matter how much data is at the helm.

With aspects in mind, keep in mind that indexing isn't always the best path you can take. Indexing doesn't always make sense – since indexes facilitate faster access to data, they're only useful when we have a lot of data that we are reading through. They also have drawbacks I've covered above, so before adding an index, think about how you would answer the following questions:

1) What's your use case?

2) Is your data set big enough for an index on a column to make sense?

3) What are the specifics of your server? How much hard drive space is available to use?

4) Have you used indexes previously? If yes, in what capacity and what were the results?

5) When adding indexes, will you need to create tables anew, or is modifying existing data enough?

The answers to the questions given above will direct you to the path you need to take. Not all use cases necessitate indexing, it doesn't always make sense to index, and your server may not have enough disk space for your index to reside on a specific column in the first place (in that case, consider prefix indexes and review the specifics of your server); sour experiences with indexes previously may be the cause of certain beliefs that need to be overcome, and methods of adding indexes onto a table will be directly dependent on your use case too.

Some of these questions may seem a little weird – for example, look at question number 5. "Why would it even matter if I create indexes anew or modify data within an existing table?" – you ask. Answers to these questions matter because behind each of them is hidden the functionality of your database:

1) Your use case depicts what type of index may be necessary for you to use.

2) The size of your data set dictates whether indexing makes sense in the first place.

3) The amount of available disk space and other specifics dictate whether indexing is an option, and if it is, directs you to a type of index.

4) Previous experience may help you overcome obstacles related to indexes.

5) Creating tables anew means that your database won't need to make a copy of the table on the disk – altering an existing table means that your database will make a copy of the table, copy all of the data there, perform all of the necessary operations, and swap the two tables.

No matter what the answers to these questions are, if you decide to index, you will have to index columns in a proper way to help your database and the queries within and when you do decide to use indexes, the first question you need an answer to will be *what to index*.

What and When to Index?

Contrary to popular belief, deciding what and when to index is pretty easy: index the column accessed by your query if that column necessitates your query to read through a lot of data, and index once you want to give your query a pointer to the data to quickly find records.

To get a concrete answer, look at your use case and take a step back. What happened to make you realize that an index on a specific column may be an option? Most of you will answer "The speed of queries reading data wasn't satisfactory." Bingo. And what speed will be considered satisfactory for your use case? Most of you won't require queries to complete in 0.00001s., but anything below a second would be awesome. Great – indexes are up to the task.

CHAPTER 11   INDEXING MYSQL

Before defining indexes on any column, look at the problematic query: it's slow because it accesses a lot of data, so make it access only the data that's necessary. Do that by

- **Looking into the types of data that are stored in the table, and especially the column you want to index.** The data types of specific columns tell you more than you can imagine; some data types aren't suitable to be indexed to begin with.
- **Selecting only the necessary data by swapping SELECT * for SELECT column.** That way you will be able to limit the number of rows that are accessed and, thus, acted on.
- **Limiting the number of rows your query needs to access with LIMIT or OFFSET clauses.** If swapping SELECT * for SELECT column doesn't work, try using the LIMIT clause.
- **Decluttering the query.** If selecting necessary data and limiting the number of results doesn't work, try decluttering the SQL query. Split the SQL query and inspect it "part by part": since all parts of your SQL query ask for something from the database, it may be wise to inspect what part of your query does what. For example, inspect the part of the query after the UNION clause if one is present: what data does it access and why? Remember the tips from the previous chapters.

After you have a good faith belief that you understand the types of data that power your columns and your query is accessing a limited set of data (I've told you to do that because when indexes are in place, your queries will further tighten the scope of data that is being accessed thus improving speed), look at the columns that are being accessed after the WHERE clause – those are the columns you need to index. You will find a couple of examples below:

1) SELECT `regdate`, `activated` FROM `users` WHERE **`user_id`** = User Input;
2) SELECT * FROM `demo_data` WHERE **`message`** = "User Input";
3) SELECT * FROM `demo_data` WHERE MATCH(message) AGAINST("User Input");

4) SELECT `message_id` FROM `demo_data` WHERE `message` LIKE "User Input%";

5) SELECT `car_brand`, `available_amount` FROM `demo_shop` WHERE `car_dealership` = "User Input" AND `car_brand` != "User Input (Checkbox)";

6) SELECT * FROM `demo_shop` WHERE `car_brand` = "User Input" UNION SELECT * FROM `another_shop` WHERE `car_brand` = "User Input";

What columns do you index and how?

1) An index on the user_id column will be enough.

2) An index on the message column will do.

3) You will need a full-text index on the message column.

4) An index on the message column will be up to the task as long as the wildcard character ("%") is at the end of the search statement.

5) This query would need two indexes: one on the car_dealership column, and another on the car_brand column. Queries with the "not equal to" ("!=") sign use indexes too!

6) This query would need two indexes on two columns between two tables. One index will need to be defined for the car_brand column in the demo_shop table, and the same query will necessitate the use of another index on the same column in the table titled another_shop.

So many nuances to consider! That's why indexes are so interesting – and so powerful. However, something this powerful and shiny necessitates the existence of preconceived notions, and to properly define and work with the indexes within your database, you will need to walk yourself through them too.

CHAPTER 11   INDEXING MYSQL

Indexing Myths, Misconceptions, and Fragmentation Issues

As far as myths go, there's no shortage of them. Not every engineer on StackOverflow will be correct, not every lecturer will help you in university, and not every colleague at work may interpret things correctly either. People understand things from their point of view – the same can be said about indexes. Some indexing advice may *sound* fair and reasonable, but when you dig in, you quickly understand that it's not the case. Here are a couple of simple examples:

Advice	Explanation
"The more indexes on your table, the better for your database."	**False** – performance is obtained when indexes are *used* by your database and once your database is configured properly, and whether they are used or not depends on your queries.
"Indexing only makes sense for simple SELECT queries."	**False** – in fact, indexing makes sense for complex queries too. All you have to do is use the EXPLAIN clause to understand whether MariaDB is making use of a given index.
"B-Tree indexes will make all SELECT queries perform faster."	**False** – the reason multiple types of indexes exist in the first place is that each index type helps developers in specific situations that differ from one another. Indexes can only help your database if they are used, too.
"Indexing once is enough – indexes don't require maintenance or upkeep."	**False** – the more fragmented your index is, the less it will be able to help your database. Fragmentation means that something is up – index pages are no longer in order or there is a lot of free space in the data pages.
"If indexing doesn't help performance, nothing else will."	**False** – indexes are not a magic pill, and for them to help, you have to consider many other things like the structure of your queries, the traffic toward your application, data types and collations, partitions, and the configuration of your database. Use indexes in conjunction with other performance optimization tips: not as a bandaid for all of your performance problems.

(*continued*)

Advice	Explanation
"Using an index on a column will make inserting data into that column unfathomably slow."	**False** – while it's true that indexes slow down `INSERT` queries, not all queries that insert data will dive into the ground because indexes are in use. Sometimes, you won't even notice a performance difference – problems often appear when we have a lot of data in a column that's indexed and we want to insert some more data, and even then, there are ways around this problem.

Ever heard of one or more of these? I'm sure you did. Myths come into the scene not because developers are stupid – far from it – but because they've done something or heard of something that produced certain results when indexes are in use.

Indexes are delicate, and for them to help your queries succeed, they need to act as an anchor for your queries – anchors may not provide necessary results because they're not fulfilling their purpose or they may become duller as they're used and may necessitate updates or a replacement.

As you work on a database day by day, you're sometimes forced to update, delete, or insert data into a column that has an index. Some of us do it so often that we don't even notice the index in the first place – such frequent maintenance of our tables and the columns within can take a toll on our indexes. Indexes are affected when we perform any action on the column in question, and some actions affect them more heavily than others do.

I've heard of a situation where a DBA has been asked to look into query performance that's been diving into the ground despite no changes being made to the database in recent times. The query performance issue seemed to appear out of thin air without any apparent reason – upon inspection, the DBA noticed that the query was making use of an index, and rebuilding the index fixed the performance issue. This is why indexes, as with everything else within your database, need upkeep. "That must've been a bug with the index or something," some of you say. No, it wasn't – *the problem lied within frequent updates to data within an indexed column and thus, index fragmentation over time.* To know whether your index is fragmented, look at its size: if the size is bigger than it "should" be, you've got problems on your hands.

CHAPTER 11 INDEXING MYSQL

Fragmentation comes in multiple colors: there is internal fragmentation and external fragmentation, meaning that either the database pages are not fully packed with data or the data pages within the index are scattered and may not be in order. When either of those things happens, queries still use the indexes, but they may slow down because they will be accessing more data than necessary.

If your index is making a difference in query performance, you need it: and if you need it, sometimes you're going to need to care for it. Think about a fragmented index as a book with some of its pages dipped in water: it'd be uncomfortable to touch, hold, and read, and the first thing that would be on your mind would be to dry those pages up or, in this case, *defragment the index*. Index defragmentation is often easy to accomplish and can be done by issuing ALTER TABLE queries into the void like so:

```
ALTER TABLE `demo_table` ENGINE = InnoDB;
```

Alternatively, you always have an option of rebuilding the table by dropping and re-loading the data into it altogether.

No matter what approach you take, remember that drying pages are only one piece of the puzzle – a puzzle that starts with your hardware at the forefront.

Your Hardware, Database, and Indexes

If there's one thing all indexes have in common is that they all take up space on the disk. They all come with a cost – a cost of time to add them to the database, a cost to your hard drive, and a cost to your queries.

This cost has a humble beginning – it all begins with the hardware within your server. You have indexes on a column because you have a database, and you have a database because you have a server – remove the hardware, and your whole application will come crashing down.

Indexes are renowned for putting a strain on your hardware – it doesn't matter what kind of processor, hard drive, or bandwidth allocation you work with, indexes are a specific appliance that "mounts" on your column, and the column "mounts" on the disk. Thus, no matter what index type you find yourself using, some of its functionality will be directly dependent on the internals of your server.

Many of us don't think of this side of indexing. It wouldn't be fair to blame the developers – after all, they're only doing their work and applying advice gained through documentation of the tools in question or practical experience.

Explore the DBA section of StackOverflow as an example, and you will quickly find questions like "My query is slow, how do I...," "blocking certain queries from being visible in the slow query log," "reorganizing or rebuilding indexes," and the like, and once you glance at the answers, many developers suggest either rebuilding queries, looking into column datatypes, or looking at the documentation – some offer you to glance into the configuration of your database, but your hardware is a rare reminder. Great hardware should be a given already, right? *Everything concerns your hardware* – from the software you run to the PHP version to the indexes on a column on a table you barely remember the name of. That's why choosing hardware is a task that shouldn't be overlooked. If you want your database to complete tasks necessary for your use case, you will need to run adequate hardware.

Coming back to indexes, keys have a special place in the heart of your database. For most of you, they're companions, but when things turn sour, they're often the first ones to blame. They've been around for ages and most of their concepts don't change – they're often taking the blame because the hardware behind your database is not equipped to deal with them.

Indexes may become a point of contention when your data set is big enough to accommodate them. They become a point of contention because they impact your hardware and as such, if your hardware isn't ready for battle, indexes can't solve necessary problems either. Indexes have an impact on your hardware because every index has index pages that contain references to where the necessary pieces of data are located. For MySQL and its counterparts, the default size of a database page is 16KB (16,385 bytes), but the size can be increased up to 64KB (65,535 bytes).

Since databases use fixed-size pages to store data and indexes, they are also stored in the buffer pool, and the larger your database page is, the more data it can work with. In MySQL, the maximum row length bound to a database page varies (the same can be said about other database management systems), but in most cases, the maximum row length will be approximately half of the database page size which is why we use data types and which is also why we cannot index the full length of TEXT-based columns, but are free to index VARCHAR.

The limitations regarding indexes should also be of interest to both your database and hardware – you cannot just mash all columns into an index even if you have petabytes of hard drive space because your database won't let you do that. Depending on what flavor of MySQL you use, you may be able to put 16 (MySQL) or 32 (MariaDB) columns into an index, but no more. Also, your table doesn't come with an unlimited number of columns either – you can run only up to 4096. Frankly, I'm yet to see tables where such amounts of columns would be necessary for any operations, so you're most likely fine on this front.

I know that many developers would find the internals of indexes a rather boring topic so I won't bore you too much on that front, but I hope that now you understand that your hardware plays a crucial role not only for your database but for the indexes within as well.

Types of Indexes

Take a look at this graph.

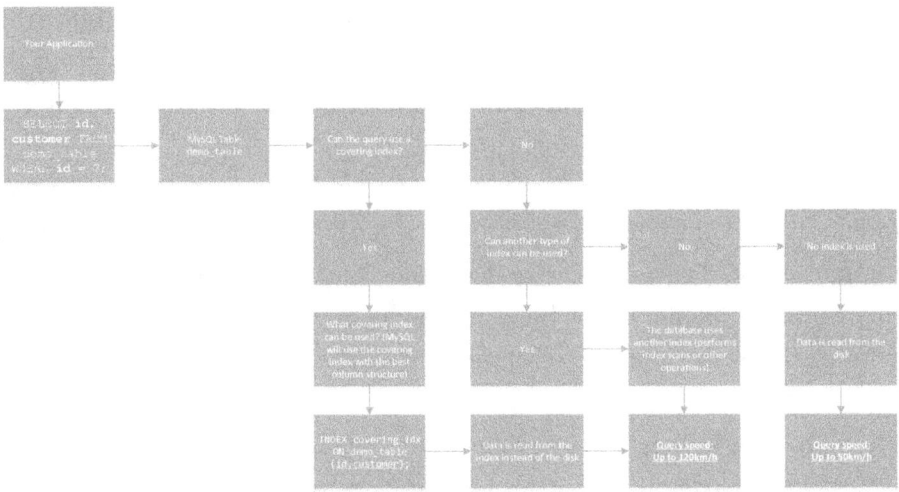

Figure 11-1. A covering index in action

This graph depicts the functionality of a covering index within a database management system. Granted, the illustration is overly simplified (queries may differ and query speed is not measured in km/h – I've added that for illustration purposes), but it gets the point across: *indexes may make your queries faster.*

Indexes may help your query – they may not. There are indeed many index types, and each index type helps a specific type of query complete faster. If you've defined an index or two in the past, chances are that you are already aware of the circumstances surrounding index types making you competent in coming up with conclusions and

CHAPTER 11 INDEXING MYSQL

decisions to employ a specific index type, but even if you didn't, index types are not that hard to understand: flick a couple of pages back and refresh your memory around index types and dive into them.

B-Tree Indexes

B-tree indexes refer to balanced tree indexes. B-tree indexes are called that way because an ideal version of such an index would hold all of its leaf nodes at the same level visually speaking, thus providing a balance. In the real world, results are often far from perfect since developers frequently add/remove data concerning the indexed column in question thus paving the way for index fragmentation, but regardless, B-Tree indexes have a firm place in the database world and will likely retain it for years to come.

To understand B-Tree indexes, an understanding of a Binary Search Tree may help. A basic illustration of a binary search tree (BST) can be seen below:

A Binary Search Tree (BST) is a tree-like structure with nodes. Nodes within a BST may have up to two children to the sides, and when you see such a structure, you begin to understand why queries using indexes are often significantly faster than those that read data from the disk.

B-tree indexes are binary tree indexes with a twist: such types of indexes allow for their members to have more than two children and that's their primary difference. Here's a basic illustration of a B-tree index.

CHAPTER 11   INDEXING MYSQL

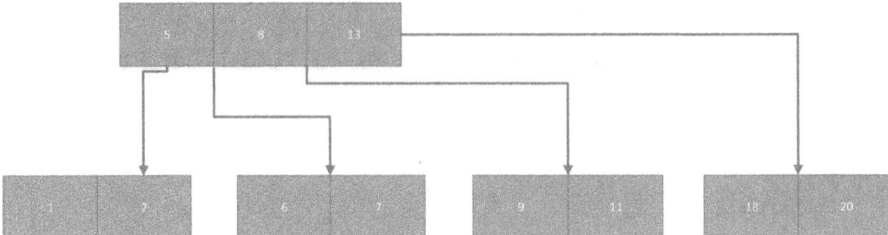

Figure 11-2. B-Tree index

B-tree indexes make query performance faster because of their structure allowing them to enable our database to skip traversing through unnecessary rows: as they use pointers to quickly locate data, the intermediate levels of the index can have many more items per node, but regardless of how many items an individual node has, the premise of B-tree indexes remains the same.

In all flavors of MySQL, B-tree indexes can be defined upon table creation or when modifying the structure of a particular table. With that being said, regardless of how you elect to define B-tree indexes, their internal functionality doesn't change. The column that they reside on, their cardinality, and other specifics might but a large majority of those specifics are related to the internals of your queries and database. The internals of your queries dictate what kind of index to choose, too.

To make good use of a B-tree index, use equality operators, BETWEEN, or LIKE without a preceding wildcard. A B-tree index will also help if you find yourself using IS [NOT] NULL clauses, and it will also be helpful when using AND clauses.

Alright, now for the examples. To test the functionality of b-tree indexes, I will create a table for demonstration purposes.

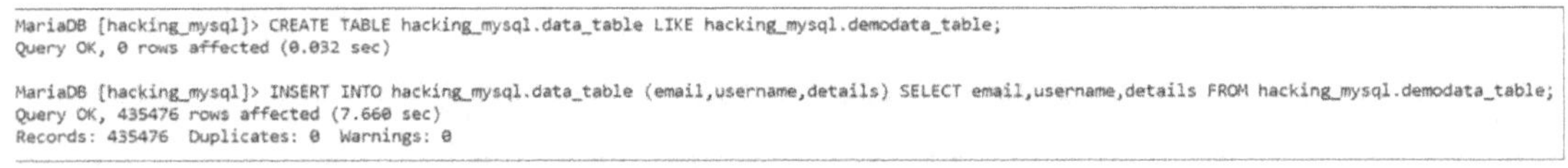

```
MariaDB [hacking_mysql]> CREATE TABLE hacking_mysql.data_table LIKE hacking_mysql.demodata_table;
Query OK, 0 rows affected (0.032 sec)

MariaDB [hacking_mysql]> INSERT INTO hacking_mysql.data_table (email,username,details) SELECT email,username,details FROM hacking_mysql.demodata_table;
Query OK, 435476 rows affected (7.660 sec)
Records: 435476  Duplicates: 0  Warnings: 0
```

Figure 11-3. Creating a table for demonstration purposes

Note my approach to the creation of the table – I didn't use a dump file to restore a table from a backup; rather, I've recreated the table structure (first query) and then inserted some (not all) of the data that existed in a previous table (second query.)

I will also note that we already had a B-tree index on the username column; thus, the speed of the INSERT query in question will be slower than usual.

222

CHAPTER 11　INDEXING MYSQL

If you generate data and then index a column that contains generated data, it's possible that the cardinality of the index will be rather low.

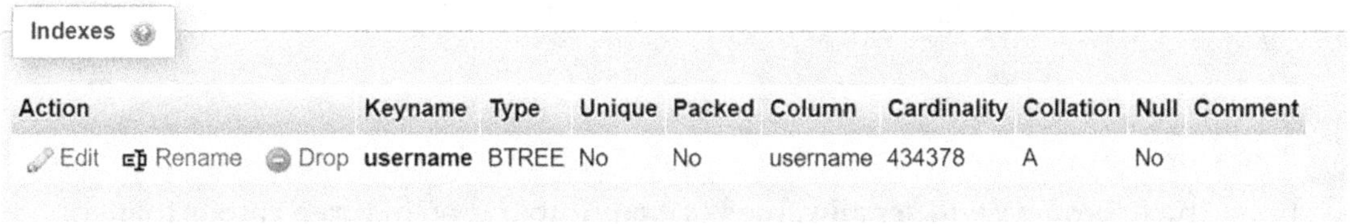

Figure 11-4. A BTREE Index on the Username Column

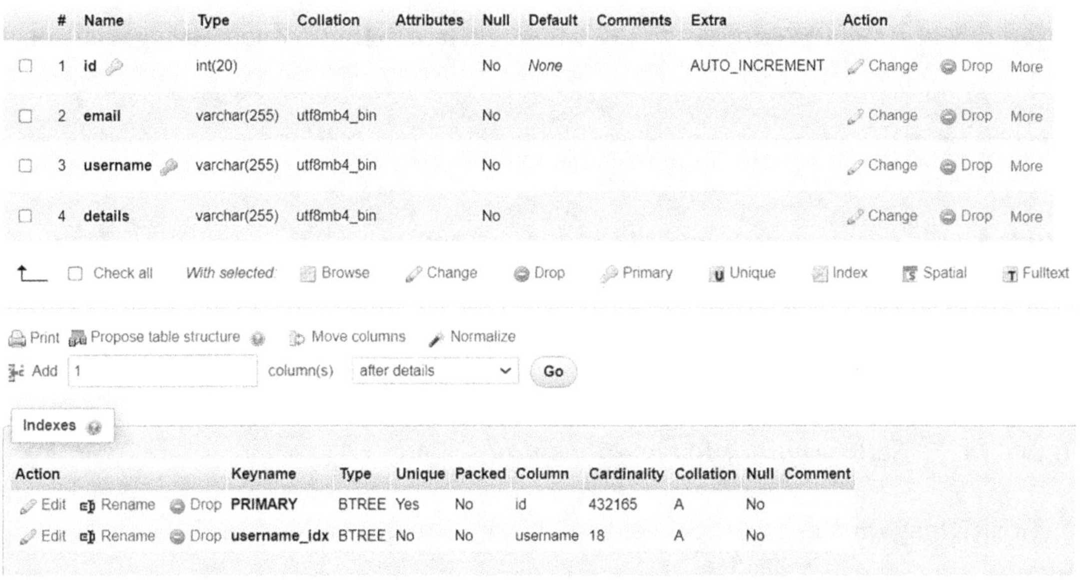

Figure 11-5. Lower cardinality of an index on a column

Now, if you're copy-pasting my actions in your own infrastructure to learn, many of you probably won't have 500k records to work with. For that, find a website that lets you generate a bunch of random data (generatedata.com is a good place to start), or restore data from a backup and anonymize if necessary. To do that, we will use a couple of queries – not all of them may be necessary for your specific use case, so take what you will and adjust the table name/columns/entries accordingly:

1. UPDATE `demo_data` SET `column` = ELT(FLOOR(RAND()*3)
   +1, 'Anonymized Row', 'Anonymous', 'Private');

2. UPDATE `demo_data` SET `id` = RAND();

223

CHAPTER 11   INDEXING MYSQL

3. UPDATE `demo_data` SET `email` = REPLACE(`email`, 'gmail.com', 'demo.com');

4. UPDATE `demo_data` SET `ip` = '127.0.0.1';

5. ...

There are many other ways you can go about this, but for this example, these will do just fine – the first query will set all values of a column to one of three values that you specify (to provide more values, increase the number RAND() is multiplied by, then add more entries), the second one will set all of the values within the id column to random values, the third query will replace all email domains of gmail.com to demo.com, and the fourth will set all IP addresses to 127.0.0.1. Feel free to think of something yourself too. Let's see how they work.

```
MariaDB [hacking_mysql]> UPDATE `data_table` SET `username` =
    -> ELT(FLOOR(RAND()*10) +1, 'DemonSlayer', 'Smooth Door Knob', 'Transformed', 'Whatever', 'Just a Guy', 'Emily', 'Samantha', 'Thomas', 'Roy is Good!', 'Rafaello');
Query OK, 435475 rows affected (24.045 sec)
Rows matched: 435476  Changed: 435475  Warnings: 0
```

Figure 11-6. *Setting usernames to random usernames*

```
MariaDB [hacking_mysql]> UPDATE `data_table` SET `email` = REPLACE(`email`, 'hotmail.com', 'demo.net');
Query OK, 81020 rows affected (4.049 sec)
Rows matched: 435476  Changed: 81020  Warnings: 0
```

Figure 11-7. *Setting emails to random emails*

Great – they work as expected. Let's run a couple of queries and see how our B-tree index is being used by MariaDB.

CHAPTER 11　INDEXING MYSQL

```
MariaDB [hacking_mysql]> EXPLAIN SELECT id,details FROM data_table LIMIT 5;
+------+-------------+------------+------+---------------+------+---------+------+--------+-------+
| id   | select_type | table      | type | possible_keys | key  | key_len | ref  | rows   | Extra |
+------+-------------+------------+------+---------------+------+---------+------+--------+-------+
|    1 | SIMPLE      | data_table | ALL  | NULL          | NULL | NULL    | NULL | 432165 |       |
+------+-------------+------------+------+---------------+------+---------+------+--------+-------+
1 row in set (0.001 sec)

MariaDB [hacking_mysql]> EXPLAIN SELECT details,id FROM data_table WHERE username = 'Smooth Door Knob' LIMIT 500;
+------+-------------+------------+------+---------------+--------------+---------+-------+-------+-----------------------+
| id   | select_type | table      | type | possible_keys | key          | key_len | ref   | rows  | Extra                 |
+------+-------------+------------+------+---------------+--------------+---------+-------+-------+-----------------------+
|    1 | SIMPLE      | data_table | ref  | username_idx  | username_idx | 1022    | const | 91618 | Using index condition |
+------+-------------+------------+------+---------------+--------------+---------+-------+-------+-----------------------+
1 row in set (0.001 sec)

MariaDB [hacking_mysql]> EXPLAIN SELECT details FROM data_table WHERE id = 777 AND username IS NOT NULL;
+------+-------------+------------+-------+----------------------+---------+---------+-------+------+-------+
| id   | select_type | table      | type  | possible_keys        | key     | key_len | ref   | rows | Extra |
+------+-------------+------------+-------+----------------------+---------+---------+-------+------+-------+
|    1 | SIMPLE      | data_table | const | PRIMARY,username_idx | PRIMARY | 4       | const | 1    |       |
+------+-------------+------------+-------+----------------------+---------+---------+-------+------+-------+
1 row in set (0.001 sec)

MariaDB [hacking_mysql]> EXPLAIN SELECT details FROM data_table WHERE username IS NOT NULL AND id = 777;
+------+-------------+------------+-------+----------------------+---------+---------+-------+------+-------+
| id   | select_type | table      | type  | possible_keys        | key     | key_len | ref   | rows | Extra |
+------+-------------+------------+-------+----------------------+---------+---------+-------+------+-------+
|    1 | SIMPLE      | data_table | const | PRIMARY,username_idx | PRIMARY | 4       | const | 1    |       |
+------+-------------+------------+-------+----------------------+---------+---------+-------+------+-------+
1 row in set (0.001 sec)
```

Figure 11-8. *Testing a B-Tree index on the username column: Round 1*

```
MariaDB [hacking_mysql]> EXPLAIN SELECT email FROM data_table WHERE username = 'Samantha' OR details = 'Referred by Thomas';
+------+-------------+------------+------+---------------+------+---------+------+--------+-------------+
| id   | select_type | table      | type | possible_keys | key  | key_len | ref  | rows   | Extra       |
+------+-------------+------------+------+---------------+------+---------+------+--------+-------------+
|    1 | SIMPLE      | data_table | ALL  | username_idx  | NULL | NULL    | NULL | 432165 | Using where |
+------+-------------+------------+------+---------------+------+---------+------+--------+-------------+
1 row in set (0.001 sec)

MariaDB [hacking_mysql]> EXPLAIN SELECT email FROM data_table WHERE details = 'Referred by Thomas' AND username = 'Samantha';
+------+-------------+------------+------+---------------+------+---------+------+--------+-------------+
| id   | select_type | table      | type | possible_keys | key  | key_len | ref  | rows   | Extra       |
+------+-------------+------------+------+---------------+------+---------+------+--------+-------------+
|    1 | SIMPLE      | data_table | ALL  | username_idx  | NULL | NULL    | NULL | 432165 | Using where |
+------+-------------+------------+------+---------------+------+---------+------+--------+-------------+
1 row in set (0.001 sec)

MariaDB [hacking_mysql]> EXPLAIN SELECT * FROM data_table WHERE details LIKE 'VPN%' AND username = 'S_mantha'
    -> UNION SELECT * FROM demodata_table WHERE username LIKE 'Samantha_';
+------+--------------+-----------------+-------+---------------+--------------+---------+-------+------+--------------------------------------+
| id   | select_type  | table           | type  | possible_keys | key          | key_len | ref   | rows | Extra                                |
+------+--------------+-----------------+-------+---------------+--------------+---------+-------+------+--------------------------------------+
|    1 | PRIMARY      | data_table      | ref   | username_idx  | username_idx | 1022    | const | 1    | Using index condition; Using where   |
|    2 | UNION        | demodata_table  | range | username      | username     | 1022    | NULL  | 67   | Using index condition                |
| NULL | UNION RESULT | <union1,2>      | ALL   | NULL          | NULL         | NULL    | NULL  | NULL |                                      |
+------+--------------+-----------------+-------+---------------+--------------+---------+-------+------+--------------------------------------+
3 rows in set (0.002 sec)
```

Figure 11-9. *Testing a B-Tree index on the username column: Round 2*

```
MariaDB [hacking_mysql]> EXPLAIN SELECT * FROM data_table WHERE username LIKE '_amantha';
+----+-------------+------------+------+---------------+------+---------+------+--------+-------------+
| id | select_type | table      | type | possible_keys | key  | key_len | ref  | rows   | Extra       |
+----+-------------+------------+------+---------------+------+---------+------+--------+-------------+
|  1 | SIMPLE      | data_table | ALL  | NULL          | NULL | NULL    | NULL | 432165 | Using where |
+----+-------------+------------+------+---------------+------+---------+------+--------+-------------+
1 row in set (0.001 sec)

MariaDB [hacking_mysql]> EXPLAIN SELECT * FROM data_table WHERE username LIKE 'Samanth_';
+----+-------------+------------+------+---------------+------+---------+------+--------+-------------+
| id | select_type | table      | type | possible_keys | key  | key_len | ref  | rows   | Extra       |
+----+-------------+------------+------+---------------+------+---------+------+--------+-------------+
|  1 | SIMPLE      | data_table | ALL  | username_idx  | NULL | NULL    | NULL | 432165 | Using where |
+----+-------------+------------+------+---------------+------+---------+------+--------+-------------+
1 row in set (0.001 sec)
```

***Figure 11-10.** Testing a B-Tree index on the username column: Round 3*

I assume that your queries would look something similar to those displayed – if they do, the lessons surrounding the usage of B-tree indexes in MySQL would be as follows (I derive those by judging whether indexes are possible to use and if they're used by MariaDB mostly looking at the `possible_keys` and key columns):

1. **For your index to be used by your query, "touch" the column.** Take a look at the first query – it has nothing to do with the username column, hence why the index on that column isn't even considered.

2. **B-tree indexes can be used when `LIMIT`, `OFFSET`, or similar clauses are in use.** `LIMIT`, `OFFSET`, and similar clauses don't neglect the usefulness of indexes within MariaDB if you use the indexed column after a `WHERE` clause.

3. **If there's a choice between a B-tree and a PRIMARY KEY index, MySQL can still elect to make use of the primary key instead, no matter whether the structure of the query "allows" MySQL to consider a different B-tree index or not.** Experiment and fiddle around to find the best fit for your queries.

4. **MySQL can consider an index, but not use it if it thinks that it wouldn't do any good for the query.**

5. **MySQL can use different indexes for different parts of the query.** This is especially true if `UNION` or other clauses are concerned.

6. **"%" is not the only wildcard that may nullify your queries.** As you may know, the "_" character signifying a single unknown character is also a wildcard. Thus, a query searching for an unknown character in front of a query is also likely to be slower than usual.

Be mindful that if you set any column to several random values, index cardinality will be rather low, and for your experience with B-tree indexes to not become sour, be mindful of the length of your index leaf structures too – the size of your indexes depends on the number of rows in the index, the number of columns, the number of indexes, and the size of the values in a column themselves.

There are ways you can predict the size of your indexes, too – approaches may differ from database to database, but for indexes based on MariaDB, you can make use of the innodb_index_stats table within the mysql database.

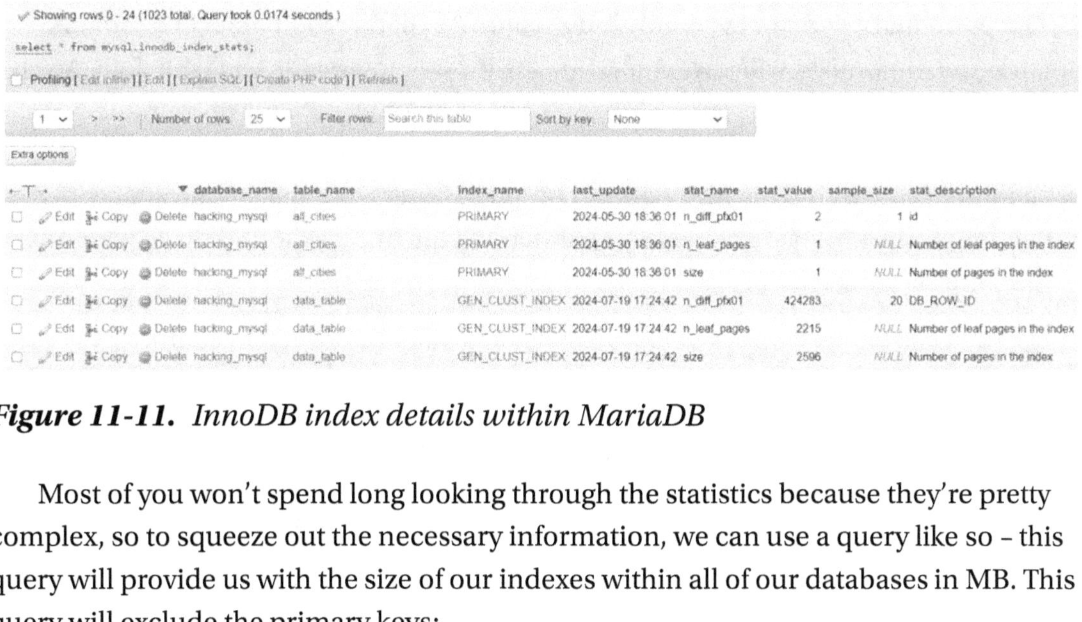

Figure 11-11. InnoDB index details within MariaDB

Most of you won't spend long looking through the statistics because they're pretty complex, so to squeeze out the necessary information, we can use a query like so – this query will provide us with the size of our indexes within all of our databases in MB. This query will exclude the primary keys:

```
SELECT database_name, table_name, index_name,
ROUND(stat_value * @@innodb_page_size / 1024 / 1024, 2) idxsize_mb
FROM mysql.innodb_index_stats
WHERE stat_name = `size` AND index_name != `PRIMARY`
ORDER BY idxsize_mb DESC;
```

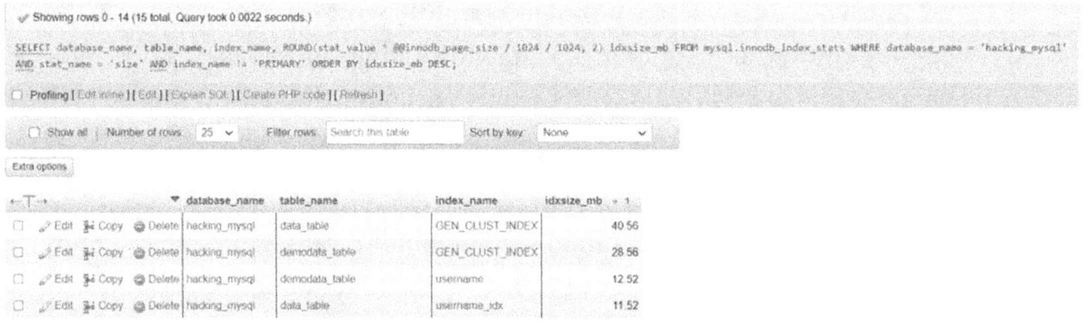

CHAPTER 11   INDEXING MYSQL

Figure 11-12. Displaying index details in a specific database

To make the size of your indexes smaller, consider minimizing the length of the data types you find yourself using and using data types that occupy less space on the disk (e.g., VARCHAR instead of TEXT) or using other types of indexes (remember – you can also index a part of the column).

Once you make sure that you only index columns that warrant indexing, remember that the query optimizer will always pick the fastest way to provide you with data. Always remember one thing – the query optimizer will search for ways to make your query faster, and if the chosen way doesn't involve your index, it's because the optimizer decided that another route would make the query complete faster. Perhaps the cardinality of your index is rather low? If not, perhaps a different type of index would make your query performance skyrocket.

Covering Indexes

For many of you, indexing won't end with a couple of B-tree indexes here or there. Every application is different, and once you've dipped your toes in the indexing water, you will likely begin searching for some other solutions that could cover you in other scenarios, too.

Enter covering indexes – in essence, they're the same thing as B-Tree indexes, but with a twist in that such indexes cover all of the columns that are required for a query to execute, hence the title.

The functionality of covering indexes doesn't differ much from B-tree indexes *because covering indexes are B-tree indexes* so there are no changes on that front, but with that being said, these kinds of indexes come with a key difference – a query using covering indexes will likely complete faster than a query using an ordinary B-tree index

CHAPTER 11   INDEXING MYSQL

because covering indexes index all columns used by the query, and thus, enable your database to read data from the index rather than the disk providing your database with drastic performance benefits as a result.

Some common misconceptions about covering indexes include saying that a covering index covers all columns in a table, which is often not the case. A useful covering index is any singular index that exists on columns we're running a SELECT query through. Another common point of contention is related to indexes that cover multiple columns. Those indexes are not covering indexes if they don't cover columns required by the query to execute, and thus, they belong in a different (yet related) category – they are multicolumn indexes.

Covering indexes are B-tree indexes so they are defined exactly as B-tree indexes are defined, but keeping in mind the specifics of this type of index, they necessitate answers to some questions beforehand. All of the most important questions would be somehow related to the columns used by our query – what columns is our query using, what data are we searching for, what data types are used by our columns, and what results do we expect?

The answers to those questions will dictate the things we need to do to make our queries work in the best way possible. First, consider your use case – what data are you searching for and what do you want to achieve? Only by answering that question will we be able to define an index that helps our database rather than just takes up space on the disk.

Once we have an answer to that question, we're free to create a table and add the necessary index. I'll modify an existing table and add a covering index on two columns – username and details – because I'm about to search for details about users registered on a mock forum (a covering index can be added on top of an existing B-tree index as well).

```
MariaDB [hacking_mysql]> ALTER TABLE `data_table` ADD INDEX `covering_idx`(`username`,`details`);
Query OK, 0 rows affected (2.247 sec)
Records: 0  Duplicates: 0  Warnings: 0

MariaDB [hacking_mysql]>
```

Figure 11-13. Adding a covering index on a table

Covering indexes are rather easy to understand – the complex part is the order of columns within them and that's the primary challenge with covering indexes: covering indexes makes your queries able to read data from the index by satisfying clear requirements. Those requirements are the backbone behind the order of the columns in the index and coming up with an order that helps your use case and the queries within is no easy feat. I'll give you an example – with a query like so:

```
SELECT user, infraction_details FROM demo_forum WHERE last_infraction = `Minor` AND referred_by = `Thomas`;
```

Which covering index would be the most efficient?

1. CREATE INDEX `covering_idx` ON `demo_forum`(`user`,`infraction_details`,`last_infraction`,`referred_by`);

2. CREATE INDEX `covering_idx` ON `demo_forum`(`referred_by`,`last_infraction`,`infraction_details`,`user`);

3. CREATE INDEX `covering_idx` ON `demo_forum`(`user`,`infraction_details`,`referred_by`,`last_infraction`);

4. CREATE INDEX `covering_idx` ON `demo_forum`(`infraction_details`,`referred_by`,`last_infraction`,`user`);

Hard question, right? All of the aforementioned indexes would constitute a proper, working covering index, but only one or two of them would be the best fit for the task, depending on what kind of MySQL flavor you find yourself using – for the users of MySQL < 8.0 and MariaDB, only the first one would cut the chase, but if you find yourself running MySQL >= 8.0, the second query is also an option because newer versions of MySQL can also perform index scans backward.

Some examples of covering indexes being used can be seen below.

```
MariaDB [hacking_mysql]> EXPLAIN SELECT id,username,details FROM data_table WHERE id = 10954;
+----+-------------+------------+-------+---------------+---------+---------+-------+------+-------+
| id | select_type | table      | type  | possible_keys | key     | key_len | ref   | rows | Extra |
+----+-------------+------------+-------+---------------+---------+---------+-------+------+-------+
|  1 | SIMPLE      | data_table | const | PRIMARY       | PRIMARY | 4       | const | 1    |       |
+----+-------------+------------+-------+---------------+---------+---------+-------+------+-------+
1 row in set (0.002 sec)

MariaDB [hacking_mysql]> EXPLAIN SELECT email,details FROM data_table WHERE username = 'Emily' AND details = 'Eats Candy';
+----+-------------+------------+------+--------------------------+-------------+---------+-------------+------+-----------------------+
| id | select_type | table      | type | possible_keys            | key         | key_len | ref         | rows | Extra                 |
+----+-------------+------------+------+--------------------------+-------------+---------+-------------+------+-----------------------+
|  1 | SIMPLE      | data_table | ref  | username_idx,covering_idx | covering_idx | 2044   | const,const | 4378 | Using index condition |
+----+-------------+------------+------+--------------------------+-------------+---------+-------------+------+-----------------------+
1 row in set (0.005 sec)

MariaDB [hacking_mysql]> EXPLAIN SELECT email,details FROM data_table WHERE details = 'Found site using Google' AND username = 'Whatever';
+----+-------------+------------+------+--------------------------+-------------+---------+-------------+------+-----------------------+
| id | select_type | table      | type | possible_keys            | key         | key_len | ref         | rows | Extra                 |
+----+-------------+------------+------+--------------------------+-------------+---------+-------------+------+-----------------------+
|  1 | SIMPLE      | data_table | ref  | username_idx,covering_idx | covering_idx | 2044   | const,const | 8782 | Using index condition |
+----+-------------+------------+------+--------------------------+-------------+---------+-------------+------+-----------------------+
1 row in set (0.003 sec)

MariaDB [hacking_mysql]> EXPLAIN SELECT * FROM data_table WHERE details = 'Found site using Google' AND id >= 555;
+----+-------------+------------+-------+---------------+---------+---------+------+--------+-------------+
| id | select_type | table      | type  | possible_keys | key     | key_len | ref  | rows   | Extra       |
+----+-------------+------------+-------+---------------+---------+---------+------+--------+-------------+
|  1 | SIMPLE      | data_table | range | PRIMARY       | PRIMARY | 4       | NULL | 216082 | Using where |
+----+-------------+------------+-------+---------------+---------+---------+------+--------+-------------+
1 row in set (0.003 sec)

MariaDB [hacking_mysql]> EXPLAIN SELECT username FROM data_table WHERE details = 'Was banned once';
+----+-------------+------------+-------+---------------+--------------+---------+------+--------+--------------------------+
| id | select_type | table      | type  | possible_keys | key          | key_len | ref  | rows   | Extra                    |
+----+-------------+------------+-------+---------------+--------------+---------+------+--------+--------------------------+
|  1 | SIMPLE      | data_table | index | NULL          | covering_idx | 2044    | NULL | 432165 | Using where; Using index |
+----+-------------+------------+-------+---------------+--------------+---------+------+--------+--------------------------+
1 row in set (0.001 sec)

MariaDB [hacking_mysql]>
```

Figure 11-14. Covering indexes in use in MariaDB

1. The first query doesn't use a covering index because I've only defined id after the WHERE clause.

2. The second query uses a covering index because it's very clear what we ask: even though such queries may not be running in the wild (we essentially select two columns after defining their values in the WHERE clause), they're a good example of when a covering index would be in use.

3. The third query uses an index by using a backward index scan (details,username.)

4. The fourth query only uses the primary key index on the id column because we're only searching for the id and nothing else.

5. The last query uses a covering index because we're after the username of a user that has specific details and the query is constructed in a way that makes it the perfect fit for a covering index without reading it backward.

Finally, keep in mind that indexes that cover too many columns while covering the columns necessary for the query to execute would also be covering indexes, but they would be overkill. To properly work with covering indexes, remember:

1. To index every column before and after a `WHERE` clause.
2. To avoid including columns you don't use.
3. That covering indexes can be read backward.
4. That one table can make use of multiple covering indexes – it all depends on the structure of your queries.

Finally, keep things simple – simple approaches are often the best.

Multicolumn (Composite) Indexes

Now, we come to multicolumn indexes. Multicolumn, or composite, indexes are often confused with covering indexes in that both types of indexes make use of multiple columns, but only covering indexes lets your database read the data from the index.

Multicolumn indexes are just what they sound like – they are indexes on multiple columns. Such indexes are also B-tree indexes, and they may or may not "cover" all of the columns required for a query to execute, but they are considered composite indexes regardless of the outcome.

Multicolumn indexes call home to various specifics unique to themselves – MySQL only allows these kinds of indexes to be of B-tree types while other database management systems such as PostgreSQL allow for GIN, BRIN, and GiST types, and some developers may even liken multicolumn indexes to a sorted array.

In MySQL, composite indexes can consist of up to 16 columns, they require queries to use some or all of the columns in the composite index, and, just like the composite indexes before them, have a crucially important feature – the order of columns within the index.

Here's a basic definition of a composite index:

```
CREATE INDEX `composite_idx` ON `demo_table`(`col_1`,`col_2`,`col_3`);
```

Composite indexes are not very complex to understand – to use them, we have to use one or more of the columns in the index in an order that we specify. The aforementioned index specification would satisfy queries that make use of the `col_1` column, both `col_1` and `col_2` columns, or all three columns combined.

CHAPTER 11 INDEXING MYSQL

Now, time for examples once again. I'll use the covering index again, but I'll start by renaming it by running a query like this – it's pretty self-explanatory:

```
ALTER TABLE `database`.`table` RENAME INDEX `covering_idx` TO
`composite_idx`;
```

That means that now our table has a composite index consisting of two columns – `username` and `details` (we can have up to 16) – upon inspection, MariaDB should return "MUL" in the Key column for the first column in a multicolumn index.

```
MariaDB [hacking_mysql]> DESCRIBE data_table;
+----------+--------------+------+-----+---------+----------------+
| Field    | Type         | Null | Key | Default | Extra          |
+----------+--------------+------+-----+---------+----------------+
| id       | int(20)      | NO   | PRI | NULL    | auto_increment |
| email    | varchar(255) | NO   |     |         |                |
| username | varchar(255) | NO   | MUL |         |                |
| details  | varchar(255) | NO   |     |         |                |
+----------+--------------+------+-----+---------+----------------+
4 rows in set (0.047 sec)

MariaDB [hacking_mysql]>
```

Figure 11-15. *"MUL" for multicolumn index in MariaDB*

Let's try them out.

```
MariaDB [hacking_mysql]> EXPLAIN SELECT * FROM `data_table` WHERE `username` = 'Emily' AND `details` = 'Eats Candy';
+----+-------------+------------+------+---------------+---------------+---------+-------------+------+-----------------------+
| id | select_type | table      | type | possible_keys | key           | key_len | ref         | rows | Extra                 |
+----+-------------+------------+------+---------------+---------------+---------+-------------+------+-----------------------+
|  1 | SIMPLE      | data_table | ref  | composite_idx | composite_idx | 2044    | const,const | 4378 | Using index condition |
+----+-------------+------------+------+---------------+---------------+---------+-------------+------+-----------------------+
1 row in set (0.002 sec)

MariaDB [hacking_mysql]> EXPLAIN SELECT username FROM data_table WHERE details = 'Was banned once';
+----+-------------+------------+-------+---------------+---------------+---------+------+--------+--------------------------+
| id | select_type | table      | type  | possible_keys | key           | key_len | ref  | rows   | Extra                    |
+----+-------------+------------+-------+---------------+---------------+---------+------+--------+--------------------------+
|  1 | SIMPLE      | data_table | index | NULL          | composite_idx | 2044    | NULL | 432165 | Using where; Using index |
+----+-------------+------------+-------+---------------+---------------+---------+------+--------+--------------------------+
1 row in set (0.001 sec)

MariaDB [hacking_mysql]> EXPLAIN SELECT `id`,COUNT(*) FROM `data_table` WHERE `details` = 'Registered from a suspicious IP address';
+----+-------------+------------+-------+---------------+---------------+---------+------+--------+--------------------------+
| id | select_type | table      | type  | possible_keys | key           | key_len | ref  | rows   | Extra                    |
+----+-------------+------------+-------+---------------+---------------+---------+------+--------+--------------------------+
|  1 | SIMPLE      | data_table | index | NULL          | composite_idx | 2044    | NULL | 432165 | Using where; Using index |
+----+-------------+------------+-------+---------------+---------------+---------+------+--------+--------------------------+
1 row in set (0.001 sec)
```

Figure 11-16. *Composite indexes: Round 1*

CHAPTER 11   INDEXING MYSQL

```
MariaDB [hacking_mysql]> EXPLAIN SELECT COUNT(*) FROM `data_table` WHERE `details` LIKE 'Ban%';
+----+-------------+------------+-------+---------------+---------------+---------+------+--------+--------------------------+
| id | select_type | table      | type  | possible_keys | key           | key_len | ref  | rows   | Extra                    |
+----+-------------+------------+-------+---------------+---------------+---------+------+--------+--------------------------+
|  1 | SIMPLE      | data_table | index | NULL          | composite_idx | 2044    | NULL | 432165 | Using where; Using index |
+----+-------------+------------+-------+---------------+---------------+---------+------+--------+--------------------------+
1 row in set (0.001 sec)

MariaDB [hacking_mysql]> EXPLAIN SELECT * FROM data_table WHERE details = 'Registered from a suspicious IP address' AND username IS NOT NULL;
+----+-------------+------------+------+---------------+------+---------+------+--------+-------------+
| id | select_type | table      | type | possible_keys | key  | key_len | ref  | rows   | Extra       |
+----+-------------+------------+------+---------------+------+---------+------+--------+-------------+
|  1 | SIMPLE      | data_table | ALL  | composite_idx | NULL | NULL    | NULL | 432165 | Using where |
+----+-------------+------------+------+---------------+------+---------+------+--------+-------------+
1 row in set (0.002 sec)
```

Figure 11-17. *Composite indexes: Round 2*

```
MariaDB [hacking_mysql]> EXPLAIN SELECT * FROM data_table WHERE username = NULL AND details = 'Registered from a suspicious IP address';
+----+-------------+-------+------+---------------+------+---------+------+------+------------------------------------------------+
| id | select_type | table | type | possible_keys | key  | key_len | ref  | rows | Extra                                          |
+----+-------------+-------+------+---------------+------+---------+------+------+------------------------------------------------+
|  1 | SIMPLE      | NULL  | NULL | NULL          | NULL | NULL    | NULL | NULL | Impossible WHERE noticed after reading const tables |
+----+-------------+-------+------+---------------+------+---------+------+------+------------------------------------------------+
1 row in set (0.003 sec)

MariaDB [hacking_mysql]> EXPLAIN SELECT username FROM data_table WHERE details = 'Was banned once';
+----+-------------+------------+-------+---------------+---------------+---------+------+--------+--------------------------+
| id | select_type | table      | type  | possible_keys | key           | key_len | ref  | rows   | Extra                    |
+----+-------------+------------+-------+---------------+---------------+---------+------+--------+--------------------------+
|  1 | SIMPLE      | data_table | index | NULL          | composite_idx | 2044    | NULL | 432165 | Using where; Using index |
+----+-------------+------------+-------+---------------+---------------+---------+------+--------+--------------------------+
1 row in set (0.002 sec)
```

Figure 11-18. *Composite indexes: Round 3*

We have results!

You can see that no matter if we query the username column and the details column or the details column and the username column, our database is still able to use the index. Sometimes MariaDB did consider using the index but decided not to because it thought the query could be completed faster without it, and on one occasion MariaDB returned with a note that said Impossible WHERE noticed after reading const tables. This error can be rather confusing for some, but it essentially means that no row that satisfied one or more criteria in your WHERE clause was found in your table. In other words, you've most likely checked for something that you weren't supposed to be checking for (a NULL value in a NOT NULL column or the other way around), or one clause didn't match any records so MariaDB didn't bother with the rest.

Covering indexes are certainly interesting, and they can be used when certain clauses are in use, too – ORDER BY will work best if you search for the leftmost column, then order by the rest using ORDER BY with an equality operator. Covering indexes can also be scanned backward.

Prefix Indexes

Covering and composite indexes are nice – what about situations where you don't have enough space to index an entire column though? In these situations, you would need to make use of a prefix index – an index that only covers some characters within a column and thus is rather small compared to other indexes but still provides enough selectivity for it to be a viable option.

Prefix indexes are defined like usual indexes, just with numbers denoting how many characters in a column should be covered. This example would add a prefix index on the first 10 characters of the demo_column in the demo_table:

```
ALTER TABLE `demo_table` ADD INDEX `prefix_idx`(demo_column(10));
```

As you can tell, indexes defined in this way would be less selective, but still provide a viable performance benefit if defined properly. That's kind of the whole point – *the challenge is defining them properly.* Aside from prefix indexes using less space on the disk, they will also be a necessity for those indexing BLOB or TEXT data types – due to their size, such data types necessitate prefix indexes to be defined no matter whether you want to define them or not.

Prefix indexes are tedious to some – developers often find the task of finding an adequate index length too much to bear because they don't have "rules" to follow to find a golden medium.

Finding a good prefix index length isn't rocket science though – a simple approach you can take involves taking a deeper dive into your use case and finding the average length of the rows concerned with it. The average length of rows should be a good starting point – aim for the length to be long enough so that its results would be as similar to an index on the entire column, but don't cover the entire column to save space on the disk.

Defining an ideal prefix index takes practice, and since such indexes can only be used for "vanilla" SQL queries and don't cover all of the values in a column, they cannot be used as covering indexes. Partial indexes cannot use the ORDER BY or GROUP BY clauses, and as such, they are not ideal for every use case either.

Spatial (R-Tree), Hash, and Clustered Indexes

Aside from prefix indexes, there is a possibility of you having a use case for spatial indexes, too. Some of you may have not even heard of them, and that's OK; spatial indexes have a very special task to fulfill – they index geometric data, and as such, columns using those kinds of indexes must store spatial data based on the POLYGON, LINESTRING, or MULTIPOINT data types. The definition of a spatial index necessitates the SPATIAL keyword in between:

ALTER TABLE `demo_table` ADD SPATIAL INDEX `spatial_idx`(`column`);

Spatial indexes work similarly to B-tree indexes in that they also make searches for exact values faster.

Spatial indexes work through Spatial Reference Identifiers (SRIDs) – these identifiers are ID values that are associated with geometric values, and to optimize data while working with spatial indexes, it's recommended to verify that all values within a column have the same SRID by running a SQL query like so:

SELECT ST_SRID(`column_title`) FROM `demo_table`;

MySQL only supports RTREE indexes with the MyISAM storage engine – MariaDB includes the Aria storage engine in the list as well.

As far as hash indexes are concerned, they work with the MEMORY and InnoDB storage engines. Such indexes don't support prefix-based queries, only work with exact match operators, and do not support the ORDER BY clause either, but as a rule, are exceptionally fast due to the data being stored in memory.

Such indexes don't have many use cases, but may sometimes be necessary for testing: when the MEMORY storage engine is in use, all of their data is held in memory and is destroyed upon shutdown, and when the InnoDB storage engine is in use, such indexes are still usable but are converted to B-tree indexes behind the scenes.

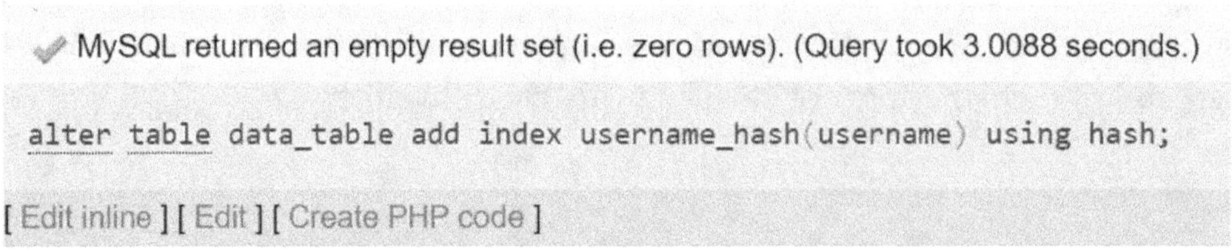

Figure 11-19. Adding a hash index on a table

Action			Keyname	Type	Unique	Packed	Column	Cardinality	Collation	Null	Comment
Edit	Rename	Drop	**PRIMARY**	BTREE	Yes	No	id	432165	A	No	
Edit	Rename	Drop	**username_hash**	BTREE	No	No	username	18	A	No	

***Figure 11-20.** Hash index is a B-tree index*

In other words, InnoDB won't error out if you define hash indexes on columns within the storage engine – it's likely to change your hash index into a b-tree index instead because it thinks that hash indexes do the same thing as b-tree indexes, so there's no need for a distinct definition.

Clustered indexes are a little different – such indexes can be used by your queries, but in most cases, MySQL and its counterparts consider such indexes to be primary keys. In other words, a clustered index is a B-tree index that contains automatically incrementing values and is defined as a primary key with an auto-increment option. Such indexes can and will be used in adherence to B-tree indexing rules.

Since clustered indexes store row data, each table can have only one index of such a type. Most of the time a clustered index will be put on the id column and will increment automatically, thus fulfilling its purpose. If an automatically incrementing column doesn't exist, MySQL will also have a clustered index because then, a clustered index will be the first UNIQUE index with its key columns defined as NOT NULL. If that's not the case either and you find yourself using InnoDB, the storage engine will generate an invisible clustered index called GEN_CLUST_INDEX and order rows by an id assigned by InnoDB.

Queries using such an index are likely to be blazing fast because when the index is in use, InnoDB is led straight to database pages that contain the data of the row, thus saving unnecessary disk I/O.

Most tables will likely make use of clustered indexes and B-tree indexes: that's a fact. No matter whether your table is storing 100,000 or 100,000,000 records, a B-tree index will certainly help. Problems arise once you need to decide on the design of your indexes: you may know the ins and outs of indexes, but all your knowledge can still make your databases grind to a halt if you don't know how to index in a way that helps your queries in your specific use case. After all this, a logical question may arise: *how do you know that?* This is a separate question that demands separate answers.

CHAPTER 11   INDEXING MYSQL

Devising the Perfect Index Design

To come up with a strategy for a perfect index design, answer a question: what do you consider a "perfect" index? For most of you, a perfect index will be an index using which query speed is faster than X. What's that X? Why that number?

To put you on a path, I'll backstep a little: around 2016, a bunch of new data breach search engines emerged; those who have followed the scene around that time will certainly remember their Twitter (now X) feeds: 50% of their tweets were focused on *"Look at us – our queries complete within 0.0003s. even under stress, and our competitor's website only sustains a speed of 0.04s! Isn't that a good reason to stop using their service and switch to ours instead?!"* or *"Our competitors are only returning 200 rows when returning results, our results aren't limited!"*

These tweets popped up because the operators of such engines were seemingly experimenting with index/database design; what index makes a certain query complete the fastest and why?

These tweets likely popped up because the operators of these search engines knew that devising the perfect index design is a tough nut to crack for many developers because most of them are well-versed in a specific language, but don't know much about databases, especially their spin-offs. Your use case may be wildly different than the use case of data breach search engines and it may be exactly the same, but regardless, if you have more than a million rows, you need to take care of a proper index design beforehand for your indexes not to cause you problems in the long run.

Many of you won't care that much about index speed in microseconds and you will be fine with the speed as long as your query completes in under a second, but keep in mind that your database needs to be stress-tested too: having your use case, stress on your database, your hardware and database capacity in mind, what's a reasonable ballpark in terms of speed? Take a wild guess taking into account the following:

- **Use case**: Your use case will refer you to a possible index type.
- **Data types**: The data types in use will hint at an index type as well. For example, if your use case necessitates TEXT columns, you'd have to consider a prefix index regardless. If your searches are based on the id column, perhaps adding a *clustered index* is enough?
- **Stress on your database**: Many of you will choose to index as so not to put more strain on your database because of visitor influx

or similar reasons; what's the load of your database at the present moment? Average load during a busy month? During the last 3 months? Does any of it have to do with query structures you are about to index?

- **Hardware and database capacity**: What hard drives are in use? What's their size and why? If you have a lot of space but run HDDs instead of NVMe drives, could you think about *covering indexes* to avoid reading data from the disk altogether? Can some data existing in your database be deleted in favor of a new one?

Take these things into account and you will be halfway there – a good start is half the work, right? Now, time for the design itself.

For this example, our use case will be a basic table in a database behind an ecommerce shop that depicts users and the latest item they've bought.

```
MariaDB [hacking_mysql]> DESCRIBE ecommerce_demo;
+---------------+--------------+------+-----+---------+----------------+
| Field         | Type         | Null | Key | Default | Extra          |
+---------------+--------------+------+-----+---------+----------------+
| id            | int(20)      | NO   | PRI | NULL    | auto_increment |
| email         | varchar(255) | NO   |     |         |                |
| username      | varchar(255) | NO   |     |         |                |
| item_purchased| varchar(255) | NO   |     |         |                |
| last_login    | datetime     | YES  |     | NULL    |                |
+---------------+--------------+------+-----+---------+----------------+
5 rows in set (0.042 sec)
```

Figure 11-21. An ecommerce shop table structure

In real life, if you're indexing a table behind an ecommerce shop, you will probably have more columns, but in this case, this table will do just fine. Right – what about our use case? We're most likely searching what item was purchased by what user using a certain system, right? With such a use case in mind, what about data types? Do we need varchar(255) everywhere? Probably not, so let's work on them – smaller data types mean less data on the disk.

```
MariaDB [hacking_mysql]> ALTER TABLE `ecommerce_demo` CHANGE `email` `email` VARCHAR(115) CHARACTER SET utf8mb4 COLLATE utf8mb4_bin NOT NULL DEFAULT '';
Stage: 1 of 2 'copy to tmp table' 0.231% of stage done
```

Figure 11-22. First stage of ALTER TABLE

```
MariaDB [hacking_mysql]> ALTER TABLE `ecommerce_demo` CHANGE `email` `email` VARCHAR(115) CHARACTER SET utf8mb4 COLLATE utf8mb4_bin NOT NULL DEFAULT '';
Query OK, 435476 rows affected (5.749 sec)
Records: 435476  Duplicates: 0  Warnings: 0
```

***Figure 11-23.** Second stage of ALTER TABLE*

Don't be surprised if you see "Stage: 1 of 2..." when running ALTER queries: MariaDB is just explaining the internal process it goes through. Also, bear in mind that you can rename columns when resetting their data types by changing the second definition of the column too.

After we've worked around with our table a little, here's what we have.

```
MariaDB [hacking_mysql]> DESCRIBE ecommerce_demo;
+----------------+--------------+------+-----+---------+----------------+
| Field          | Type         | Null | Key | Default | Extra          |
+----------------+--------------+------+-----+---------+----------------+
| id             | int(20)      | NO   | PRI | NULL    | auto_increment |
| email          | varchar(115) | NO   |     |         |                |
| username       | varchar(75)  | NO   |     |         |                |
| item_purchased | varchar(50)  | NO   |     |         |                |
| last_login     | datetime     | YES  |     | NULL    |                |
+----------------+--------------+------+-----+---------+----------------+
5 rows in set (0.048 sec)
```

***Figure 11-24.** An ecommerce table with optimized data types*

Much better – we can get ready for indexing.

To do that, we need to look at our application functionality: what does it do? What options does the user have within the search engine? *What data is searched for and displayed?* The last question is particularly important because the answer to it determines the query structure and the query structure determines the index design.

Let's say that we're searching for the last purchased item to determine the last login date of a certain customer to check if the customer is still logging in to the shop and his email so we can contact him offering discounts and other details. That's an answer to the biggest part of our question – what to index. We usually index the column that's being searched for, so in this case, we need to have an index on an `item_purchased` column. If there's nothing else to assist our search efforts (any other columns we add would necessitate the presence of AND/OR clauses), our search on that front is over.

To decide on an index type, we need to once again dig into our use case: in this case, it's pretty clear that we're going to need a B-tree index due to the nature of the app, but do we need a full-text index? In this case, probably not; full-text indexes are only necessary if:

a) We want to have the capability to include Boolean characters in our search query to tell the query to include/exclude something from the search results, etc. – that's what the Boolean search mode is all about.

b) We rely on "implied knowledge" in that we search for "cheese" and we want our result set to contain "cheddar cheese," "blue cheese," etc. – that's why the query expansion mode exists.

c) We have larger text fields like TEXT that we intend to run queries on.

d) Adhere to all of the full-text search rules: full-text indexes have a minimum string length for searches (three characters for InnoDB, four characters for MyISAM) as well as a list of stopwords for the storage engine in question including words like "the," "it," "on," etc., so we'd have to make sure that our search query does not include those too.

Do we need our B-tree index to be a covering index? It all depends on how many records we have and on the structure of our query. If our data set isn't huge, a covering index is probably not necessary, but if the data set is bigger and we change our use case for it to necessitate other data than the purchased item or relevant to the purchased item (e.g., the type of purchased item, amount, etc.), a covering index will help. In this case, we can have a covering index (we have 500k rows and we want to see what users purchased what items), but a B-tree index will do fine too, and we don't need it to be a prefix index either.

So, based on these facts, how do we define our indexes? In this case, everything's simple. Our query looks like so:

```
SELECT email,last_login FROM `ecommerce_demo` WHERE `item_purchased` = <search query here>;
```

Based on that and our use case, we need to index the item_purchased column – we will name it search_idx (indexes can have any name, and if not set, the name will be the name of the column):

```
ALTER TABLE `ecommerce_demo ` ADD INDEX `search_idx`(`item_purchased`);
```

CHAPTER 11   INDEXING MYSQL

Done – wasn't hard, was it? From having no idea what and how to index to having a functional index on a table in minutes. How did that happen? Answering a couple of questions acted like a funnel that led you to the answer: if you know what questions to ask, you will find the answer.

Indexing for Performance and Big Data

After your index design is very good (let's face it – nothing's ever 100% perfect), your data has grown and some time has flown by; some of you will find yourself re-evaluating your index design choices. Re-evaluations of index design may happen for a couple of reasons, but most of them will have something to do with changes to your use case, data, or the experience you've gained.

When you have a lot of data, the index structures you've defined may no longer be as effective as they've been. Some of you may not even work with the same data as before – perhaps you've built a different project having to deal with way more data than the other. That's normal – things change and your indexes need to evolve together with them.

When things change, it's important to not get carried away and remember that databases don't change much. Changes are related to your use case instead, which in other words, means that most of the things you will find yourself doing won't differ too much from the actions you took when ordinary data sets were involved.

A billion records are a lot of data, and if you need to index that much data, the first thing you have to come back to is your use case once again: what necessitates that much data in a database and what is your application doing? Is data written to the tables within the database and how often or is your database a read-only environment? *Why do you need to extract insights from that much data?*

Answer these questions, evaluate the basics of indexes, and you will stumble upon a path you should take once again. Many of you will be surprised to notice that the actions you need to take don't differ much from what you would usually do – it just necessitates more consideration than usual. Here's an example:

If we decide to index our columns, we once again have to know what the backbone of our application is doing, and if we have hundreds of millions of rows we need to query through, it's in our best interest to limit as much data as possible. How did hundreds of millions of rows appear in our table in the first place? Are all of them necessary and could we add a unique index to deal with duplicates? What do we need to be shown to the user and how?

CHAPTER 11   INDEXING MYSQL

If you have that much data, the search functionality within your website may differ too. For some, having that much data necessitates an advanced, detailed search accessible within the application – the purpose of such an appliance would be to act on two fronts:

1. Help users/customers further refine what they're searching for and what they expect to find.

2. Help your database access data in a way that eliminates certain rows from consideration even before an index is considered for use.

A perfect example of this are car-related websites that let you search for things across multiple categories – I'll provide examples in brackets and explain why later on:

1) The brand of the car (e.g., "**Toyota**")

2) Specific title of the car (e.g., "Toyota **Corolla**")

3) The year the car was made (e.g., "**2019** Toyota Corolla")

4) The type of gas that powers the car (e.g., "**Gasoline** 2019 Toyota Corolla")

5) The price of the car (e.g., "Gasoline 2019 Toyota Corolla **Under $10,000**")

6) Whether the car has been in an incident or not (e.g., "Gasoline 2019 Toyota Corolla Under $10,000 **without Accidents**")

7) The number of previous owners on the car (e.g., "Gasoline 2019 Toyota Corolla Under $10,000 without Accidents **with Less than 3 Owners**")

8) How do you want to pay for the car (e.g., "Gasoline 2019 Toyota Corolla Under $10,000 without Accidents with Less than 3 Owners **Available Through a Lease**")

And so on. All of these clauses have something to say – and have a big impact your indexes and the database behind them. Many such websites use rather simple queries to conduct searches through data – the more filters they have, the less data the database has to query through, and thus, once an applicable index that further lessens the amount of accessible data is involved, queries still complete quickly. That's the primary reason why you might see "156,521,776 cars in the listing" and "query completed in 0.12sec." at the same time.

On the other hand, constructing indexes to help such queries may not be an easy task – building queries adhering to all of the points specified by the user is likely to necessitate many clauses to access various columns of data from the table (we may need AND/OR, etc.); we may need to access data in different tables (we use the UNION clause for that and to use it, both tables need to have the same structure) or different databases altogether. As far as indexes on bigger data sets are concerned, both DESCRIBE and EXPLAIN are good points.

```
MariaDB [hacking_mysql]> DESCRIBE car_data;
+-----------+-------------+------+-----+---------+----------------+
| Field     | Type        | Null | Key | Default | Extra          |
+-----------+-------------+------+-----+---------+----------------+
| id        | int(5)      | NO   | PRI | NULL    | auto_increment |
| car_brand | varchar(20) | NO   |     |         |                |
| car_model | varchar(30) | YES  |     | NULL    |                |
| year      | int(4)      | YES  |     | NULL    |                |
| car_vin   | varchar(30) | YES  |     |         |                |
+-----------+-------------+------+-----+---------+----------------+
5 rows in set (0.048 sec)
```

Figure 11-25. *car_data table*

Notice the data types that we're using – all data types are carefully thought out and have reasonable length applied to them. Now, if we're searching for all of the fields (excluding the ID field), we would need four separate indexes on four fields, right? Not necessarily. In this case, we can use a composite index instead, because we sort of implicitly know the order of the choices of the user – first, he'd have to choose the car brand (e.g., "Toyota"), then – the model (e.g., "Corolla"), and only after that can he choose the rest of the options including the year and define a possible VIN unique identifier if our application necessitates that. It's impossible to choose the model before the brand or the year before the model, and so, we sort of implicitly know what's going to happen after what. Our index may even be covering if all fields are required to be used by our application! Let's use that to our advantage when building the index:

```
ALTER TABLE `car_data` ADD INDEX `composite_idx`(`car_brand`,`car_model`,`year`,`car_vin`);
```

Now, to craft a query, we need to consider the data we need to return: in this specific case, we likely need to select everything except the ID because the nature of such websites necessitates informing the customer with a lot of data. The result page may include the title of the car, the year, type, VIN code, what it's powered with, what transmission it has, and in what city the owner lives. Tables focused on such use cases are likely to be bigger, but our demo table not having many columns is not a problem either.

For our use case, we also know when an exact match is necessary. We won't need to involve wildcards or `LIKE` queries inside of this, so that's out of the question too. Here's how we go about this:

1. Our app would most likely list the available car brands and provide all data in the table, so that's `SELECT * FROM ` car_data` WHERE ` car_brand` = 'BRAND'`.

2. Once a brand is chosen, our app would list the models of the cars for selection – once a model is selected, we would need to consider it (`AND car_model = 'Model'`).

3. Once the model is selected, the user would also be able to select the range of years the model would need to be made (`AND year [>=|<=] YEAR`).

All things considered, a query searching for a 2015 or newer Toyota Corolla through the app would look like this:

```
SELECT * FROM `car_data` WHERE car_brand = 'Toyota' AND car_model = 'Corolla' AND year >= 2015;
```

Let's see if the query uses any indexes.

```
MariaDB [hacking_mysql]> EXPLAIN SELECT * FROM `car_data` WHERE `car_brand` = 'Acura' AND car_model = 'CL' AND year >= 1997;
+----+-------------+----------+-------+---------------+---------------+---------+------+------+--------------------------+
| id | select_type | table    | type  | possible_keys | key           | key_len | ref  | rows | Extra                    |
+----+-------------+----------+-------+---------------+---------------+---------+------+------+--------------------------+
|  1 | SIMPLE      | car_data | range | composite_idx | composite_idx | 210     | NULL |    7 | Using where; Using index |
+----+-------------+----------+-------+---------------+---------------+---------+------+------+--------------------------+
1 row in set (0.001 sec)
```

Figure 11-26. Seeing if a query uses indexes

Regardless of how many rows are returned and although we're not even searching for a VIN (that was the last column in the covering index), we see that both the `possible_keys` and key columns include the name of our index. Our database has found the data using the index – woohoo!

The same rules apply to many other data sets, including data breach search engines. Do you think data breach search engines with billions of records run other types of queries? Return to the last chapter or have a look below.

```php
<?php
foreach(explode(',', $Results['tables']) as $Upcoming_Table) {
    $Search_Query = $Database->prepare("SELECT * FROM `$Upcoming_Table` WHERE $Column = :SearchQuery [LIMIT ...];");
    $Search_Query->execute(array(":SearchQuery" => $SearchQuery));
    $Results = $Search_Query->fetch([PDO::FETCH_ASSOC]);
}
?>
```

Figure 11-27. *Loop searching through 10 billion records*

This loop searches through more than 10 billion records! You've seen queries that look more complex than this, didn't you? Simple things are often the best – and big data sets are no exception.

Really – all you need to do to index big data sets boils down to simple things:

1. Your use case and the bits and pieces available inside of it
2. Proper data types
3. The understanding of index types and things surrounding them
4. Accessing a limited set of data
5. Returning a limited set of data

The bottom line is this: when choosing an index, consider your use case, choose data types that don't put much of a strain on your database, educate yourself about the ups and downs of each index type that you can use before making a choice, and make sure to access a limited set of data before involving indexes in the first place.

Adhering to this advice will let you define indexes that help your database instead of acting like a spoke in a wheel, but as always, nothing's a guarantee – test the advice you receive again and again before even considering applying anything in a real-world environment.

Summary

Indexing is the backbone behind many modern-world applications: properly defined indexes excel at making SELECT queries blazing fast, and indexing can help even if you find yourself obstructed by a variety of factors like low disk space on the hard drive, inability to use certain data types, or other circumstances. Indexes do that by minimizing the amount of readable data in the database, but indexing is not the only way to make query performance skyrocket.

Enter partitions – mini tables inside of your table that split data into easy-to-access chunks further minimizing the scope of accessible data and further improving the performance of certain types of queries.

CHAPTER 12

Optimizing Partitions

When indexes don't help or help only partially, developers seek out other ways to improve their query performance. One of those ways is partitions – partitioning is a concept that lets users divide a database into several independent parts that still get treated as one part by the database layer.

Partitioning is a known concept for users of many database management systems – users of MySQL are no exception. Tables within databases are partitioned for the data within them to be more manageable and accessible or for load-balancing purposes. In MySQL, MariaDB, and Percona Server, only two storage engines support partitioning: those storage engines are InnoDB and NDB.

Why Partition Data?

To understand why we partition data, we need to understand the purpose of partitioning in the first place. In this regard, partitioning acts similarly to indexing. Once we access data in partitions, our database reads through less data (e.g., 15 million rows instead of 100 million), and thus, our queries can complete faster. *Partitioning can also be used together with indexing* to make the performance of read operations even faster – such an approach may be beneficial for those possessing billions of records.

Partitions are beneficial because their purpose is to split big data sets into smaller, manageable pieces, and since each partition contains a subset of data, managing data split into these subsets becomes much easier. Partitioning data helps with scalability, manageability, and improved performance at the price of space – just like indexes, partitions come with files unique to themselves that store data relevant to that partition, and those files take up space on the disk. Partitions are stored separately from one another, and your database considers a partition to be a separate table while still treating the table and the partitions within as one object through the SQL layer. This is done to alleviate data access burdens and make partitions easier to access and use.

CHAPTER 12 OPTIMIZING PARTITIONS

When to Partition Data?

To answer probably the most important question in this realm, I'll start with an example I've seen on Stack Overflow. The main points of this example are as follows (I'll call the user who asked the question user X, and the user who gave an accepted answer user Y):

1. User X said that he runs a table with approximately 2 million rows and 39 columns and that the table is growing every day. Then, touched upon a point that queries through such a data set take a very long time, and said that someone (likely a colleague of his at work) suggested that he partition the large table.

2. User X had a couple of questions:

    a. When is it time to partition data?

    b. Is partitioning the table likely to improve the performance of queries?

    c. If he partitions the table, will partitioning necessitate changes to any `SELECT`, `INSERT`, or other statements that are being run?

    d. Will partitioning take a long time to perform?

    e. If partitioning would be helpful, how to go about it? How to identify column(s) that should be partitioned and columns that should be left intact?

    Many users chimed in to give suggestions – a suggestion that was accepted by the user X answered the questions the following way:

    a. Probably never.

    b. Partitioning is likely to decrease the performance of queries a little. Queries taking a long time usually do so because of a lack of an applicable index, possibly a composite one. The way you craft the query also has an effect, and the design of your queries probably affects them way more than partitions would.

    c. It depends.

    d. It depends.

e. Partitioning wouldn't be helpful since your table has around 2 million rows. Start by optimizing the performance of slow-running queries and think about partitioning once you have bigger data sets to work with.

Why did the user Y answer questions in such a way? What's hidden behind his words? Let's find out:

a. For partitioning to be particularly effective, one needs to have big data sets to work with. "Big" means something with tens of millions of rows at the very least. Thus, by saying "probably never," he meant "you don't have enough data to necessitate partitioning."

b. For partitioning to be effective, it has to work in conjunction with queries, not replace them and work for them instead. The user needs to take care of query design first and add any applicable indexes, then if that doesn't help, turn to partitions.

c. It depends because no queries were ever provided for inspection – if queries through 2 million rows are already slow, there are enough problems aside from partitioning.

d. It depends on the configuration of your database and the resources of an applicable server – everything comes down to the storage engine in question, too (I'd guess user X is using InnoDB), and for partitioning to be completed as quickly as possible, certain parameters need to be optimized properly and data needs to be inserted in a way that doesn't obstruct the database.

e. If queries are already slow, partitioning 2 million rows isn't likely to do much good – in fact, it may do more harm than good because if your queries are a mess on 2 million rows to begin with and your data is growing, I can only imagine what happens once you reach data exceeding 8 digits.

The answers may seem a little mean to some, but they have a lot of weight – in this case, partitioning isn't necessary, because there simply isn't enough data to warrant it. So, when does one decide it's time to partition data?

There is no "one-rule-fits-all" solution here; the time to partition data arrives when you've optimized your schemas, queries, and indexes, and see that none of your approaches help increase the performance of your queries to a satisfactory level. The performance of your queries may still be declining because you search through a lot of data and your database thinks that this much data is too much to handle. That isn't likely to happen for many of you, but once or if that happens, it's time to think about partitions. Some of you may decide whether your use case necessitates partitions without doing that: if you already know that your use case necessitates users searching through more than 100 million rows, is it worth your time or effort to postpone partitioning? No.

In other words, partition your tables when you know that you're going to store a lot of rows inside a table. Exceeded 100 million rows in one table? Time to partition. Have reasons to believe that your data set will exceed 100 million rows in one table? Partition. Optimized both your database and queries with indexes, but queries are still slow? Consider partitioning. One thing you shouldn't be doing, though, is indexing/partitioning everything you see: everything has a price, and both indexes and partitions will slow down queries that update, insert, or delete data. In other words, partition carefully and only after fully understanding the implications of a given partitioning type.

Internals of Database Partitioning

Partitioning splits data into separate tables, but for many, it's hard to understand because your database deals with partitioning in silence: it doesn't show information on partitioned tables once you run `SHOW TABLES` or provide much information by default, so if you don't know ways to see what's going on behind the hood partitioning-wise, you may have a tough time advising fellow developers what to do and what's wrong. Thankfully, MySQL and its counterparts do provide ways for developers to obtain information about partitions existing in a database. One can use the `SHOW CREATE TABLE` statement.

CHAPTER 12 OPTIMIZING PARTITIONS

```
MariaDB [hacking_mysql]> SHOW CREATE TABLE demo_partitioned;
+------------------+----------------------------------------------------------
| Table            | Create Table
+------------------+----------------------------------------------------------
| demo_partitioned | CREATE TABLE `demo_partitioned` (
    `data_int` int(117) DEFAULT NULL
) ENGINE=InnoDB DEFAULT CHARSET=utf8mb4 COLLATE=utf8mb4_unicode_ci
 PARTITION BY LIST (`data_int`)
(PARTITION `partition_1` VALUES IN (1,2,3,4,5) ENGINE = InnoDB,
 PARTITION `partition_2` VALUES IN (6,7,8,9,10) ENGINE = InnoDB) |
+------------------+----------------------------------------------------------
1 row in set (0.001 sec)
```

Figure 12-1. *SHOW CREATE TABLE in MariaDB*

Alternatively, one can understand if a table is partitioned through the SHOW TABLE STATUS option – inspecting the Create_options column will do the trick (note that this query doesn't display the actual partitions, just whether the table is partitioned or not).

Update_time	Check_time	Collation	Checksum	Create_options	Comment	Max_index_length	Temporary
NULL	NULL	utf8mb4_unicode_ci	NULL			0	N
NULL	NULL	utf8mb4_unicode_ci	NULL			0	N
NULL	NULL	utf8mb4_unicode_ci	NULL			0	N
NULL	NULL	utf8mb4_unicode_ci	NULL			0	N
NULL	NULL	utf8mb4_unicode_ci	NULL	partitioned		0	N
NULL	NULL	utf8mb4_unicode_ci	NULL			0	N
NULL	NULL	utf8mb4_bin	NULL			0	N
NULL	NULL	utf8mb4_bin	NULL			0	N
NULL	NULL	utf8mb4_unicode_ci	NULL			0	N

Figure 12-2. *Partial output of SHOW TABLE STATUS in MariaDB*

SHOW TABLE STATUS won't display the names and types of partitions, but it will provide many other useful information such as the engine the table is running, how many rows exist in a table, what's the average data length, index length, whether the table has an automatically incrementing column, what it's collation looks like, etc.

For those wanting to do things through the CLI, we can understand if data is partitioned if we inspect the data directory in MariaDB or MySQL and see [table_name]#p#[title].ibd but for the file name to not be misinterpreted, the output would require a bit of knowledge to understand what everything means (table_name refers to the table name, #p# refers to the partition, and title refers to the name of the partition while .ibd refers to the data file.)

CHAPTER 12 OPTIMIZING PARTITIONS

As an example, I'll list the files available within the `hacking_mysql` database. Take a look – what partitions do you see here and on what table?

```
C:\wamp64\bin\mariadb\mariadb10.10.2\data\hacking_mysql>ls
all_cities.frm                      demodata_table.ibd
all_cities.ibd                      ecommerce_demo.frm
car_data.frm                        ecommerce_demo.ibd
car_data.ibd                        json_demo.frm
db.opt                              json_demo.ibd
demo.frm                            messages.frm
demo.ibd                            messages.MYD
demo_data.frm                       messages.MYI
demo_data.ibd                       messages_old.frm
demo_partitioned#p#partition_1.ibd  messages_old.ibd
demo_partitioned#p#partition_2.ibd  mock_data.frm
demo_partitioned.frm                mock_data.ibd
demo_partitioned.par                normalization_example.frm
demo_table.frm                      normalization_example.ibd
demo_table.ibd                      old_demo_data.frm
demodata_table.frm                  old_demo_data.ibd
```

Figure 12-3. *Data files in MariaDB*

We see two partitions under the names of `partition_1` and `partition_2`. These partitions reside on the `demo_partitioned` table that runs the InnoDB storage engine – got the idea?

Granted, files won't say what type of partitioning is in use, so that's a downside. The type of partitioning may determine the effectiveness of partitions themselves, and so when thinking about whether to partition your tables and how to do it, it's wise to return to the roots and understand the options permitted by partitioning in the first place.

Types of Partitioning in MySQL

Options permitted by partitions in MySQL and its counterparts directly depend on the type of partitioning you find yourself using. Available partitioning types in MySQL and its counterparts include four partitioning types – each of those partitioning types comes with its upsides and downsides and those are as follows:

1. **Partitioning by RANGE or RANGE COLUMNS**: Partitioning data by range is one of the most frequently used ways to partition data in MariaDB and MySQL. Partitioning data by range enables us to spin up separate partitions for data falling within a given range, so partitioning by range would allow you to store rows with values less than 100 in one partition, values less than 50 in another, and use another partition for values less than 25. Partitioning by RANGE COLUMNS lets users provide MySQL with a list of one or more columns to be used when defining partitioning ranges, too.

2. **Partitioning by LIST or LIST COLUMNS**: Such a partitioning type accepts a list of values as the partitioning key. When such a partitioning type is in use, data falls into partitions based on whether it's included in the list or not.

3. **Partitioning by HASH**: Partitioning by hash ensures an even distribution of data across a number of defined partitions. Only numeric expressions are accepted as the partitioning key.

4. **Partitioning by KEY**: Partitioning by key is similar to partitioning by hash, but where partitioning by hash takes user input, partitioning by key takes input provided by the server (i.e., an internal hashing function is used). As a result, we only need to define the number of partitions.

Aside from these types of partitioning, many database management systems support subpartitioning, and MySQL is not an exception.

Partitioning by RANGE is perhaps one of the most frequent ways to partition data in MySQL. Such a partitioning type is rather easy to understand. Take a look at this example:

```
CREATE TABLE `demo_partitioned` (
`first_name` VARCHAR(30) NOT NULL DEFAULT '',
`last_name` VARCHAR(30) NOT NULL DEFAULT '',
`work_department_id` SMALLINT(20) NOT NULL DEFAULT 0,
`salary` INT(10) NOT NULL DEFAULT 10000
)
```

```
PARTITION BY RANGE (work_department_id) (
PARTITION p0 VALUES LESS THAN (5),
PARTITION p1 VALUES LESS THAN (10),
PARTITION p2 VALUES LESS THAN (15),
PARTITION p3 VALUES LESS THAN (20),
PARTITION p4 VALUES LESS THAN (25),
PARTITION p5 VALUES LESS THAN (30)
);
```

What do you think is happening here? We partition the column `work_department id` into six separate partitions (p0 is also a partition – we just start counting from 0.) All values less than 5 are stored in the partition titled p0, values less than 10 are stored in the partition p1, and so on. Such an approach makes our table bigger by default (96kB instead of 16kB), but also makes our data reside in separate "sub-tables" of which we have six.

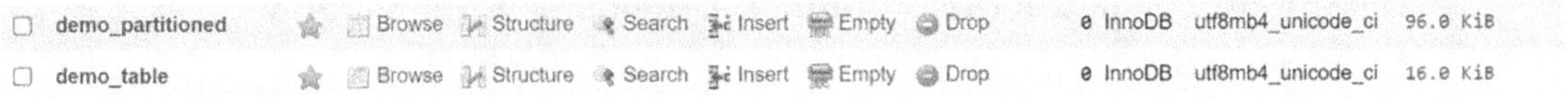

Figure 12-4. Partitioned table is bigger.

One thing you should note when making use of partitioning is that when partitioning a column, the column that you use in the partitioning expression must be a part of a unique key if composite indexes are explicitly defined. That means that if you include the id column in a table and try to partition the table in the same way, you may face an error as follows:

```
#1503 - A PRIMARY KEY must include all columns in the table's partitioning function
```

Coming back to partitioning by range, everything's self-explanatory: the value of 27 would be stored in the partition titled "p5," a value of 3 would be stored in the partition titled p0, and so on. If we insert a value that is outside the partition bounds, an error would appear. Such an error can be solved by adding a single additional partition with the value of MAXVALUE – in other words, every value that remains:

```
PARTITION p6 VALUES LESS THAN MAXVALUE
```

From now on, any values that don't match the values defined in partitions 0 to 5 will reside in partition number 6. If you use this approach, be wary of putting too many values in a partition with MAXVALUE; such an approach is beneficial, but only beneficial once all of your other partitions work in unison. If you have two partitions and the MAXVALUE partition holds 90% of the total values, something's wrong and you should reconsider your approach.

Aside from that, partitioning by range can also consider string values – then, one could use partitioning by RANGE COLUMNS instead of partitioning by RANGE and everything would look like so:

```
CREATE TABLE `demo_partitioned` (
`first_name` VARCHAR(30) NOT NULL DEFAULT '',
`last_name` VARCHAR(30) NOT NULL DEFAULT '',
`work_department_id` VARCHAR(20) NOT NULL DEFAULT '',
`salary` INT(10) NOT NULL DEFAULT 10000
)
PARTITION BY RANGE COLUMNS (work_department_id) (
PARTITION p0 VALUES LESS THAN ('a'),
PARTITION p1 VALUES LESS THAN ('b'),
PARTITION p2 VALUES LESS THAN ('c'),
...
PARTITION p3 VALUES LESS THAN MAXVALUE
);
```

Notice that the work_department_id column now has a VARCHAR data type.

Partitioning by LIST is quite self-explanatory, too: this partitioning type lets us define partitions based on values as the partitioning keys. The partitioning expression must be either a column value or an expression based on it that returns an integer value. Here's an example (note that if you provide integers as partitioning keys, if the column has a default value, it should also be an integer):

```
CREATE TABLE `demo_partitioned_list` (
`first_name` VARCHAR(30) NOT NULL DEFAULT '',
`last_name` VARCHAR(30) NOT NULL DEFAULT '',
`work_department_id` INT(20) NOT NULL DEFAULT 0,
`salary` INT(10) NOT NULL DEFAULT 10000
)
```

CHAPTER 12   OPTIMIZING PARTITIONS

```
PARTITION BY LIST(work_department_id) (
PARTITION p0 VALUES IN (1,3,5,7),
PARTITION p1 VALUES IN (2,4,6,8),
PARTITION p2 VALUES IN (10,12,14,16),
PARTITION p3 VALUES IN (11,13,15,17)
);
```

Such a partitioning definition would come up with four partitions, and as mentioned before, values not matching those defined in the partitions would be rejected.

```
MariaDB [hacking_mysql]> INSERT INTO demo_partitioned_list VALUES ('John', 'Doe', 5, 10000);
Query OK, 1 row affected (0.003 sec)

MariaDB [hacking_mysql]> INSERT INTO demo_partitioned_list VALUES ('Josh', 'Doe', 8, 10000);
Query OK, 1 row affected (0.002 sec)

MariaDB [hacking_mysql]> INSERT INTO demo_partitioned_list VALUES ('Jack', 'Doe', 16, 10000);
Query OK, 1 row affected (0.014 sec)

MariaDB [hacking_mysql]> INSERT INTO demo_partitioned_list VALUES ('James', 'Doe', 28, 10000);
ERROR 1526 (HY000): Table has no partition for value 28
MariaDB [hacking_mysql]>
```

Figure 12-5.   *No partition for a given value*

Granted, one can use `INSERT IGNORE INTO` instead, but if you choose such an approach, don't be surprised that certain values will be missing.

```
MariaDB [hacking_mysql]> INSERT INTO demo_partitioned_list VALUES ('James', 'Doe', 28, 10000);
ERROR 1526 (HY000): Table has no partition for value 28
MariaDB [hacking_mysql]> INSERT IGNORE INTO demo_partitioned_list VALUES ('James', 'Doe', 28, 10000);
Query OK, 0 rows affected, 1 warning (0.001 sec)

MariaDB [hacking_mysql]> SELECT * FROM demo_partitioned_list WHERE work_department_id = 28;
Empty set (0.014 sec)
```

Figure 12-6.   *No values in a partition*

If partitioning by `LIST` is not your type or if you use columns of data types other than integer, keep in mind that partitioning by `LIST COLUMNS` is also possible.

Partitioning by `HASH` isn't anything out of the ordinary, either – such a partitioning type enables us to split values within a table evenly. All we need to define is an integer defining the count of applicable partitions, and then MySQL will split applicable values evenly across all of the partitions:

```
CREATE TABLE `demo_partitioned_hash` (
`first_name` VARCHAR(30) NOT NULL DEFAULT '',
`last_name` VARCHAR(30) NOT NULL DEFAULT '',
`work_department_id` INT(20) NOT NULL DEFAULT 0,
`salary` INT(10) NOT NULL DEFAULT 10000
)
PARTITION BY HASH(salary)
PARTITIONS 4;
```

Hash partitioning relieves you of the burden of specifying a partition to store values in – your database will decide that for you.

As far as hash partitioning is concerned, there were talks in Stack Overflow saying that the name of a hash partition can be determined by running a query like so (here [input] determines your input and the [number] is the number of partitions):

```
SELECT partition_name from information_schema.partitions
where table_name = 'table_name'
and partition_ordinal_position = 1+ ABS(MOD([input], [number]));
```

Finally, we have partitioning by key. Partitioning a table by key works almost the same as partitioning a table by hash, the only difference being the partitioning function used. When partitioning by key is in use, the function will be derived from the server. Also, keep in mind that when partitioning by key is being used, all columns that are used as part of the partitioning expression must form a part or an entirety of a primary key and we also have to specify the number of partitions necessary. Partitioning by key looks like this:

```
CREATE TABLE `demo_partitioned_key` (
`id` INT(20) NOT NULL AUTO_INCREMENT PRIMARY KEY,
`first_name` VARCHAR(30) NOT NULL DEFAULT '',
`last_name` VARCHAR(30) NOT NULL DEFAULT '',
`work_department_id` INT(20) NOT NULL DEFAULT 0,
`salary` INT(10) NOT NULL DEFAULT 10000
)
PARTITION BY KEY(id)
PARTITIONS 2;
```

CHAPTER 12 OPTIMIZING PARTITIONS

No matter the type of partitioning used, your database will use a partitioning function to determine what partition to put the data in. One of the primary benefits of partitioning is that it helps your database split large data sets into smaller chunks that can be more easily "absorbed" or used by your application. Also, keep in mind that some types of partitioning will limit you regarding the data types available for you to use.

Aside from helping access data faster, partitions can also be used for data pruning.

```
MariaDB [hacking_mysql]> SHOW CREATE TABLE demo_partitioned_list;
+----------------------+----------------------+
| Table                | Create Table         |
+----------------------+----------------------+
| demo_partitioned_list | CREATE TABLE `demo_partitioned_list` (
  `first_name` varchar(30) NOT NULL DEFAULT '',
  `last_name` varchar(30) NOT NULL DEFAULT '',
  `work_department_id` int(20) NOT NULL DEFAULT 0,
  `salary` int(10) NOT NULL DEFAULT 10000
) ENGINE=InnoDB DEFAULT CHARSET=utf8mb4 COLLATE=utf8mb4_unicode_ci
 PARTITION BY LIST (`work_department_id`)
(PARTITION `p0` VALUES IN (1,3,5,7) ENGINE = InnoDB,
 PARTITION `p1` VALUES IN (2,4,6,8) ENGINE = InnoDB,
 PARTITION `p2` VALUES IN (10,12,14,16) ENGINE = InnoDB,
 PARTITION `p3` VALUES IN (11,13,15,17) ENGINE = InnoDB) |
+----------------------+----------------------+
1 row in set (0.001 sec)

MariaDB [hacking_mysql]> INSERT INTO demo_partitioned_list VALUES ('John', 'Doe', 4, 60000);
Query OK, 1 row affected (0.013 sec)

MariaDB [hacking_mysql]> ALTER TABLE demo_partitioned_list DROP PARTITION p1;
Query OK, 0 rows affected (0.044 sec)
Records: 0  Duplicates: 0  Warnings: 0

MariaDB [hacking_mysql]> SELECT * FROM `demo_partitioned_list` WHERE first_name = 'John' AND last_name = 'Doe' AND work_department_id = 4 AND salary = 60000;
Empty set (0.007 sec)
```

Figure 12-7. Pruning data in partitions

If your table is partitioned and you find yourself in a situation where you know that results will be in one or more partitions and you know that some partitions are unnecessary, removing partitions will help reclaim some space on the disk.

Partition pruning can also be performed by the query optimizer in the sense that when queries with any of the equality signs (=,<,>,<=,>= or <>) or the IN clause are in use, the optimizer will only scan through data in a partition that contains the value. If you use such an approach to partition pruning, no data will be removed from the partitions themselves – they just won't be searched through.

Partitioning Tips: Subpartitioning, Limitations, NULL Values, and More

When it comes to partitioning, MySQL and its counterparts do have a special trick up their sleeves: the first rule to remember in this realm is that as a DBMS, *MySQL treats NULL values as being less significant than other values.* That doesn't mean that NULL values are not stored in partitions – they are – but some types of MySQL partitioning treat NULL values differently than others do.

If you use partitioning by RANGE, bear in mind that any NULL values used to determine the partition will be inserted into the lowest possible partition. Partitioning by LIST will allow NULL values to be inserted if one of its lists contains NULL values. For tables partitioned by HASH or KEY, if a value that yields NULL is inserted into a partition, the value is treated as if it's a zero (0).

Subpartitioning is another rather interesting thing you should keep in mind – if we partition partitions, we subpartition. Subpartitions are explicitly defined and often look something like this:

```
CREATE TABLE `demo_subpartitioned` (
`first_name` VARCHAR(30) NOT NULL DEFAULT '',
`last_name` VARCHAR(30) NOT NULL DEFAULT '',
`join_date` DATE NOT NULL,
`salary` INT(10) NOT NULL DEFAULT 10000
)
PARTITION BY RANGE(YEAR(join_date))
SUBPARTITION BY HASH(salary)
(
        PARTITION p0 VALUES LESS THAN (60000),
        PARTITION p1 VALUES LESS THAN (80000),
        PARTITION p2 VALUES LESS THAN MAXVALUE
);
```

In this example, we partition the join_date by range and then add a subpartition for the salary. When defining any partition including subpartitions, we need to adhere to all of the rules of partitioning (see below).

CHAPTER 12   OPTIMIZING PARTITIONS

Finally, when defining partitions, remember a couple of key rules:

1. As of MySQL 8.4, partitioning is only supported by the InnoDB and NDB storage engines. MariaDB adds more storage engines to the mix – they are MERGE, SPIDER, and CONNECT.

2. Partitions are tables within your table, but the SQL layer will still "glue everything together" and won't display separate tables per partition. Partitions can be observed by running the SHOW CREATE TABLE or SHOW TABLE STATUS queries.

3. Partitions have a couple of types – partitioning by range lets us define separate partitions for data falling within a given range, partitioning by range columns lets users provide a list of columns that MySQL should partition by range, partitioning by list accepts a list of values as partitioning keys, partitioning by hash ensures an even distribution of data across several partitions, and partitioning by key takes an internal hashing function as the partitioning key.

4. Partitioning has limitations (see above).

5. Partitions are not only useful to supplement search operations – they can be pruned, thus freeing up space on the disk and getting rid of the data inside of partitions, too.

6. If you use VALUES LESS THAN, you must define values in a strictly increasing manner.

7. Partitions can be used with indexes and vice versa. If a table uses both partitions and indexes, its size will be significantly larger than usual, but at the same time, your database will have an easier time reading data.

8. MAXVALUE means "everything not defined in other partitions."

It's wise to stop at indexing for a second – partitions are divisions of data that are still treated as a whole data set by your database. As such, *columns that are partitioned can also be indexed* – and using both partitions and indexes can boost your query performance to levels you can't even imagine. To understand the concept, consider a table with 1 billion rows: for the sake of an example, we'll say that all rows within that table are split equally across 10 partitions: that's already 100 million rows in a table separated from the rest (remember – your database treats partitions as tables). Indexing will help further maximize the efficiency of your `SELECT` queries by sorting data and knowing what subset of the data to access when you search for it. In other words, without indexes or partitions, your database would have to read through 100% of the data, with partitions alone that percentage drops down to 10% or even less (depending on how many partitions are specified), and indexes will help sort that 10% of data to help your database access even less data when searching for a specific row.

Another thing to note is that MariaDB allows you to convert partitions to tables and vice versa. If we use a query like `CONVERT PARTITION ... TO TABLE ...`, our partition will be converted into a table, and if we use a query like `CONVERT TABLE ... TO [partition definition]`, our table will be converted into a partition. This feature is in place in MariaDB starting from MariaDB 10.7. See example below.

```
MariaDB [hacking_mysql]> ALTER TABLE `demo_partitioned_list` CONVERT PARTITION `p0` TO TABLE `table_list`;
Query OK, 0 rows affected (0.055 sec)
Records: 0  Duplicates: 0  Warnings: 0

MariaDB [hacking_mysql]> SHOW TABLES;
+-------------------------+
| Tables_in_hacking_mysql |
+-------------------------+
| all_cities              |
| car_data                |
| demo                    |
| demo_data               |
| demo_partitioned        |
| demo_partitioned_hash   |
| demo_partitioned_key    |
| demo_partitioned_list   |
| demo_subpartitioned     |
| demo_table              |
| demodata_table          |
| ecommerce_demo          |
| json_demo               |
| messages                |
| messages_old            |
| mock_data               |
| normalization_example   |
| old_demo_data           |
| table_list              |
+-------------------------+
19 rows in set (0.004 sec)

MariaDB [hacking_mysql]>
```

Figure 12-8. Converting a partition into a table

CHAPTER 12   OPTIMIZING PARTITIONS

The same can be said about converting tables into partitions, too.

```
MariaDB [hacking_mysql]> ALTER TABLE `demo_partitioned_list` CONVERT TABLE `table_list` TO PARTITION `p0` VALUES IN (1,3,5,7,9);
Query OK, 0 rows affected (0.045 sec)
Records: 0  Duplicates: 0  Warnings: 0

MariaDB [hacking_mysql]> SHOW TABLES;
+------------------------+
| Tables_in_hacking_mysql |
+------------------------+
| all_cities             |
| car_data               |
| demo                   |
| demo_data              |
| demo_partitioned       |
| demo_partitioned_hash  |
| demo_partitioned_key   |
| demo_partitioned_list  |
| demo_subpartitioned    |
| demo_table             |
| demodata_table         |
| ecommerce_demo         |
| json_demo              |
| messages               |
| messages_old           |
| mock_data              |
| normalization_example  |
| old_demo_data          |
+------------------------+
18 rows in set (0.004 sec)

MariaDB [hacking_mysql]>
```

Figure 12-9. *Converting a table into a partition*

Keep in mind that partitions, like tables, can also be analyzed, checked, repaired, or optimized with a query like so:

ALTER TABLE [table_name] ANALYZE|CHECK|REPAIR|OPTIMIZE PARTITION [partition names];

```
MariaDB [hacking_mysql]> ALTER TABLE `demo_partitioned_list` ANALYZE PARTITION p0;
+-----------------------------------+---------+----------+----------+
| Table                             | Op      | Msg_type | Msg_text |
+-----------------------------------+---------+----------+----------+
| hacking_mysql.demo_partitioned_list | analyze | status   | OK       |
+-----------------------------------+---------+----------+----------+
1 row in set (0.005 sec)

MariaDB [hacking_mysql]> ALTER TABLE `demo_partitioned_list` CHECK PARTITION p0;
+-----------------------------------+-------+----------+----------+
| Table                             | Op    | Msg_type | Msg_text |
+-----------------------------------+-------+----------+----------+
| hacking_mysql.demo_partitioned_list | check | status   | OK       |
+-----------------------------------+-------+----------+----------+
1 row in set (0.001 sec)

MariaDB [hacking_mysql]> ALTER TABLE `demo_partitioned_list` REPAIR PARTITION p0;
+-----------------------------------+--------+----------+----------+
| Table                             | Op     | Msg_type | Msg_text |
+-----------------------------------+--------+----------+----------+
| hacking_mysql.demo_partitioned_list | repair | status   | OK       |
+-----------------------------------+--------+----------+----------+
1 row in set (0.001 sec)

MariaDB [hacking_mysql]> ALTER TABLE `demo_partitioned_list` OPTIMIZE PARTITION p0;
+-----------------------------------+----------+----------+----------+
| Table                             | Op       | Msg_type | Msg_text |
+-----------------------------------+----------+----------+----------+
| hacking_mysql.demo_partitioned_list | optimize | status   | OK       |
+-----------------------------------+----------+----------+----------+
1 row in set (0.006 sec)

MariaDB [hacking_mysql]>
```

Figure 12-10. Analyzing, checking, repairing, and optimizing a partition

Partitions can be reorganized – a partition can be split into multiple partitions, merged with existing partitions, or renamed. Oh, and you can change their internal structure (i.e., what values they cover) too.

Partitions can be split like so:

```
ALTER TABLE `table_name` REORGANIZE PARTITION `p1` INTO (
PARTITION `reorg_p1` VALUES LESS THAN (2000),
PARTITION `reorg_p2` VALUES LESS THAN (3000)
);
```

Merged like so:

```
ALTER TABLE `table_name` REORGANIZE PARTITION `p0`,`p1` INTO (
    PARTITION p2 VALUES LESS THAN (3000)
);
```

And renamed like so:

```
ALTER TABLE `table_name` REORGANIZE PARTITION `p0` INTO (
PARTITION `p0_renamed` VALUES LESS THAN (1000)
);
```

Finally, you can also reduce the number of partitions from a column. To do that, make use of the COALESCE PARTITION statement (this statement applies to all partitions as a whole, not to any single partition):

```
ALTER TABLE `demo_table` COALESCE PARTITION 2;
```

After you have dipped your toes in the partitioning water, also keep in mind that partitioning has a couple of limitations unique to itself:

1. You cannot use stored procedures, functions, or user-defined variables as partitioning expressions.
2. All storage engines excluding NDB support up to 8,192 partitions. For NDB, the number depends on the version of NDBCluster in use.
3. Partitioning expressions don't allow the operators |, &, ^, <<, >>, or ~.
4. Partitioned tables on InnoDB don't support foreign keys.
5. ALTER TABLE ORDER BY If we run statements like ALTER TABLE ORDER BY on a partitioned column, we should be mindful that only values within a partitioned column will be ordered.
6. Adding FULLTEXT indexes on a partitioned table is impossible.
7. One cannot use the ENUM data type to denote partitioning keys.
8. A partitioning key cannot be a subquery.
9. You cannot partition log tables.

CHAPTER 12   OPTIMIZING PARTITIONS

10. If subpartitions are defined, they must be partitioned by HASH or by KEY.

11. Starting from MySQL 8.4, MySQL uses 130kB of memory per partition for buffering to improve the performance of LOAD DATA INFILE statements.

Even with all of these limitations in sight, partitioning is a really helpful companion to many – with a well-optimized database, query structure, and wise indexing decisions, partitioning will help you overcome performance burdens when reading data.

Before choosing to partition though, weigh all other decisions you've made – inspect the database structure, data types and character sets, indexes that may reside on any columns within your table, and other things: partitioning will only be helpful as an assisting, not a replacing tool. If you find yourself running different flavors of MySQL (e.g., MariaDB or Percona Server), pay extra attention to the storage engines available within your server, too: since partitioning is directly dependent on the storage engine you find yourself using, and since different flavors of MySQL come with different storage engines, those engines will allow you to perform a bunch of interesting things with partitions too. Users of MariaDB will be aware of MERGE, SPIDER, and CONNECT: in this sphere, SPIDER would allow you to conduct data sharding by moving partitions of the same table across different servers, and CONNECT would enable you to build tables with partitions running different storage engines that may not support partitioning.

Here's an example of the CONNECT storage engine being used to power partitioning in MariaDB:

```
CREATE TABLE `demo_table` (
`id` INT(5),
`account_name` VARCHAR(20) NOT NULL DEFAULT '',
`assigned_supportagent` VARCHAR(20) NOT NULL DEFAULT '',
key(`account_name`)
) ENGINE = SPIDER COMMENT = 'wrapper "mysql", table "demo_table"'
PARTITION BY RANGE COLUMNS(`account_name`)
(
PARTITION `p1` VALUES LESS THAN ('L') COMMENT = 'Values stored in server Mercury',
PARTITION `p2` VALUES LESS THAN (MAXVALUE) COMMENT = 'Values stored in server Venus'
);
```

In this case, all values up to K (K precedes L) would be stored in the server titled Mercury, and the rest of them would be stored in the server titled Venus. Interesting! We have much more to learn though.

Summary

Partitioning is a method to split tables inside of your database into several different tables – your database will treat partitions as a bunch of different tables under the hood, but since the SQL layer will still treat partitions as one table, you won't ever be able to see your partitions as separate tables in any SQL clients or phpMyAdmin. However, you will be assisted with statements like `SHOW TABLES` or `SHOW CREATE TABLE`: the first statement will show whether partitions are in place on a specific table, and the second statement will provide you with a query that lets you recreate a table with partitions.

Partitions are only one piece of the cake though and partitioning shouldn't be done carelessly – partition only once you have enough data to warrant it (think 100 million rows or more), and do so only once you're well-acquainted with the internals of partitioning in the first place.

Whatever you do, remember that partitioning is only a piece related to your tables, tables that are behind a database that contains data. To avoid issues, that database needs to be backed up properly and often, and to come up with a proper backup plan, you need to plan for recovery too. Grab a coffee – time to backup.

CHAPTER 13

Optimizing Backups and Recovery

You do take backups, don't you? Seriously – backup and recovery procedures exist for a reason, and that reason has nothing to do with making your life as a developer or DBA harder or more complex. Every developer knows why they should back up their most precious asset – data – but not everyone does.

Not everyone backs up data – such is the reality of the web today. Sure, perhaps for you, there's no need to back up data every day – but that's not a reason to forget backups altogether, is it?

In this ever-changing world, backups are a necessity; backups are in place to protect the data of your organization from hardware failure, human errors, or even natural disasters. Many forget about them – some neglect them. Regardless of what's the reason behind you not backing up your data, backups are a necessity, and if taking them is not already a routine for your DBAs, it should become one.

When it comes to databases, many DBMS offers multiple different ways to take database backups and restore them. MySQL and MariaDB are no exception to the rule, but before digging deeper into what may be involved when you find yourself in the MariaDB backup and recovery realm, first, we have to understand why, when, and how people back up databases like MySQL in the first place.

Why, When, and How to Backup MariaDB?

Data is backed up for it to be restored in the future when disaster strikes. Backups are done differently depending on the application and your use case in question, and just as there are multiple ways for someone to mess up and lose all of the data in your database, there are multiple ways to back up the data inside of MySQL or any of its counterparts too. This book has a focus on MariaDB, so the options shown here will likely differ for those using Percona Server, MySQL, or even newer versions of MariaDB that will be released in the future.

As for why you should back up data in MariaDB, everything's pretty obvious – backing up and testing your database backups frequently will help you avoid headaches that may occur once disaster strikes. If you don't yet, implement backups into your routine as a developer – you may not need to complete them every single day, so come up with a plan for what backup frequency is deemed acceptable by you and your database, and act accordingly. Add backups to your development routine, and you will never regret your decision.

If you haven't yet, back up your data now. Then, come up with a feasible backup interval that won't hurt your workflow and that will lessen the amount of headaches you get once the hardware holding your assets crashes.

Then, to back up the data inside of MariaDB, the first thing I would advise you to do is to have a look at backups from a birds-eye view and decide on a couple of things. Consider answering the following questions:

- **What kind of data are you backing up?** In other words, what's the use case behind the database powering your application and what kind of backup are you taking?

- **How much data do you need to back up and why?** Backing up bigger data sets will necessitate different actions you need to take.

- **Did you take backups before and what types of backups were they?** Did you take logical backups? Physical backups? Both? How often?

- **Are your backup processes manual or automated?** Why?

- **How often do you need your data to be backed up?** In other words, what backup frequency does your application necessitate and why?

- **What medium are you backing up data into?** Are you backing up data into a cloud service, a separate VPS, a Network Attached Storage device, perhaps an external hard drive, or even a USB?

CHAPTER 13   OPTIMIZING BACKUPS AND RECOVERY

- **Do you follow backup best practices?** Here, I'm talking about things like "bulletproof backups" that necessitate backups of data to be stored in a variety of different locations so that you can access the data to restore it when necessary regardless of the magnitude of the incident that caused you to lose it in the first place.

Answer these questions to obtain knowledge about a variety of different things. These things may include, but are not limited to, the following:

1) Whether you will have to take logical or physical backups and what are your options when it comes to restoring them.

2) You will know how better to back up your data.

3) You will know whether you can use your experience gained in the past to help your database in its present state.

4) You will be aware of the variety of backup scripts you can use when backing up the data inside of your database.

5) Finally, you will know the approximate number of backups a specific device can store and how often you need to rotate backups (i.e., what number of backups to retain/delete, etc.).

All in all, understanding these things will point you toward a direction you need to consider when backing up data. For example, if your backups are logical, you would need to look into tools helping you back up SQL statements that recreate data. On the other hand, if your backups are physical, you will know that no matter what you do, you will need to take copies of the files within your database, and thus, you will be forced to look only at the tools that can take physical copies of data – copies of files and not of SQL statements that recreate data that's stored inside files.

From there, appliance gates will open – you will now know what appliances you should be using to back up data in the way you desire. Users choosing to back up data in a logical way may use appliances like `mariadb-dump`, while users taking physical backups may use simple commands available within Windows or Linux.

Do note that physical backups may be a little harder to restore because such backups in MariaDB can only be restored on similar hardware that runs the same database management system and the same (or relatively unchanged) version of MariaDB. That's the case because physical backups back up data that is subject to changes as time goes along. As such, the restoration of physical backups is often less flexible, though such backups may be faster and less resource-intensive at the same time.

If you know that you back up data into the cloud with a limited amount (say, 5GB) of space, you will have a basis for an assumption on how many backups can your specific cloud account store. In other words, being delicately aware of your use case will help you assume how frequently should you back up data, too. It turns out that everything is much simpler than it seems, right?

When it comes to actually backing up your data, the way you will back up data is, once again, directly related to what kind of backups you need to take – physical backups will necessitate you to back up files from the database; logical backups will necessitate you back up statements that recreate data. One can take logical types of backups "by hand" using tools like the Export functionality of your favorite SQL client, while physical backups will necessitate some more knowledge.

Backup Types and Tools

When it comes to backup types available in MySQL, there are multiple types of data backup strategies you can choose from. The types of MySQL backups are split into multiple categories: some people put backups in categories according to how data is backed up (if we back up SQL statements, our backups will be logical, and if we back up files, our backups will be physical). Some people split backups into categories based on whether backups are hot or cold (hot backups backup data while a system behind it is being actively used and cold backups backup data once the system is down), or whether they're completed online or offline. Backups can also be full, incremental, differential, or snapshot-based. Backups also can be compressed.

So many distinct features of backups, right? We will get into them, but first, backup types. I'll start by putting everything in place by using a table:

What's Backed Up?	Database State When Backups Are Made	Full, Incremental, or Differential Backups?
If SQL queries are being backed up, we are taking *logical backups*. If files within the database are being "touched" and backed up, we are taking *physical backups*.	Backups will be considered hot when they're being taken with a database being *online*. Backups will be considered cold when they're being taken with a database being *offline*.	*Full backups* back up everything in a database (all data). *Differential backups* back up data that has been changed since the last full backup has been taken. *Incremental backups* only back up data that has changed since the last full or incremental backup.

So, as you can see, backups differ in a couple of aspects. They differ in

- The data we back up – we can back up SQL statements that recreate data or the data itself.

- The state of the database when we back up data – the database can be online or offline.

- The actual types of backups we make – database backups can be full, differential, or incremental.

Coming back to backup types, full backups refer to the process of backing up all data related to your use case in a single backup operation. This type of backup is called a "Full backup" because it makes a full – a complete – copy of the data assets controlled by the organization. In the database world, full backups often refer to backing up all tables within all databases excluding databases used/created by the system.

To make a full backup of data residing in MariaDB, first decide whether you're taking a physical or logical backup. Then, follow the appropriate steps.

To take a logical backup of data residing inside MariaDB, consider a `mysqldump` equivalent – `mariadb-dump`. `mariadb-dump` takes a logical backup of the data existing in MariaDB, and at the time this book is being written, it's one of the best ways to back up MariaDB-based database instances running mid-sized data sets. Up until MariaDB 11.0.1, `mysqldump` was a symlink to `mariadb-dump` – that's no longer the case. To take a backup with `mariadb-dump`, navigate to the MariaDB bin directory through the CLI, then

CHAPTER 13 OPTIMIZING BACKUPS AND RECOVERY

invoke `mariadb-dump` to see the available options. Familiarize yourself with the available options, then invoke `mariadb-dump` and add the option necessary for your backup by invoking `mariadb-dump` like so:

mariadb-dump [OPTIONS]

The options relevant to `mariadb-dump` are numerous and will be displayed on the screen once the tool is invoked.

```
mariadb-dump
Usage: mariadb-dump [OPTIONS] database [tables]
OR     mariadb-dump [OPTIONS] --databases DB1 [DB2 DB3...]
OR     mariadb-dump [OPTIONS] --all-databases
OR     mariadb-dump [OPTIONS] --system=[SYSTEMOPTIONS]]
For more options, use mariadb-dump --help
mariadb-dump --help
mariadb-dump  Ver 10.19 Distrib 10.10.2-MariaDB, for Win64 (AMD64)
Copyright (c) 2000, 2018, Oracle, MariaDB Corporation Ab and others.

Dumping structure and contents of MariaDB databases and tables.
Usage: mariadb-dump [OPTIONS] database [tables]
OR     mariadb-dump [OPTIONS] --databases DB1 [DB2 DB3...]
OR     mariadb-dump [OPTIONS] --all-databases
OR     mariadb-dump [OPTIONS] --system=[SYSTEMOPTIONS]]

Default options are read from the following files in the given order:
C:\WINDOWS\my.ini C:\WINDOWS\my.cnf C:\my.ini C:\my.cnf C:\wamp64\bin\mariadb\mariadb10.10.2\my.ini
b10.10.2\data\my.ini C:\wamp64\bin\mariadb\mariadb10.10.2\data\my.cnf
The following groups are read: mysqldump mariadb-dump client client-server client-mariadb
The following options may be given as the first argument:
--print-defaults        Print the program argument list and exit.
--no-defaults           Don't read default options from any option file.
The following specify which files/extra groups are read (specified before remaining options):
--defaults-file=#       Only read default options from the given file #.
--defaults-extra-file=# Read this file after the global files are read.
--defaults-group-suffix=# Additionally read default groups with # appended as a suffix.

  -A, --all-databases Dump all the databases. This will be same as --databases
                      with all databases selected.
  -Y, --all-tablespaces
                      Dump all the tablespaces.
  -y, --no-tablespaces
                      Do not dump any tablespace information.
  --add-drop-database Add a DROP DATABASE before each create.
  --add-drop-table    Add a DROP TABLE before each create.
                      (Defaults to on; use --skip-add-drop-table to disable.)
  --add-drop-trigger  Add a DROP TRIGGER before each create.
  --add-locks         Add locks around INSERT statements.
                      (Defaults to on; use --skip-add-locks to disable.)
  --allow-keywords    Allow creation of column names that are keywords.
```

Figure 13-1. The options available to use within mariadb-dump

CHAPTER 13 OPTIMIZING BACKUPS AND RECOVERY

Some of the most popular options available for you to use include but are not limited to (two values mean you can choose either and multiple values are explained):

Option	Use Case or Meaning
-A --all-databases	Use these options when you need to back up all data within all databases.
-B --databases	These options dump only the specified databases. When these options are in use, MariaDB will treat the first title argument as the database title. Database names should be separated by spaces (see example below).
--add-drop-database --add-drop-table --add-drop-trigger --add-locks	Depending on which option is used, add a DROP DATABASE option before creating each database anew, a DROP TABLE option before creating tables, a DROP TRIGGER option before creating triggers, or add some locking statements before running INSERT queries.
--lock-all-tables -x	Lock all tables across all databases during the time the backup is running.
--lock-tables -l	When a database is dumped, tables will be locked before the data inside of them will be backed up.
--no-autocommit	INSERT statements will be preceded with the SET autocommit=0 option, and once all data is inserted into a table, a COMMIT will commence.
--no-data -d	Tables will be backed up without any internal information related to them (contents).
--order-by-size	The backup operation is ordered by size: smallest tables first, largest tables last.
--order-by-primary	If a primary key exists on a table, table rows are sorted according to it. If no primary key exists, rows are sorted according to the first unique index.

A couple of examples of mariadb-dump in use can be seen below.

CHAPTER 13   OPTIMIZING BACKUPS AND RECOVERY

```
mariadb-dump -uroot --databases demo2 demo3 > C:/wamp64/tmp/backup.sql
mariadb-dump -uroot --databases demo2 > C:/wamp64/tmp/backup_demo2.sql
```

Figure 13-2. *Backing up databases using mariadb-dump*

```
mariadb-dump -uroot --lock-tables hacking_mysql car_data > C:/wamp64/tmp/hackingmysql_cardata.sql
```

Figure 13-3. *Backing up the data in the car_data table within the hacking_mysql database. Before the table is dumped, a LOCK TABLE statement is added.*

```
mariadb-dump -uroot -p -A -x > C:/wamp64/tmp/backup_alldata.sql
Enter password: ******************
```

Figure 13-4. *Backing up all data across all databases while locking all tables across all databases*

To use `mariadb-dump` for a partial backup, back up only some tables or databases. For an incremental backup, come up with a way to identify changes to databases or tables within, then back up data that changed since the previous backup and new data that has been created.

However, no matter how powerful `mariadb-dump` might seem to be, it should be noted that the tool only takes logical backups. If you want physical backups to be taken, you're going to make use of tools built from a different caliber: one of those is `Mariabackup`, which can be used to perform physical backups of data behind InnoDB, MyRocks, Aria, or MyISAM tables. The tool can take full, incremental, or partial backups as well as restore data. According to MariaDB, `Mariabackup` should be considered as a replacement for Percona XtraBackup since MariaDB doesn't provide official support for XtraBackup and has no plans to do so for the near future – the issue is known but Percona XtraBackup still isn't supported in MariaDB, and that's why MariaDB suggests users use `Mariabackup` can be used with options similar to Percona XtraBackup like so:

```
mariabackup [--backup|--prepare] [--copy-back|--move-back] [options]
```

To backup data using `mariabackup`, make use of the `--target-dir` option to tell MariaDB what directory the backup should be stored in and specify the user and password that can take backups like so:

```
mariabackup --backup --target-dir=/tmp/backups/ --user=hackingmysql --password=verystrongpassword
```

Since `mariabackup` works similarly to Percona XtraBackup, backups taken using `mariabackup` need to be prepared for restoration before restoring the backup since the data files need to be consistent: for that, run a query with the `--prepare` option – don't forget to specify the directory where your backup is located:

```
mariabackup --prepare --target-dir=/tmp/backups/
```

Other available options like `--copy-back` or `--move-back` will specify whether the backup files need to be copied or moved back to the `datadir` directory of the database server – if you want to keep a copy of the data for yourself for whatever reason, use `--copy-back`. Otherwise, use `--move-back`. You will use them when restoring the backup:

```
mariabackup --copy-back --target-dir=/tmp/mariadb/backup/
```

To take incremental backups using `mariabackup`, take a full backup with the `--target-dir` and `--incremental-basedir` options:

```
mariabackup --backup --target-dir=/tmp/mariadb/incremental1 --incremental-basedir=/tmp/mariadb/backup/ --user=root --password=verystrongpassword
```

These commands would create files storing incremental changes to data, thus allowing you to restore a backup as an incremental backup.

To restore the incremental backup, prepare the backup once again (see example above), and then apply incremental changes to the full backup making use of the `--incremental-dir` option:

```
mariabackup --prepare --target-dir=/tmp/mariadb/backup --incremental-dir=/tmp/mariadb/incremental1
```

Only after applying all incremental backups to the base backup will you be able to restore the backup using the `--move-back` or `--copy-back` options and making use of the `--target-dir` option like usual:

```
mariabackup --copy-back --target-dir=/tmp/mariadb/backup/
```

Aside from knowing your way around backup types, there will be situations where you will need to back up massive amounts of data, compress and secure your backups, and of course, restore everything you've backed up when issues have occurred, too.

Backup Compression and Security

Just as backups can be taken, they can be compressed, too. Backup compression enables developers and database administrators to save space on the disk when storing backups and restoring compressed backups often reduces disk I/O so that's a win-win all around.

The same can be said about security – backups can be encrypted when they're being taken and decrypted when they're being restored. Encryption and decryption are done via OpenSSL, while compression and decompression are often done via gzip or 7Zip. I'll start from compression, then move into security, and finally, join the two.

Here's the thing – backup compression in MariaDB isn't complex, nor is it a thing you should learn anew if you were using MySQL or Percona Server in the past. For most of you, MariaDB backup compression and decompression will be achieved using `gzip` and encryption will be achieved by using `openssl` – when compressing and encrypting backups, most of you will also make use of `mariabackup`, so there's no need to invent a bike on this front either.

A basic use case of `mariabackup` to compress files when backing them up would necessitate the `gzip` feature and would look as follows (as always, replace `username` with the applicable username):

```
mariabackup --user=[username] --backup --stream=xbstream | gzip > [backupnamehere].gz
```

Here the `--user` option specifies a user that takes the backup, the `--backup` option specifies that we're taking a backup, the `--stream` option specifies `xbstream` as an option to copy and compress backups in parallel, and finally, the `gzip` option specifies that we want to compress the backup using GZip.

CHAPTER 13   OPTIMIZING BACKUPS AND RECOVERY

To compress backups, you can also use 7Zip instead – here, a very similar logic applies:

`mariabackup --user=[username] --backup --stream=xbstream | 7z a --si [backupnamehere].xb.7z`

To decompress backups taken with `gzip`, we would use `gunzip` like so:

`gunzip -c [backupnamehere].gz | mbstream -x`

To decompress backups taken with 7Zip:

`7z e [backupnamehere].xb.7z -so | mbstream -x`

Not very complex, is it? There are other approaches you can use to compress backups if you wish, but GZip and 7Zip should provide you with a good enough starting point.

When it comes to encryption, everything's also simple: many people using GZip will elect to encrypt their backups using OpenSSL, and doing that would look almost identical to the last example, just with OpenSSL and AES-256 options added into the mix – don't forget to specify the password you'd encrypt the backup with after the `-k` parameter (the `.enc` extension specifies that the backup is encrypted):

`mariabackup --user=[username] --backup --stream=xbstream | gzip |` **`openssl enc -aes-256-cbc -k [encryptionpw]`** `> [backupnamehere].gz.enc`

To decrypt the same backup, use GZip with the `-d` (decryption) option like so and make sure to specify the backup as the input after the `-in` parameter:

`openssl enc -d -aes-256-cbc -k [encryptionpw] -in [backupnamehere].gz.enc |gzip -d| mbstream –x`

To encrypt backups taken by using 7Zip, add the `-p` option while specifying the password you need to encrypt the backup with through the CLI after invoking 7z – 7Zip should have the AES-256 encryption mode built into the tool.

To compress and secure logical backups, you can also use `mariadb-dump` or `mysqldump` and pipe its output to a compression resource like GZip or 7Zip as well. Users of `mysqldump` should already be aware of such an option:

`mysqldump -u[username] [databasename] | gzip > backup.sql.gz`

Everything works the same way with `mariadb-dump` as well, just note that the 7Zip option won't be supported, so if you're compressing logical backups, you're going to have to use `gzip/gunzip` instead.

```
Command Prompt
mariadb-dump -uroot demo2 | gzip > C:/wamp64/tmp/backup.sql.gz
mariadb-dump -uroot demo2 | 7zip > C:/wamp64/tmp/backup.7z
'7zip' is not recognized as an internal or external command,
operable program or batch file.
mariadb-dump -uroot demo2 | 7z > C:/wamp64/tmp/backup.7z
'7z' is not recognized as an internal or external command,
operable program or batch file.
```

Figure 13-5. *mariadb-dump with gzip and 7zip options*

Backup compression and security aren't rocket science, and with some effort and education, your backups can take up less space on the disk and be stored in an encrypted fashion, too. Cool, yeah?

Backing Up Big Data Sets

To back up bigger data sets (let's say that "big data" is anything in the 100 million rows realm), you once again would need to come back to the basics and understand that backups will be quick if they come with as little overhead as possible and that you will have to wait for a while for the backups to complete anyway (after all, you're copying over bigger data sets, right?)

Advice relevant to tools like `mariabackup` and `mariadb-dump` still applies: *everything's still valid*, but when backing up bigger data sets, keep in mind that small things make a lot of difference. For those backing up bigger data sets with `mariadb-dump`, I'd suggest

1. Specifying what kind of databases and/or tables within you need to back up by specifying them as options when invoking `mariadb-dump` as to not back up everything that exists.

2. Fiddling with the `--max-allowed-packet` option to set the maximum allowed packet length that should be sent/received (maximum – 1GB).

CHAPTER 13   OPTIMIZING BACKUPS AND RECOVERY

3. Enclosing INSERT statements with the --no-autocommit option to turn off automatic commits for bulk inserting operations.

4. Looking into the --add-drop-database or --add-drop-table options if/when necessary. Not a performance-enhancing option, but you wouldn't have to drop databases/tables, and the backup would recreate them for you instead.

5. Backing up data row-by-row instead of buffering data before backing it up for memory reasons (you do have a lot of data, right?) – for that, use --opt or --quick.

6. Avoiding using the -c or --complete-insert options for your INSERT statements to skip specifying column names – if you have a lot of columns within your tables and your use case necessitates logical backups, skipping column names should make your backup size significantly smaller.

7. Setting the default character set with --default-character-set if necessary. The default character set set by MariaDB will be utf8mb4, but if you need to adjust the character set because you store characters from a different language, the --default-character-set setting is the way to go. Alternatively, use the set-charset option to add SET NAMES default_character_set to the backup.

8. Fiddling with the -K or --disable-keys option if you have indexes on the table. This option will add the necessary keys (indexes) on the table after all of the rows are inserted.

9. Making use of the --fields-terminated-by or --fields-escaped-by options. With them, fields in the backup will be terminated or escaped by a string of your choice.

10. Looking into the -f or --force option. This option would let the backup continue running even if errors would be encountered – very useful for all kinds of use cases!

CHAPTER 13   OPTIMIZING BACKUPS AND RECOVERY

Again – this is nothing revolutionary, just some of the default options you can use. I don't promise that your backups will complete in an instant – they almost certainly won't – but good things come to those who wait, right?

However, if you don't want/need to use `mariabackup` or `mariadb-dump`, you have another option that I've talked about numerous times already – you can use `SELECT ... FROM ... INTO OUTFILE/LOAD DATA INFILE` – something like this will work:

```
SELECT * FROM 'table_name' INTO OUTFILE '/tmp/table_backup.txt' FIELDS
TERMINATED BY '|' [other options...];
```

The problem with this approach is that if you have a lot of tables (which you almost certainly do), running the same query manually all the time becomes infeasible. To automate at least a part of your work, you can make use of built-in scheduling tasks like so:

```
CREATE EVENT event_daily ON SCHEDULE EVERY 1 DAY
STARTS CURRENT_DATE [+ INTERVAL X DAY + INTERVAL Y MINUTE]
DO
Query here...
```

Such an event would run every day starting the date you specify (e.g., if you specify `INTERVAL 1 DAY + INTERVAL 1 MINUTE`, the event would start tomorrow at 00:01), and would run any query after the `DO` specification meaning that if you provide a query like `UPDATE 'customers' SET 'days_retained' = 'days_retained' + 1`, it would update the days_retained column of the customer table and add 1 more day to the customer's retention period. The same would work with backups with `SELECT * INTO OUTFILE` – specify an event like so:

```
CREATE EVENT event_daily ON SCHEDULE EVERY 1 DAY
STARTS CURRENT_DATE + INTERVAL 1 DAY
DO
SELECT * FROM `your_table` INTO OUTFILE '/tmp/your_table_backup.txt' FIELDS
TERMINATED BY '|';
```

Then, MariaDB would provide you with a backup file called your_table_backup.txt consisting of everything within your_table with fields terminated by the | character every single day. Of course, the problem with this approach would be that you would have to create another script that would move the file out of the /tmp/ directory to somewhere else every single day because two files of the same simply can't co-exist, but backing up in such a way would be possible too. If you can't be bothered to come up with scripts/solutions for moving files out of the /tmp/ directory, you can give the file a name related to the current date, but that'd be a little more complex to prepare. Nonetheless, it is possible when we use a query like so:

```
SET @backup_prepare = CONCAT("SELECT * FROM `your_table` INTO OUTFILE 
'C:/wamp64/tmp/backups/", DATE_FORMAT(NOW(), '%d%m%Y'), ".csv'");
PREPARE x FROM @backup_prepare;
EXECUTE x;
DROP PREPARE x;
```

Once done, our backup would reside in the backups directory inside of the tmp directory.

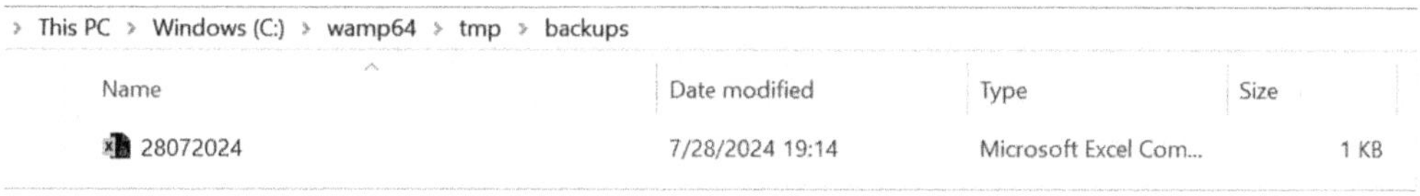

Figure 13-6. File made with SELECT ... INTO OUTFILE

Not everyone will make use of `SELECT ... INTO OUTFILE` and it's not a fit for every use case, but as the statement allows us to back up raw data, it's a very good fit for those working with bigger data sets.

Recovering MariaDB

When backing data up, you've thought about preparing for the worst. Preparing for the worst is necessary because the worst can sometimes come your way in the form of data corruption, disk failures, power outages, hosting mishaps, and other things: once it does, you need to know how to recover the data you've backed up.

There's little use in backing up data without testing how to recover it on a different server: only when the data is recovered can you feel safe and assured that backups haven't been made in vain.

To recover logical backups using `mariadb-dump`, invoke `mariadb-dump` like so where `backup.sql` is the name of your backup:

```
mariadb-dump -u[username] [database_name] < backup.sql
```

Provide a password if necessary (if you haven't defined one within my.ini or my.cnf, you should be prompted for one), and your backup should be restored inside the database you have just specified. There's usually no need to specify character sets or collations – a backup has been made with those in mind, and these settings should be restored as necessary.

Take note that you can also restore *parts* of your logical backup by venturing into the backup file itself (opening it up) and then copying over the necessary `CREATE TABLE` and `INSERT INTO ...` statements, too. It's not at all necessary to restore the file as a whole, and while such an approach may not be for everyone, it's entirely possible to restore parts of your data, too.

Coming back to restoration, to restore compressed backups (most of them will have the .gz – GZip – extension), use something like `gunzip` – replace `database_name` with the name of your database:

```
gunzip < backup.sql.gz | mysql -uroot [-ppassword] database_name
```

With physical backups, prepare them with the `--prepare` option as I've already shown earlier on:

```
mariabackup --prepare --target-dir=/tmp/backup/
```

Then, stop MariaDB, empty the data directory or ensure it's empty, and run `mariabackup` with either the `--copy-back` or `--move-back` option:

```
mariabackup --copy-back --target-dir=/tmp/backup/
```

That's it – no high-grade math stuff is necessary here either (you would have to ensure that the backup resides in the `target-dir` – don't forget that).

Recovering Big Data

When recovering bigger data sets, apply the same practices. Granted, you will wait for longer for the backup to be restored, but if the backup was taken in a way that helps your database in the first place, it should contain at least some of the options available within `mariadb-dump` that help it to be restored as quickly as possible (see the options in the "Backing Up Big Data Sets" heading).

If you've backed up data inside of your MariaDB instance by running SELECT ... INTO OUTFILE ... (read: if your backups are composed of raw data), they can be restored by running queries akin to the following (you may want to replace the file and table names as well as the character the fields are terminated by to adhere to your use case):

```
LOAD DATA INFILE '/tmp/backup_file.csv' INTO TABLE `table_name` FIELDS TERMINATED BY ',';
```

That's it – if your database is optimized, restoring millions or even billions of rows in such a fashion shouldn't be a very hard task either.

Backup and Recovery Pitfalls

After knowing how to back up and recover your most precious data, you should also be aware of backup and recovery pitfalls.

Start from the basics – inspect the last backup you took on a high level. What do you notice? A file with X MB|GB|TB in size. That's right – all backups come with a certain weight. The bigger your data set is, the bigger the weight will be. What kind of a file is it? Did you perform a full logical backup? A partial logical backup? A raw data backup? Is all of the data in the backup really necessary or can you back up only necessary data to save space on the disk? *Can the backup be restored?*

One of the biggest backup and recovery pitfalls is related to data restoration – you'd be surprised how often people back up, but don't try to restore their assets! Now imagine being in dire need to restore data and being unable to do so. Not a very good scenario, is it? Always test the backups you take – the more data you have, the more applicable this advice will become.

Next, make sure to automate at least some of your backup tasks – I've already provided an example of how you could go about optimizing and automating a backup of billions of rows, and if you can automate backups in regard to billions of rows of data, what makes you think you're incapable of automating smaller backup tasks? Seriously – make use of events to automate backup tasks, or take a look into cronjobs if necessary.

When testing whether backups can be restored, consider the locations where the backups are stored, too: are your backups making use of the cloud or are they using hard drives/SSDs in a separate server? If they are, perhaps it'd be wise to move data to the cloud and avoid the costs associated with another server? If that's not an option, perhaps consider storing the backups in a "rolling fashion" so that only backups not older than, say, 1 month, are stored? Think of how much space you'd save!

Also, make good use of hot backups – they exist for a reason and they provide users with an excellent way to back up data while not obstructing any operations running within the database management system: just because MariaDB doesn't support XtraBackup, doesn't mean that `mariadb-dump` won't help! To this day, many situations make `mariadb-dump` an indispensable component of your database.

If you're using stored procedures, triggers, or functions to power your data, keep in mind that these are stored separately from your data, and as such, they need to be backed up separately as well. No need to invent a bike here (the `--routines` flag should be more than enough), but as you're backing up, take care of these too.

Don't forget about the configuration files, either – if you restore data on another server, it's likely that you will want an identical configuration to power that database server, too. In such a situation, it's only natural that not having a configuration file backed up would mean trouble for you and your database.

Finally, consider the place where you store the backups – if it's necessary to store backups on another server, store them in a place inaccessible to the public (i.e., below `public_html`).

Pitfalls for Big Data

All the same applies to big data sets too – backups of big data sets are backups too, eh?

From practical experience, I can tell you that many pitfalls for the backup/restoration of bigger data sets are somehow related to the following:

1. Backing up/restoring logical backups using an improperly configured database, then complaining that backup restore times are rather slow

2. Not following best practices when using `LOAD DATA INFILE` to restore raw backups

3. Indexing and/or partitioning

Yup – these three basic things! Starting from the top, if you've taken logical backups for your bigger data sets, you must've known what you're doing. I hope your database is optimized and that indexes are added after the data is inserted into your tables because, otherwise, you're just asking for a headache.

Bulk INSERT operations for bigger data sets will always be rather slow (yes, even if your database is optimized to the max), and unless you've exchanged those operations for LOAD DATA INFILE, you're going to need to brace for impact on your database. Information will still be written, albeit not in such a quick fashion as with LOAD DATA INFILE.

To ensure that logical backups complete as quickly as possible, defer auto-commit operations (remember – autocommit=0 goes before INSERT operations, COMMIT comes at the end); if a primary key is present on your table, consider adding it before data is inserted because if a primary key will be in place beforehand, MySQL (and MariaDB too) will check for the integrity of the PRIMARY KEY during each INSERT operation. The same goes for indexes. On the same note, if multiple types of indexes are in place within your tables, first ask yourself whether you even need many types of indexes to be present – do you need that B-Tree and FULLTEXT index to be mashed together? What kind of use case do these indexes assist? What kind of full-text search operations are necessary, if at all?

LOAD DATA INFILE also has consequences, and you're welcome to familiarize yourself with them by searching for "LOAD DATA INFILE slow" through StackOverflow. Let me explore one of such use cases with you, and you'll quickly understand what I want to tell you – I'll call the user who asked the question person A, and the one who answered – person B. The problem was as follows:

1. Person A started a thread on StackOverflow saying that he was loading a file of approximately 100GB in size into a table inside of one of his databases using LOAD DATA INFILE.

2. Person A continued that "<...> I'm trying it now using InnoDB <...> The load starts fast at around 10MB/sec <...> after some GB of data is inserted, it slows down to the 2–3MB/sec range <...>".

3. Person A also stated that the size of his InnoDB buffer pool is around 8GB and that he's running a couple of queries before running LOAD DATA INFILE – these queries being the following:

```
SET @@session.sql_log_bin=0;
SET autocommit=0;
SET unique_checks=0;
SET foreign_key_checks=0;
ALTER TABLE 'tbl_name' DISABLE KEYS;
```

4. Person A also said that it seems to him that InnoDB doesn't support loading bigger data sets that are over a few GB in size into tables.

The problem here is pretty clear – `LOAD DATA INFILE` starts quickly but slows down after a while even though options that would supposedly help the database are in place. Why? Let's explore the accepted answer by person B. It was stated that

1. `DISABLE KEYS` wouldn't work with InnoDB because such a statement shuts down updates to secondary indexes on MyISAM, but since the system tablespace in InnoDB includes a structure to deal with secondary indexes, InnoDB doesn't deal with indexes in the same way as MyISAM does, so such an option is not necessary.

2. Setting `autocommit` to off piles up data in ibdata1, so user A should consider keeping it turned on.

3. User B stated that the MVCC and ACID features exclusive to InnoDB often make the storage engine act as a bottleneck when inserting bigger data sets into it and that setting the `ROW_FORMAT` to a value of `Fixed` would further speed up `INSERT` queries on MyISAM tables at the expense of making the table significantly larger to deal with.

4. Other users chimed in to support what the user B said saying that MyISAM as a storage engine is simple, but in this case, so are the requirements of the user A, and because of that, everything should be fine. If the user is facing any further problems, he might need to split the files into separate parts. If the user is running a powerful server, he should also consider optimizing the server for both MyISAM and InnoDB as necessary, but to do that, he would need to modify both mechanisms.

Most of this advice is OK, but some of it is outdated by now – first off, never use MyISAM in a production environment if your use case doesn't warrant `COUNT(*)` queries. As I've already told you in the chapter about storage engines, as MySQL advanced, most of the features originally available within the MyISAM storage engine became obsolete and are now available in InnoDB. When `LOAD DATA INFILE` is in use, you can keep `autocommit` functions at default, but the advice relevant to `DISABLE KEYS` still stands.

For most of you, things won't be so complex and you don't need to overthink things – just optimize your database, and when recovering big data sets make use of `LOAD DATA INFILE` that makes use of the optimized parameters (examples of `LOAD DATA INFILE` in use can be found throughout this chapter). Make sure that indexes and any applicable keys are loaded into the database after the data has been inserted, too, and you should be good to go.

Summary

Backing up your data is a necessity – there's no doubt about that. Just as your data needs to be backed up, though, it has to be recovered properly, and I sincerely hope that the advice in this chapter has helped you refine both your data backup and recovery procedures to meet your goals as necessary.

No matter how you elect to backup or restore your data, always keep in mind that backups do have a friend – his name is replication. Database replicas aren't backups and they aren't a replacement for backups, but rather, they are a way to ensure that what's happening on one database server is quickly replicated on the other. Let's get into them now.

CHAPTER 14

Optimizing Replication

Like backups, replication is top of mind for many DBAs across the globe. Properly built replication architectures ensure increased data availability, thus making it a fundamental strategy for database architectures as well as disaster recovery. However, as fundamental as replication may seem, one should consider both the benefits and drawbacks of such an appliance.

Understanding Replication

At a high level, replication in database management systems is quite easy to understand: replication helps copy data over to another server (of which there can be more than one) and keep data across those servers in sync, and by doing so, helps improve database availability and reliability. In the MySQL world, replication comes in a couple of flavors: we can have synchronous, semi-synchronous, or asynchronous replication as well as statement-based, row-based, or mixed-mode replication, too. MariaDB only supports asynchronous and semi-synchronous replication and comes with a Galera Cluster appliance.

Synchronous replication makes sure that changes are received and applied before committing them while asynchronous replication commits the transaction at the instant it's received without waiting for the reply from replica servers. Semi-synchronous replication aims to provide a compromise between the two by ensuring that one or more of the replica servers have confirmed the changes to data. When it comes to replication formats available in MySQL and MariaDB, there is statement-based replication that replicates `INSERT`, `UPDATE`, and `DELETE` statements on another server and row-based replication that replicates the changes to rows, hence the name. Row-based replication is said to be more precise; it offers more compatibility in comparison to statement-based replication and is the default replication mode in MySQL and MariaDB. Mixed-mode replication offers the best of both worlds where the server chooses the best way to replicate data based on a specific scenario.

CHAPTER 14   OPTIMIZING REPLICATION

Some of you may undoubtedly be familiar with replication and some of its upsides, but nonetheless, I feel the need to introduce you to some of the terms surrounding replication:

Term	Meaning
Master or Master Server	The database server that serves as the primary source of data.
Slave or Slave Server	The database server that acts as a read-only copy of the Master Server.
Source or Source Server	The same as a Master Server.
Secondary, Secondary Server, Replica or Replica Server	The same as a Slave Server.

I bet you've heard most (or at least some) of the terms mentioned above since many of you will be familiar with what replication can provide. What you may not be aware of, however, is the fact that replication terminology has changed a little during the years: while many DBAs may be aware of a master-slave and a master-master topology, you should also be aware that in 2020, MySQL has acknowledged the negative connotations of the initial terminology like "master" and "slave" and has announced that the team is moving toward implementing numerous terminology changes that should soon be introduced into MySQL: the team has also stated that they're thinking of replacing the word "blacklist" with "blocklist" and the word "whitelist" with the word "allowlist."

All references to these words won't be removed in a single release because it's simply impossible to do – according to the MySQL team, the new syntax will be the recommended syntax instead of an alternative one.

Configuring and Implementing Replication

Regardless of the issues concerning the syntax, for replication to bear its fruit, one has to choose the type of replication to implement, and then configure it as necessary. To configure and implement replication, you would first need to have two or more servers with MySQL installed, configured, and running.

Once you're sure that MySQL is installed, configured, and running on both of the servers, start configuring replication. In this example, we will configure master-slave replication, and I'll get into the possible types of replication afterward. With that being

CHAPTER 14   OPTIMIZING REPLICATION

said, the basic steps to configure replication in MySQL are as follows (take note that locations of binary logs on a Windows architecture may differ and can be found in the C:\ProgramData\MySQL\MySQL Server *.* or other locations depending on the configuration within my.ini – consult the value of the log-bin variable):

1. Take a backup of data existing in MySQL or MariaDB, a backup of my.ini or my.cnf, and then stop MySQL (MariaDB).

2. Open up my.ini or my.cnf and uncomment the log_bin and server_id options. The server_id will let your database distinguish between multiple servers in a replication setup, and the log_bin variable allows MySQL to read through the binary log which is a necessity for replication (the directory may differ). Additionally, you may want to include the name of the database you desire to replicate by specifying the database name after the binlog_do_db parameter:

   ```
   [mysqld]
   log_bin = /var/log/mysql/mysql-bin.log
   server_id = 1
   binlog_do_db = testdb
   ```

3. Ensure that the secondary (slave) server has a user with enough permissions to deal with replication by either creating a user or granting him privileges like shown – keep in mind that we use mysql_native_password instead of caching_sha2_password because we may not possess an encrypted connection between our servers, and FLUSH PRIVILEGES saves our privileges:

   ```
   CREATE USER '[username]'@'[slaveserver_ip]' IDENTIFIED
   WITH mysql_native_password BY '[password]';
   GRANT REPLICATION SLAVE ON *.* TO
   '[username]'@'[slaveserver_ip]';
   FLUSH PRIVILEGES;
   ```

4. Since replication reads changes from the log file, we need to retrieve its position. To do so, lock the database so the position doesn't "move" as data is modified by running a query like FLUSH TABLES WITH READ LOCK.

5. Then, obtain status information on the binary log file by issuing a SHOW MASTER STATUS query. The output of the query should provide you with the name of the bin file in the form of mysql-bin.000002 or similar, the position (e.g., "761" or similar), and other parameters such as what database is replicated in the Binlog_Do_DB column or what database is ignored in the Binlog_Ignore_DB column, and other information. Remember the name of the bin file and the position that's shown, if possible copy and paste it into another location – you are going to need it in a minute.

6. We're assuming that this is a fresh master-slave configuration and that we don't have any data on the master server yet – as such, we can unlock the database by running UNLOCK TABLES.

7. Come back to the slave server, open up my.ini or my.cnf, change the server-id variable to a value of 2 (the numbers mustn't clash), and then set the other applicable variables to the same values as in the master server (e.g., the log_bin variable should have the value of the bin file in the SHOW MASTER STATUS query – in this case, it's mysql-bin.000002, the binlog_do_db variable should have the value of the Binlog_Do_DB variable in the master server, etc.).

8. While still modifying my.ini or my.cnf, adjust the relay-log variable to the location of the log file inside of the slave server. If you're under a Linux architecture, most likely the value will be something like /var/log/mysql/mysql-relay-bin.log.

9. Save changes and restart MySQL or MariaDB.

10. Instruct the slave server on the location of the binary log file and its contents. This is a single query with values derived from the values in the SHOW MASTER STATUS query – the SOURCE_USER and SOURCE_PASSWORD are the username and password values of the user you've created for replication:

```
CHANGE REPLICATION SOURCE TO
SOURCE_HOST='ip_of_master_server',
SOURCE_USER='replication_user',
SOURCE_PASSWORD='replication_user_password',
SOURCE_LOG_FILE='mysql-bin.000002',
SOURCE_LOG_POS=761;
```

Now you're free to start the replication process! Run `START REPLICA` on the slave server, and you should be good to go. The status of the replica server can be inspected by running `SHOW REPLICA STATUS` – when such a query is run, MariaDB would return with the state of the replica server (e.g., "Waiting for master to send event," while `Source_host` and `Source_user` will be the IP and the username of the master server.

If your master server has data you want to migrate, "upload" the backup of the data to the slave server by using `scp` (here, `backup.sql` is the name of your backup, and `slave_user` and `slave_ip` are the username and IP of the slave server, respectively). I move the backup to a `/tmp/` directory to ease an upcoming data import process:

```
scp backup.sql slave_user@slave_ip:/tmp/
```

Once done, head back to the slave server, create a database, and import the backup from the `/tmp/` directory. The rest of the steps don't change.

Types of Replication

As already mentioned, replication in MariaDB and MySQL comes in a couple of flavors: MySQL supports synchronous, semi-synchronous, and asynchronous replication, while MariaDB supports asynchronous and semi-synchronous replication options as well as provides support for Galera Cluster.

I've already let you in on the secrets of synchronous, asynchronous, and semi-synchronous replication, and as far as Galera Cluster is concerned, on MariaDB it only supports the InnoDB storage engine though the team is experimenting with support for MyISAM and Aria. The downside of the Galera Cluster is that the cluster appliance is largely only available on Linux architectures, but it has a couple of upsides unique to itself including providing its users with virtually synchronous replication, meaning that while replication is done synchronously, database nodes are written and committed to asynchronously, or independently. Users of the Galera Cluster can direct reads and writes to any database node, it's based on certification-based replication, and failed database nodes are automatically removed from the database cluster without any kind of interruption to operations.

Taking into account that Galera Cluster nodes are highly available and scalable, that it has features ensuring no replica lag, and its ability to not lose any transactions as per the features defined above, it's easy to see why Galera Cluster is the go-to solution for many developers and DBAs, too.

The default type of replication available within MariaDB, though, is asynchronous master-slave replication (primary-replica) replication. There is also support for master-master replication and the so-called multi-master replication as well.

The "default" type of replication available within MariaDB was also the very first replication option available for the users of MySQL and only necessitates you to own one primary server and one or more replica (slave) servers. In such a replication setup, both read and write operations will be distributed across multiple database servers, and as such, the load for the database would be balanced. The example of setting up replication available above is a good example of a primary-replica database replication setup.

Another popular type of database replication has to do with a master-master replication setup. This type of replication requires you to have at least two servers that act as "masters" (i.e., that accept read and write queries). Each primary (master) server can run several replica servers while taking advantage of asynchronous replication capabilities.

If you have multiple primary servers, you would have to make use of Galera Cluster and have the benefit of all of the features described above.

If discerning the features, the upsides and downsides of each type of replication in MariaDB seem a little complex; I've also split everything into the table below:

Type of Database Replication	Explanation and Features
Master-slave replication	The default mode of replication in MariaDB. Such a replication setup is in use when we possess one primary server and multiple replica servers.
Master-master replication	A replication setup with at least two servers acting as primary servers. Each primary server can have multiple nodes (slave servers).
Multi-master replication	A replication setup where there is more than one database node (server) that acts as a primary server. Any MariaDB Server may be used to both write and read data. In MariaDB, this setup would be the same as the Galera Cluster.

No matter what type of replication you elect to use, remember that all types of replication will read events written to the binary log before replicating them. As such, the binary log is the crucial part as it remembers the modifications of contents within a MariaDB database. In other words, binary logs record changes to data that have occurred to be executed by other servers and bring the data to a consistent manner with the primary server. Binary logs reside in the `datadir` of MariaDB.

In the database world, replication is also home to a couple of concepts unique to itself: there is a concept of "replication lag" (delayed replication), a concept of servers having a global transaction ID (GTID), a concept of servers reading the binary log that contains a record of all of the changes made to the database, and others – they're also important because when dealing with replication, coming across them is inevitable.

Replication lag is quite easy to understand – as the title suggests, this term refers to servers being out-of-sync with other servers when any kind of replication is set up. The "lag" refers to the difference between the state a server is returning and the "current" state of the server (the state available to see/use). Replication lag occurs when things aren't "fast enough," for example, when the replicas don't receive or apply changes to data fast enough, when the master server can't send data changes to the replicas fast enough, etc.

Replication lag can be reduced by minimizing the duration of transactions on the source database (use the query optimization tips we've talked about – they're all applicable), minimizing network latency, or making sure our disk I/O operations are powerful enough.

When it comes to GTIDs, they refer to global transaction identifiers, and they are unique across the entire replication topology. A GTID "appears" when a transaction is written to the binary log and every transaction will be assigned an auto-incrementing ID. Naturally, this also means that transactions not written to the binary log will not receive a GTID. Once a transaction with a GTID has been committed on a server, no other transaction with the same GTID will be executed. For some, global transaction identifiers can be similar to hashes, and each GTID is represented like so – `hash-like source_id:transaction_id` and will consist of a server identifier (most likely `server_uuid`) and a numeric transaction ID. A transaction ID of #1337 means that it's the 1337th transaction to be committed on the server:

```
7B17FA77-84FD-44D7-9B11-N65FF2978613:1337
```

CHAPTER 14 OPTIMIZING REPLICATION

Replication Notes and Tips

Just as replication is powerful, there are a couple of things you should take note of beforehand to not drown in its capabilities!

Replication offers so much more than just a few auto-incrementing GTIDs; replication requires binary logging to be enabled on the master server, and as that happens, each replica server adds some load onto the primary server. On a high level, replication works like so:

1. The primary server reads its binary log and notices changes to data.

2. The slave (replica) server copies the binary log events to its relay log.

3. The slave (replica) server repeats the events in the relay log, thus updating its data.

The binary log notifies the replica of changes to data, which are then read into the relay log – events in the relay log are replayed, and data is updated. The binary log files and the relay log files are generally formatted in the same way, and relay log events in MariaDB can be inspected by running a query like SHOW RELAYLOG EVENTS – in this case, an empty result set will indicate that replication isn't set up.

```
MariaDB [hacking_mysql]> SHOW RELAYLOG EVENTS;
Empty set (0.002 sec)

MariaDB [hacking_mysql]>
```

Figure 14-1. SHOW RELAYLOG EVENTS in MariaDB

Once replication is set up, it will always involve multiple database servers and accounts that must be instructed to connect to and read from the primary server (see instructions in headings below). All that means that at a high level, replication looks like this:

CHAPTER 14 OPTIMIZING REPLICATION

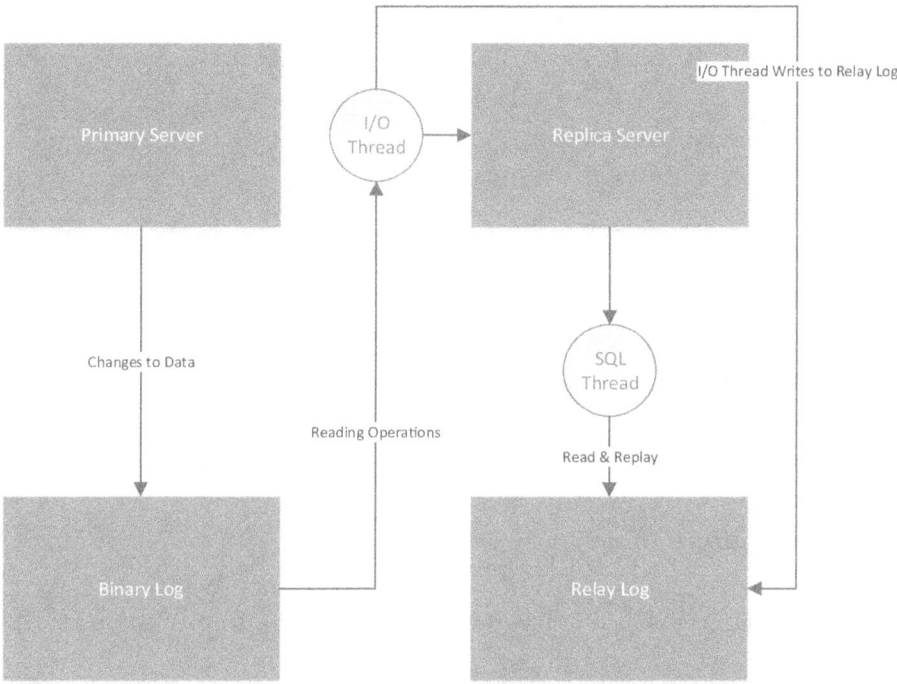

Figure 14-2. Replication in relational database management systems

Thus, replication is not exactly rocket science – what replication also isn't is a backup or a substitute for a backup. Yes, replication does copy data to another server, and this is very similar to what your backups would do, but the core difference between any type of replication and backups is the fact that once data on the master server is updated, data on the replica servers will be updated as well.

Securing Replication

Once you find yourself aware of the internals of replication, you will inevitably think about the security of the data you replicate too. To ensure the security of the asset so vital to your business – data – it's crucial to take care of security and privacy measures beforehand and act keeping in mind the specifics of replication.

To ensure your data is being transferred securely, ensure that SSL/TLS is enabled on the primary server, or better yet, on both primary and replica servers. Ensuring that TLS is enabled isn't very hard and can be done either via my.ini (my.cnf in Linux) or by observing the output of simple SQL queries like `status`.

299

CHAPTER 14 OPTIMIZING REPLICATION

```
MariaDB [hacking_mysql]> status
--------------
mysql  Ver 15.1 Distrib 10.10.2-MariaDB, for Win64 (AMD64), source revision 695f20f1b55949ae5e4870805cf0b056457ec932

Connection id:          3
Current database:       hacking_mysql
Current user:           root@localhost
SSL:                    Not in use
Current pager:          stdout
Using outfile:          ''
Using delimiter:        ;
Server:                 MariaDB
Server version:         10.10.2-MariaDB mariadb.org binary distribution
Protocol version:       10
Connection:             localhost via TCP/IP
Server characterset:    latin1
Db     characterset:    utf8mb4
Client characterset:    utf8mb4
Conn.  characterset:    utf8mb4
TCP port:               3307
Uptime:                 1 min 0 sec

Threads: 1  Questions: 4  Slow queries: 0  Opens: 17  Open tables: 10  Queries per second avg: 0.066
--------------
```

Figure 14-3. *The output of status in MariaDB*

Note the SSL part – if SSL is used, you will see a different output, such as `Cipher in use is DHE-RSA-AES256-SHA` or similar.

You can also find out if your server is using SSL via the configuration file: open up the file and if you see TLS system variables like `ssl_cert`, `ssl_key`, and `ssl_ca` defined under the `[mariadb]` tab, you're golden.

The output of `status` is also interesting because it provides the character sets of the database, connection and client, uptime, the TCP port you may use to connect to MariaDB (port may be useful for those using MariaDB to power content management systems like WordPress, vBulletin, IPBoard, or MyBB).

Regardless, if your server is using SSL, you would likely need to tell MariaDB to use TLS for your replication setup by running a `CHANGE MASTER` query to include SSL options – to achieve this, take a look into `MASTER_SSL`, `MASTER_SSL_CA`, `MASTER_SSL_CAPATH`, `MASTER_SSL_CERT`, `MASTER_SSL_KEY`, `MASTER_SSL_VERIFY_SERVER_CERT`, and other TLS-related options that are available to use with the `CHANGE MASTER` query.

Set these options up, and you should be good to go – it's really that simple.

Of course, you will also need to adhere to privacy standards like HIPAA and GDPR if they apply to your business, but I'll let you in on their secrets in the last part of this book where I cover security.

Summary

Replication is a difficult beast to tame – that beast comes in many shapes and sizes, and in essence, it's a process that helps ensure the availability of data. Replication has a couple of types, one can replicate rows or SQL statements, and as with everything database-related, replication has issues unique to itself, but regardless, it's a perfect mechanism to ensure that data "lives" in another server without manual intervention.

Replication is not the only friend of your database though – security is paramount too. Heard of the most recent data breaches? Yup – they're scary. Breaches over a decade ago were no "better" too with tens or even hundreds of millions of people impacted, and in such an environment, it's crucial you properly secure your database if you don't want to see the name of your company in the news regarding the next major data breach.

CHAPTER 15

Optimizing for Security

Now that you know a thing or two about storage engines, things that break your MariaDB instances and the queries within, understand your server and know how to optimize your server, what goes into optimizing specific storage engines, schemas, data types, collations, queries themselves, know how to optimize MariaDB for bigger data sets and a thing or two about indexing, partitioning, backups and replication, it's high time to learn how to optimize your database management system for security, isn't it?

Security is paramount – it's the reason some of you've picked this book up in the first place, isn't it? Perhaps you've even suffered a data breach and have been recommended this book to know how to deal with security issues surrounding your MySQL or MariaDB instance?

Understanding Security in MariaDB

I'll begin by stating the obvious – securing MariaDB and MySQL in general isn't nearly as hard as you think it is. Sure, there are certain specifics related to MariaDB you will need to know, but in general, security-related issues can be split into a couple of categories:

1. General security guidelines
2. Access control
3. User security
4. Security-related components and plugins
5. Enterprise-level security controls

CHAPTER 15   OPTIMIZING FOR SECURITY

Would you look at that – so many categories, right? I agree that categories in the MariaDB security realm may seem to be few and far between, but when you think about it, every MariaDB security issue has its roots somewhere in one or more of those categories and as you read along, you should be able to quickly understand that this is indeed the truth.

Let's begin by looking into your database in general – the first thing you need to inspect from a security standpoint would be the classes of data your database is storing. That can be done by having a closer look into your use case in general – assuming you use MariaDB to house a forum where users interact with one another (CMS), your database will contain multiple tables, of which

- Some will contain log data.

- Some will contain attachments and data related to them (their types, who attached what, etc.).

- Some will contain ban filters.

- Some will contain data related to anti-spam operations (think CAPTCHAs, etc.).

- Some will contain forum event-related data.

- Some will contain user group data (i.e., data on ordinary users, moderators, administrators, VIP users or donators, other user groups, etc.).

- Some will contain details on the users themselves (user ranks, usernames, email addresses, infraction details, messages sent/received, hashed and salted passwords, administrative remarks, etc.).

- Some will contain details related to the installation of the CMS and whether the installation is locked or not, etc. (once the installation is finished, many content management systems lock the directory for it not to be accessible from the outside).

- Some will contain details relevant to the documentation of the CMS.

- Some may contain data on polls that have been created on the forum and what users voted on what polls during what time, etc.

- Some may contain data relevant to the reputation of the users (e.g., a reputation of 100% may mean a "clean slate," while a reputation of 20% means you should double-check the advice given by the user because many users reported him for something).

- Some may contain data related to the threads and messages sent and received through the forum.

- Some will contain message and attachment metadata or similar things.

Thus, even though you may think your forum isn't very popular compared to other forums, the forum will still have data you need to take care of and secure. There's still something for attackers to steal!

Granted, many attackers will only be interested in the user table of your forum and the details within (stolen data is what brings "revenue" to the business of the attackers since the data is often sold on the dark web and then re-used for identity theft, credential stuffing, and other types of attacks), but other data classes shouldn't be discounted either – taking the 2015 Experian data breach as an example, the data breach was said to have included not only sensitive user login information, but also user genders, income levels, phone numbers, addresses, credit status information, family details, and many other sensitive data classes. Other data breaches may include the aforementioned threads and posts within the forum, messages that have been sent back and forth over the years, and so on.

What I'm trying to say here is the things that are included in your database depend on your use case – you would need to protect everything inside of a database to begin with, but for a CMS use case, you would need to pay extra attention to SSL, the password hashing function that is being used, whether passwords are salted, and what kind of user data is stored.

Start from your user table because user data brings the most value to a potential attacker (as stated before, user data can be and often is sold to other nefarious parties and the data is then used for identity theft attacks) – review the password hashing function that is being used, whether your hashes are salted (salts slow down password cracking when a lot of hashes are being cracked), and try to look at everything from the standpoint of a hacker – if *you* would be an attacker, what would you do and what data would be of value to you? Ask any security expert, and you will quickly receive advice saying that there have been stolen user databases (read: user tables attackers have acquired from a bigger data set and parsed them before selling them off) sold on the dark web for tens of thousands of dollars: what makes you think your database/use case will not be worth "looking into?"

After the user table, inspect other tables storing data of interest to a potential nefarious party (these may include messages and metadata, too – you never know what users are chatting about), and then, you will start to have a good picture of what security measures already exist and what can be improved.

The landscape each of you will see will differ – it should differ because no one use case is the same, but that's also what makes security so exciting. For those of you running content management systems, the beginnings of security could look something like this.

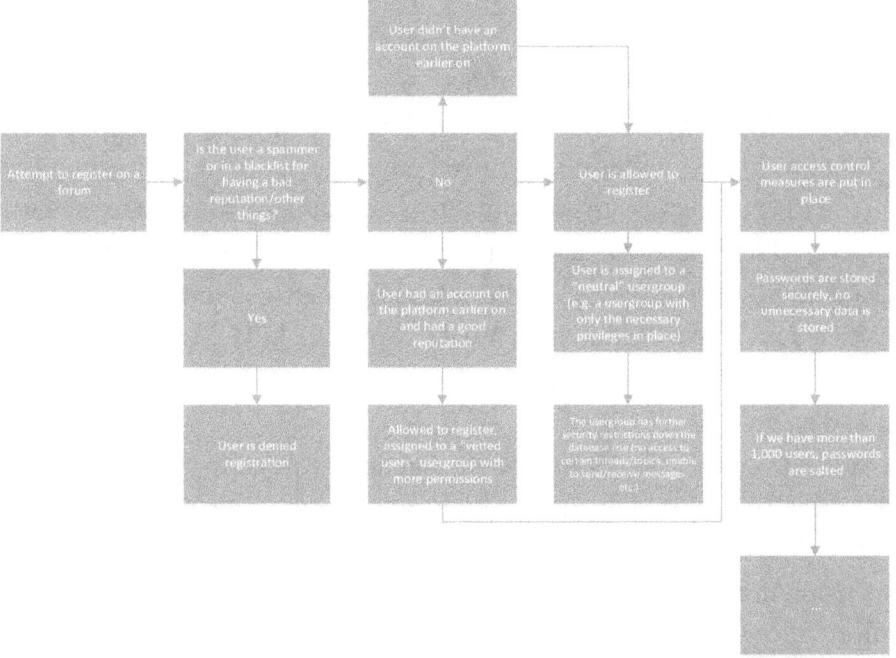

Figure 15-1. *User registration on a forum from a security standpoint*

Yes, there are many things you need to consider – and all of them have something to do with the security categories mentioned above.

This specific use case, as you can discern already, has more to do with general security guidelines, access control, and user security, but a server behind the CMS may also be using security-related components and plugins to complete certain actions depicted in the graph. Thus, all components of the security chain are equally important, and even though each of them may involve your database working on different things, they all work in unison to push your database forward on the security landscape:

Guidelines	What's Involved?
General security guidelines	Carefully evaluating the use case, then securing and hardening the server as a whole during the architecture, design, and implementation phases of the project.
Access control	Not letting users access parts of the forum they shouldn't be able to access, usergroups, warnings, reputation, and related things.
User security	Hashing/salting passwords using a secure mechanism such as BCrypt or Blowfish and advising users on how to further the security of their account when registering on the forum and once they have registered.
Components and plugins related to security	Installing and setting up plugins and appliances that work in conjunction with the CMS to perform a wide range of duties starting from not allowing users to upload certain types of files via upload forms that may be available on the forum (.exe, .pdf, .php, files having a double extension, etc.) to informing administrators of unauthorized access via email or SMS and locking down the entire forum once a data breach is detected by the appliance.

However, regardless of what your use case is, you're going to start securing your MariaDB installation from the bottom, and you're on the bottom once you decide to *install* MariaDB.

Securing MariaDB upon Installation

Ask any experienced DBA "How do I secure MariaDB upon installation?" and the first answer you're going to hear will have something to do with a Unix script called `mariadb-secure-installation`. The downside of this script is that it's only available on Unix (Linux) architecture, and you won't be able to make use of its features on Windows-based servers (Windows users can complete some of the steps themselves to achieve similar results), but that doesn't negate its usefulness. The script can be invoked by typing `mariadb-secure-installation` without any additional arguments, and when invoked, will guide you through the actions you need to perform to secure a freshly installed instance of MariaDB. The script

1. Allows you to change the password for the main user of your database (the root user.) Make sure that the password used by the root user is strong.

2. Removes anonymous users inside of MariaDB. This step is important because, by default, fresh installations of MariaDB will include an anonymous user (i.e., enable anyone to log in to the server without an account.) No production environment should contain anonymous accounts.

3. Sets boundaries for the root user and only allows him to connect from localhost and not from other places.

4. Removes the database named "test" that can be accessed by anyone. As its name suggests, this database is set up for testing purposes and should be removed in a production environment.

5. Reloads the privilege tables (saves all changes made through the completion of previous steps).

These steps will mark the beginning of your security journey with MariaDB. Yes, they're nothing revolutionary, but they will help you set a strong footing when beginning to build anything MariaDB-based. If you're running MariaDB on any Unix server, always run `mariadb-secure-installation`, and after securing your MariaDB installation, make sure to put security first in all phases of your application – architect, design, and implement all of your systems with security in mind. Be mindful of the libraries and frameworks used by your application, code to reduce attack surfaces, sanitize all inputs provided by the user, never provide direct user input to the database, parameterize, encode output if necessary, validate input, harden your environment, and if applicable, add a firewall on your application, on your database, or both. I'll walk you through the security measures you can take in the security part of this book.

CHAPTER 15   OPTIMIZING FOR SECURITY

General Security Measures

After your MariaDB installation is safe, it's time to follow general security measures when building any applications interacting with this database management system. Follow these rules:

1. Never provide user input straight into a database and always sanitize user input before passing it on to a database or/and tables within.

2. If you store user data, store only what's necessary and encrypt or hash sensitive data such as passwords. Consider salting data if you have more (~thousands) of users.

3. Limit user privileges and build upon the "must know" principle: if the answer to the question "Does this user have to know this?" begins with "No," don't show them the information and restrict their access. Remember – the fewer people access sensitive data, the less probability for it to be stolen.

4. Code systems that are secure by design and harden them whenever applicable/possible – "security by design" means that security is integrated into systems from their inception and is not an additional thing that is "built" on top of them.

5. Code for performance, but keep security in mind. Have a look through the recent edition of OWASP top 10 and apply those principles to your application at every corner possible. Handle errors properly and be careful about exposing potentially sensitive data to the end user.

6. Make use of threat modeling – after you're done working on a specific feature within your software, examine your code for security vulnerabilities and, better yet, ask a security-minded friend to review the code for you. Perhaps he'd notice a vulnerability that crossed your eyesight?

Follow these security measures and you will certainly ensure a bright future for both your application and database; however, do keep in mind that these steps and measures are only the tip of the iceberg. To ensure that your application, database, and the data within are safe, ensure that you instruct your developers/employees/users on safety measures benefitting them in their specific scenario, and stay updated in the security space by reading cybersecurity news to keep on top on whatever is happening within the industry.

Over time, the advice to further the security within your application and/or database may change, basic fundamentals will likely stay intact. Keep in touch with the industry, attend conferences, workshops, and seminars, read blogs, books, and whitepapers, and you will have a nice head-start toward security in the database realm.

Summary

Optimizing MariaDB for security may seem like a tough feat; however, when you discern the things behind the security landscape of the database management system, you quickly realize that everything's simpler than it sounds.

Security in MariaDB doesn't require you to be a senior-level security engineer to protect all of your assets: all you need is to follow general security advice, then advice relevant to your specific use case/scenario and you should be good to go.

With that being said, the optimization part of this book is effectively over – now we're reaching the ~~hacking~~ security realm.

PART IV

Securing MySQL

CHAPTER 16

The World of Security in MySQL

Now that you're somewhat aware of the security world within MariaDB, it's time to dive deeper into the things you can do to secure your relational database management system, isn't it? In this chapter, I'll provide you with a deeper dive into the general security guidelines we've talked about, then talk more about access control and user security, walk you through MariaDB components and plugins that help you keep your data safe, talk about using firewalls together with MariaDB or MySQL, and walk you through a couple of enterprise-level security controls. After that, we'll dip into security guidelines for specific use cases, talk about password management, account locking, security plugins, and backup security and attacks targeting your database.

General Security Guidelines and Measures Revisited

So, where did we stop? Right – I've walked you through general security guidelines and mentioned secure coding practices. The truth is, if you want to build a secure database, the things you need to start from aren't exactly related to the database to begin with: security must be built-in into everything you do. Remember when you first started thinking about the project? About its features? It'd be great if you thought of security guidelines applicable to your use case before developing those features. Contrary to popular belief, that's not very hard to do if you just act on standards like OWASP or the NIST framework. Standards will ensure you won't drown in the loads of features you need to implement/work on and if you follow them properly, you will enhance your database security, the privacy of your users, and the safety of your code by multiple times. Following standards like the OWASP Top 10 or the NIST framework isn't a bad practice, but it depends on where you apply them.

CHAPTER 16   THE WORLD OF SECURITY IN MYSQL

The NIST framework will be very useful for those running a business or managing it because the framework is designed to make businesses of all sizes better understand, manage, and reduce the risk of cyber-attacks and better protect their assets. The NIST framework has five different aspects:

1. **Identification**: According to the framework, first you need to identify the kind of data you're protecting. This step includes listing all equipment, hardware, software, applicable plugins, and other appliances you may be using. Since NIST is targeting organizational behavior, this step also includes computers, laptops, tablets, phones, point-of-sale devices, and so on. And yes, this step also includes listing any and all appliances you're using to protect your data at present such as firewalls, too.

2. **Protection**: Surely, protecting your hardware and software assets is easier said than done, but the framework suggests a couple of ways you can go about this: consider using firewalls, encrypt your data, test your backup strategy, and introduce security policies into your organization.

3. **Detecting**: Take measures to ensure that you and your team are the first ones to know when an incident occurs. That means monitoring your networks and devices for unauthorized access, disallowing devices like USB sticks, external hard drives, and network-attached storage devices to be plugged into networks, etc.

4. **Responding**: The NIST framework also notes the need to have a plan to notify customers, employees, and users of your software that you've suffered a data breach. Have a plan to investigate the hack, and report the attack to law enforcement if necessary.

5. **Recovery**: Finally, the framework recommends you have a plan to recover your data, equipment, and parts of your software that were affected by the data breach. The plan should be tested regularly to ensure it's up to the task and usable.

Taking care of the internals of your organization (social engineering is still a thing), it's time to familiarize yourself with the OWASP framework. The OWASP framework generally changes every 4-5 years as new vulnerabilities are added/removed from the list, but regardless, it does provide a good starting point for those securing their databases and applications. Here's what the recent – 2021 – edition of the OWASP Top 10 has to say, with flaws ranging from the most to the least important:

Security Issue	Explanation
Broken access control	Broken access control occurs when an application allows anyone to access pages that should be available only for people with certain privileges (e.g., administrators, paid users, etc.)
Cryptographic failures	Cryptographic failures (e.g., unencrypted or improperly encrypted data, improperly hashed passwords, etc.) often leads to compromise.
Injection	Injection occurs whenever we pass unvalidated user input straight into a database. The 2021 edition of OWASP considers Cross-site Scripting part of Injection, presumably because of its "injectory" nature (attackers have to inject payloads, test for XSS using input fields, etc.).
Insecure design	Applications should be built securely by design: the 2021 edition of OWASP mentions the necessity for more secure design patterns and principles.
Security misconfiguration	An application may be susceptible to security misconfiguration if it has unnecessary features enabled (e.g., directory listing is enabled where it's not necessary, improper error handling that reveals directories with sensitive data inside of them, disabling security updates, etc.).
Vulnerable and outdated components	Applications using vulnerable and outdated components are more susceptible to data breaches. After an attacker finds out that a platform uses outdated components, he or she may proceed to exploit known vulnerabilities within the software to gain access to the internals of your system, thus harming your company, customers, users, employees, and everyone else in the process.
Identification and authentication failures	Such vulnerabilities refer to failures to properly verify the identity of the user, permitting brute-force or other attacks via login or registration forms, permitting weak passwords to be used, etc. Ineffective ways to reset passwords may also fall under this category.

(*continued*)

CHAPTER 16   THE WORLD OF SECURITY IN MYSQL

Security Issue	Explanation
Software and data integrity failures	This vulnerability category refers to software that fails to protect against integrity violations. A prime example of this would be the inclusion of stylesheets of scripts without the integrity attribute that provides a SHA-384 hash of the script and thus, if the script changes even one bit, the hash won't be the same and the stylesheet or javascript file will no longer be loaded into the system, etc.
Security logging and monitoring failures	This vulnerability category refers to failure to adequately log and monitor security-related issues, the missing of auditable events, and related issues (e.g. not logging administrative IP addresses that have logged in to a system to have an indicator of a possible data breach, etc.)
Server-Side Request Forgery (SSRF)	This vulnerability occurs when an attacker manipulates a server into making requests to internal resources, then furthering an attack.

Along with NIST and OWASP, don't forget the basics – filter user input and sanitize it wherever possible (various programming languages offer various functions suitable for this specific task), and don't provide user input to a database without filtering it to avoid SQL injection attacks (I'll walk you through those in a second), and you should pave a way for beginning securing your applications and database.

Access Control

After taking care of the basics, don't forget your database. Database security often starts with access control – users who aren't 100% required to see/access specific content aren't able to access it. Make sure that all of your users have strong passwords (use a password manager if possible) and that they're only able to access databases from a specified host rather than any host possible.

After that, keep in mind that accounts within MariaDB are a global phenomenon, that is, an account is not "linked" to a specific database or tables within in any way, shape, or form, but it can be assigned to have a form of control over data in databases with permissions. Users can be created with a user that has the CREATE USER privilege, or with the root user. Users can be created like so:

```
CREATE USER 'username'@host IDENTIFIED BY 'passwordhere';
```

CHAPTER 16 THE WORLD OF SECURITY IN MYSQL

So, to create a demo user in localhost, we would use a query like so:

CREATE USER 'demouser'@localhost IDENTIFIED BY 'demopassword';

```
Copyright (c) 2000, 2018, Oracle, MariaDB Corporation Ab and others.

Type 'help;' or '\h' for help. Type '\c' to clear the current input statement.

MariaDB [(none)]> CREATE USER 'demouser'@localhost IDENTIFIED BY 'demopassword';
Query OK, 0 rows affected (0.009 sec)

MariaDB [(none)]>
```

Figure 16-1. *Creating a demo user on localhost*

Once you create a user, it should be listed in a list of users when you run a query like SELECT user FROM mysql.user – don't be surprised if you see multiple root users either; they're for different hosts (127.0.0.1 and ::1 is the same thing just under a different expression too).

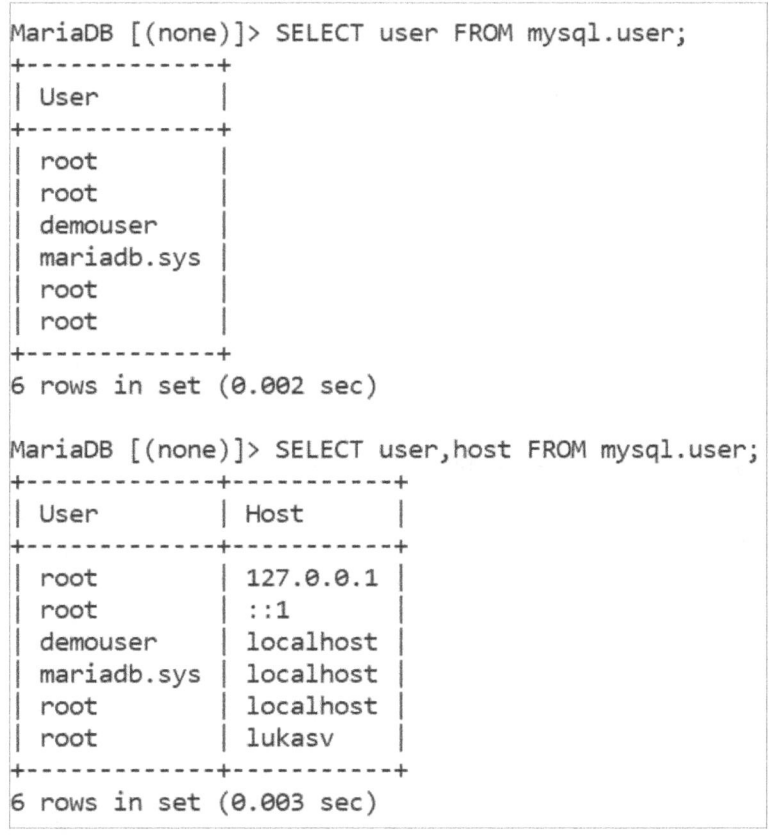

Figure 16-2. *Multiple root users*

CHAPTER 16   THE WORLD OF SECURITY IN MYSQL

Now that your user is created, it has to be assigned privileges. Privileges can be granted in a couple of ways:

1) You can grant all privileges on every database and every host.

2) You can grant a type of privilege on every database and every host.

3) You can grant all privileges on a certain database or a certain host.

4) You can grant all privileges on a certain table within a certain database within all hosts or a certain host.

Privileges can be set up using a query like the one below:

```
GRANT [ALL PRIVILEGES/SPECIFIC PRIVILEGE] ON database.table TO 'username'@host;
```

Afterward, they can be inspected using a SHOW GRANTS FOR query like the one below (keep in mind that beforehand, it'd be wise to issue a query like FLUSH PRIVILEGES for peace of mind too):

```
SHOW GRANTS FOR 'user'@host;
```

Let's have a gander here.

```
MariaDB [(none)]> GRANT SELECT ON hacking_mysql.* TO 'demouser'@localhost;
Query OK, 0 rows affected (0.006 sec)

MariaDB [(none)]> SHOW GRANTS FOR 'demouser'@localhost;
+-----------------------------------------------------------------------------------------------------------------+
| Grants for demouser@localhost                                                                                   |
+-----------------------------------------------------------------------------------------------------------------+
| GRANT USAGE ON *.* TO `demouser`@`localhost` IDENTIFIED BY PASSWORD '*0756A562377EDF6ED3AC45A00B356AAE6D3C6BB6' |
| GRANT SELECT ON `hacking_mysql`.* TO `demouser`@`localhost`                                                     |
+-----------------------------------------------------------------------------------------------------------------+
2 rows in set (0.014 sec)
```

Figure 16-3. *Granting a SELECT privilege*

Our demouser now has the SELECT privilege. All privileges available in MariaDB can be inspected using the SHOW PRIVILEGES query.

CHAPTER 16 THE WORLD OF SECURITY IN MYSQL

```
MariaDB [(none)]> SHOW PRIVILEGES;
+------------------------+-------------------------------------+-------------------------------------------------------+
| Privilege              | Context                             | Comment                                               |
+------------------------+-------------------------------------+-------------------------------------------------------+
| Alter                  | Tables                              | To alter the table                                    |
| Alter routine          | Functions,Procedures                | To alter or drop stored functions/procedures          |
| Create                 | Databases,Tables,Indexes            | To create new databases and tables                    |
| Create routine         | Databases                           | To use CREATE FUNCTION/PROCEDURE                      |
| Create temporary tables| Databases                           | To use CREATE TEMPORARY TABLE                         |
| Create view            | Tables                              | To create new views                                   |
| Create user            | Server Admin                        | To create new users                                   |
| Delete                 | Tables                              | To delete existing rows                               |
| Delete history         | Tables                              | To delete versioning table historical rows            |
| Drop                   | Databases,Tables                    | To drop databases, tables, and views                  |
| Event                  | Server Admin                        | To create, alter, drop and execute events             |
| Execute                | Functions,Procedures                | To execute stored routines                            |
| File                   | File access on server               | To read and write files on the server                 |
| Grant option           | Databases,Tables,Functions,Procedures| To give to other users those privileges you possess  |
| Index                  | Tables                              | To create or drop indexes                             |
| Insert                 | Tables                              | To insert data into tables                            |
| Lock tables            | Databases                           | To use LOCK TABLES (together with SELECT privilege)   |
| Process                | Server Admin                        | To view the plain text of currently executing queries |
| Proxy                  | Server Admin                        | To make proxy user possible                           |
| References             | Databases,Tables                    | To have references on tables                          |
| Reload                 | Server Admin                        | To reload or refresh tables, logs and privileges      |
| Binlog admin           | Server                              | To purge binary logs                                  |
| Binlog monitor         | Server                              | To use SHOW BINLOG STATUS and SHOW BINARY LOG         |
| Binlog replay          | Server                              | To use BINLOG (generated by mariadb-binlog)           |
| Replication master admin| Server                             | To monitor connected slaves                           |
| Replication slave admin| Server                              | To start/stop slave and apply binlog events           |
| Slave monitor          | Server                              | To use SHOW SLAVE STATUS and SHOW RELAYLOG EVENTS     |
| Replication slave      | Server Admin                        | To read binary log events from the master             |
| Select                 | Tables                              | To retrieve rows from table                           |
| Show databases         | Server Admin                        | To see all databases with SHOW DATABASES              |
| Show view              | Tables                              | To see views with SHOW CREATE VIEW                    |
| Shutdown               | Server Admin                        | To shut down the server                               |
| Super                  | Server Admin                        | To use KILL thread, SET GLOBAL, CHANGE MASTER, etc.   |
| Trigger                | Tables                              | To use triggers                                       |
| Create tablespace      | Server Admin                        | To create/alter/drop tablespaces                      |
| Update                 | Tables                              | To update existing rows                               |
+------------------------+-------------------------------------+-------------------------------------------------------+
```

Figure 16-4. SHOW PRIVILEGES in MariaDB

In this regard, MariaDB is rather generous because it doesn't only provide a list of privileges that can be granted but also provides the context in which the privileges are applicable in and provides a couple of words as comments where to apply them. The SHOW PRIVILEGES query will be very useful for those who aren't aware of what privileges to grant by heart and don't want to spend time reading the documentation either.

When it comes to passwords, users within MariaDB can set their passwords by themselves or rely on the root user to set passwords for them – root users can then run the SET PASSWORD or ALTER USER queries to accomplish the task.

After you know how to grant and save privileges and know a thing or two about resetting passwords, dig into access control. When working on access control, it's wise to understand the environment users are using in the first place: what's the environment created by your use case and why?

Once you understand the environment in use by the customers or users of your application, it's time to think about access control. If you find yourself to be a part of an organization, you can think about implementing privileges based on *role-based access control (RBAC)*: such an approach links privileges to organizational roles and provides users with the ability to obtain privileges that are directly connected to their role within an organization. In the MySQL/MariaDB world, RBAC may be implemented in a sense that developers within an organization would have CRUD and data altercation privileges on a database or two (e.g., they could have the Insert, Select, Update, Delete, Alter, Index, Trigger, Slave monitor, Replication slave, and some other privileges) while their direct managers (e.g., an engineering manager or a CTO) could have some more privileges including the File privilege, Create view and Create user privileges, as well as the Grant option privilege. Role-based access control is rather simple and seldom requires many thoughts.

If you don't find yourself in an organization, you could make use of a spreadsheet to list out what parts are necessary for a given user to access and grant privileges based on that.

User Security

When it comes to user security, everything's also closely connected to access privileges: newer versions of MySQL and MariaDB come with roles that in essence are collections of privileges, and thus, when a role is granted to a user, we grant all privileges connected to that role.

Roles have two components – first, we create them, and then we grant privileges to the role so that once the role is granted to a user, the user can possess the necessary privileges connected to that role. Roles can be created with the CREATE ROLE statement:

```
CREATE ROLE role_name;
```

Once roles are created, we need to grant privileges to that role using the GRANT statement like so:

```
GRANT [permission] ON [database].[table] TO [role];
```

If we want to grant all privileges on all tables within the demo_database database to a role named demo_role, we can do that like so:

```
GRANT ALL PRIVILEGES ON demo_database.* TO demo_role;
```

We can grant all other privileges to roles and in such a way build "role profiles" (tailor one profile for managers, another for developers, third for DBAs, fourth for support engineers, etc.), then grant the roles to a specific user like so:

```
GRANT demo_role TO demo_user;
```

Roles can also be granted to roles, and a user would need to set the role before using it using SET ROLE by accessing MariaDB through his account and setting a role using SET ROLE [role_name].

Roles consist of privileges and privileges are the pillar of user security. Another pillar of user security within MariaDB has to do with password choices where you need to ask yourself two questions:

1) Do you always create unique passwords for every service you use?

2) Do your passwords contain uppercase and lowercase letters, special characters, and numbers, and consist of 20 or more characters in length?

If you don't answer "yes" to both of these questions, you've got problems. You've got problems because you certainly have more than a couple of accounts you use to access services on the web, not even counting logins to access all kinds of applications both online and offline.

Frequently, those applications require login details, and when those are provided, they match the details you provide with your username or email and a hashed password in their database, and if everything checks out, grant you access to their service. The problem with such an approach is that whenever sensitive data is stored in a database, the service becomes a target for hackers who see the data as something to sell to other hackers to further identity theft/credential stuffing attacks. To access the data though, they not only need to break the application but access the account in the database that has the appropriate privileges to select/update data, proceed with a data dump, or at least select some users within a database into some other source.

User security is the pillar that helps you protect your application and database from such attacks – make sure to use a password manager (better yet, make the use of password managers mandatory across your entire organization across all teams), protect the accounts that have any sort of access to the database with strong passwords, make sure that all user/customer accounts in the database have strong passwords too (passwords should be 8 or more characters in length, have uppercase and lowercase characters as well as special symbols) but don't enforce too rigid of a ruleset (it's a two-sided sword and you can even lose customers who won't bother with it) and avoid running MySQL/MariaDB as root since the root user has the FILE privilege which can be used and abused to create unnecessary files.

CHAPTER 16   THE WORLD OF SECURITY IN MYSQL

Many users of MariaDB would also suggest making a user with a random/"normal" name the root user and disabling access for the root user altogether. This way you would benefit from security through obscurity – if an attacker would try to access the root account, he would fail and probably move on to other, easier, targets. For that, you can make use of roles once again:

1. `CREATE ROLE rootprivilege WITH ADMIN your_user@localhost`

2. `GRANT ALL ON *.* TO rootprivilege WITH GRANT OPTION`

3. `Switch to your_user@localhost, then DROP USER root, root@localhost, root@...`

4. `GRANT rootprivilege TO account@localhost`

Now you have a privilege called `rootprivilege` that you can grant to any user to make them have God-level access, but no root user. Isn't that cool?

MariaDB Components and Plugins That Keep Data Safe

Aside from privileges and roles, both MySQL and MariaDB come with a bunch of components and plugins that help keep your database safe. MySQL plugins can, once again, be split into separate categories: there are authentication plugins, connection-control plugins, plugins and components helping validate passwords, as well as enterprise solutions such as MySQL Enterprise Audit and MySQL Enterprise Firewall.

Authentication plugins describe pluggable authentication methods available within MySQL/MariaDB (native pluggable authentication, SHA-256 pluggable authentication, LDAP pluggable authentication, FIDO pluggable authentication, etc.); connection-control plugins refer to plugins that check attempts to connect and introduce a delay to the responses given by the database when it's necessary. Failed logins are also logged in the `CONNECTION_CONTROL_FAILED_LOGIN_ATTEMPTS` table.

Plugins and components helping validate password strength include a well-known component called `validate_password`, and the component can be installed/uninstalled like so:

`[UN]INSTALL COMPONENT 'file://component_validate_password';`

By default, the `validate_password` component enables you to implement a database-wide password strength policy and deny the usage of passwords that don't match certain criteria, for example, aren't over 8 characters long, etc.

To modify the way `validate_password` checks for password strength, modify system variables beginning with "`validate_password.`" Such variables may include, but are not limited to

- `validate_password.policy`: Available values include LOW, MEDIUM (default), and STRONG or the corresponding numeric values of 0, 1 (default), and 2. A policy using the LOW setting will check for password length, the level of MEDIUM will check for password length as well as numeric, lowercase, uppercase, and special characters, and the level of STRONG will check for password length as well as numeric, lowercase, uppercase, and special characters, as well as use a dictionary file.

- `validate_password.number_count`: Takes a numeric value that counts how often numbers appear in the password. Default value – 1.

- `validate_password.special_char_count`: Takes a numeric value that counts the occurrences of special characters. Default value – 1.

- `validate_password.length`: Takes a numeric value that specifies the minimum possible password length. This parameter has a default value of 8, and the numeric value can be either decreased or increased as necessary.

- `validate_password.mixed_case_count`: Denotes the minimum number of mixed-case (lowercase and uppercase) characters that are required if the password policy is set to MEDIUM or HIGH.

- …

When it comes to enterprise solutions, both MySQL and MariaDB offer enterprise-level solutions such as MySQL/MariaDB Enterprise Audit and MySQL Enterprise Firewall. Those two solutions, as their titles suggest, act as enterprise-level auditing and firewall appliances. The enterprise-level database firewall protects data within your MySQL database by detecting or blocking the execution of SQL statements as configured (if SQL statements don't match a predefined allowlist, they will be denied execution or still execute, but the database will notify administrators of policy violations), blocking SQL injection attacks, detecting database intrusions, and logging both allowed and blocked SQL queries.

MySQL Enterprise Audit enables us to monitor, log, and, if necessary, block the execution of queries running within our database. The plugin needs to be installed, and once it's installed, it sets up and writes to an audit log file (which can be renamed and/or have its format changed if necessary) as well as enables the audit log files to be encrypted and/or compressed if necessary.

The downside of both the enterprise-level firewall and the audit plugin is, of course, the enterprise-level pricing: both the firewall and the audit plugin can set you back thousands of dollars. Thankfully, other solutions such as web application firewalls generally cost less, and they're well-equipped to protect your applications and databases in one go.

Firewalling MariaDB

Another thing you can do to secure MariaDB and MySQL includes having a firewall installed on your application. The firewall *can* be MySQL Enterprise Firewall – but it doesn't have to. You can also put a firewall on MySQL or MariaDB through a CDN appliance like CloudFlare, Sucuri, or Imperva if you feel like it and can pay money to improve the security of your application, but if you are strapped for money or other resources, *you can also build your own firewall.* It may sound difficult, but it isn't – all you need to do is to essentially create a file, then use a loop that loops through every POST/GET/whatever you specify request to see if there are any blacklisted queries in the request. Afterward, if suspicious queries are identified, the firewall should block the request and return an error message to the user. If not, the request should pass through as usual.

Once you're done, title the file appropriately with an extension applicable to your programming language (firewall.ext anyone?), then include the file into every file you want/need to protect.

To let you in on a secret, *that's exactly how CDN-based firewalls operate, too, just instead of including a file in every file you need to protect, they use DNS servers to filter the traffic.* Again – the context is the same and the actions taken by the firewall are also largely the same; it's just the approach that differs. Oh, and you may save a couple thousand dollars too (and learn something in the process). Win-win, isn't it?

CHAPTER 16   THE WORLD OF SECURITY IN MYSQL

Summary

In this chapter, we revisited general security guidelines applicable to MySQL and MariaDB and familiarized ourselves with access control, user security, components, and plugins that keep our data safe, and also security controls applicable to our database. Each of those things has a place in your database, and each of those things may be applied differently to a different use case, which is why now I'll walk you through security guidelines applicable to specific use cases and teach you how to further secure your database instance.

CHAPTER 17

Securing Your Database Instance

Now that the basics of security are out of the way, let's dig deeper into how you can secure your most precious assets from data theft. In this chapter, I'll walk you through numerous methodologies that will help you apply security guidelines for your specific use case, we'll dig more into account categories, password management, account locking, security plugins, backups, SQL injection, and other attacks that may someday target your database instance.

Security Guidelines for Specific Use Cases and Defense in Depth

Truth be told, security guidelines and appliances often have to be applied and used differently depending on the use case. Think about it – having your things stolen because you've left the door unlocked and went on vacation for a month and having your things stolen because you've been threatened at gunpoint is different, right? The same can be said about security – while basic security principles don't change, some principles may have to be applied differently depending on your use case. For easier understanding, I've split everything into a table once again:

CHAPTER 17   SECURING YOUR DATABASE INSTANCE

Use Case/Scenario	Applicable Guidelines
A simple calculator belonging to an individual	The basics of security, input sanitization for XSS, SSL, if the app is behind a login, GDPR.
Course-selling company	GDPR is not applicable if the company doesn't store client data (e.g., stores only course-related information such as the duration, price, etc., and people enquire using a form) or is based outside the EU and doesn't work with data from EU citizens.
	May make use of NIST.
	The basics of security, SSL, input sanitization, OWASP Top 10 if applicable.
A directory (listing) of cars with a search functionality belonging to an individual who created the application as a hobby	The basics of security, OWASP Top 10, input sanitization.
An e-shop selling any kind of product belonging to an organization	GDPR, NIST, OWASP Top 10, input sanitization, and firewall appliance. Possibly enterprise-level solutions such as MySQL Enterprise Audit and/or MySQL Enterprise Firewall.

As you can see, not all use cases necessitate enterprise-level solutions such as Enterprise Audit/Enterprise Firewall, and not every use case necessitates NIST and/or GDPR. With that being said, every appliance whether it targets the web or not will necessitate security measures being taken – the extent of those security measures depends on the specifics of the application, so make sure to carefully evaluate your use case before choosing to do one thing or another in the security space. Knowing the best practices applicable to your use case isn't rocket science – you just need to look at your use case from a bird's eye view and with a clear head. You can also ask a friend to take a "fresh look" if you'd like – perhaps there's something you've missed?

Security experts will also be aware of defense in depth which aims to layer a set of security mechanisms to further the security of an application and protect the data stored within that application. The concept of defense in depth is that if one layer of security/defense fails, others will still be in place to disrupt a potential attack. Here's an example – say we have a basic web application with a login form using a web-based firewall (WAF) that is hashing user passwords with BCrypt. Its login forms are protected from brute-force

CHAPTER 17 SECURING YOUR DATABASE INSTANCE

attacks; aside from username/password forms, the application requires a two-factor code to log in; once a login is initiated, the app checks for a geolocation match for the user (if the location doesn't match the location used when registering, access is denied); and users who haven't been active for more than 5 minutes are automatically logged out. Judging by that, we can safely say that

1) If an attacker finds a security flaw on the website, he will have to bypass the firewall to exploit it and "bear fruits," which is a tough feat.

2) If the attacker bypasses the firewall and wants to find the username/password of an administrative user, he will have to exploit the flaw such that he possesses a username and a BCrypt hash of the user (presumably by using SQL injection) because brute-force attacks won't work. His actions would be somewhat limited thanks to the firewall.

3) If an attacker successfully mounts an SQL injection attack such that he's granted access to the database, he'd have to extract data from the database, and if the user he's using doesn't have the SELECT privilege (SELECT queries are necessary to dump data out of the database), he's out of luck.

4) If the user accessed by the attacker has all privileges and he's able to extract a username/hash combination, he'd need to "crack" that BCrypt hash. Brute-force attacks on a BCrypt hash would be very time-consuming to accomplish (the same can't be said about hashes like SHA1 or MD5).

5) Even if the attacker cracks the BCrypt hash, obtains the password of the user, and wants to log in to the administration control panel, he'd quickly be stopped by a two-factor authentication window which would send an SMS/email message to the account owner with an ID that needs to be entered.

6) Even if an attacker would somehow possess the 2FA ID code by accessing the email/phone of the owner, it's possible that the control panel wouldn't provide the attacker with anything "of interest" to begin with.

Is cracking all of these steps worth the time for an attacker? The most likely answer is no, and it's all thanks to your Defense in Depth practices.

Account Categories and Reserved Accounts

Aside from roles, users of newer versions of MySQL and MariaDB should also be familiar with account categories and reserved accounts.

MySQL is surrounded by a concept of account categories of which there are two – we have system users and regular users. In other words, a user in MySQL can either be a system user or a regular user and that's distinguished by whether a user has the SYSTEM_USER privilege or not:

GRANT SYSTEM_USER ON [database].[table] TO [username];

Accounts without the privilege will be regular users – accounts with the privilege will be system users. Easy, right? With that being said, keep in mind that the SYSTEM_USER privilege is only accessible for users of MySQL and not people using the MariaDB ecosystem because MariaDB will error out instead.

```
MariaDB [(none)]> GRANT SYSTEM_USER ON *.* TO demouser;
ERROR 1064 (42000): You have an error in your SQL syntax; check the manual that corresponds to your MariaDB server version for the right syntax to use near 'ON *.* TO demouser' at line 1
MariaDB [(none)]>
```

Figure 17-1. *Granting a SYSTEM_USER privilege in MariaDB*

However, both MySQL and MariaDB do offer the concepts of reserved accounts and roles. One should consider an account to be "reserved" if it's exclusively used for administrative purposes, accounts that are used internally by some features of MySQL or MariaDB, and others. Reserved accounts in MySQL and MariaDB are as follows:

Reserved Account	Explanation
'root'@'localhost'	The main – root – user account that has godlike privileges across all tables in all databases. This account can control other accounts. This account can be renamed for "security through obscurity" purposes or deleted altogether.

Reserved Account	Explanation
`'mysql.sys'@'localhost'`	Engineers turn to the `mysql.sys` account if the root account is renamed or deleted and problems occur. This account cannot be used to login to MariaDB, but it's used by the sys schema to power views, procedures, and functions – it's a locked account.
`'mysql.session'@'localhost'`	This account is used by plugins that access the database/server. Locked account.
`'mysql.infoschema'@'localhost'`	This account helps us view the information_schema table. Locked account.

In other words, reserved accounts are reserved for your database to accomplish specific tasks, and some of them (excluding the `root` account) are locked so they cannot be accessed from the outside.

Password Management and Account Locking

Account locking is also closely related to database security. Account locking has been available in MariaDB since MariaDB 10.4.2 and in MySQL since MySQL 8.0.19, and it's a feature that enables users to disable other accounts from being used or accessed. Account locking/unlocking works like so:

```
ALTER USER 'username'@'host' ACCOUNT [LOCK|UNLOCK];
```

```
MariaDB [(none)]> SET PASSWORD FOR 'demouser'@'localhost' = PASSWORD("");
Query OK, 0 rows affected (0.004 sec)

MariaDB [(none)]> ALTER USER 'demouser'@'localhost' ACCOUNT LOCK;
Query OK, 0 rows affected (0.015 sec)

MariaDB [(none)]> exit
Bye
mysql -udemouser
ERROR 4151 (HY000): Access denied, this account is locked
```

Figure 17-2. Locking an account in MariaDB

CHAPTER 17 SECURING YOUR DATABASE INSTANCE

In the example above, I set the password for `'demouser'@'localhost'` to an empty string so that I would be able to log in without specifying a password, then locked it, tried to log in, and got an error saying that this account is locked. We can even issue a SHOW CREATE USER command to make sure that's the case (example below). The same works the other way around, too.

```
Copyright (c) 2000, 2018, Oracle, MariaDB Corporation Ab and others.

Type 'help;' or '\h' for help. Type '\c' to clear the current input statement.

MariaDB [(none)]> SHOW CREATE USER 'demouser'@'localhost';
+------------------------------------------------+
| CREATE USER for demouser@localhost             |
+------------------------------------------------+
| CREATE USER `demouser`@`localhost` ACCOUNT LOCK |
+------------------------------------------------+
1 row in set (0.001 sec)

MariaDB [(none)]> ALTER USER 'demouser'@'localhost' ACCOUNT UNLOCK;
Query OK, 0 rows affected (0.004 sec)

MariaDB [(none)]> SHOW CREATE USER 'demouser'@'localhost';
+-----------------------------------+
| CREATE USER for demouser@localhost |
+-----------------------------------+
| CREATE USER `demouser`@`localhost` |
+-----------------------------------+
1 row in set (0.001 sec)

MariaDB [(none)]> exit
Bye
mysql -udemouser
Welcome to the MariaDB monitor.  Commands end with ; or \g.
Your MariaDB connection id is 12
Server version: 10.10.2-MariaDB mariadb.org binary distribution

Copyright (c) 2000, 2018, Oracle, MariaDB Corporation Ab and others.

Type 'help;' or '\h' for help. Type '\c' to clear the current input statement.

MariaDB [(none)]>
```

Figure 17-3. *Unlocking an account in MariaDB*

In the example above, we've made sure our account was locked, then unlocked it, made sure it's unlocked, and logged in to it. Simple when you understand the concept, isn't it?

CHAPTER 17 SECURING YOUR DATABASE INSTANCE

When it comes to password management, such capabilities are mostly exclusive to MySQL. MySQL can

- Expire passwords and require them to be changed.
- Help you implement restrictions on password reuse.
- Generate strong and secure passwords as well as verify them.
- Lock accounts after too many consecutive incorrect login attempts.

Here's what password expiration looks like.

```
MariaDB [(none)]> ALTER USER 'demouser'@'localhost' PASSWORD EXPIRE;
Query OK, 0 rows affected (0.015 sec)

MariaDB [(none)]> ALTER USER 'demouser'@'localhost' PASSWORD EXPIRE INTERVAL 1 MONTH;
ERROR 1064 (42000): You have an error in your SQL syntax; check the manual that corresponds to your MariaDB server version for the right syntax to use near 'MONTH' at line 1
MariaDB [(none)]> ALTER USER 'demouser'@'localhost' PASSWORD EXPIRE INTERVAL 30 DAY;
Query OK, 0 rows affected (0.004 sec)

MariaDB [(none)]> ALTER USER 'demouser'@'localhost' PASSWORD EXPIRE NEVER;
Query OK, 0 rows affected (0.004 sec)

MariaDB [(none)]> ALTER USER 'demouser'@'localhost' PASSWORD EXPIRE DEFAULT;
Query OK, 0 rows affected (0.002 sec)

MariaDB [(none)]>
```

Figure 17-4. *Expiring passwords in MariaDB*

Keep in mind that the PASSWORD EXPIRE syntax only supports day-based values: we can't make a password expire in 1 month since that raises an error, but we're free to expire a password after 30 days if we so desire.

We can also set a password reuse policy by making use of the password_history and password_reuse_interval variables. We're free to prohibit the rotation of any of the last 3 passwords when a password is changed as well as prohibit any passwords to be used if they've been used within the last, say, 90 days:

password_history=3
password_reuse_interval=90

The same statements can be run at runtime by using SET PERSIST queries or also when creating or altering a user (here X denotes a numeric value):

CREATE USER 'demouser'@'localhost' PASSWORD HISTORY X;
CREATE USER 'demouser'@'localhost' PASSWORD REUSE INTERVAL 90 DAY;
ALTER USER 'demouser'@'localhost' PASSWORD REUSE INTERVAL 90 DAY PASSWORD HISTORY 3;

CHAPTER 17   SECURING YOUR DATABASE INSTANCE

Some policies can be set to require users to specify the currently used password before changing it to prevent errors – that can be done by setting the `password_require_current` variable to ON.

Use the `RANDOM PASSWORD` clause to set the password of users to a random password, and keep in mind that users can be set to have dual passwords by making use of the `RETAIN CURRENT PASSWORD` clause like so:

```
ALTER USER 'demouser'@'somehost' IDENTIFIED BY 'complex_password' RETAIN CURRENT PASSWORD;
```

The `RETAIN CURRENT PASSWORD` clause retains the password of an account but adds the specified password as a secondary password the user can use to log in.

Last but not least, accounts can be locked after a specified amount of failed login attempts like so (here X represents a numeric value):

```
CREATE USER 'demouser'@'localhost' IDENTIFIED BY 'password' FAILED_LOGIN_ATTEMPTS 5 PASSWORD_TIME [UNBOUNDEDIX];
```

Once users are secure, it's time to come back to your data.

SQL Injection, Input Sanitization, and MariaDB

SQL injection is the pillar of many attacks targeting applications and database management systems – according to OWASP, injection-based attacks were the #1 attack vector in 2010, 2013, and 2017, and in 2021, injection moved into third place. Regardless, injection attacks remain an immensely important point of contention for those aiming to protect their infrastructure from hackers for a couple of reasons:

1) Injection attacks are rather easy to find.

2) Attackers can use injection attack vectors in a couple of ways.

3) The impact of a successfully mounted injection attack is often very severe.

The risks of injection attacks remain rampant despite the warnings of security experts, and there's a good reason for that: just as not every MySQL DBA will know his/her way around all components of the database management system, not every developer will be security-savvy and may write sloppy code as a result. In fact, many

CHAPTER 17 SECURING YOUR DATABASE INSTANCE

developers are very well aware of the risks posed by SQL injection, but they may not be aware of what to do to prevent such attacks.

The answer to the question "How to prevent SQL injection attacks targeting my database?" is rather simple and twofold:

1) Never trust user input.

2) Never provide user input straight into a database query.

That's it, really – not a very hard task to accomplish, is it? In developer terms, "never trust user input" translates to "sanitize all input fields" and "never provide user input straight into a query" translates to "parameterize your queries so that the input provided by the user cannot modify the syntax of your query to act unexpectedly."

The sanitization of user input fields can be done in a couple of ways, but the most popular and recommended way to accomplish such a task is by the usage of functions available in programming languages – I'll use PHP as an example:

Function to Sanitize Data	Explanation
filter_var()	The filter_var() function allows the developer to discern whether a certain variable is formatted in a way consistent with a chosen filter. For example, filter_var($variable, FILTER_VALIDATE_BOOLEAN) would return true if the variable is a boolean value, and false if otherwise enabling a developer to take the value returned by the function and return an error if the value of false is returned.
filter_input()	The filter_input() function allows the developer to discern whether input provided by the user confirms with a chosen filter. For example, filter_input(INPUT_GET, $user_provided_value, FILTER_SANITIZE_SPECIAL_CHARS); would filter and sanitize any special characters provided in a $user_provided_value variable that is passed via a GET parameter.
htmlspecialchars() htmlentities()	htmlspecialchars converts all special characters in the string to HTML entities. htmlentities act similarly by converting all applicable characters in the string to HTML entities, thus preventing Cross-site Scripting (XSS) attacks in the process.

CHAPTER 17   SECURING YOUR DATABASE INSTANCE

Function to Sanitize Data	Explanation
mysqli_real_escape_string()	mysqli_real_escape_string() escapes special characters. This function is also unique in that it takes into account the charset in the database, and as such, it has its benefits, but keep in mind that the best way to protect your database from SQL injection attacks is to use parameterized statements (see Corner cases of SQL Injection for more information).

The sanitization of user input fields is helpful, but when SQL injection is concerned, it is recommended to prevent such an attack by using prepared statements. Prepared statements look like so (PHP-based example).

```php
<?php
$server = "localhost";
$username = "root";
$password = "password";
$dbname = "database_name";
$connection = new mysqli($server, $username, $password, $dbname);
if($connection->connect_error) {
    die("Double-check your configuration: ".$conn->connect_error);
}
...
$user_input_col1 = $_POST['user_input_1'];
$user_input_col2 = $_POST['user_input_2'];
$sql_query = $connection->prepare("SELECT * FROM `demo_table` WHERE `column` = ? OR `column_2` = ?");
$sql_query->bind_param("ss", $user_input_col1, $user_input_col2);
$sql_query->execute();
...
$connection->close();
?>
```

Figure 17-5. Parameterized statements in PHP

The code above does a couple of things:

1) Connects to a database server.

2) Assigns user input passed via a POST request to two parameters.

3) Parameterizes an SQL query to accept two parameters because there are two input values provided by the user.

4) Binds two parameters into the SQL query and executes it (we use "s" to specify a string value, but we can also specify integers with i, double-based values with d, or BLOB values with b).

Prepared statements make the query no longer susceptible to SQL injection because *the query and user input are sent to the server separately*, thus eliminating the root cause of the SQL injection problem.

Corner Cases of SQL Injection

mysqli_real_escape_string() and input parameterization both have benefits unique to themselves, but neither of them has the cure for all of your database problems. When used properly, they are capable of protecting your database from SQL injection attacks, but they don't forbid you from passing user input straight into a database. I've seen cases where a person has used PDO and put a variable into their SQL query – in that case, can you expect protection? You've just nullified everything that you've been told!

Also, keep in mind that *PDO defaults to emulating prepared statements with MySQL*, which for very, very rare cases (when the gbk Chinese character set is in use) may make issues worse rather than alleviate them because the aforementioned character set is considered to be vulnerable and if it's in use, running certain statements would still result in a successful execution of the query, thus paving the way to another successful SQL injection attack.

Disable this behavior by disabling the emulation of prepared statements by setting the PDO attribute ATTR_EMULATE_PREPARES to FALSE:

```
$PDO->setAttribute(PDO::ATTR_EMULATE_PREPARES, FALSE);
```

Alternatively, avoid using the gbk character set – more information can be found here (https://stackoverflow.com/questions/5741187/sql-injection-that-gets-around-mysql-real-escape-string/12118602).

Other Attacks Targeting Your Database

Once you have a good grasp of how SQL injection may be used to harm your database, think of other attacks as well. Attackers aren't likely to limit themselves to a single attack vector, and if injection attacks fail, they will almost certainly try other attack vectors to steal data from your organization or access your application. I've covered other attack vectors in this book, and I'll come back to my recommendations once again:

CHAPTER 17 SECURING YOUR DATABASE INSTANCE

1) **Follow the recent edition of the OWASP Top 10.** OWASP doesn't only provide a list of the top 10 most impactful security issues that harm applications and databases but also provides actionable tips centered around how you can prevent the outlined security flaws from being introduced into your application as well as provides detailed advice related to when an application may be susceptible to an attack, example scenarios when such an attack may take place, and ways to prevent it. If an attack does take place, the tips provided by OWASP will provide a good basis to contain the scale of a data breach and protect your applications from further exploitations of security vulnerabilities.

2) **Take note of older editions of OWASP and other security-related frameworks.** Some attacks may drop in the rating list; some may be included. It's wise to know ways to protect from them all. For example, CSRF isn't a part of the recent edition of OWASP, but it doesn't mean that the attack ceased to be dangerous, does it?

3) **Make use of firewall solutions.** Firewall solutions protect your application from an attacker exploiting security flaws, and as such, even if your code would be susceptible to a security vulnerability, it couldn't be exploited. There's no need to choose the most expensive firewall solution for your use case either – simple things will do just fine.

4) **Chat with the security engineering team if you have access to one.** Software engineering and the database world can be scary as it is – why not listen to some fresh insight about how to deal with issues?

5) **To continue staying on top of cyber security news, follow security blogs** such as the ones being written by BreachDirectory, Cybernews, Rapid7, and others. Video content on cybersecurity is an awesome place to start too.

CHAPTER 17   SECURING YOUR DATABASE INSTANCE

To top it off, continue educating yourself on software, database, and security issues by attending conferences and workshops, reading the documentation of products you find yourself using, and reading books such as this one – you will never know what you'll come across.

You are capable of combating attacks targeting your database – apply your knowledge to thwart them all.

Summary

This chapter has walked you through a variety of methods to protect your database instance and the data within. Many of those methods have lots to do with following standards and following given advice by reputable sources.

Now, let me walk you through some more things necessary to know for those working with bigger data sets – security doesn't end here, does it?

CHAPTER 18

Security and Big Data

1. The architecture of the server, application, and database are important because those things help uncover simple, but important things ranging from the versions of plugins we're allowed to use to the limits of PHP versions that can be installed on our server (PHP versions are dependent on your operating system and older versions of operating systems will not power newer versions of PHP). If the architecture of our application, server, or database is already problematic, problems need to be squashed before we move on, because they will only get bigger if we don't do that.

2. The amount of data available within our database will point us in a direction in regard to where it's stored (e.g., if we have a billion rows, it'd be safe to assume that some of the tables within our database would be partitioned, and each partition comes with a certain weight on the disk, so if one partition weighs around 10GB, one might assume that such things are stored in a hard drive having an appropriate limit for space), and the space where data is stored is likely to answer additional questions: is the space a hard drive? An SSD? A NVMe drive?

3. The data classes within our database once again tell us whether we're susceptible to GDPR or other regulations.

4. The measures we take to protect our data at present will inevitably have an impact on the measures we'll take when our data gets bigger. It's unlikely that we'll need to reevaluate our entire security strategy when our data grows to a level where we consider it "big data," but it's entirely possible that we'd have to add some security methods/appliances that we didn't have before to improve our security posture.

CHAPTER 18   SECURITY AND BIG DATA

To put it simply, *we secure big data sets just as we'd secure data sets of "ordinary" size while also keeping mindful of the basics and securing data using measures applicable to our specific use case.* Let's consider a couple of security measures and see what they would mean in a big data context:

Security Measure	Meaning in Big Data Context
Data encryption/hashing	Passwords should be hashed with a function that's considered hard to crack – Blowfish or BCrypt – and encryption should be applied to everything you need to protect to scramble the text into ciphertext that needs to be decrypted with a key.
Data masking	Data masking is the obfuscation of data. The more data you have, the more important data masking may become in the sense that you may have a lot of data that is valuable to attackers and data masking would help obfuscate sensitive data that may be used to somehow cause harm.
Data segmentation	When bigger data sets are involved, data segmentation is one of the best ways to group data with similarities into groups based on chosen parameters so it can be used more effectively. Perhaps you would even consider backing up segments of data instead of backing up the entire data set to begin with?
"Right to be forgotten" (data erasing upon request)	EU-based companies are subject to the so-called "right to be forgotten" where if a user/customer asks to delete his/her data, the data should be promptly deleted without any further questions/charges. If you run a big data-based project and store EU-based user data to facilitate their access to any part of your product, you have to comply with this law.
CDN to protect against DoS/DDoS attacks	Big data sets are usually necessary to complete an objective – and objectives must be secured from outside threats such as DDoS attacks. DDoS attacks are very easy to launch, and a CDN like the one provided by Sucuri, Imperva, or CloudFlare can help you mitigate this risk.

(continued)

Security Measure	Meaning in Big Data Context
Firewall and/or audit appliances	When your data gets bigger, it's natural that you will have more data to protect – a properly installed firewall appliance will protect you from threats posed to your application/database and an audit appliance will help you evaluate your security posture at all times. Many audit and firewall appliances are integrated because they act as integral parts of one another and help you inspect and track the steps of an attacker and forbid him from accessing certain areas of your application/website as a result.
Effective access control	The more data you have, the more important the control who accesses that data becomes. Make sure to follow the "need to know" access control guideline, and you should be good to go.
Traffic analysis	It's important to analyze traffic to your application/website often to identify potentially malicious actors/attacks. A sudden shift from 10,000 requests a day to 70,000,000 requests an hour may indicate a DDoS attack, and the existence of "/script.php?id=8 SELECT @@version" in the request list may indicate a possible SQL injection attack vector. Traffic analysis applies when you run smaller data sets, too, but once your data sets get bigger, the importance of traffic analysis is likely to increase.
Backup strategy	It's important to always have and test your backup strategy. As your data grows, the importance of a proper backup strategy is likely to become more and more paramount – come up with a backup strategy applicable to your use case by following the tips outlined in this book (if necessary, back up raw data to guarantee faster restoration times), and make sure your backups can be restored.
Threat detection and incident response plan	It's always important to have threat detection and incident response plans at hand. As your data grows, your application will be likely to become a target for all kinds of attacks, and no matter if they're executed successfully or not, you *have* to have means to detect and preempt them.
GDPR & NIST	As your data gets bigger, it's crucial to adhere to the regulations of GDPR and NIST. They may not apply to your specific case, but if they do, you have to make sure to follow them to the tea to avoid hefty fines and other issues down the way.

CHAPTER 18   SECURITY AND BIG DATA

To secure bigger data sets during the transfer, storage, and displaying phases, think of security in the very first steps of your system development lifecycle. Then, no matter if your use case already deals with big data or will deal with it in the future, you will be in safe hands.

Security, Big Data, and Code in the Initial Phases of Your SDLC

There's no specific methodology to "secure big data operations" because there are no "big data operations" to begin with. SELECTs will remain SELECTs, INSERTs will remain INSERTs, and UPDATEs and DELETEs will retain their functionality as well. What people mean when they say "How do I secure big data sets?" is "How to secure the code that accesses bigger data sets?" and that can and should be done *by implementing security in the initial phases of your SDLC and never forgetting it in the long run.* You need to

1) Write code in adherence to regulations and security methodologies

2) Perform threat modeling in adherence to your use case

3) Perform regular vulnerability scanning and, if possible, automate the process

4) Inspect, update, delete, or mask the data inside of your database if necessary

5) Conduct code reviews

In other words, the majority of the things you need to do won't change – what changes is your approach to those things. Let me explain:

1) Writing code in adherence to security regulations may mean "not storing data that are not necessary to store" instead of "storing data and deleting it within 6-12 hours of getting a request."

2) By taking on threat modeling early on in the system development life cycle, you will be better equipped to counter the threats that are posed to your application(s) and database. Proper threat modeling may even help you build out your database/table

structure because if you identify data that would be of interest to an attacker but is not necessary to store, you can make a decision to not store it in the first place, and thus, be less susceptible to a certain type of attack.

3) In the big data realm, regular vulnerability scanning combined with threat modeling enables you to not only identify possible threats by *scanning* but also presume how they could be exploited by *threat modeling* and thus, be better equipped to preempt them before they take place. For some, bigger data sets also provide the ability to further threat modeling capabilities by using AI-based threat modeling based on the structure of the data.

4) Frequent inspecting, updating, or deleting of data may be necessary to ensure that we no longer store unnecessary data to adhere to regulations.

5) Conducting code reviews helps to identify and preempt possible security flaws that may arise. These days, before a commit is added to any repo, it can even be subjected to automatic static and/or dynamic code analysis processes that identify and fix vulnerabilities without you doing any work!

When designing software, think of security as a default measure that comes with everything you do. Ships are a perfect example of what I want to say – if you build a ship so that *it displaces as much water as possible* instead of plugging holes when you see water coming in, your ship is way less likely to sink if controlled properly. The second way of dealing with problems is also an option, but it's unlikely to save you.

If your ship displaces as much water as possible, it doesn't matter whether it floats through a pond, river, lake, sea, or ocean, it will be unlikely to sink if you control it properly. *The same goes for your data* – adhere to security and privacy regulations, make use of threat modeling and regular vulnerability scanning, inspect your data frequently, and if necessary – update it and conduct code reviews, and you should be good to go. Notice that I don't say that "you won't suffer a data breach" because a guarantee can never be given and everything can be made more secure, but those actions will certainly fortify your data castle and fend off attackers.

CHAPTER 18   SECURITY AND BIG DATA

Before jumping into security limitations, one thing to always keep in mind is that there's no such thing as 100% security – and there is unlikely to ever be. Systems can be secured, but absolute security is a myth. Everything can be hacked – we, as developers, have a task to harden our infrastructure to the level that a breach would be unfeasible to conduct.

As far as threat scanning and modeling are concerned, I've even heard of stories where certain people preparing for the defense of their Master's or PhD thesis worked with big data sets, threat modeling, and classifier algorithms to predict the probability of a data breach or some statistics related to them. If I remember correctly, the person I'm talking about employed a Naive Bayes Classifier to predict the probability of an upcoming data breach which is an even more interesting approach because such classifiers work best when we have a lot of data to "feed" them with and the hacking space sure has a lot of data to offer.

Data, Script Kiddies & Co.

Some of you may also be wondering whether there are ways to protect your big data sets from being misused or used for fraudulent purposes. This doesn't apply to everyone – to protect big data against misuse/fraud, your data generally needs to be displayed in a place readily accessible by the user first and pose a big enough threat to employees, users of the software, clients, or the general public. You see, by saying "protecting from misuse," I mean "protecting data from being used to cause harm" – in other words, protecting the way data is *used* rather than protecting the way it's stored. If your use case necessitates you working with sensitive data, you need to pay attention to this too.

To give you an example, I'll once again focus on data breach search engines and various bulletin forums. If you've been around the security industry starting around 2015 until 2017, you've most likely noticed a couple of odd things, the main ones of those being (1) the appearance of data-mining data breach search engines and (2) the activity on forums of questionable nature, hence our focus.

Those two things were related because the operators of data breach search engines or people related to them advertised their "services" to attract paying customers who would pay money to access data in data breaches. The services were said to be advertised on hacking forums and then went further through word of mouth.

The services were advertised on hacking forums because some of the clientele for those operating such services aside from software engineers, security enthusiasts, and engineers were wanna-be hackers (so-called "script kiddies"). Script kiddies were the perfect audience for such services because

a) Such people often use existing scripts and services to potentially cause harm to other people or services.

b) Data breach engines available back in the day quickly grew to infamy for providing people access to data for questionable purposes often without verifying that those who search for the data own it (i.e., those searching for email addresses own such email addresses, those searching for usernames own these usernames, etc.).

The combination of these two things – access to sensitive data and clientele based on script kiddies served a purpose – data was misused and often used to further illicit access to accounts and/or services. While the nature of such services also attracted people wanting to ensure that they are not at risk of identity theft (i.e., it had a legitimate use case, too), security experts presumed that most of the data within such services attracted nefarious parties who were paying to access the data so they could attack and take over accounts on the web.

It wasn't long until some of such services shut down by themselves, and some were even shut down by law enforcement because those bigger data sets were data leaks acquired from other services used to facilitate identity theft attacks! Data derived from leaked data breaches was being misused and allegedly used for fraudulent purposes – not what we all want to see on the web, is it? The bottom line is that if you build data breach search engines, do so ethically intending to minimize cybercrime on the web, not to further it: otherwise things aren't going to end nicely.

Of course, not many of you would've even heard of such use cases, and your use case may be far from data breach search engines and that's fine, but protecting data against it being misused and being used for questionable purposes still stands and there is one important thing to do here – before storing/displaying data, think about the other side of things first: is there anyone who could exploit the way data is stored/provided for the user to harm other people without any special skills or software? If your answer to that question is "yes," you've got problems on your hands. Data breach search engines are just one example of this, and I'm almost sure that as time goes by, other similar "use cases" will also appear.

Besides these use cases, you need to take care of personal security – even the highest security of data within your database instance is likely to be quickly nullified if you use one password across 57 different services or stick a password to your MySQL database on your front desk. Use password managers, security features available within browsers, don't share too much information about yourself on social media and elsewhere on the web, and if necessary, use encrypted communication channels too.

Also, think about using modern browsers like Google Chrome or the like. It's a safe bet that if you're reading this book, most of you are already using one, but keep in mind that Chrome is a very advanced browser that has security features some of you wouldn't even think about – it has many advanced features like the ability to mask the IP addresses of its users using proxy servers, the ability to detect weak passwords and others, and some privacy-paranoid users may even consider alternative browsers like Brave: the browser blocks ads, trackers, and protects from browsers being fingerprinted by default, thus furthering your security.

Finally, there's no need to be paranoid about personal and corporate security in daily life as long as you understand that hackers will always be there and data within publicly available systems will always be a target. Don't store unnecessary data, when you're storing data, only store data you need, to be in safe hands, employ security practices, be sensible about things, and avoid pushing things too far. Also, coming back to your database, be mindful of possible pitfalls related to big data security as well.

What Happens If...?

Last but not least, I'll let you in on secrets related to what you should expect should flaws like SQL injection, improper access control, or mistakes like the usage of weak passwords be exploited and how to go about fixing them.

As a website/app owner, suspect a compromise if you come across any or all of the following points:

1) Any files being missing/having their content changed at odd times that you know no one worked on the system

2) Unusual or a lot of entries in any kind of log files

3) Anomalies in account/user activity

4) Weird login/registration attempts

5) Sudden and unreasonable increase in database read volume

6) Anomalies on the DNS front

7) Numerous requests for unusual files in unusual locations

8) Unexpected software being installed or updated

9) Suspicious changes in configuration or other core files

10) A deface page on any or all of your pages (obviously)

Most of the time, these IoCs (Indicators of Compromise) are a good telling point saying that your system/application has suffered an attack and needs immediate support.

Even having multiple Indicators of Compromise in mind, an attack will likely be difficult to detect and mitigate because no attacker will leave a text file saying "I've breached your system using SQL injection via the following endpoint: /api.php?request=<payload> where I've used a blind union-based SQL injection attack. This attack was made possible by your mismanagement of access control privileges, thus allowing me to access the API without paying for it in the first place. I've also defaced the index page and backdoored the forum of your website, backdoors can be found in the admin.php script on line 227 and in the install.php script on line 56."

Not all Indicators of Compromise will be the same either, and these days, after finishing an attack, hackers will clear all of the applicable logs from the system, too.

To combat this, I'd advise you to create a system that backs up your logs to a remote server every day/week/month/whatever frequency you necessitate. That way, even if access logs are cleared, you would still be able to access them via another server, thus making it significantly easier for you to identify what'd happened and why. After accessing the logs, remember the OWASP Top 10 and skim through these security vulnerabilities while aiming to see indicators of compromise coming from any of the flaws in the OWASP list.

Once a potential indicator of compromise is identified, lock your systems down (make the entire perimeter of an application unaccessible, only accessible via a login, etc.), then follow these steps:

1. Contain the data breach.

2. Remove access for everyone, except yourself (that may be as simple as setting up .htaccess settings within your application – don't sweat).

3. Maintain the settings of your audit/firewall appliance.

4. Back up all of the logs (if necessary, including the firewall logs) and assess the boundaries of the data breach – aim to answer questions *what* has been breached? *How* could it have been breached? *When* (at least approximately) could the data breach taken place?

5. Act on the data breach response plan applicable to your use case – if necessary, notify managers and the clients of the breach, have some discussions back & forth, consider involving your security engineering team/related people or involve outside experts for an audit, and wait until it completes before resetting any passwords or performing related activities (if you reset passwords at this stage, an attacker who might have retained control will simply re-gain access to them).

6. Act on the advice in the data breach audit plan that has been laid out.

7. Reset passwords.

Many things can be said about the points above, but in my opinion, the most important ones would be related to how and when the data breach took place. This is why you back up your log files because if the content of them (or even the files themselves) is deleted which happens more often than you would think, they would still retain their value in the sense that they will act as a helping hand for you to initially investigate the data breach and identify the possible IP addresses, requests made, and other details about the perpetrators.

From the requests that have been made, often you will have a good enough birds-eye view to identify problematic places in your application or website and even tell what flaws were exploited within these places. For example, a bunch of requests like these in the access.log:

```
127.0.0.1 - [27/Mar/2024 : 17:36:42 +0300] "Get /admin/ HTTP/1.1" 200 1254 "https://website.com/admin/login.php"
127.0.0.1 - [27/Mar/2024 : 17:38:00 +0300] "Get /admin/ HTTP/1.1" 200 1254 "https://website.com/admin/panel.php"
```

```
127.0.0.1 - [27/Mar/2024 : 17:39:42 +0300] "Get /admin/ HTTP/1.1" 200 1254
"https://website.com/panel.php?do=backup"
127.0.0.1 - [27/Mar/2024 : 17:42:00 +0300] "Get /admin/ HTTP/1.1" 200 1254
"https://website.com/panel.php?do=modifyroles"
127.0.0.1 - [27/Mar/2024 : 17:53:00 +0300] "Get /admin/ HTTP/1.1" 200 1254
"https://website.com/admin/logout.php"
```

Combined with a request like this in the error.log:

```
[Fri Mar 27 10:42:29.902022 2024] [core:error] [pid 35708:tid 4328636416]
[client 127.0.0.1] File does not exist: https://website.com/backup/
backup.sql
```

May indicate the following:

1. An IP of 127.0.0.1 is likely to belong to or be somehow related to an attacker.

2. The attack took place on or around March 27 and could've taken the attacker the whole day to complete (approximate timeline: 10AM–6PM).

3. The attacker has attempted to locate a backup of the database. The request has taken place at 10:42AM and was unsuccessful (the request was in the error.log).

4. The attacker accessed the admin panel of the website at 17:38:00 GMT +3 and stayed there for 15 minutes.

5. During those 15 minutes, the attacker has attempted to take a backup of the data within the website and modify the roles (privileges?) of certain users, perhaps even himself. Judging by the fact that taking the backup has taken a couple of minutes (the attacker proceeded to modify roles not even three minutes later), we can assume that the attacker didn't export all data from the database and exported only a small portion of our data cake (the user table, anyone?).

Log files are likely to have thousands, or even hundreds of thousands, of requests, and not all requests will be malicious – and that's why you have to pay so much attention to the contents of the log files. When you do, experience and attention will likely point you in the right direction. You will be able to identify problematic sides of an application or a script, patch them, and together with your application and database head toward a more prosperous future. So few requests, so much information!

After the cause of the breach is identified (and your application remains locked to the outside world), you can start working on remedying issues. Once you're confident that the security flaws are squashed and after you've scanned the perimeter of your application for other kinds of security flaws and issues (the OWASP top 10 is always a good place to start) and cleaned up your infrastructure, you can issue a mandatory password reset for those logging in to your application, then start re-opening your application to the outside world.

Keep in mind that if your infrastructure has suffered a data breach once, it can suffer a data breach again – don't assume that attackers have gotten tired and remain vigilant. Always follow the best practices in the security world, read cybersecurity blogs, and stay updated, and no matter how much data you have, your database and the application built on top of it should thrive.

Summary

Security is a crucial aspect within any kind of database, and it's even more paramount when bigger data sets are concerned. When securing bigger data sets, keep in mind the three Vs (Volume, Velocity, Variety) and the phases – transfer, storage, and display – you need to secure data in. Follow security best practices and frameworks, adhere to ways to squash the most prominent attacks on the web and beyond consulting with the OWASP Top 10, and remain vigilant.

Aside from these three Vs, be mindful of what the future upholds for you, your application, and your database too. Threats evolve – the ways you are protecting your database and application against them should too.

If the unfortunate strikes your database, whatever you do remember to not reset passwords until after you've completed the steps necessary to secure your application. Make sure to keep your users/visitors/customers informed on what's happening too and tell them everything they need to know, because chances are they will figure everything out regardless.

Be smart around social media, protect your devices, beware of phishing attacks, shop safely, use password managers to avoid password reuse, and, perhaps most importantly, *keep things simple* and retain a cool head on your shoulders.

Keep things simple, because when your data castle is burning, you need a way to escape before finding a firehose or calling firefighters.

I hope that this book helped you do it all – you now understand how your database castle can be broken, how to make use of the data in your database castle in a performant way, and how to secure the entire castle from intruders, too.

Do contact me via the contacts at the beginning of this book, and tell me what you've thought of it – I'm eager to hear your thoughts on this.

Until then – au revoir.

APPENDIX

Things You Wish You Knew, but Don't

Why, hello there! Or hello again, if you didn't skip to the appendix. Not all books have an appendix – and, indeed, not all of them need it. This book doesn't "need" it either per se; however, the appendix contains a bunch of valuable (and perhaps weird) information you can put to use.

Schrödinger's Tables

Have you ever had a situation where SHOW TABLES shows a table in the list, but it's impossible to issue any kind of SQL query on it because it seemingly disappears when you do so? Creating the table is impossible because it exists:

```
mysql> CREATE TABLE 'demo_table' (
'a' VARCHAR(5) NOT NULL ''
) ENGINE = InnoDB;
ERROR 1051 (42S02): Table 'demo_table' already exists
```

And dropping the table is impossible because it *doesn't* exist:

```
mysql> DROP TABLE 'demo_table'
ERROR 1051 (42S02): Unknown table 'demo_table'
```

Such tables are known as Schrödinger's tables – they can be called that way because the concept behind them is derived from a physics phenomenon called a Schrödinger's cat – a cat that is both alive and dead at the same time. From time to time, you may see errors like the one above when working with MariaDB or its counterparts: if you do, that most likely means that InnoDB is lost in its own world – in its own tablespace. In particular, this error occurs when the InnoDB's copy of the data dictionary is out of sync with the data dictionary files in `.frm` files. Upon checking the error log, many of you will see an error like so suggesting that the error may have occurred because you've copied and pasted data files together, hoping they would click with ibdata1 – they won't:

```
170426 17:44:16 InnoDB: Error: table 'hacking_mysql/demo_table' does not exist in the InnoDB internal
InnoDB: data dictionary though MySQL is trying to drop it.
InnoDB: Have you copied the .frm file of the table to the
InnoDB: MySQL database directory from another database?
```

"Have you copied the .frm file of the table to the MySQL database directory from another database?" Well, you most likely did, didn't you? If you did, everything's self-explanatory: the entries in the .frm file wouldn't match the entries in the InnoDB tablespace, hence the appearance of errors like the one above. Never copy data files from one InnoDB-based server to another: that's just asking for problems like the one above: the error above occurred because the `ibdata1` file "saw" the data file, but the .frm file related to that data file was either corrupt or missing.

Lesson   Never copy over .frm and/or .ibd files to another server if you cannot ensure that the tablespace ID of the .ibd file matches the tablespace ID in the metadata of ibdata1. Doing so is just asking for trouble.

Having Fun with ibdata1

The ibdata1 is the tablespace behind the main storage engine in MySQL – InnoDB. Sometimes, the InnoDB tablespace will be the reason behind errors like "Unable to lock ibdata1 error: 11" and notes like "InnoDB: Check that you do not aleady have another mysqld process using the same InnoDB data or log files."

These errors say that MariaDB/MySQL wasn't able to lock the `ibdata1` file which is an error that occurs upon restarting MySQL. This error likely means that MySQL has tried to restart with an old MySQL process still running. Think of deleting a file that's still open – your OS will throw an error, right? That's what InnoDB does.

The safest way to stop this particular InnoDB-related error is to stop your database, then start the process anew: `systemctl stop mysql.service` / `systemctl start mysql.service` should do. In some cases, the MySQL process won't be running so it won't be able to be stopped, and in that case, you would need to identify the process running on applicable ports (3306 if you run MySQL or 3307 if you run MariaDB.) Linux users will be able to issue a command like this:

`lsof -i:3306`

This command will provide the ID of the process that runs on the port 3306. Kill the process, then restart your database, and the error should be gone.

In the past, users of InnoDB were facing yet another annoying problem: InnoDB would store all of its data in one data file that would often become rather gigantic. Newer versions of the database management system don't have such a problem thanks to the `file-per-table` variable being set to 1 on most newer versions of the software, but earlier on, that was a problem because the architecture of the storage engine necessitates four types of database pages, which were the following:

1. Table data pages
2. Index data pages
3. Table metadata
4. Multiversion Concurrency Control (MVCC) data to support ACID compliance and transaction isolation

Back in the day, all of those details were stored in the same place – ibdata1 – and were "glued together" with the .ibd files in a sense that .ibd files provided InnoDB with a link to the data pages in the filespace and vice versa. The core problem was that MySQL wasn't able to reduce the size of its tablespace, and even if some space were freed, MySQL would reuse the space later. Later on, MySQL defaulted the variable `file-per-table` to 1 which, to a large extent, fixed this issue.

Having Fun with Indexes

As far as indexes are concerned, there also are a couple of things you need to keep in mind and these are as follows:

APPENDIX   THINGS YOU WISH YOU KNEW, BUT DON'T

Note	About
Most MySQL index types are B-tree indexes.	`INDEX`, `UNIQUE`, `PRIMARY KEY`, and `FULLTEXT` index types are stored in B-tree data structures while spatial indexes use R-tree data structures. Hash indexes are supported by the `MEMORY` storage engine; however, not all types of indexes within the storage engine will be hash indexes.
There is a maximum limit for secondary indexes, but there's no limit to the amount of indexes that can reside on a single column.	MySQL has a limit for secondary indexes on a table (a singular table permits up to 64 secondary indexes for one column); however, there's no limit for the indexes or their types that reside on a column. In other words, if you want to have 2 full-text indexes, 1 b-tree index, and one unique index on a column, you're free to do so.
You can make use of partitions *and* indexes at the same time.	Many developers and even power users of MySQL elect to use either indexes or partitions to further the performance of read-based queries in their infrastructure. However, some may be blind to the fact that they can use both indexes and partitions to further the performance of read-based operations. Keeping this in mind will be very useful if the primary use case of your application is a search engine or a similar appliance.
Some storage engines support instant removal/adding of indexes, and when some storage engines are in use, indexes can be moved from one server to another without downtime or issues related to data corruption.	Those using MyISAM can enjoy life without their data being connected to a tablespace file, and because that's the case, data (.MYD) and index (.MYI) files can be moved around servers with no hassle, which can't be said about any other storage engine. InnoDB doesn't have such a capability, but since starting in 2018, the MySQL team has implemented instant DDL operations that enable users to make instant changes to their table structure when applicable, in some cases, MySQL can only modify metadata instead of the table structure itself. That can be done by specifying `ALGORITHM=INSTANT` at the end of the `ALTER TABLE` statement and is effective when we're adding the last column in a table or some other scenarios. Newer versions of MySQL will also make use of the `INSTANT` algorithm first (if applicable) and then try everything else.

(continued)

APPENDIX   THINGS YOU WISH YOU KNEW, BUT DON'T

Note	About
Index usage can be verified by digging into the EXPLAIN plan or other types of queries.	The query execution – EXPLAIN – plan is a very useful tool when working with indexes because not only does it provide the type of index used by the query, but also provides the names of possible keys (indexes) that could but may or may not have been used by your database, assisting you in further investigation.

For those interested in more information about these points, return to the chapter on indexes.

Query That Breaks MySQL 5.7

Older versions of MySQL (we're talking about MySQL 5.7 for this example) had a couple of weird things up their sleeves too. One of such things is full-text indexes. The problem wasn't related to full-text indexes by themselves per se; however, it did occur when all of the following were true:

1) We had a bigger data set (>100M and above).

2) Our data set had a column with data consisting of "@" signs (think email addresses or similar things).

3) We were searching for anything consisting of an "@" sign, and our query was using a full-text index – that is, we used the MATCH() AGAINST() query.

4) Optionally, the query can use a search mode applicable for full-text indexes (e.g., the Boolean mode, etc.)

Here's an example – on a properly configured database, such a query would complete almost instantaneously even if a table would have hundreds of millions of records:

```
SELECT * FROM 'demo_table' WHERE MATCH(column) AGAINST("example" IN
BOOLEAN MODE);
```

Whereas a query like the following would make MySQL 5.7 timeout or take hundreds of times more time to execute at best because it would have the "@" sign present:

```
SELECT * FROM 'demo_table' WHERE MATCH(column) AGAINST("example@demo.com"
IN BOOLEAN MODE);
```

In 2021, I've dug into the issue with Jonathan Gennick and Charles Bell: I remember that Jonathan initially thought that the "@" character might be treated as some kind of an escape character, while Charles suggested escaping the character with something like demo\@test.com, but that hasn't helped the use case either: a SQL query fetching results without an "@" sign was able to return 2 results in 0.0137 sec. while a query fetching results with the "@" sign has returned a single (1) result in 8.6970 sec. Eventually, the anomaly was classified as a bug and obtained the bug ID #104263…

I've initially came across this bug when building BreachDirectory a decade ago or so; at first, I thought I need to switch to "a more durable database," but as we can see, that wasn't the case…

Reliably Using MyISAM

Aside from the main storage engine in MySQL, MyISAM can be used as well. Now, whether you can "reliably use MyISAM" is up for debate because of the reasons described throughout this book, but you can always *combine* MyISAM with something else to achieve the desired effect – for example, assuming the row count within your table doesn't change, a MyISAM-based table can provide you with the exact count of the number of rows within it, then you can make use of an InnoDB-based normalized table to store the record count in a column and display the record count via an application or a website. Easy and no long waiting times for the page to load! Did I mention that your database will be normalized too?

Even to this day, MyISAM can become the go-to storage engine for certain tasks – you just have to use it wisely!

Building APIs and Interacting with Big Data

MySQL, MariaDB, or Percona Server can also be used as a back-end data supplier for your API service. In fact, the BreachDirectory API is built on nothing else than a mix of PHP and MariaDB, and there are billions of records in the database: surprising, isn't it?

No matter what you use to build an API – Laravel, Symfony, CodeIgniter, CakePHP, or perhaps you're building an API yourself using plain PHP or a different programming language, there are a couple of things you need to keep in mind regardless if your API works with big data sets or "normal-sized" data:

1. Your API will most likely provide JSON-based output.

2. Your API will involve and act on API keys or similar things to identify a user that's using the API.

3. Your API will most likely have a limit of queries that can be made for a single user. That limit may be set per day, week, month, or year. A different frequency can also be chosen.

4. If you have a lot of databases/tables within your database, it's likely that you will have to use a loop like `foreach` to loop through each of the databases/tables within, query data with an SQL query or two, and return results.

5. When executing `SELECT` queries, your user would have to define the type of search query if it's necessary (e.g., email address, username, or domain for data breach search engines), then provide the query itself via another parameter.

6. The query would need to be sanitized according to its type (e.g., email addresses would make use of `FILTER_VALIDATE_EMAIL`, etc.)

7. Your API will likely need to update the number of queries a user has made by running an `UPDATE` query after each `SELECT` query has been executed.

8. Your API will likely need to be rate-limited (that can be done via PHP, MariaDB, or both).

APPENDIX   THINGS YOU WISH YOU KNEW, BUT DON'T

Think about your application and database in each of these steps – providing JSON-based output likely means that you're going to issue a header in line of `Content-type: application/json; charset=utf-8` to tell your application that content will be in JSON format and should be provided as UTF-8 data and nothing else. API keys mean that your application will have to generate and provide API keys to each user, limiting the amount of queries may have to do with API plans that provide the user with no more than X amount of queries during a calendar month (that's also why your API needs to update the number of queries a user has run – you need to keep track of those and some of you may use that for internal statistics purposes, too), and rate-limiting your API will help you to prevent abuse and users who may use the API for questionable purposes.

Coming back to the database, perhaps the most important thing I've learned when building APIs would be the importance of rate limiting and carefully selecting data that's presented to the user. These things will ring a bell for everyone who has built API services in the past, and no matter whether they've dealt with big data sets or not, these things are crucial – rate limiting will most likely be done via PHP and it will prevent your database from timing out and affecting your application in return, while presentable data can be selected in both ways: we can either not store the data in the database in the first place or if storing the data is necessary, we should not provide it to the end user when it's not necessary.

With that being said, if we look at everything from a birds-eye view, interacting with big data sets is not that different from our everyday interactions with ordinary-sized data, is it? If we assume that we use REST-based API services, we need to remember a couple of things and we're golden.

First, *REST-based architectures are stateless.* Stateless means that when sending a request, we must identify ourselves (that's what API keys are for) and then clearly define our requests to help our database further limit accessible data (search types with a search query, anyone?)

It's also wise to remember that *some REST API requests can be cached.* GET requests can be cached, POST requests are not cached by default but one can "ask" them to be cached with a Cache-Control header, and two kinds of requests cannot be cached at all – these are PUT and DELETE. Last but not least, REST APIs can make use of data in MySQL or any other database management system no matter if your application is a web app, a mobile application, or an Internet of Things (IoT) device.

Preparing for the Future

After you have a deep understanding of the tables involved in MySQL/MariaDB, understand what breaks your database, queries and understand their components, optimize your server, storage engines, schemas, and data types, find yourself properly indexing and partitioning data, your backup and recovery procedures are optimized, and you have a good enough understanding of security measures that involve your database, your database is on a good path.

Sure, you may face things like Schrödinger's tables or mess up your data structure from time to time, but you have tools to deal with those problems too – and even if you don't, there's always things like Stack Overflow and/or developer forums. No book is guaranteed to squash all of your database problems; however, I'd argue that you know more than one that helped you get rid of many.

I hope that this book has been one of them – I hope that this book helped you harness and better understand how to uncover the diamonds in your database performance, security, and availability space, put them to the test when necessary, and break them when the use case necessitates you to do so.

I hope that you've enjoyed reading this book as much as I've enjoyed writing it: I'd love to hear your feedback on how I did, so don't hesitate to get in touch with me (you can find ways to contact me through my blog at lukasvileikis.com and I'll usually respond promptly), check whether your data is at risk of identity theft by making use of BreachDirectory.com, and until next time.

Summary

I bet you haven't heard of a concept called Schrödinger's tables in database management systems before, have you? The tablespace of your database – ibdata1 – can also be a fun place depending on how you look at it, index structures are (or can be) fun as well, and MyISAM can be used reliably in some situations, too.

I hope that you've enjoyed reading about the SQL query that breaks older instances of MySQL and that this newly acquired knowledge will be useful in your daily work, when running workshops or in conferences, and I hope that the knowledge centered around API solutions will prove useful sometime in the future too.

APPENDIX   THINGS YOU WISH YOU KNEW, BUT DON'T

When it comes to the future, don't forget to think about the way ahead either, and think about the mistakes you've made in the past as a learning curve allowing you to become a better data, software, database, or security professional.

To wrap it up, I hope that you've enjoyed reading this book. I hope that the contents of the appendix were as interesting as the rest of the book – and for those interested to consume some more of my content or use the services I'm involved in, I promise that the rest of my content and services are just as interesting and beneficial to everyone involved, too.

Index

A

Access control, 316–320, 343
Account categories, 330–331
Account locking, 331–334
ACID, 41, 42
    and big data, 205, 206
    properties, 150–153
ALTER queries, 137, 191, 199
ALTER TABLE queries, 218, 240
ALTER USER query, 319
Amazon S3 servers, 20
APIs and big data, 361, 362
Architecture of DBMS
    character sets and collations, 54
    client, 53
    server, 53
    storage, 54
Architecture of MySQL
    client, 4
    components, 4
    layers, 5
    server, 4
    storage, 4
ARCHIVE storage engine, 28, 29
Authentication plugins, 322–324
autocommit parameter, 173, 174
Auto-increment option, 237

B

Backups, 223, 269, 349
    big data sets, 280–283
    birds-eye view, 270–271
    commands, 277
    compression and security, 278–280
    logical or physical, 271
    in MariaDB, 270–273
    and recovery pitfalls, 285–286
    SQL statements, 271
    strategy, 343
    types and tools, 272–278
BASE, 152, 153
Basic Multilingual Plane (BMP), 53
Bcrypt/Blowfish, 128, 328, 329
Big data, 89, 249, 251, 341, 342, 344–346
    and ACID, 205, 206
    and APIs, 361, 362
    breached data, 197
    data analysis, 207, 208
    database, 195
    data types, 165–166
    exfiltrating data, 197
    hackers operate, 197
    Linux options, 207
    LOAD DATA INFILE, 206
    indexing, 242–246
    and MariaDB, 196–204
    with MySQL, 196
    NoSQL databases, 196
    optimizing MySQL, 196
    optimizing queries, 192, 193
    optimizing schemas, 165–166
    parsing, 207

INDEX

Big data (*cont.*)
  pitfalls, 286–289
  recovering, 284
  Script kiddies, 346–348
  search engine, 207
  security, 348
  sets, 280–283
  and storage engines, 204–205
  unique indexes, 207
Big-data-based search engine, 125
BINARY and VARBINARY data types, 50
Binary logs, 297
Binary search tree (BST), 221
BIT data type, 49
BLACKHOLE storage engine, 28, 29
BLOB and TEXT data types, 50, 164
BMP, *see* Basic Multilingual Plane (BMP)
Brachistochrone, 127
Breached data, 197
Broken access control, 315
BST, *see* Binary search tree (BST)
B-tree indexes, 84, 210, 241
  backups, 223
  BST, 221
  copy-pasting, 223
  data types, 228
  demonstration purposes, 222
  equality operators, 222
  InnoDB index, 227
  in MySQL, 222, 226–227
  query performance, 222
  random mails, 224
  SELECT queries, 183, 184
  username column, 222, 225
  values, 224
Buffers, 143
Built-in scheduling tasks, 282

C

CALL procedure, 98
Car-related websites, 243
CDNs, 45, 116, 127, 135, 137
CHAR and VARCHAR data types, 50
Character sets and collations, 48, 81–84
CloudFlare, 45, 137
Clustered indexes, 211, 236–238
CMS use case, 305
COALESCE PARTITION statement, 266
Code for performance, 309
Code reviews, 345
Code systems, 309
Coding for MySQL performance and security
  advanced features, 125, 126
  application and database, 127
  architecture, 127
  backup your data, 126
  Bcrypt/Blowfish, 128
  benchmark and profile, 124, 125
  brachistochrone, 127
  clean code, 126, 127
  code profilers, 125
  completely secure application/completely secure database, 127
  CSRF tokens, 126
  index for high performance, 125
  load balancers, 124
  server components, 125
  terminate connections, 124
  user input, 124
Coffman's conditions, 193
Composite indexes, 211, 232
Compression, 278–280
Configuration file, 166
Configuring MySQL

disk I/O, 145–147
parameters
    buffers, 143
    file-per-table feature, 144
    files, 140
    ibdata1, 143, 144
    InnoDB, 142–144
    Linux users, 142
    my.ini with comments, 141
    my.InnoDB settings in my.ini, 141, 142
    MyISAM, 144
    scratch, 140
    Windows users, 140
Constructing indexes, 244
CONVERT PARTITION ... TO TABLE query, 263–264
count_cities, 98
Covering indexes, 210, 220, 231
    B-tree indexes, 229
    columns, 232
    details column, 234
    functionality, 228
    in MariaDB, 231
    multicolumn indexes, 232–234
    order of columns, 229
    requirements, 230
CREATE queries, 66, 197
CREATE PROCEDURE, 98
CREATE ROLE statement, 320
CREATE TABLE and INSERT INTO ... statements, 284
CRUD (Create, Read, Update, and Delete)
    queries, 62
    operations, 35
    triangle, 169
Cryptographic failures, 315
CSRF tokens, 126

CSV storage engine, 27, 28
Cybercrime, 347
Cyber security, 339

D

Database, 195
    backups, 273
    performance, 43, 77, 138
    in shared hosting, 115
Database management systems, 128, 129, 136, 139, 196, 197, 205
Data breaches, 46, 238, 246, 349
    boundaries, 350
    infrastructure, 352
    people access, 347
    search engines, 89, 345, 346
Data control language (DCL), 62, 68, 97
Data definition language (DDL), 62, 65–67, 97
Data encryption, 342
Data fragmentation, 195
Data manipulation language (DML), 62–65, 97
Data masking, 342
Data pruning, 260
Data segmentation, 342
Data types, 47, 48, 53, 64
    characters, 78–79
    character sets, 151–153, 159
    and collations, 48, 49, 51–53, 159
    database instance, 77
    date and time, 78
    date, time, spatial, and JSON, 161, 162
    define, 47
    ENUM, 80
    errors, 159, 160
    integer, 51

Data types (*cont.*)
    JSON, 78, 80
    numeric, 78, 160, 161
    numeric data, 49
    optimizing schemas, 165–166
    right, 164–165
    SET, 80
    spatial, 78
    spatial (geospatial) to store geographic data, 50
    storage requirements, 162–164
    store date and time values, 49
    to store string values, 50
    string, 78, 160
    use cases, 79
    utf8mb4, 159
DATE data type, 49
Date and time data types, 78
DATETIME data type, 49
Date, time, spatial, and JSON data types, 161, 162
DBAs, 24, 62, 106, 108, 192, 195
DBMS, 41
DCL, *see* Data control language (DCL)
DDL, *see* Data definition language (DDL)
DDoS attacks, 45, 137, 342
Deadlocks, 192, 193
Debian, 21
DECIMAL and NUMERIC data types, 49
Decluttering, query, 214
Dedicated server, 115, 116, 139
"Default" type of replication, 296
DELETE queries, 170, 191, 192, 203
Descending index, 84
DISABLE KEYS, 288
Disk I/O, 145–147
DML, *see* Data manipulation language (DML)

Documentations, 93–95, 128
Duplicate indexes, 107–108

E

e-commerce shop, 239
Enterprise-level database, 323
Enterprise-level security controls, 47
ENUM data type, 50, 80
Equality operators, 86, 222
ERD schemas, 75, 76
Error codes, MySQL, 119–120
    42000, 106
    can't create/write file, 106
    DBMS, 104
    error 1040 (too many connections), 104
    error 1045 (access denied), 105
    error 1064 (syntax error), 105
    error 1114 (table is full), 105
    error 1659 (timestamp), 105
    error 2006 (server connection closed), 105
    error 2008 (client ran out of memory), 105
    error 2013 (lost connection during query), 105
    HY000, 106
    packet too large, 106
    partitioning, 105
Error messages
    error codes, 104–106
    error condition, 103
    error number, 103
    format, 104
    in MariaDB, 103
    MariaDB syntax error, 104
    SQLSTATE value, 104
    troubleshoot, 104

INDEX

Errors
    condition, 103
    understanding and
        simulating, 117–120
EXPLAIN, 102, 110–114
    operation, 85
    query, 201

F

FEDERATED and EXAMPLE storage
    engines, 34, 35
Federated table, 35
file_per_table, 144
File-per-table feature, 144
filter_input() function, 335
filter_var() function, 335
Firewalling MariaDB, 324
Firewall solutions, 338
FLOAT and DOUBLE
    data types, 49
FLUSH PRIVILEGES, 105
FLUSH TABLES WITH READ LOCK
    query, 293
foreach loop, 200
Fragmentation, 218
Full backup, 273
Full-text indexes, 240

G

Galera Cluster, 291, 295
GDPR & NIST, 343
GEN_CLUST_INDEX, 237
Global transaction ID (GTID), 297
Google Chrome, 348
Greek character set, 53
GROUP BY clauses, 235

H

hacking_mysql database, 254
Hardware, 239
Hardware testing, 147–150
Hash indexes, 210, 236–238
Hash partitioning, 255, 259
HDD storage, 139
htmlspecialchars, 335

I

ibdata1, 20, 121, 143, 144, 356–357
Imperva, 137
incrementing_id column, 107
Indexed Sequential Access Method
    (ISAM), 24
Index design, perfect, 238–243
Indexes, 84–86, 116, 170, 179, 357–359
    advices, 216–218
    Big Data, 242–246
    B-tree indexes, 183, 184, 221–228
    columns, 215, 217
    covering index, 228–232
    databases, 218–220
    DBMS, 210
    definition, 214
    disk space, 212
    functionality, 212–214
    hardware, 218–220
    high performance, 125
    index scan, 184
    index seek, 184
    in MariaDB, 209–213
    misconceptions, 216–218
    myths, misconceptions, and
        fragmentation issues, 216–218
    ORDER BY clause, 185

INDEX

Indexes (*cont.*)
    performance, 242–246
    SELECT queries, 182, 183
    UPDATE queries, 188
    WHERE clause, 214–215
Injection-based attacks, 334–337
InnoDB, 7, 20, 26, 94, 121, 125, 136, 144, 156, 204, 355
    ACID compliance, 26
    applications, 156
    buffer pool, 116
    buffer pool and log files, 157
    checkpointing operations, 146
    component, 67
    configuration, 12
    configure, 146
    data file, 144
    delete data, 144
    detect read-only transactions, 158
    features, 25
    flush method, 145
    ibdata1, 20, 24
    innodb_adaptive_hash_index, 13
    innodb_buffer_pool_dump_at_shutdown, 13
    innodb_buffer_pool_dump_now, 13
    innodb_buffer_pool_instances, 13
    innodb_buffer_pool_load_at_startup, 13
    innodb_buffer_pool_size, 14, 18
    innodb_data_file_path, 14, 18
    innodb_default_row_format, 14
    innodb_doublewrite, 15
    innodb_file_per_table, 15, 18
    innodb_flush_log_at_trx_commit, 15, 19
    innodb_flush_method, 16, 19
    innodb_force_recovery, 16
    innodb_ft_enable_stopword, 16
    innodb_ft_max_token_size, 16
    innodb_ft_min_token_size, 16
    innodb_io_capacity, 16
    innodb_lock_wait_timeout, 17
    innodb_log_buffer_size, 17, 19
    innodb_log_files_in_group, 17
    innodb_log_file_size, 17
    innodb_max_dirty_pages_pct, 17
    innodb_optimize_fulltext_only, 17
    innodb_page_size, 17
    innodb_purge_threads, 17
    innodb_read_io_threads, 17
    innodb_redo_log_capacity, 20
    innodb_stats_on_metadata, 17
    innodb_strict_mode, 18
    innodb_thread_concurrency, 18
    innodb_undo_log_truncate, 18
    innodb_write_io_threads, 18
    log files, 25
    MyISAM into, 11
    parameters, 18, 142
    primary contestant, 24–26
    read-only operations, 157
    row formats, 163
    settings, 12
    skip_innodb_doublewrite, 15
    storage engine, 6
    system tablespace, 20
    tables, 144
    tablespace file, 25, 143
    tables with records, 91
    variables, 158
innodb_adaptive_hash_index, 13
innodb_buffer_pool_dump_at_shutdown, 13

innodb_buffer_pool_dump_now, 13
innodb_buffer_pool_instances, 13
innodb_buffer_pool_load_at_startup, 13
innodb_buffer_pool_size, 14
innodb_data_file_path, 14
innodb_default_row_format, 14
innodb_doublewrite, 15
innodb_file_per_table, 15
innodb_flush_log_at_trx_commit, 15
innodb_flush_method, 16, 122
innodb_force_recovery, 16
innodb_ft_enable_stopword, 16
innodb_ft_max_token_size, 16
innodb_ft_min_token_size, 16
InnoDB index, 227, 236, 237
innodb_io_capacity, 16
innodb_lock_wait_timeout, 17
innodb_log_buffer_size, 17
innodb_log_files_in_group, 17
innodb_log_file_size, 17
innodb_max_dirty_pages_pct, 17
innodb_optimize_fulltext_only, 17
innodb_page_size, 17
innodb_purge_threads, 17
innodb_read_io_threads, 17
innodb_stats_on_metadata, 17
innodb_strict_mode, 18
innodb_thread_concurrency, 18
innodb_undo_log_truncate, 18
innodb_write_io_threads, 18
Input sanitization, 334–337
INSERT operations, 287
INSERT queries, 63, 65, 128, 170, 173–176, 189, 197, 217
Internet, 129
ISAM, *see* Indexed Sequential Access Method (ISAM)

J

JOIN operations, 184, 201
JOIN queries, 116, 117
JSON, 362
JSON data type, 50, 78, 80

K

Key partitioning, 255, 259
KILL operation, 68

L

Last_query_cost, 100
LIKE clause, 201
LIKE queries, 245
LIMIT clause, 201
List/list columns partitioning, 255
Load balancers, 124
LOAD DATA INFILE, 199, 200, 206, 287–288
LOCK TABLE statement, 276
log_bin and server_id options, 293
Logical backups, 271–273

M

MariaDB, 3, 4, 35–37, 48, 51, 67, 84, 110, 128, 138, 196, 197, 205, 216, 227, 334–337, 355, 361, 363
  backups, 269–272
  B-tree index, 224
  calling a procedure, 98
  character sets and collations, 52, 81, 82
  columns, 219
  components and plugins, 322–324
  covering index, 231

INDEX

MariaDB (*cont.*)
    data files, 254
    default behavior, 148
    defining procedures, 98
    error messages, 103
    functionality, 212–214
    index type, 210
    Last_query_cost, 101
    mariadb-slap, 148
    MERGE, SPIDER, and CONNECT, 267
    MUL, 233
    MyBB 1.8.38 database, 149
    with mysqlslap, 177
    and partners, 210
    Planet, 129
    procedures, 99
    query cache in, 171, 172
    recovering, 283–284
    replication types, 296–299
    reserved accounts, 330–331
    secured installation, 307–308
    SHOW STATUS Query, 111
    SQL query, 99, 100
    syntax error, 104
    working, 212
    your_table_backup.txt file, 282
MariaDB and big data
    database management system, 197
    deleting, 203–204
    inserting, 198–200
    reading, 200–202
    updating, 202–203
mariadb-dump, 274–276, 286
mariadb-secure-installation, 308
mariadb-show, 150
mariadb-slap, 128
Master-master replication, 296
Master-slave replication, 296

max_allowed_packet variable, 106
MEMORY and TempTable storage
    engines, 26, 27
MERGE storage engine, 29, 30
Mixed-mode replication, 291
mod_security for firewall, 137
MongoDB, 196, 204
Multicolumn (composite) indexes, 232–234
Multi-master replication, 296–297
Multiple root users, 318
Multiversion Concurrency Control
    (MVCC) data, 20
MyISAM, 7, 11, 20, 29, 30, 35, 144, 158,
    191, 360
    cheap, 24
    data inconsistency, 25
    deprecated, 26
    features, 25
    flip side, 25
    functions, 24
    InnoDB's ibdata1, 24
    InnoDB's tablespace, 24
    MRG_MyISAM, 29
    non-transactional storage
        engine, 24, 25
    storage, 288
    storage engine, 176
MyRocks
    bulk loading, 23
    data, 22
    installed and enabled, 21
    memory, 23
    operating system, 21
    ps-admin, 21
    RocksDB, 21, 22
    rocksdb_bulk_load, 22
    rocksdb_column_default_value_as_
        expression, 22

INDEX

rocksdb_create_checkpoint, 22
rocksdb_db_write_buffer_size, 22
rocksdb_error_if_exists, 22
secondary indexes, 23
sudo command, 21
unsorted data, 23

MySQL, 3, 292, 324
architecture, 4–5
ANDs or ORs, 55
backups types, 272–278
B-tree indexes, 222–229
character sets and collations, 81
communication, 55
configuration files, 6, 7
data types, 159–166
default replication mode, 291
history, 3–4, 41
indexes, 209–213
keys, 209
NULL values, 261–268
partitioning types, 254–260
performance, 56
queries (*see* Queries)
RDBMS, 6
reserved accounts, 330–331
search engine, 55
slow query performance, 56–59
SQL queries, 55, 56
storage, 6
storage engines, 7–9
UTF-8, 83
See also Security

MySQL 5.7, 359–360
MySQL Enterprise Audit, 324
MySQL Enterprise Firewall, 324
mysqli_real_escape_string(), 336, 337
mysqlslap, 128, 148, 150

N

NDBCluster, 30–32
Network Database (NDB) storage engine
configuration file, 32
data node, 30
installing and using, 31–33
management node, 31–33
management service, 33
MySQL NDB Cluster, 31
NDBCluster, 30–33
service, 32
shared-nothing architecture, 30
SQL node, 31
NIST framework, 314
Non-relational databases, 196
NoSQL databases, 196
NULL values, 90–92, 95, 261–268
Numeric data types, 78, 160, 161
NVMe drives, 145
NVMe SSD, 139

O

OFFSET clause, 201
Online/offline data backups, 273
Online transaction processing (OLTP) queries, 205
Operating memory, 133, 134, 138
Optimization a server
ACID properties, 150–153
advice, 134
budget, 135
choice previously, 135
choosing server and hard drives, 139–140
configuring, 140–147
data, 133

INDEX

Optimization a server (*cont.*)
    database, 133
    database configuration, 133
    database management system, 134
    experience, 135
    flexibility, 135
    fortifications, 134
    hardware testing, 147–150
    location and maintenance requirements, 135
    mistakes cost, 135
    operating memory, 133, 134
    performance of MySQL, 138, 139
    remove blockers, 136
    search engine, 134
    security measures, 134
    slow-running queries, 133
    use case, 135
    webserver issues, 136–138
Optimization of storage engines
    autocommit, 158
    backup strategy, 157
    buffer pool and log files of InnoDB, 157
    configuration file, 155
    craft and select indexes, 157
    database collections, 156
    data partitions, 157
    and data types, 155
    data types and character sets, 156
    InnoDB, 156, 158
    InnoDB detect read-only transactions, 158
    load and extract data, 157
    MyISAM, 158
    START TRANSACTION READ ONLY statement, 158
    type of data/data classes, 157
Optimizers query, 99–103

Optimizing SQL queries
    big data, 192, 193 (*see also* Big data)
    data, 169
    data types, 169
    deadlocks, 192, 193
    DELETE queries, 170, 191, 192
    indexes, 170
    INSERT queries, 170, 173–176
    query cache, 171–173
    SELECT queries, 170, 177–187
    SHOW PROFILES, 170
    slow SQL queries, 169
    types, 169
    UPDATE queries, 170, 187–191
ORDER BY clause, 235, 236
OWASP framework, 313, 315–317
OWASP Top 10, 338, 349

P

Parameterized statements, 336
Parsers query, 99–103
Partition data, 250–251
    definition, 258
    by hash, 255
    internals, 252–254
    by key, 255
    by list/list columns, 255
    limitations, 266–267
    NULL values, 261–268
    purpose, 249
    by range/range columns, 255
    rules, 262
    schemas, queries, and indexes, 252
    SQL layer, 249
    subpartitioning, 261–268
    sub-tables, 257–263
    tables, 252

INDEX

values, 258
Partitioning, 95, 105, 125, 165
Partitions, 179
    and big data, 89
    by COLUMNS, 87
    disk space, 86
    function, 87
    by HASH, 87
    by KEY, 87
    by LIST, 87
    in MariaDB, 92
    mini tables, 86
    MySQL, 89
    NULL values, 90–92
    pruning, 90–92
    by RANGE, 87, 88
    subpartitions, 87, 88
    tables with and without, 90, 91
    tables with records, 91, 92
    types, 86
PASSWORD EXPIRE syntax, 333
Password management, 331–334
Percona Server, 3, 4, 9, 35, 48, 84, 136, 196, 197, 210
    character sets and collations, 81
    free and an open source, 20
    MyRocks, 21–23
    TokuDB, 23
    XtraDB, 9, 21
Perfect schema design
    data reality, 77
    designs, 74
    devise, 74
    ERD schemas, 75, 76
    performance improvement/restructurization, 75
    pick small data types, 77
    principles, 77
    simple column type, 77
    SQL clients, 75, 76
    structure of database, 75
Performance hiccups, 43–45
Performance of MySQL, 138, 139
Physical backups, 271–273
Plugins, 322–324
PostgreSQL, 204, 232
Prefix indexes, 211, 235–236
Primary contestant of InnoDB
    DBAs, 24
    MyISAM, 24–26
PRIMARY KEY index, 85, 211, 226
Problematic use cases
    availability issues, 45
    availability, performance, and security, 42
    performance hiccups, 43–45
    security problems, 46–47
Pruning, 90–92, 95, 260

Q

Queries
    avoid complicating things, 93
    avoid over-optimizing your database, 93
    avoid repeating bad practices, 92
    breaking, 62
    cache, 112, 171–173
    character sets and collations, 81–84
    CRUD, 62
    data types, 77–80
    DBAs, 62
    DCL, 62, 68
    DDL, 62, 65–67
    developers, 62
    DML, 62–65

INDEX

Queries (*cont.*)
    documentations, 93–95
    indexes, 84–86
    INSERT, SELECT, UPDATE,
        DELETE, 61
    optimization, 92
    optimizer, 101
    partitions, 86–92
    perfect schema design, 74–77
    performance, 99
    SHOW CHARACTER SET, 51
    slow performance, 68–74
    structure, 62
    TCL, 62, 68
    transactions, 63
    types, 43
    written, 61
Queries dislike
    columns, 107
    duplicate indexes, 107–108
    EXISTS instead of IN, 108
    EXPLAIN, 110–114
    SHOW STATUS, 110–114
    stored procedures and triggers, 108–110
Query components
    and error message, 103–106
    parsers and optimizers, 99–103
    query performance, 99
    and stored procedures, 97–99

R

RAND(), 224
RANDOM PASSWORD
    clause, 334
Random values, 227
Range/range columns partitioning, 255
RBAC, *see* Role-based access
    control (RBAC)

RDBMS, storage engines, 6
Recovering
    big data, 284
    MariaDB, 283–284
Recovery pitfalls, 285–286
Relational database management
    systems, 299
Replication
    configuration, 292–295
    implementation, 292–295
    lag, 297
    notes and tips, 298–299
    security, 299–300
    synchronous, 291
    types, 295–298
    Reserved accounts, 330–331
REST-based API, 362
REST-based architectures, 362
Right data type, 164–165
Right schema, 48
    brainstorm, 48
    choose, 48
    databases and tables, 48
    server, 48
    use case, 48
RocksDB, 21, 22
Role-based access control (RBAC), 320
Root user, 322
R-Tree indexes, 210

S

Sanitization, 336
Schemas, 75
Schrödinger's tables, 355–356, 363
Script kiddies, 346–348
Search engine, 134, 207
secure-file-priv, 199

376

INDEX

Security, 278–280
    access control, 316–320
    account categories, 330–331
    account locking, 331–334
    Big Data, 344–346, 348
    categories, 303
    components and plugins, 322–324
    data available, 341
    firewalling MariaDB, 324
    guidelines, 313–316, 327–330
    injection-based attacks, 334–337
    installation, MariaDB, 307–308
    landscape, 307
    in MariaDB, 304–305
    measures, 309–311, 313–316
    PHP versions, 341
    replication, 299–300
    reserved accounts, 330–331
    union-based SQL, 349
    website/app owner, 348
Security guidelines
    enterprise-level security controls, 47
    general, 46
    MySQL security components and plugins, 47
    user security and access control, 46
Security misconfiguration, 315
Security-related frameworks, 338
SELECT … INTO OUTFILE, 283
SELECT privilege query, 318, 329
SELECT queries, 65, 84, 170, 201, 202, 209, 211, 216, 229, 263
    access as little data, 184
    application and search, 177
    BETWEEN … AND and the IN clauses, 185
    BreachDirectory, 177
    columns, 180
    condition-based filtering, 185
    DESCRIBE in action, 180
    DISTINCT clause, 186
    EXPLAIN, 180, 181
    full table scans, 186
    indexes, 182–185
    investigate the tables, 180
    investigation process, 179
    JOIN operations, 184
    LIMIT clause, 185, 186
    MariaDB with mysqlslap, 177
    NULL, 185
    performance, 177, 184, 186
    search for answers, 179–180
    self-explanatory, 177
    SHOW PROCESSLIST, 177–179
    SQL query profiler, 181
    table structure, 181
SELECT user FROM mysql.user, 317
Server components and interaction with MySQL, 125
    bandwidth, 122
    hard drives, 122
    InnoDB flush method, 121, 122
    MySQL infrastructure, 120, 121
    mysqlslap, 122, 123
    operating memory, 122
    operating system, 122
    processor, 121
    storage engine, 121
    stress testing, 123
Server resources
    CPU information, 116
    dedicated server, 116
    file system, 117
    innodb_buffer_pool_size, 116
    innodb_log_file_size, 116
    join_buffer_size, 117

INDEX

Server resources (*cont.*)
   memory capacity, 116
   mysqld, 117
   nproc, 116
   partitioning, 116
   shared hosting, 115
   statistics, 116
   table_open_cache and max_
      connections, 117
   version, 116
   VPS, 116
SET data type, 50, 80
SET PASSWORD query, 319
SET PERSIST queries, 333–334
SET ROLE, 321
Shared hosting, 115
Shared server, 139
SHOW CHARACTER SET, 83
SHOW CREATE TABLE statement, 252–253
SHOW MASTER STATUS query, 294
SHOW PRIVILEGES query, 319
SHOW RELAYLOG EVENTS, 298
SHOW REPLICA STATUS query, 295
SHOW STATUS, 110–114
SHOW TABLES, 355
SHOW TABLE STATUS, 253
skip_innodb_doublewrite, 15
Slow query performance
   DELETE, 59
   disable monitoring, 69
   and doesn't load, 68
   enable monitoring, 69
   full-text search, 57
   INNER JOIN, 57
   INSERT, 58
   is response time, 68
   monitoring, 70
   NULL values, 58
   profiling, 70–72
   query structure, 56
   replace ID with your query ID, 70
   SELECT, 57, 58
   status codes, 72–74
   subtasks, 69, 74
   UPDATEs, 58
   wildcards, 57
Slow-running queries, 133
Slow SQL queries, 169
Software engineering, 338
Solid-state drives, 116
Spatial data types, 78
Spatial indexes, 236–238
Spatial Reference Identifiers (SRIDs), 236
SphinxSE, 36
SQL clients, 76
SQL injection attacks, 334–337, 348
SQL query, in loop, 200
SQLSTATE codes, 118–120
SQL statements, 271, 273
SQLSTATE value, 103, 104
SRIDs, *see* Spatial Reference
      Identifiers (SRIDs)
SSD drives, 145
Stack Overflow, 129
Stateless, 362
Storage, 11
Storage engines, 4, 117, 121, 155, 171
   ARCHIVE, 8, 28, 29
   and big data, 204–205
   BLACKHOLE, 8, 28, 29
   CSV, 8, 27, 28
   EXAMPLE, 9, 34, 35
   FEDERATED, 9, 34, 35
   InnoDB, 7, 8, 11–20, 24–26
   innodb_buffer_pool_size, 6
   innodb_data_file_path, 6

key_buffer_size, 6
log_error, 6
log_error_verbosity, 6
LSM-based, 22
MariaDB, 11–20, 35–37
max_allowed_packet, 6
MEMORY, 27
MEMORY (HEAP before MySQL 4.1), 8
MERGE, 29, 30
MERGE (formerly MRG_MyISAM), 9
MyISAM, 7
NDB, 30–33
optimization, 155–159
Percona Server, 9, 20 (*see also* Percona Server)
Percona XtraDB, 9
port, 6
principle of, 6, 7
and row-based databases, 205
TempTable, 8, 27
vanilla, 205
Storage requirements, 162–164
Stored procedures, 98–100, 108–110, 179
Storing data, 205
String-based data types, 78, 160
Subpartitioning, 261–268
Sucuri, 137
Synchronous replication, 291
Syntax errors, 65
System tablespace, 20
SYSTEM_USER privilege, 330

T

Table schemas, 47, 48
TCL, *see* Transaction control language (TCL)
TCP port, 300

TEXT columns, 238
Threat detection, 343
Threat modeling, 309
Threat scanning, 346
TIME data type, 49
Timestamp, 105
TIMESTAMP data type, 49
TokuDB, 23
Traffic analysis, 343
Transaction control language (TCL), 62, 68, 97
Transactions, 63
Triggers, 109, 110, 120, 125

U

Ubuntu, 21
Understanding and simulating errors
    categories, 117
    database management system, 117
    MySQL error codes, 119–120
    SQLSTATE code, 117–119
    triggers, 120
UNION queries, 201
Union-based SQL, 349
uniq statement, 186
Unique index, 85
UPDATE queries, 63, 170, 202
    ALTER queries, 191
    copy of table, 189
    data in tables, 187
    default value on column, 189
    importing data, 190
    indexes, 188
    locking in mind, 188, 189
    LIMIT clause, 187
    partitions, 188
    column after SET defines, 187

INDEX

UPDATE queries (*cont.*)
    table creation, 189, 190
    value, 190
    WHERE clause, 187
Use cases, 238, 275
    security, 327–330
Use cases of MySQL
    ACID, 41, 42
    database management system, 41
    DBMS, 41
    industries, 41
    problematic, 42–47
Username column, 223
User registration, 306
User security, 320–322
User table, 305, 306
utf8mb4, 53, 83
UTF-8 unicode, 52

V

validate_password component, 323
VPS, 115, 116, 139
Vulnerabilities, 315–316
Vulnerability scanning, 345

W

Web-based firewall (WAF), 328
Webserver issues
    avoid optimizing your application, 137
    backup strategy, 137
    CDN, 137
    infrastructure, 138
    low on disk space, 137
    operating memory, 138
    overloaded, 137
    running old, outdated versions of software, 136
WHERE clause, 231, 234
Wildcard, 86
WordPress, 136

X

XtraDB, 9, 21, 136

Y, Z

YEAR data type, 49

GPSR Compliance

The European Union's (EU) General Product Safety Regulation (GPSR) is a set of rules that requires consumer products to be safe and our obligations to ensure this.

If you have any concerns about our products, you can contact us on

ProductSafety@springernature.com

In case Publisher is established outside the EU, the EU authorized representative is:

Springer Nature Customer Service Center GmbH
Europaplatz 3
69115 Heidelberg, Germany

www.ingramcontent.com/pod-product-compliance
Lightning Source LLC
LaVergne TN
LVHW080310260326
834688LV00038B/1040